$16.50

XX X X

Functional Equations in Economics

APPLIED MATHEMATICS AND COMPUTATION

A Series of Graduate Textbooks, Monographs, Reference Works

Series Editor: ROBERT KALABA, University of Southern California

No. 1 MELVIN R. SCOTT
Invariant Imbedding and its Applications to Ordinary Differential Equations: An Introduction, 1973

No. 2 JOHN CASTI and ROBERT KALABA
Imbedding Methods in Applied Mathematics, 1973

No. 3 DONALD GREENSPAN
Discrete Models, 1973

No. 4 HARRIET H. KAGIWADA
System Identification: Methods and Applications, 1974

No. 5 V. K. MURTHY
The General Point Process: Applications to Bioscience, Medical Research, and Engineering, 1974

No. 6 HARRIET H. KAGIWADA and ROBERT KALABA
Integral Equations Via Imbedding Methods, 1974

No. 7 JULIUS T. TOU and RAFAEL C. GONZALEZ
Pattern Recognition Principles, 1974

No. 8 HARRIET H. KAGIWADA, ROBERT KALABA, and SUEO UENO
Multiple Scattering Processes: Inverse and Direct, 1975

No. 9 DONALD A. PIERRE and MICHAEL J. LOWE
Mathematical Programming Via Augmented Lagrangians: An Introduction with Computer Programs, 1975

No. 10 J. SUSAN MILTON and CHRIS P. TSOKOS
Probability Theory with the Essential Analysis, 1976

No. 11 WOLFGANG EICHHORN
Functional Equations in Economics, 1978

No. 12 SIDNEY J. YAKOWITZ
Computational Probability and Simulation, 1977

No. 13 RAFAEL C. GONZALEZ and PAUL WINTZ
Digital Image Processing, 1977

No. 14 RAFAEL C. GONZALEZ and MICHAEL G. THOMASON
Syntactic Pattern Recognition, 1978

Functional Equations in Economics

WOLFGANG EICHHORN

Institut für Wirtschaftstheorie
und Operations Research
University of Karlsruhe

1978

Addison-Wesley Publishing Company
Advanced Book Program
Reading, Massachusetts

London • Amsterdam • Don Mills, Ontario • Sydney • Tokyo

Library of Congress Cataloging in Publication Data

Eichhorn, Wolfgang.
Functional equations in economics.

(Applied mathematics and computation; no. 11)
Includes bibliographical references and indexes.

1. Economics, Mathematical. 2. Functional equations. I. Title.
HB135.E34 330'.01'51 77-24419

ISBN 0-201-01948-5
ISBN 0-201-01949-3 pbk.

American Mathematical Society (MOS) Subject Classification Scheme (1970):
39A15, 39A20, 39A25, 39A30, 90A15, 90B30

Printed in the United States of America

ABCDEFGHIJK-HA-798

Dem Andenken
an meinen Vater

MAX EICHHORN

6.9.1904 — 25.6.1972

Gründer der Volkssternwarte Hof
und Planer, Erbauer und Stifter
ihres Spiegelteleskops

Founder of the public observatory of the city of Hof
and designer, builder, and donor
of its telescope

CONTENTS

SERIES EDITOR'S FOREWORD

Execution times of modern digital computers are measured in nanoseconds. They can solve hundreds of simultaneous ordinary differential equations with speed and accuracy. But what does this immense capability imply with regard to solving the scientific, engineering, economic, and social problems confronting mankind? Clearly, much effort has to be expended in finding answers to that question.

In some fields, it is not yet possible to write mathematical equations which accurately describe processes of interest. Here, the computer may be used simply to simulate a process and, perhaps, to observe the efficacy of different control processes. In others, a mathematical description may be available, but the equations are frequently difficult to solve numerically. In such cases, the difficulties may be faced squarely and possibly overcome; alternatively, formulations may be sought which are more compatible with the inherent capabilities of computers. Mathematics itself nourishes and is nourished by such developments.

Each order of magnitude increase in speed and memory size of computers requires a reexamination of computational techniques and an assessment of the new problems which may be brought within the realm of solution. Volumes in this series will provide indications of current thinking regarding problem formulations, mathematical analysis, and computational treatment.

Functional equations are an old and important part of applied mathematics. It is well known that the logarithmic, exponential, and trigonometric functions satisfy relations such as

$$\log xy = \log x + \log y, \ \exp(x+y) = \exp(x)\exp(y) \text{ and } \sin(x+2\pi) = \sin x.$$

But to what extent do such relations characterize these functions?

If we have two factors of production in the amounts x and y, respectively, and denote the amount produced by $f(x, y)$, we may require that for $k > 0$ we have $f(kx, ky) = kf(x, y)$. Which functions, differentiable or not, satisfy this relation?

Such areas in economics as the theory of index numbers, aggregation, and growth abound with functional equations. It is to the formulation and solution of such equations that this pioneering volume is devoted. It will be especially welcomed by economists and mathematicians; additionally, it will lend insights and pose particular challenges to specialists in computer science, econometrics, and operations research.

Robert Kalaba

PREFACE

The solution of functional equations is one of the oldest topics of mathematical analysis. Though it is difficult to state a definition of the concept "functional equation," Aczél [1966, p. 1] gives "a somewhat loose paraphrase of what is generally meant by this expression" when he says:

Functional equations are equations, both sides of which are terms constructed from a finite number of unknown functions (of a finite number of variables) and from a finite number of independent variables. This construction is effected by a finite number of known functions of one or several variables (including the four species) and by finitely many substitutions of terms which contain known and unknown functions into other known and unknown functions. The functional equations determine the unknown functions. We speak of functional equations or systems of functional equations, depending on whether we have one or several equations. (Also, a single functional equation can determine several desired functions occurring within the equation; as a result, the number of equations is not related to the number of functions to be determined.)

By this definition, which underlies the present book, functional equations in the broader sense (e. g., operator equations; differential, integral, integro-differential, and functional differential equations; and the equations for the value functions in dynamic programming, such as Bellman's functional equation) are excluded.

The number of the independent variables of the functional equations considered in this book is always greater than the minimum number of variables of the functions of the equations. Hence, difference equations, iteration equations, equations defining implicit functions, and so on, will not be considered here.

Aczél's [1966] book, which excludes exactly the same classes of functional equations, contains many applications of functional equations to different fields of science, such as geometry, nomography, physics, mechanics, probability theory, and information theory. But it presents only one application to economics, namely, the determination of the interest formula (pp. 105–106).

Since then, many papers have been published in which functional equations are applied to the formulation and solution of economic problems. It is interesting to note that in most cases these applications do not involve the usual assumptions of calculus, like differentiability or continuity, which perhaps points to new roles for mathematics in economics.

It is the purpose of this book to give the first comprehensive treatment of a subject field that might be called "functional equations in economics."

Concerning the form of presentation of the material, in most cases we first point out applications to economics in order to raise interest in a functional equation, and then we solve the equation and give further details and applications. Thus we hope to maintain a good balance between the theory of functional equations and its applications to economics.

These applications refer to such different fields of economics as

business mathematics (Chapter 1);
price and advertising policies of firms (Chapters 1, 3, and 11);
the theory of production (Chapters 1–6, 9, 10, and 12);
the theory of growth and technical progress (Chapters 1 and 5);
the theory of index numbers (Chapters 3, 8, and 9);
the theory of the price index (Chapters 3 and 8);
the theory of aggregation (Chapter 6);
the theory of the price and quantity level and Fisher's equation of exchange (Chapter 7);
the theory of multisectoral growth (Section 11.4);
the budget equation (Section 11.5).

We point out here that many of the applications to production theory can also be considered, in another interpretation, as applications to utility theory.

The book consists of four parts:

1. functional equations for scalar-valued functions of a single variable (Chapters 1 and 2);
2. functional equations for scalar-valued functions of several variables (Chapters 3–7);
3. systems of three or more functional equations for a single scalar-valued function of several variables (Chapters 8–10);
4. functional equations for vector-valued and set-valued functions of several variables (Chapters 11 and 12).

The functional equations occurring in the first and second part (such as Cauchy's and Pexider's equations, the functional equations of the homogeneous functions, and the generalized distributivity and associativity equation) can be found, for instance, in Aczél's [1966] book. In the present book, however, many of them had to be solved on *restricted domains* for reasons that are consequences of the very nature of the economic problems considered.

To the best of my knowledge, this is the first *book* that investigates the systems of functional equations (determining price indices, production functions, and the effectiveness of a production process) of Part 3 and the functional equations for vector-valued and set-valued functions of Part 4 (playing an important role in the theories of production and multisectoral growth). Aczél's book also contains vector-valued functional equations, but they are different from those considered here.

For all essential results presented in this book the full proofs are given, so that there is no need to consult other sources in this respect. The end of each proof is marked by ■.

The book consists of thirteen chapters. Each chapter starts with introductory remarks sketching both the problems raised and the results obtained. The theorems, corollaries, remarks, assumptions, and several of the formulas and definitions are identified by triple numbers: the first number refers to the chapter, the second to the section, and the third indicates order within the given section; hence, (7.4.5) refers to the fifth item in the fourth section of Chapter 7.

Most of the mathematical symbols in this book are well known. Nevertheless, we place at the reader's disposal, in the first section of Chapter 13, an explanation of the symbols used. The two remaining sections of the chapter provide some mathematical and economic details that may be helpful to readers who require additional background in mathematics or economics.

Some topics in this book are based on papers by the author that have been published in various journals, several of them in German. Concerning the style and language of the book, I quote from the Preface to J. Pfanzagl's *Theory of Measurement*, Physica-Verlag, Würzburg, Wien, 1971:

> Readers might wonder why an author whose native language is German and who lives in a German-speaking country publishes a book in English only. The reasons are patent: he would miss most of his potential readers if the book were published in the German language only. He will not miss any potential reader if the book is published only in English. Let me close by expressing the hope that the reader will excuse all shortcomings in this text due to my insufficient command of the English language.

Acknowledgments

The author is indebted to several persons and institutions for their extremely valuable help in connection with the preparation of the present work.

I am indebted to the Faculty of Mathematics of the University of Waterloo, the department of economics of the University of Southern California, and the Institut für Gesellschafts- und Wirtschaftswissenschaften of the University of Bonn. Visiting professorships at these places provided stimulating occasions for both teaching and learning about the material in this book.

János D. Aczél, who has taught me a great deal about functional equations, gave me his encouragement and approval while I was engaged in writing the manuscript. His readiness to help whenever necessary was truly outstanding. The whole book derived great benefit from his suggestions aimed at improving both the mathematical content and the style.

Warmest thanks also go to my friend and colleague Frank Stehling, who also read the whole manuscript and rendered possible many valuable improvements.

Frank Stehling and Fritz Pokropp added highlights to this book by writing Chapters 5 and 6, respectively, on subjects (such as the theory of technical progress and aggregation problems in production theory) on which they are leading experts.

I am particularly indebted to Ronald W. Shephard, Rolf Färe, and Eginhard Muth for many suggestions concerning Chapters 4, 11, and 12, which were completed when they joined my institute as visiting professors. Chapter 12 could have never been written if the theory of production correspondences as developed by my friend Ronald W. Shephard had not existed.

Chapters 7, 8, and 9 on index numbers benefited from a careful revision by Georg Hasenkamp, to whom I offer my sincere thanks. Thanks are also due to John Muellbauer and R. Robert Russell for suggestions concerning several details of Chapter 8.

I thank Robert Kalaba, editor of the Applied Mathematics and Computation series, for including this book in it.

Last but not least I am obliged to my friends and colleagues at our institute, Ralph Bürk, Helmut Funke, Wilhelm Gehrig, Klaus Spremann, and Joachim Voeller, with whom I had stimulating discussions about the topics of this book. All of them read parts of the drafts of the manuscript. These drafts and the final manuscript were carefully and patiently typed by Gebhard Erny and Mrs. Ingeborg Kasper. Thanks are also due to Friedrich Allendorf, who drew the figures.

W. Eichhorn

Functional Equations in Economics

Part I

Functional Equations for Scalar-Valued Functions of a Single Variable

1

Cauchy's Functional Equations

As will be shown later, the problem of solving Cauchy's [1821] functional equations

$$f(x+y)=f(x)+f(y) \quad \text{where} \quad (x,y)\in \mathbb{R}^2, \quad f\colon \mathbb{R}\to\mathbb{R},^1 \qquad (1.0.1)$$

$$g(x+y)=g(x)+g(y) \quad \text{where} \quad (x,y)\in \mathbb{R}_+^2, \quad g\colon \mathbb{R}_+\to\mathbb{R}, \qquad (1.0.2)$$

$$h(x+y)=h(x)\,h(y) \quad \text{where} \quad (x,y)\in \mathbb{R}_+^2, \quad h\colon \mathbb{R}_+\to\mathbb{R}, \qquad (1.0.3)$$

$$l(xy)=l(x)+l(y) \quad \text{where} \quad (x,y)\in \mathbb{R}_{++}^2, \quad l\colon \mathbb{R}_{++}\to\mathbb{R}, \qquad 1.0.4)$$

$$m(xy)=m(x)\,m(y) \quad \text{where} \quad (x,y)\in \mathbb{R}_+^2, \quad m\colon \mathbb{R}_+\to\mathbb{R}, \qquad (1.0.5)$$

arises in various fields of economics. In the following, the solutions of (1.0.1) –(1.0.5) that are not everywhere discontinuous are determined. Applications are made to business mathematics, the price and advertising policies of firms, the theory of production, and to the theory of growth and technical progress.

1.1 Business Mathematics: Two Properties of an Interest Formula

The following example, which is taken from Aczél [1966, pp. 105–106], provides motivation for studying Eqs. (1.0.2) and (1.0.3).

Let us consider a capital market that is perfect in the following sense:

(a) The amount $A(K, t)$ to which a capital K increases during a time interval of length t by interest compounding does not change by dividing K into separate

[1] For the definitions of symbols and terms not defined in the context see Chapter 13.

Wolfgang Eichhorn, Functional Equations in Economics.

ISBN 0-201-01948-5/01949-3 PBK

investments K_1 and K_2 $(K = K_1 + K_2,\ K_1 \geqq 0,\ K_2 \geqq 0)$:

$$A(K_1 + K_2, t) = A(K_1, t) + A(K_2, t). \tag{1.1.1}$$

(b) The amount to which $A(K, t_1)$ increases during a time interval of length t_2 is equal to the amount to which K increases during a time interval of length $t_1 + t_2$:

$$A(A(K, t_1), t_2) = A(K, t_1 + t_2). \tag{1.1.2}$$

As we will see in Section 1.5, the problem of determining all interest formulas, that is, all strictly monotonically increasing functions A satisfying (1.1.1) and (1.1.2), requires analysis of Eqs. (1.0.2) and (1.0.3). This will be done in Sections 1.2–1.4. The problem itself is then solved in Section 1.5.

In passing, it may be noted that the system (1.1.1), (1.1.2) arises not only in business mathematics but also in economic (as well as organic) growth theory and in the theories of absorption, of heating or cooling, and of radioactive and chemical decay.

1.2 Cauchy's Basic Equation $f(x + y) = f(x) + f(y)$

The following two theorems about Cauchy's basic equation

$$f(x + y) = f(x) + f(y) \quad \text{where} \quad (x, y) \in \mathbb{R}^2, \quad f: \mathbb{R} \to \mathbb{R}, \tag{1.2.1}$$

are important for solving most of the equations in this book.

1.2.2 **Theorem.** *Let f satisfy Eq. (1.2.1). Then*

$$f(ru) = rf(u) \tag{1.2.3}$$

for all real u and rational r; in particular

$$f(r) = f(1)\, r = cr \tag{1.2.4}$$

for all rational r ($c = f(1)$ a constant).

Proof (see Aczél [1966, pp. 31–32]). From (1.2.1) it follows by induction that

$$f(x_1 + x_2 + \cdots + x_n) = f(x_1) + f(x_2) + \cdots + f(x_n)$$

for all real $x_1, x_2, \ldots, x_n$ and for all positive integers n.
By putting $x_\nu = x$ ($\nu = 1, 2, \ldots, n$), we obtain

$$f(nx) = nf(x). \tag{1.2.5}$$

Putting

$$x = (m/n)\, u \quad (m \text{ and } n \text{ positive integers}),$$

that is,

$$nx = mu,$$

we get

$$f(nx) = f(mu).$$

Because of (1.2.5), this can be written

$$nf(x) = mf(u) \quad \text{or} \quad f\left(\frac{m}{n}u\right) = \frac{m}{n}f(u),$$

that is,

$$f(ru) = rf(u) \tag{1.2.6}$$

for all real u and for all *positive* rational r.

From (1.2.1) follows

$$f(x) = f(x) + f(0),$$

that is, $f(0) = 0$, and so (1.2.6) is also valid for $r = 0$.

For *negative* x, replacing y by $-x$ in (1.2.1), we get

$$f(x) + f(-x) = f(0) = 0,$$

that is,

$$f(-x) = -f(x),$$

so (1.2.6) remains true for negative r.

Assertion (1.2.4) follows by setting $u = 1$ in (1.2.3). ■

We note that in neither the theorem nor its proof was a continuity assumption made.

Obviously, every function f given by

$$f(x) = cx \qquad (c = f(1) \text{ an arbitrary real const})$$

satisfies (1.2.1).

1.2.7 **Corollary.** *If in Theorem 1.2.2 the additional assumption is made that f is continuous everywhere, then*

$$f(x) = f(1)\,x = cx \tag{1.2.8}$$

for all real x ($c = f(1)$ a constant).

Proof. Take limits on both sides of (1.2.4). ■

The corollary remains true if "everywhere" is replaced by "at a single point". This follows from

1.2.9 **Theorem.** *Let f satisfy (1.2.1). If there exists no real constant c such that $f(x) = cx$ for all x, then the graph $\{(x, z) \mid x \in \mathbb{R}, z = f(x)\}$ of f is dense in $\mathbb{R}^2$.*

Proof. If f satisfying (1.2.1) is different from f^* with $f^*(x) = cx$, then there exist at least two real numbers $x_1 \neq 0$, $x_2 \neq 0$ such that

$$\frac{f(x_1)}{x_1} \neq \frac{f(x_2)}{x_2}.$$

This implies that the vectors $(x_1, f(x_1))$ and $(x_2, f(x_2))$ are both linearly independent. Then the *real* linear combinations

$$\varrho\cdot(x_1, f(x_1)) + \sigma\cdot(x_2, f(x_2)) \qquad ((\varrho, \sigma) \in \mathbb{R}^2)$$

span the whole plane $\mathbb{R}^2$ and the *rational* linear combinations

$$r\cdot(x_1, f(x_1)) + s\cdot(x_2, f(x_2)) \qquad (r \text{ and } s \text{ rational})$$

are dense in $\mathbb{R}^2$. But then the points

$$(x, f(x)) \quad \text{where} \quad x = rx_1 + sx_2 \qquad (r \text{ and } s \text{ rational}),$$

are also dense in $\mathbb{R}^2$, since from $f(rx_1) = rf(x_1)$ and $f(sx_2) = sf(x_2)$ (see Theorem 1.2.2) we have

$$\begin{aligned}(rx_1 + sx_2, f(rx_1 + sx_2)) &= (rx_1 + sx_2, rf(x_1) + sf(x_2)) \\ &= (rx_1, rf(x_1)) + (sx_2, sf(x_2) \\ &= r\cdot(x_1, f(x_1)) + s\cdot(x_2, f(x_2)). \quad \blacksquare\end{aligned}$$

A straightforward consequence of Theorem 1.2.9 is

1.2.10 **Corollary.** *If f satisfying (1.2.1) has a property that excludes the density of the graph of f in $\mathbb{R}^2$, then*

$$f(x) = cx = f(1)\,x \tag{1.2.8}$$

for all real x ($c = f(1)$ a constant).
Examples of such properties are

continuity at a single point x_0; (1.2.11)
monotonicity in an arbitrarily small interval; (1.2.12)
boundedness in an arbitrarily small interval; (1.2.13)
nonnegativity or positivity of $f(x)$ for sufficiently small positive x. (1.2.14)

Proof. The first assertion and the statements concerning examples (1.2.12)–(1.2.14) are obvious. If f is *continuous* at x_0, then, given any $\varepsilon > 0$ there exists a $\delta > 0$ such that the portion of the graph over $]x_0 - \delta, x_0 + \delta[$ is completely included in the rectangle

$$\{(x, z) \mid |x - x_0| < \delta, \quad |f(x) - f(x_0)| < \varepsilon\},$$

that is, the graph of f is not dense in $\mathbb{R}^2$. $\blacksquare$

For weaker conditions on f than (1.2.11)–(1.2.14) which yield (1.2.8), see Aczél [1966, pp. 34–35] and the literature quoted there.

1.3 Cauchy's Basic Equation with Restricted Domain

Many applications in economics (e.g., (1.1.1)) require the solution of the equation

$$g(x + y) = g(x) + g(y) \quad \text{where} \quad (x, y) \in \mathbb{R}_+^2, \quad g: \mathbb{R}_+ \to \mathbb{R}, \qquad (1.3.1)$$

rather than the solution of (1.2.1).

1.3.2 **Theorem.** *Every solution of (1.3.1) can uniquely be extended to a solution of*

$$f(x + y) = f(x) + f(y) \quad \textit{where} \quad (x, y) \in \mathbb{R}^2, \quad f: \mathbb{R} \to \mathbb{R}. \qquad (1.2.1)$$

Proof. The proof proceeds in five steps.

1. Every $z \in \mathbb{R}$ can be written as $z = x - y$, where $x \in \mathbb{R}_+$, $y \in \mathbb{R}_+$. Define

$$f(z) = f(x - y) = g(x) - g(y) \qquad \text{for} \quad x \in \mathbb{R}_+, \quad y \in \mathbb{R}_+. \qquad (1.3.3)$$

2. By (1.3.3), f is well defined on $\mathbb{R}$ because

$$x - y = u - v,$$

that is,

$$x + v = u + y \qquad (x \in \mathbb{R}_+, y \in \mathbb{R}_+, u \in \mathbb{R}_+, v \in \mathbb{R}_+),$$

implies

$$g(x) + g(v) = g(u) + g(y) \qquad \text{or} \qquad g(x) - g(y) = g(u) - g(v).$$

3. That f satisfies (1.2.1) can be shown as follows: For every $z \in \mathbb{R}$, $w \in \mathbb{R}$ there exist $x \in \mathbb{R}_+$, $y \in \mathbb{R}_+$, $u \in \mathbb{R}_+$, $v \in \mathbb{R}_+$ such that $z = x - y$, $w = u - v$ and

$$\begin{aligned} f(z + w) &= f[(x - y) + (u - v)] = f[(x + u) - (v + y)] = \\ &= g(x + u) - g(v + y) \\ &= g(x) - g(y) + g(u) - g(v) = f(x - y) + f(u - v) \\ &= f(z) + f(w). \end{aligned}$$

4. f is an extension of g since for all $x \in \mathbb{R}_+$ we have

$$f(x) = f((x + x) - x) = g(x + x) - g(x) = g(x) + g(x) - g(x) = g(x).$$

5. The extension f of g is unique, that is, all solutions f of (1.2.1) equal to g on $\mathbb{R}_+$ are of the form (1.3.3). This is because for an arbitrary solution ψ,

$$\psi(x - y) = \psi(x) - \psi(y) = g(x) - g(y) = f(x - y)$$

for all $x \in \mathbb{R}_+, y \in \mathbb{R}_+$. ■

1.3.4 **Remark.** We can formulate Theorem 1.3.2 also as follows: *Every homomorphism g of the semigroup S of the nonnegative reals under addition into the group G of the reals also under addition can uniquely be extended to a homomorphism of G into G.* For generalizations see Aczél, Baker, Djoković, Kannappan, and Radó [1971, pp. 263–271].

1.3.5 **Remark.** Replacing $\mathbb{R}_+$ by $\mathbb{R}_{++}$ in (1.3.1) and in the foregoing proof, we see that (1.3.2) also remains true in case (1.3.1) with $\mathbb{R}_{++}$ instead of $\mathbb{R}_+$.

1.3.6 **Remark.** According to Theorem 1.3.2 every solution of (1.3.1) (or of (1.3.1) with $\mathbb{R}_{++}$ instead of $\mathbb{R}_+$) is obtained by taking an arbitrary solution f of (1.2.1), and by restricting f to nonnegative (or positive) x's. As a consequence of thiswe have

1.3.7 **Corollary.** *If a solution of (1.3.1) (or of (1.3.1) with $\mathbb{R}_{++}$ instead of $\mathbb{R}_+$) has one of the properties (1.2.11)–(1.2.14), then it can be written in the form*

$$g(x) = cx = g(1)\,x,$$

where $c = g(1)$ is a constant that, in case (1.2.14), is nonnegative or positive, respectively.

1.4 Cauchy's Equation $h(x + y) = h(x)\,h(y)$

The results of Sections 1.2 and 1.3 can easily be applied to solve Cauchy's equations

$$h(x + y) = h(x)\,h(y) \quad \text{where} \quad (x, y) \in \mathbb{R}_+^2, \quad h: \mathbb{R}_+ \to \mathbb{R}, \quad (1.4.1)$$

$$h(x + y) = h(x)\,h(y) \quad \text{where} \quad (x, y) \in \mathbb{R}^2, \quad h: \mathbb{R} \to \mathbb{R}, \quad (1.4.2)$$

and

$$h(x + y) = h(x)\,h(y) \quad \text{where } (x, y) \in \mathbb{R}_{++}^2, \; h: \mathbb{R}_{++} \to \mathbb{R}. \quad (1.4.3)$$

Let us start with (1.4.2), (1.4.3) and prove

1.4.4 **Lemma.** *If a function satisfying Cauchy's equation (1.4.2) or (1.4.3) is zero at a single point x_0, then it is zero everywhere.*

Proof. In case $h : \mathbb{R} \to \mathbb{R}$, the assertion follows from

$$h(x) = h((x - x_0) + x_0) = h(x - x_0)\, h(x_0) = 0 \quad \text{for all} \quad x \in \mathbb{R}. \tag{1.4.5}$$

In case $h : \mathbb{R}_{++} \to \mathbb{R}$, (1.4.5) shows that $h(x) = 0$ only for $x > x_0$. If there exists a

$$t_0 \in]0, x_0[\qquad \text{such that} \quad f(t_0) \neq 0,$$

then take a positive integer n such that $nt_0 \geqq x_0$. Applying (1.4.5) and (1 4.3), we obtain

$$0 = h(nt_0) = h(t_0)^n \neq 0,$$

which is impossible. So, $h(x) = 0$ for all $x \in \mathbb{R}_{++}$. ■

Note that the same argument is valid for *positive* x in the case of Eq. (1.4.1). As a matter of fact, the statement of the lemma is not true in this case, as the counterexample

$$h(x) = \begin{cases} 1 & \text{for} \quad x = 0, \\ 0 & \text{for} \quad x > 0 \end{cases} \tag{1.4.6}$$

shows.

In the following the foregoing trivial solutions are excluded. From (1.4.1) or (1.4.2) or (1.4.3) with $x = y = t/2$ we obtain

$$h(t) = h(t/2)^2 > 0$$

for any nontrivial h; that is, any nontrivial function satisfying (1.4.1) or (1.4.2) or (1.4.3) is positive valued. Taking the logarithm on both sides of (1.4.1) or (1.4.2) or (1.4.3), we get

$$\log h(x + y) = \log h(x) + \log h(y).$$

With

$$\phi(x) := \log h(x) \tag{1.4.7}$$

this becomes Eq. (1.2.1) if the domain of h is $\mathbb{R}$, (1.3.1) if the domain of h is $\mathbb{R}_+$, or

$$\phi(x + y) = \phi(x) + \phi(y) \qquad \text{where} \quad (x, y) \in \mathbb{R}^2_{++}, \quad \phi: \mathbb{R}_{++} \to \mathbb{R}. \tag{1.4.8}$$

Since (1.4.7) is equivalent to

$$h(x) = e^{\phi(x)},$$

we have

1.4.9 **Theorem.** *If h satisfies (1.4.2) or (1.4.3), then*

$$h(x) = e^{\phi(x)} \quad \text{or} \quad h(x) = 0 \quad \textit{for all } x \tag{1.4.10}$$

where ϕ is a suitably chosen solution of the basic Cauchy Eq. (1.2.1) (or of (1.2.1) with $(x, y) \in \mathbb{R}^2_{++}$). If h satisfies (1.4.1), then it has the form (1.4.6) or (1.4.10), where ϕ is a solution of (1.3.1).

If, in (1 4.10), h is continuous at a single point x_0 or monotonic in an arbitrarily small interval, then the same is true for ϕ, and we conclude from (1.4.9), (1.2.10), and (1.3.7):

1.4.11 **Corollary.** *Excluding the trivial solution h with $h(x) = 0$ for all x and the trivial solution (1.4.6), every solution of (1.4.1) or (1.4.2.) or (1.4.3) that is continuous at a single point or monotonic in an arbitrarily small interval can be written in the form*

$$h(x) = e^{cx} \qquad (c \text{ a real const}). \tag{1.4.12}$$

Every function h given by (1.4.12) is a solution of (1.4.1) or (1.4.2) or (1.4.3).

The statement of this corollary is the reason why $h(x + y) = h(x)\,h(y)$ is called the *functional equation of the exponential function.*

1.5 Applications of Sections 1.3 and 1.4 to 1.1: The Interest Formulas

According to Section 1.1, the problem of determining all interest formulas is equivalent to the problem of determining all strictly increasing functions A satisfying

$$\begin{aligned} A(K_1 + K_2, t) &= A(K_1, t) + A(K_2,t) \qquad \text{where} \quad (K_1, K_2) \in \mathbb{R}^2_{+}, \\ A&: \mathbb{R}^2_{+} \to \mathbb{R}, \end{aligned} \tag{1.5.1}$$

and

$$A(A(K, t_1), t_2) = A(K, t_1 + t_2) \qquad \text{where} \quad (t_1, t_2) \in \mathbb{R}^2_{+}, \quad A: \mathbb{R}^2_{+} \to \mathbb{R}. \tag{1.5.2}$$

1.5.3 **Theorem.** *Let A be a strictly increasing function satisfying (1.5.1) and (1.5.2). Then there exists a constant $q > 1$ such that*

$$A(K, t) = Kq^t. \tag{1.5.4}$$

Every function A given by (1.5.4) is a solution of (1.5.1), (1.5.2).

Proof. The second assertion is obvious. The first follows from (1.3.7) and (1.4.11): According to (1.3.7), every strictly increasing solution of (1.5.1) can be written in the form

$$A(K, t) = h(t)\,K \qquad \text{where} \quad h(t) > 0.$$

Because of (1.5.2), $h(t)$ satisfies

$$h(t_1 + t_2) = h(t_1)\, h(t_2),$$

where $h\colon \mathbb{R}_+ \to \mathbb{R}_{++}$ is strictly increasing. Then, from (1.4.11),

$$h(t) = e^{ct} \qquad (c > 0 \text{ a real constant}),$$

or, with $q = e^c > 1$,

$$h(t) = q^t. \qquad \blacksquare$$

Theorem 1.5.3 can be briefly phrased as follows: *Every interest formula has the form (1.5.4), where $q > 1$ is a constant, and every formula (1.5.4) with $q > 1$ is an interest formula.*

1.6 Theory of the Firm: A Model of the Price and Advertising Policy

Let the market position of a single-product firm be such that its sales S depend only on the price p of its product and on the advertising expenditure w. Let the sales function $S\colon \mathbb{R}_+ \times \mathbb{R}_{++} \to \mathbb{R}$ satisfy the equations[2]

$$\left.\begin{array}{l} S(p + \pi, w) = \psi(\pi, w)\, S(p, w) \quad \text{where} \quad (p, \pi) \in \mathbb{R}_+^2, \\ \psi\colon \mathbb{R}_+ \times \mathbb{R}_{++} \to \mathbb{R}, \quad \psi(0, w) = 1 \quad \text{for all} \quad w > 0, \quad S(0, 1) > 0, \\ \pi \to \psi(\pi, w) \text{ nonconstant and nonincreasing} \end{array}\right\} \qquad (1.6.1)$$

and

$$\left.\begin{array}{l} S(p, \lambda w) = S(p, w) + T(p, \lambda) \qquad \text{where} \quad (\lambda, w) \in \mathbb{R}_{++}^2, \\ T\colon \mathbb{R}_+ \times \mathbb{R}_{++} \to \mathbb{R}, \qquad T(p, 1) = 0 \qquad \text{for all} \quad p \geqq 0, \\ \lambda \to T(p, \lambda) \quad \text{nonconstant and nondecreasing.} \end{array}\right\} \qquad (1.6.2)$$

Equation (1.6.1) says that for every given advertising expenditure the sales at price $p + \pi$ are equal to the sales at price p times a real number $\leqq 1$ that is a nonincreasing function of π. The assumption $S(0, 1) > 0$ assures that there are sales if the price is zero and advertising expenditure is 1.

Equation (1.6.2) says that for every given price p, a *multiplicative* change in advertising expenditure w yields an *additive* change in sales. For instance, sales are increased by increases in advertising. This increase is a function of the factor λ, by which advertising expenditures are multiplied, and the price.

1.6.3 **Remark.** If Eq. (1.6.2) were assumed to be valid also for $w = 0$, then $T(p, \lambda) \equiv 0$, contradicting the assumption that $\lambda \to T(p, \lambda)$ is nonconstant.

---

[2] The reason why w is assumed to be positive rather than nonnegative will be made clear by Remark 1.3.6.

The foregoing model gives rise to the following questions:

(a) What does the class $\mathcal{C}$ of sales functions S satisfying (1.6.1) and (1.6.2) look like?

(b) Does there exist a maximum of the profit function P given by

$$P(p, w) = pS(p, w) - K(S(p, w)) - w \tag{1.6.4}$$

where K is the cost function of the firm and S is a sales function of class $\mathcal{C}$?

(c) If yes, for any K and $S \in \mathcal{C}$, does there exist a unique price and advertising policy for the firm, that is, one and only one pair (p^*, w^*) maximizing (1.6.4)? If yes, how is it calculated?

Problems (a)–(c) will be solved in Section 1.8 under the assumption that the cost function $K: \mathbb{R}_+ \to \mathbb{R}_{++}$ is additive in the following sense:

$$\left.\begin{array}{l} K(x + \xi) = K(x) + L(\xi) \qquad \text{with} \quad (x, \xi) \in \mathbb{R}_+^2, \\ L: \mathbb{R}_+ \to \mathbb{R}_+, \qquad L(0) = 0, \qquad L(\xi) \not\equiv \text{const}, \\ x \text{ represents the sales and } \xi \text{ an increment of the sales.} \end{array}\right\} \tag{1.6.5}$$

Before doing this, we have to consider Cauchy's equation

$$l(xy) = l(x) + l(y) \qquad \text{where} \quad (x, y) \in \mathbb{R}_{++}^2, \quad l: \mathbb{R}_{++} \to \mathbb{R} \tag{1.6.6}$$

since Eq. (1.6.2) can be reduced to it by setting $w = 1$, $p = \bar{p}$, $S(\bar{p}, 1) = a$. Thus (1.6.2) becomes $T(\bar{p}, \lambda) = S(\bar{p}, \lambda) - a$, where $T(\bar{p}, w) = l(w)$ satisfies

$$l(\lambda w) = l(w) + l(\lambda).$$

1.7 Cauchy's Equation $l(xy) = l(x) + l(y)$

Since x and y are assumed to be positive, Cauchy's Eq. (1.6.6) can be written

$$l(e^{\log xy}) = l(e^{\log x}) + l(e^{\log y}),$$

that is,

$$l(e^{\log x + \log y}) = l(e^{\log x}) + l(e^{\log y}).$$

With

$$l(x) = l(e^{\log x}) = f(\log x),$$

this becomes

$$f(\log x + \log y) = f(\log x) + f(\log y).$$

If l is not everywhere discontinuous, then the same is true for f. Then, because of (1.2.10),

$$l(x) = f(\log x) = c \log x \qquad (c \in \mathbb{R} \text{ a constant}).$$

We have proved

1.7.1 **Theorem.** *If l, satisfying Cauchy's equation*

$$l(xy) = l(x) + l(y) \qquad \textit{where} \quad (x, y) \in \mathbb{R}^2_{++}, \quad l\colon \mathbb{R}_{++} \to \mathbb{R}, \quad (1.7.2)$$

is not everywhere discontinuous (i.e., if it is continuous at least at one point or monotonic on an arbitrarily small interval), then there exists a constant $c \in \mathbb{R}$ such that

$$l(x) = c \log x \qquad \textit{for all} \quad x \in \mathbb{R}_{++}. \qquad (1.7.3)$$

Every function l given by (1.7.3) is a solution of (1.7.2).

This theorem is the reason Eq. (1.7.2) is called the *functional equation of the logarithm.*

If the domain of l includes 0, then clearly, $l(x) \equiv 0$ is the only solution of $l(xy) = l(x) + l(y)$. If the domain of l is $\mathbb{R}\backslash\{0\}$, then $l(x) = c \log|x|$ is the most general solution of $l(xy) = l(x) + l(y)$ that is continuous at a single point; see Aczél [1966, pp. 39–41].

1.8 Application of Sections 1.3, 1.4, and 1.7 to 1.6: Optimal Price and Advertising Policy of a Firm

Let us first determine the class $\mathscr{C}$ of sales functions $S\colon \mathbb{R}_+ \times \mathbb{R}_{++} \to \mathbb{R}$ satisfying (1.6.1) and (1.6.2) (see problem (a), Section 1.6).

Putting $w = 1$ in (1.6.2), we obtain

$$T(p, \lambda) = S(p, \lambda) - S(p, 1),$$

which satisfies

$$T(p, \lambda w) = T(p, \lambda) + T(p, w).$$

But then, according to (1.7.1),

$$T(p, w) = b(p) \log w$$

where $b(p) > 0$ for all $p \geqq 0$ because of the assumptions on T (see (1.6.2)); and

$$S(p, w) = \beta(p) + b(p) \log w \qquad \text{where} \quad \beta(p) = S(p, 1) \quad \text{and} \quad b(p) > 0. \qquad (1.8.1)$$

The sales function S also has to satisfy Eq. (1.6.1). With $p = 0$ this equation becomes

$$S(\pi, w) = \psi(\pi, w)\, S(0, w).$$

According to (1.8.1), $S(0, w) \neq 0$ except for exactly one w, say $\bar{w}$. Obviously, $\psi(\pi, \bar{w})\, S(0, \bar{w}) = S(\pi, \bar{w}) \equiv 0$. For all $w \neq \bar{w}$ we have

$$\psi(\pi, w) = \frac{S(\pi, w)}{S(0, w)},$$

which satisfies

$$\psi(p + \pi, w) = \psi(p, w)\, \psi(\pi, w). \tag{1.8.2}$$

According to Corollary 1.4.11, every solution of (1.8.2) having the properties listed in (1.6.1) can be written in the form

$$\psi(p, w) = e^{c(w)\, p}$$

where $c(w)$ is a negative constant depending on w. Hence

$$S(p, w) = \gamma(w)\, e^{c(w)\, p} \qquad (\gamma(w) = S(0, w)). \tag{1.8.3}$$

Note that (1.8.3) contains, for $\gamma(\bar{w}) = S(0, \bar{w}) = 0$, the above-mentioned case in which $S(p, \bar{w}) \equiv 0$.

A function of class $\mathscr{C}$ has to have the form (1.8.3) as well as the form (1.8.1):

$$\gamma(w) e^{c(w)\, p} = \beta(p) + b(p) \log w. \tag{1.8.4}$$

Putting first $w = 1$, then $p = 0$, and then $w = 1$, $p = 0$ simultaneously, we obtain

$$\beta(p) = \gamma(1)\, e^{c(1)\, p}, \tag{1.8.5}$$

$$\gamma(w) = \beta(0) + b(0) \log w, \tag{1.8.6}$$

and

$$\gamma(1) = \beta(0), \tag{1.8.7}$$

respectively. Note that $\beta(0) = \gamma(1) = S\,(0,1) > 0$, according to the assumption on S in (1.6.1). With (1.8.5)–(1.8.7), (1.8.4) becomes

$$(\gamma(1) + b(0) \log w)\, e^{c(w)\, p} = \gamma(1)\, e^{c(1)\, p} + b(p) \log w. \tag{1.8.8}$$

Setting $w = e$ we obtain from (1.8.8)

$$b(p) = (\gamma(1) + b(0))\, e^{c(e)\, p} - \gamma(1)\, e^{c(1)\, p},$$

setting $w = e^2$, we have

$$b(p) = \left(\frac{\gamma(1)}{2} + b(0)\right) e^{c(e^2)\, p} - \frac{\gamma(1)}{2}\, e^{c(1)\, p}.$$

Since, by assumption, $\gamma(1) = S(0,1) > 0$, $b(0) > 0$, the right-hand sides are equal for all $p \geqq 0$ if and only if $c(e^2) = c(e) = c(1)$. Hence

$$b(p) = b(0)\, e^{c(1)p} \tag{1.8.9}$$

and, inserting this into (1.8.4), we obtain

$$c(w) = c(1). \tag{1.8.10}$$

With (1.8.6), (1.8.10) the function S given by (1.8.3) becomes

$$S(p, w) = (\beta(0) + b(0) \log w)\, e^{c(1)\, p},$$

and this is just the same as (1.8.1) with (1.8.5), (1.8.9). Obviously, every function S given by

$$S(p, w) = (a + b \log w)\, e^{-cp} \qquad (a, b, c \text{ positive constants})$$

is a solution of (1.6.1), (1.6.2) that is, belongs to class $\mathcal{C}$.

We have proved

1.8.11 **Theorem.** *A function S belongs to the class $\mathcal{C}$ of sales functions satisfying Eqs. (1.6.1) and (1.6.2) if and only if*

$$S(p, w) = (a + b \log w)\, e^{-cp} \tag{1.8.12}$$

where a, b, c are arbitrary positive constants.

1.8.13 **Remark.** The functions S given by (1.8.12) seem to be a suitable class of sales functions for the following reasons.

(i) The graph

$$\left\{ (p, x) \,\middle|\, \begin{array}{l} p \geqq 0,\ x = S(p, w) = (a + b \log w)\, e^{-cp} > 0, \\ w \geqq 1 \text{ fixed}, \quad a > 0,\ b > 0,\ c > 0 \text{ constants} \end{array} \right\}$$

is strictly convex (from below) and strictly decreasing (see Fig. 1.8.14).

(ii) The graph

$$\left\{ (w, x) \,\middle|\, \begin{array}{l} w \geqq 1, \quad x = S(p, w) = (a + b \log w)\, e^{-cp} > 0 \\ p \geqq 0 \text{ fixed}, \quad a > 0, \quad b > 0, \quad c > 0 \text{ constants} \end{array} \right\}$$

is strictly concave and strictly increasing (see Fig. 1.8.15). At least in the middle of the usual range of the advertising expenditures, this conforms with empirical results (see, e.g., Rao [1970]).

(iii) Another justification to the foregoing form of the sales functions S is the so-called Weber–Fechner law. It states that in the middle of a continuum of stimuli the intensity of perception of an individuum is a linear function of the logarithm of the intensity w of the stimulus: $a + b \log w$. This law is confined to *individual* response functions, but it may also be valid if the individual

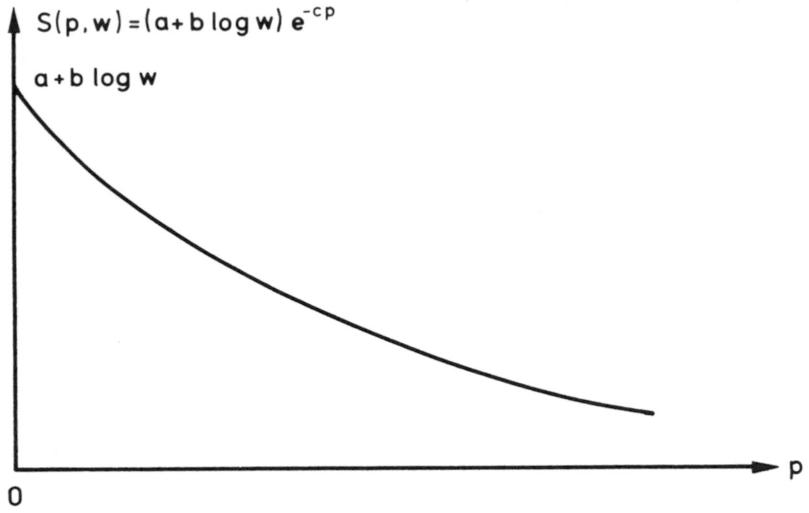

1.8.14 Figure. Graph of the function $p \to (a + b \log w)\, e^{-cp}$.

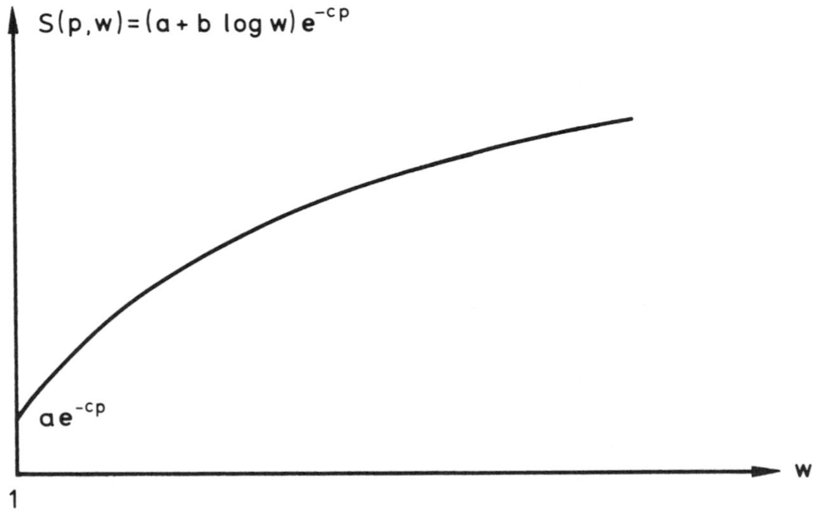

1.8.15 Figure. Graph of the function $w \to (a + b \log w)\, e^{-cp}$.

advertising response functions are aggregated; see in this connection Rao [1970, p. 17].

We now proceed to solve problems (b) and (c) of Section 1.6. Let a single-product firm have a sales function S of class $\mathscr{C}$ and a cost function $K: \mathbb{R}_+ \to \mathbb{R}_{++}$. Its profit Π, which depends on both the price p of the product and the advertising expenditure w, is then

$$\Pi(p, w) = pS(p, w) - K(S(p, w)) - w. \tag{1.8.16}$$

The problem of maximizing P can be solved if properties of the cost function are known. Let the cost function be additive in the following sense:

$$K(x + \xi) = K(x) + L(\xi) \tag{1.8.17}$$

where x is the firm's output and $K(x)$ the (minimum) cost of x; ξ represents increments of output; and $L: \mathbb{R}_+ \to \mathbb{R}_+$ is a nonconstant function of the increment ξ. Then

$$L(\xi) = K(\xi) - K(0)$$

satisfies

$$L(\xi + \xi^*) = L(\xi) + L(\xi^*), \qquad L: \mathbb{R}_+ \to \mathbb{R}_+, \quad L(\xi) \neq \text{const.}$$

According to Corollary 1.3.7, L then has the form

$$L(\xi) = \beta\xi \qquad (\text{the constant } \beta > 0 \text{ since } L(\xi) \geqq 0,\, L(\xi) \not\equiv \text{constant}),$$

that is, the cost function K has the form

$$K(x) = \alpha + \beta x \tag{1.8.18}$$

where $\alpha = K(0) \geqq 0$ is the fixed cost and $\beta > 0$ is the marginal cost.

1.8.19 **Theorem.** *Let the profit function Π of a single-product firm be given by (1.8.16) where $S: \mathbb{R}_+ \times \mathbb{R}_{++} \to \mathbb{R}$ is the sales function satisfying (1 6.1), (1.6.2) and $K: \mathbb{R}_+ \to \mathbb{R}_+$ is the cost function satisfying (1.8.17). Then the following statements are valid:*

(i) Given any price p greater than marginal cost β, there exists one and only one advertising expenditure $w(p) > 0$ that maximizes profit (1.8.16).

(ii) Given any advertising expenditure $w \geqq 1$[3] there exists one and only one price $p^* > \beta$ that maximizes profit (1.8.16). This price p^* does not depend on w.

[3] This can be sharpened to $w > e^{-(a/b)}$ where a and b are the positive constants occurring in (1.8.12).

(iii) If the constant b[4] *in (1.8.12) is greater than c* $e^{1+c\beta}$ *where c is the damping factor (see (1.8.19)) and* β *is the marginal cost (see (1.8.18)), then there exists one and only one optimal price and advertising policy* (p^*, w^*).

(iv) *Let* (p^*, w^*) *be such an optimal price and advertising policy. If the constant a*[5] *in (1.8.12) satisfies the inequality*

$$a > \alpha c\, e^{1+c\beta} - b(\log b - \log c - c\beta - 2), \tag{1.8.20}$$

then (and only then) $\Pi(p^*, w^*) > 0$.

Proof. As we have seen, the assumptions of our theorem yield the classes of sales and cost functions given by (1.8.1) and (1.8.18), respectively. Inserting (1.8.12) and (1.8.18) into (1.8.16), we obtain the profit at (p, w):

$$\Pi(p, w) = (p - \beta)(a + b \log w)\, e^{-cp} - \alpha - w \tag{1.8.21}$$

where a, b, c, α, β are positive constants.

(i) From

$$\frac{\partial \Pi(p, w)}{\partial w} = (p - \beta)\frac{b}{w} e^{-cp} - 1 = 0$$

and

$$\frac{\partial^2 \Pi(p, w)}{\partial w^2} = (p - \beta)\frac{-b}{w^2} e^{-cp} < 0 \qquad \text{for all} \quad p > \beta,\ w > 0,$$

it follows that

$$w = (p - \beta)\, be^{-cp} > 0 \qquad \text{for} \quad p > \beta \tag{1.8.22}$$

is the unique advertising expenditure that maximizes the profit (1.8.21) given the price $p > \beta$.

(ii) If $w > e^{-(a/b)}$, then

$$\frac{\partial \Pi(p, w)}{\partial p} = (a + b \log w)\, e^{-cp}\,(1 - (p - \beta)\, c) = 0$$

if and only if

$$p = p^* = (1/c) + \beta. \tag{1.8.23}$$

Note that p^* does not depend on w. Inserting this into

$$\frac{\partial^2 \Pi(p, w)}{\partial p^2} = (a + b \log w)\,(-c)\, e^{-cp}\,(2 - (p - \beta)\, c),$$

---

[4] Obviously b influences the saturation quantity (i.e., the quantity sold if $p = 0$) whenever $w > 1$.

[5] If $w = 1$, then a is the saturation quantity.

we get

$$\frac{\partial^2 \Pi(p^*, w)}{\partial p^2} = (a + b \log w)(-c)\, e^{-1-c\beta} < 0 \qquad (w > e^{-(a/b)}),$$

that is, at $p = p^*$ we obtain a *local* maximum of the graph

$$\{(p, q) \mid p \geqq 0, \quad q = \Pi(p, w), \quad w \text{ fixed}, w > e^{-(a/b)}\}.$$

That this maximum is *global* follows easily from the shape of (1.8.21).

(iii) If $b > ce^{1+c\beta}$, then (1.8.22) with (1.8.23) becomes

$$w = w^* = \frac{b}{c} e^{-1-\beta c} > 1,$$

that is, the condition $w > e^{-(a/b)}$ in (ii) is fulfilled. Since

$$\frac{\partial^2 \Pi(p^*, w^*)}{\partial p^2} < 0, \qquad \frac{\partial^2 \Pi(p^*, w^*)}{\partial p\, \partial w} = 0, \qquad \frac{\partial^2 \Pi(p^*, w^*)}{\partial w^2} < 0,$$

the above proves the following: If $b > ce^{1+c\beta}$, then there exists a unique point (p^*, q^*) at which the profit (1.8.21) assumes its maximum, namely

$$(p^*, w^*) = \left(\frac{1}{c} + \beta, \frac{b}{c} e^{-1-c\beta}\right). \tag{1.8.24}$$

(iv) Inserting (1.8.24) into (1.8.21), we obtain immediately that $\Pi(p^*, w^*) > 0$ if and only if inequality (1.8.20) is valid. ■

1.8.25 **Example.** Let the sales function given by (1.8.12) have the following constants:

$$a = e^{13} \approx 442{,}412.3, \qquad b = e^{12} \approx 162{,}755.0, \qquad c = 1.$$

Let the fixed and marginal costs be

$$\alpha = 9e^{10} \approx 198{,}238.6, \qquad \beta = 1$$

(see (1.8.18)). Then, according to (1.8.24), the optimal price and advertising policy is

$$p^* = \frac{1}{c} + \beta = 2, \qquad w^* = \frac{b}{c} e^{-1-c\beta} = e^{10} \approx 22{,}026.5,$$

and the maximum profit is

$$\Pi(p^*, w^*) = (p^* - \beta)(a + b \log w^*)\, e^{-cp^*} - \alpha - w^* = e^{11} \approx 59{,}874.1.$$

At (p^*, w^*) the sales and cost are

$$S(p^*, w^*) = (a + b \log w^*)\, e^{-cp^*} = (e^{13} + e^{12}\, 10)\, e^{-2} \approx 280{,}139.2$$

and

$$K(S(p^*, w^*)) = \alpha + \beta\cdot(a + b \log w^*)\, e^{-cp^*} = 9e^{10} + S(p^*, w^*) \approx 478{,}377.8,$$

respectively.

1.9 Theory of Production: A Problem Yielding Cauchy's Equation $m(xy) = m(x)\,m(y)$

Let

$$\Phi: \mathbb{R}^n_+ \to \mathbb{R}_+$$

be a *production function*,[6] that is, a function associating with each input vector

$$\mathbf{x} = (x_1, \ldots, x_n) \in \mathbb{R}^n_+$$

the largest output (of a single commodity) obtainable with $\mathbf{x}$, namely $\Phi(\mathbf{x})$. It is natural to assume at least the following properties of Φ.

There is at least one input vector $\mathbf{x}^* \geqq \mathbf{0}$ such that

$$\Phi(\mathbf{x}^*) > 0; \tag{1.9.1}$$

$$\lambda \to \Phi(\lambda\mathbf{x}^*) \text{ is nondecreasing } (\lambda \in \mathbb{R}_+); \tag{1.9.2}$$

$$\Phi(\lambda^*\mathbf{x}^*) > \Phi(\mathbf{x}^*) \qquad \text{for some} \quad \lambda^* > 1. \tag{1.9.3}$$

A function $\Phi: \mathbb{R}^n_+ \to \mathbb{R}$ is called *homogeneous of degree r* ($r \in \mathbb{R}_+$) if it satisfies the functional equation

$$\Phi(\lambda\mathbf{x}) = \lambda^r\Phi(\mathbf{x}) \qquad \text{for all} \quad (\lambda, \mathbf{x}) \in \mathbb{R}^{n+1}_+. \tag{1.9.4}$$

Here λ^r is defined as follows:

$$\text{If } r = 0, \quad \text{then} \quad \lambda^r = \lambda^0 = 1 \qquad \text{for all} \quad \lambda \in \mathbb{R}_+.$$

$$\text{If } r \in \mathbb{R}_{++}, \quad \text{then} \quad \lambda^r = \begin{cases} e^{r \log \lambda} & \text{for all} \quad \lambda \in \mathbb{R}_{++}, \\ 0 & \text{for} \quad \lambda = 0. \end{cases} \tag{1.9.5}$$

An extension of the class of production functions that are homogeneous of degree r ($r \in \mathbb{R}_{++}$) may perhaps be obtained as follows (see Lancaster [1968, p. 334]. Replace (1.9.4) by

$$\Phi(\lambda\mathbf{x}) = m(\lambda)\,\Phi(\mathbf{x}) \tag{1.9.6}$$

where

$$m: \mathbb{R}_+ \to \mathbb{R}_+ \tag{1.9.7}$$

---

[6] An extensive list of properties that are often assumed for production functions can be found in Section 13.3 (see (13.3.1)–(13.3.6)).

has, as a consequence of (1.9.6) with (1.9.1)–(1.9.3), the properties

$$m(1) = 1; \tag{1.9.8}$$

$$m \text{ is nondecreasing;} \tag{1.9.9}$$

$$\text{there is some } \lambda^* > 1 \text{ such that } m(\lambda^*) > m(1) = 1. \tag{1.9.10}$$

Whereas the graphs

$$\{(\lambda, \varrho) \mid \lambda \in \mathbb{R}_+, \varrho = \lambda^r; r \in \mathbb{R}_{++}\}$$

are only parabolas ($r \neq 1$) or a ray ($r = 1$), the set of graphs

$$\{(\lambda, \varrho) \mid \lambda \in \mathbb{R}_+, \varrho = m(\lambda); m \text{ a function (1.9.7) with (1.9.8)–(1.9.10)}\}$$

contains, for instance, $\int$-shaped curves like that drawn in Fig. 1.9.11.

It may be noted that Shephard's [1970, p. 22] system A.1–A.6 (i.e., (13.3.1)–(13.3.6)) of properties of a production function allows for $\int$-shaped product curves in the case of proportional scale variation, that is, $\lambda \to \Phi(\lambda \mathbf{x})$. Levenson and Solon [1966] have considered production functions with this property explicitly.

We can prove that functional equation (1.9.6) with (1.9.7)–(1.9.10) *excludes* solutions for which the graph of m is a curve of the kind drawn in Fig. 1.9.11. To show this, we compare

$$\Phi(\lambda\mu \cdot \mathbf{x}) = m(\lambda\mu)\Phi(\mathbf{x}) \qquad ((\lambda, \mu, \mathbf{x}) \in \mathbb{R}_+^{n+2})$$

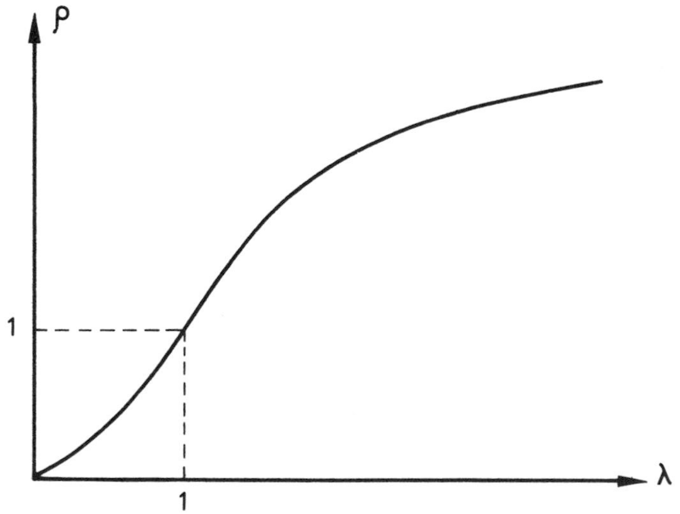

1.9.11 Figure. Example of an $\int$-shaped curve.

with

$$\Phi(\lambda \cdot \mu \mathbf{x}) = m(\lambda)\Phi(\mu\mathbf{x}) = m(\lambda)\, m(\mu)\, \Phi(\mathbf{x}) \qquad ((\lambda, \mu, \mathbf{x}) \in \mathbb{R}_+^{n+2})$$

in the case in which $\mathbf{x} = \mathbf{x}^*$, that is, when $\Phi(\mathbf{x}^*) > 0$. It follows that

$$m(\lambda\mu) = m(\lambda)\, m(\mu) \qquad \text{where} \quad (\lambda, \mu) \in \mathbb{R}_+^2, \quad m\colon \mathbb{R}_+ \to \mathbb{R}_+. \tag{1.9.12}$$

This is Cauchy's equation (1.0.5) with range $\mathbb{R}_+$ instead of $\mathbb{R}$.

1.9.13 **Theorem.** *If m, satisfying Cauchy's equation*

$$m(\lambda\mu) = m(\lambda)\, m(\mu) \qquad \textit{where} \quad (\lambda, \mu) \in \mathbb{R}_+^2, \quad m\colon \mathbb{R}_+ \to \mathbb{R} \quad (\textit{or } \mathbb{R}_+), \tag{1.9.14}$$

is nondecreasing in an arbitrarily small interval, then either there exists $r \in \mathbb{R}_+$ such that

$$m(\lambda) = \lambda^r \qquad \textit{for all} \quad \lambda \in \mathbb{R}_+ \qquad (\textit{see } (1.9.5)) \tag{1.9.15}$$

or

$$m(\lambda) = 0 \qquad \textit{for all} \quad \lambda \in \mathbb{R}_+ \tag{1.9.16}$$

or

$$m(\lambda) = \begin{cases} 0 & \text{for} \quad \lambda = 0, \\ 1 & \text{for} \quad \lambda \in \mathbb{R}_{++}. \end{cases} \tag{1.9.17}$$

Conversely, every function m given by (1.9.15), (1.9.16), or (1.9.17) is a solution of (1.9.14)

Proof. The last assertion is obvious. In order to prove the remaining assertions, let us first set $\mu = 0$ in (1.9.14). We obtain $m(0) = m(\lambda)m(0)$, whence either $m(\lambda) \equiv 1$ or $m(0) = 0$. The identity $m(\lambda) \equiv 1$ is (1.9.15) with $r = 0$.

With $\mathbb{R}_{++}$ instead of $\mathbb{R}_+$, (1.9.14) can be written as

$$m(e^{\log \lambda + \log \mu}) = m(e^{\log \lambda})\, m(e^{\log \mu}).$$

Setting

$$m(\lambda) = m(e^{\log \lambda}) =: h(\log \lambda),$$

we obtain

$$h(\log \lambda + \log \mu) = h(\log \lambda)\, h(\log \mu).$$

If m is nondecreasing in an arbitrarily small interval, then the same is true for h. Then, because of (1.4.11),

$$m(\lambda) = h(\log \lambda) = e^{r \log \lambda} = \lambda^r \qquad (r \in \mathbb{R}_+, \lambda \in \mathbb{R}_{++}) \tag{1.9.18}$$

or

$$m(\lambda) = 0 \qquad \text{for all} \quad \lambda \in \mathbb{R}_{++}. \tag{1.9.19}$$

Extending the domain $\mathbb{R}_{++}$ of (1.9.18) and (1.9.19) to $\mathbb{R}_+$, we easily see that the remaining assertions of the theorem are true. ∎

Since Eq. (1.9.6) in conjunction with the properties (1.9.7) and (1.9.1)–(1.9.3) implies Eq. (1.9.12) in conjunction with the properties (1.9.8)–(1.9.10), we have

1.9.20 **Corollary.** *A function $\Phi\colon \mathbb{R}^n_+ \to \mathbb{R}_+$ with the properties (1.9.1)–(1.9.3) (e.g., a production function) satisfies the functional equation*

$$\Phi(\lambda\mathbf{x}) = m(\lambda)\Phi(\mathbf{x}) \qquad \textit{where} \quad (\lambda, \mathbf{x}) \in \mathbb{R}^{n+1}_+, \quad m\colon \mathbb{R}_+ \to \mathbb{R}_+ \tag{1.9.21}$$

if and only if it is homogeneous of degree r where $r \in \mathbb{R}_{++}$.

Similar versions of this corollary have been proved by the author [1968a]; [1970, pp. 104–107] and, independently, by Kats [1970]. McElroy [1969] and Whitaker and McCallum [1971] proved it under differentiability conditions.

1.9.22 **Remark.** Note that the results of this section remain true when the domain $\mathbb{R}^n_+$ of Φ is replaced by a *cone of $\mathbb{R}^n_+$ with vertex* $\mathbf{0}$, that is, by a subset $C \subseteqq \mathbb{R}^n_+$ satisfying $\lambda\mathbf{x} \in C$ for all $\lambda \in \mathbb{R}_+$ whenever $\mathbf{x} \in C$.

1.9.23 **Remark.** As follows from the proof of Theorem 1.9.13, *a function $m\colon \mathbb{R}_{++} \to \mathbb{R}$, which is monotonic in an arbitrarily small interval or continuous at a single point, satisfies*

$$m(\lambda\mu) = m(\lambda)\, m(\mu) \qquad \textit{where} \quad (\lambda, \mu) \in \mathbb{R}^2_{++} \tag{1.9.24}$$

if and only if

$$m(\lambda) = \lambda^r \qquad \textit{for all} \quad \lambda \in \mathbb{R}_{++}\ (r \in \mathbb{R}) \tag{1.9.25}$$

or

$$m(\lambda) = 0 \qquad \textit{for all} \quad \lambda \in \mathbb{R}_{++}. \tag{1.9.26}$$

The complete set of solutions of $m(\lambda\mu) = m(\lambda)\, m(\mu)$ that are continuous at a single point can be found in Aczél [1966, pp. 39–41] for (λ, μ) from $\mathbb{R}^2$, $\mathbb{R}^2_+$, $\mathbb{R}^2_{++}$, or $(\mathbb{R}\backslash\{0\})^2$.

A true extension of the class of the homogeneous functions (see (1.9.4)) can be obtained by introducing the functional equation

$$\Phi(\lambda\mathbf{x}) = m(\lambda, \mathbf{x}/|\mathbf{x}|)\Phi(\mathbf{x}) \tag{1.9.27}$$

where

$$\Phi\colon \mathbb{R}^n_+ \to \mathbb{R}, \tag{1.9.28}$$

$$(\lambda, \mathbf{x}) \in \mathbb{R}^{n+1}_+, \qquad |\mathbf{x}| := (x_1^2 + \cdots + x_n^2)^{1/2} \neq 0, \tag{1.9.29}$$

$$m\colon \mathbb{R}_+ \times \{\mathbf{y} \mid \mathbf{y} \in \mathbb{R}^n_+, |\mathbf{y}| = 1\} \to \mathbb{R}. \tag{1.9.30}$$

When there exists $\mathbf{x} \geq \mathbf{0}$ such that $\Phi(\mathbf{x}) \neq 0$, then, in the same way that (1.9.6) implied (1.9.12), Eq. (1.9.27) yields

$$m(\lambda\mu, \mathbf{x}/|\mathbf{x}|) = m(\lambda, \mathbf{x}/|\mathbf{x}|)\, m(\mu, \mathbf{x}/|\mathbf{x}|). \tag{1.9.31}$$

For each special value of $\mathbf{x}/|\mathbf{x}|$, (1.9.31) is an equation of the form (1.9.14). Hence, Theorem 1.9.13 can be applied, and since $\Phi(\mathbf{x}) = 0$ implies $\Phi(\lambda\mathbf{x}) = 0$ for all $\lambda \in \mathbb{R}_+$, we have

1.9.32 **Corollary.** *A function* $\Phi: \mathbb{R}_+^n \to \mathbb{R}_+$ *with properties (1.9.1)–(1.9.3) (e.g., a production function) satisfies functional equation (1.9.27) in conjunction with (1.9.29) and (1.9.30) if and only if it satisfies the functional equation*

$$\Phi(\lambda\mathbf{x}) = \lambda^{g(\mathbf{x}/|\mathbf{x}|)}\,\Phi(\mathbf{x}) \tag{1.9.33}$$

where

$$\mathbf{x} \geq \mathbf{0}, \qquad g(\mathbf{x}/|\mathbf{x}|) \in \mathbb{R}_{++}, \qquad \lambda \in \mathbb{R}_+.$$

In other words, a production function Φ satisfying Eq. (1.9.27) in conjunction with (1.9.29) and (1.9.30) is *homogeneous along rays*

$$\{\mathbf{y} \mid \mathbf{y} = \lambda\mathbf{x},\ \lambda \in \mathbb{R}_+;\ \mathbf{x} \geq \mathbf{0},\ \text{fixed}\}$$

where the degree r *(*$r \in \mathbb{R}_{++}$*) of homogeneity depends on the particular ray along which the input vector in question lies.*

Functional equation (1.9.27) was introduced and solved by the author [1969; 1970, pp. 104–111] and, independently, by McElroy [1969] (in a somewhat more restricted form and under differentiability assumptions). It was subsequently considered by Aczél [1969, pp. 59–62] and Goldman and Shephard [1972], and has been generalized by Shephard [1974a] and by Färe and Shephard [1977] for technologies with *multiple* outputs. See, in this connection, Sections 12.4 and 12.5. Some further results about Eq. (1.9.27) can be found in Section 4.7.

1.10 Theory of Technical Progress: Further Problems Yielding Cauchy's Equation $m(xy) = m(x)\,m(y)$

The following is taken from a joint paper by Eichhorn and Kolm [1974].

Let $\Phi: \mathbb{R}_+^3 \to \mathbb{R}$ be a production function[7] depending not only on the two productive factors capital K and labor L but also on t. We consider t as time or, alternatively, as an index of the state of technology. The assumption $t \geqq 0$ does not restrict generality.

An assumption on Φ needed later is the following:

There exists at least one vector $(K^*, L^*) > (0, 0)$
such that $t \to \Phi(K^*, L^*, t)$ is nondecreasing (1.10.1)
and nonconstant for $t > 0$.

[7] For an intuitive definition of a production function, see the beginning of Section 1.9. See also Remark 13.3.7.

This says that the output $\Phi(K^*, L^*, t)$ obtainable by the fixed input vector (K^*, L^*) increases with time, that is, with technical progress.

Technical progress is called *output augmenting* if there exist two functions

$$\Phi_1: \mathbb{R}_+^2 \to \mathbb{R}_+ \quad \text{and} \quad \phi_1: \mathbb{R}_+ \to \mathbb{R}_+$$

such that Φ with property (1.10.1) can be written as

$$\Phi(K, L, t) = \phi_1(t)\Phi_1(K, L). \tag{1.10.2}$$

If, in addition, Φ is *linearly homogeneous* with respect to K and L, that is, if

$$\Phi(\lambda K, \lambda L, t) = \lambda\Phi(K, L, t) \qquad \text{for all} \quad (K, L, t) \in \mathbb{R}_+^3 \quad \text{and} \quad \lambda \geqq 0, \tag{1.10.3}$$

then inventions are called *Hicks neutral* (see Sato and Beckmann [1968] or Krelle [1969, pp. 129–131]; the reason for this name will become clear in Section 5.1).

From (1.10.1) and (1.10.2) it follows that

$$\phi_1 \quad \text{is nondecreasing and nonconstant for} \quad t > 0, \tag{1.10.4}$$

and from (1.10.2) and (1.10.3) that Φ_1 is linearly homogeneous.

Technical progress is called *labor augmenting* if there exist two nondecreasing functions

$$\Phi_2: \mathbb{R}_+^2 \to \mathbb{R}_+ \quad \text{and} \quad \phi_2: \mathbb{R}_+ \to \mathbb{R}_+$$

such that

$$\Phi(K, L, t) = \Phi_2(K, \phi_2(t)\, L). \tag{1.10.5}$$

It is called *capital augmenting* if there exist two nondecreasing functions

$$\Phi_3: \mathbb{R}_+^2 \to \mathbb{R}_+ \quad \text{and} \quad \phi_3: \mathbb{R}_+ \to \mathbb{R}_+$$

such that

$$\Phi(K, L, t) = \Phi_3(\phi_3(t)\, K, L). \tag{1.10.6}$$

If, in addition, Φ is linearly homogeneous with respect to K and L, then inventions are called *Harrod neutral* in case (1.10.5) and *Solow neutral* in case (1.10.6) (see Sato and Beckmann [1968] or Krelle [1969, pp. 124–127, 131–133]; the reason for these names will become clear in Section 5.1).

Note that property (1.10.1) of Φ, together with the assumption that the functions $\Phi_2, \Phi_3, \phi_2, \phi_3$ are nondecreasing, implies that $\Phi_2, \Phi_3, \phi_2, \phi_3$ are nonconstant.

1.10.7 **Theorem.** *Let $\Phi: \mathbb{R}^3_+ \to \mathbb{R}_+$ with property (1.10.1) be a function that can be expressed in each of the three forms (1.10.2), (1.10.5), and (1.10.6), where*

$$\phi_1 \quad \text{is nondecreasing and nonconstant for} \quad t > 0, \tag{1.10.8}$$

$$\Phi_2 \quad \text{and} \quad \Phi_3 \quad \text{are nondecreasing}, \tag{1.10.9}$$

$$\left.\begin{array}{l}\phi_2 \quad \text{and} \quad \phi_3 \quad \text{are continuous and strictly increasing from} \\ \phi_2(0) = 0, \quad \phi_3(0) = 0^{8} \quad \text{to infinity for} \quad t \to \infty.\end{array}\right\} \tag{1.10.10}$$

That is, interpreting Φ as a production function, suppose technical progress to be at the same time

(i) *output augmenting,*
(ii) *labor augmenting, and*
(iii) *capital augmenting,*

and let (1 10.1), (1.10.8)–(1.10.10) be valid. Then

$$\Phi_1(K, L) = CK^{\alpha} L^{\beta} \qquad (C, \alpha, \beta \text{ positive constants}),$$

that is,

$$\Phi(K, L, t) = \phi(t)\, K^{\alpha} L^{\beta} \qquad (\phi(t) = C\phi_1(t); \text{ see } (1.10.2)). \tag{1.10.11}$$

Thus Φ is the Cobb–Douglas[9] *function with respect to K and L. Every function given by (1.10.11) can be expressed in each of the three forms (1.10.2), (1.10.5), and (1.10.6) with suitably chosen functions $\Phi_1, \Phi_2, \Phi_3, \phi_1, \phi_2$, and ϕ_3.*

Proof. Since the last assertion is obvious, we have only to prove the first part of the theorem. If Φ can be expressed in each of the forms (1.10.2), (1.10.5) and (1.10.6), then

$$\Phi_2(K, \phi_2(t) L) = \phi_1(t) \Phi_1(K, L) \tag{1.10.12}$$

and

$$\Phi_3(\phi_3(t) K, L) = \phi_1(t) \Phi_1(K, L). \tag{1.10.13}$$

Because of (1.10.10) we can write

$$t = \phi_i^{-1}(\tau) \qquad (i = 2, 3) \tag{1.10.14}$$

rather than $\phi_i(t) = \tau$, where ϕ_i^{-1} is the inverse of ϕ_i. Substituting (1.10.14) into (1.10.12) and (1.10.13), we obtain

$$\Phi_2(K, \tau L) = \psi(\tau)\, \Phi_1(K, L) \qquad \left(\psi(\tau) = \phi_1(\phi_2^{-1}(\tau)),\ \tau \geqq 0\right) \tag{1.10.15}$$

[8] If we assume $\phi_2(0) = a$, $\phi_3(0) = b$ ($a \geqq 0$, $b \geqq 0$ constants), the theorem does not change essentially.

[9] See Cobb and Douglas [1928] and Douglas [1934].

and

$$\Phi_3(\tau K, L) = \chi(\tau)\Phi_1(K, L) \qquad \left(\chi(\tau) = \phi_1(\phi_3^{-1}(\tau)), \tau \geqq 0\right), \quad (1.10.16)$$

respectively. Hence, for $\tau = 1$,

$$\Phi_2(K, L) = \psi(1)\Phi_1(K, L), \qquad \Phi_3(K, L) = \chi(1)\Phi_1(K, L). \quad (1.10.17)$$

Here $\psi(1) \neq 0$, $\chi(1) \neq 0$, since otherwise $\Phi_2(K, L) \equiv 0$ or $\Phi_3(K, L) \equiv 0$, and hence, because of (1.10.5) or (1.10.6) $\Phi(K, L, t) \equiv 0$, contradicting (1.10.1). With (1.10.17), (1.10.15) and (1.10.16) can be written

$$\Phi_1(K, \tau L) = \frac{\psi(\tau)}{\psi(1)}\Phi_1(K, L) = m(\tau)\Phi_1(K, L) \qquad \left(m(\tau) = \frac{\psi(\tau)}{\psi(1)}\right)$$

and

$$\Phi_1(\tau K, L) = \frac{\chi(\tau)}{\chi(1)}\Phi_1(K, L) = n(\tau)\Phi_1(K, L) \qquad \left(n(\tau) = \frac{\chi(\tau)}{\chi(1)}\right),$$

respectively. From here we obtain, as from (1.9.6),

$$m(\sigma\tau) = m(\sigma)\, m(\tau) \quad \text{and} \quad n(\sigma\tau) = n(\sigma)\, n(\tau),$$

respectively. Assumptions (1.10.1), (1.10.5), and (1.10.10) imply that m and n are functions mapping $\mathbb{R}_+$ into $\mathbb{R}_+$ that are nondecreasing and nonconstant for $\tau > 0$. Hence, by (1.9.13),

$$m(\tau) = \tau^\beta, \qquad n(\tau) = \tau^\alpha \qquad (\alpha, \beta \text{ positive constants}).$$

Hence

$$\Phi_1(K, L) = \Phi_1(K \cdot 1, L) = K^\alpha \Phi_1(1, L \cdot 1) = K^\alpha L^\beta \Phi_1(1, 1) = CK^\alpha L^\beta,$$

and the theorem is proved. ■

Note that neither differentiability nor homogeneity assumptions were made in the theorem.

Assume now that Φ, in (1.10.7), is homogeneous of degree $r > 0$ (see (1.9.4)) with respect to K and L; that is, that Φ_1 is homogeneous of degree $r > 0$. *Then only one of the equations (1.10.12), (1.10.13), that is, only (i), (ii), or (i), (iii), is needed to prove that Φ_1 is Cobb–Douglas.* This follows from the fact that Φ_1, if homogeneous of degree $r > 0$, can be written in either of the forms

$$\Phi_1(K, L) = \Phi_1\left(K \cdot 1, K\frac{L}{K}\right) = K^r \Phi_1\left(1, \frac{L}{K}\right) \qquad (K > 0),$$

$$\Phi_1(K, L) = \Phi_1\left(L\frac{K}{L}, L \cdot 1\right) = L^r \Phi_1\left(\frac{K}{L}, 1\right) \qquad (L > 0).$$

A special case of this result is the following theorem, due to Uzawa [1961]:[10]

[10] His proof requires differentiability assumptions up to the order 2.

1.10.18 **Corollary.** *If a production function* $\Phi: \mathbb{R}_+^3 \to \mathbb{R}_+$, $(K, L, t) \to \Phi(K, L, t)$, *is linearly homogeneous with respect to K and L, then either (i′) Hicks neutrality (of inventions, technical progress) and (ii′) Harrod neutrality, or (i′) and (iii′) Solow neutrality imply that, under the corresponding relevant assumptions of Theorem 1.10.7,* Φ *is the (linearly homogeneous) Cobb–Douglas function with respect to K and L.*

Let us now generalize the forms of technical progress considered in the foregoing. Technical progress is called *both factors augmenting* if there exist three nondecreasing functions

$$\Phi_4: \mathbb{R}_+^2 \to \mathbb{R}_+, \qquad \phi_4: \mathbb{R}_+ \to \mathbb{R}_+, \qquad \phi_5: \mathbb{R}_+ \to \mathbb{R}_+$$

such that

$$\Phi(K, L, t) = \Phi_4(\phi_4(t)\,K, \phi_5(t)\,L). \tag{1.10.19}$$

Note that if $\phi_4(t) \equiv 1$ or $\phi_5(t) \equiv 1$, (1.10.19) reduces to the labor-augmenting (see (1.10.5)) or capital-augmenting (see (1.10.6)) case, respectively.

1.10.20 **Theorem.** *Let* $\Phi: \mathbb{R}_+^3 \to \mathbb{R}_+$ *with property (1.10.1) be a production function that can be expressed in the output-augmenting form (1.10.2) as well as in the "constant-factor-mix-augmenting" form*

$$\Phi(K, L, t) = \Phi_4(\phi_4(t)\,K, \phi_4(t)\,L). \tag{1.10.21}$$

If Φ_4 *is nondecreasing and* ϕ_4 *has the form described in (1.10.10), then* Φ *is homogeneous with respect to K and L.*

Proof. From the assumptions of the theorem,

$$\Phi_4(\phi_4(t)\,K, \phi_4(t)\,L) = \phi_1(t)\Phi_1(K, L).$$

Since ϕ_4 has the form described in (1.10.10), this can be written as

$$\Phi_4(\tau K, \tau L) = \phi_1(\phi_4^{-1}(\tau))\Phi_1(K, L) \tag{1.10.22}$$

where ϕ_4^{-1} is the inverse of ϕ_4. Using arguments analogous to that in the proof of (1.10.7) we obtain, from (1.10.22),

$$\Phi_4(K, L) = \varrho(1)\Phi_1(K, L) \qquad [\varrho(\tau) = \phi_1(\phi_4^{-1}(\tau))],$$

$$\Phi_1(\tau K, \tau L) = p(\tau)\Phi_1(K, L) \qquad \left[p(\tau) = \frac{\varrho(\tau)}{\varrho(1)}\right],$$

$$p(\sigma\tau) = p(\sigma)\,p(\tau),$$

$$p(\tau) = \tau^\gamma \qquad (\gamma \text{ a positive constant}).$$

Hence Φ_1 is homogeneous. But then, because of (1.10.2), Φ is homogeneous with respect to K and L. ■

1.10.23 **Remark.** The theorem does not remain true if (1.10.21) is replaced by (1.10.19). For instance,

$$\Phi(\phi_4(t)\,K,\ \phi_5(t)L) = \phi_1(t)\Phi_1(K, L)$$

is fulfilled by

$$\phi_1(t) = t^{1/2}, \qquad \phi_4(t) = t, \qquad \phi_5(t) = t^{2/3},$$

$$\Phi_1(K, L) = \Phi_4(K, L) = K^{1/2} + L^{3/4}.$$

Clearly Φ_1 is *not* homogeneous.

Let Φ have the form (1.10.19) with the exception that $\phi_5(t)$ is replaced by $\phi_4(t)\,\phi_5(t)$. If, in addition, Φ is linearly homogeneous with respect to K and L, then inventions are called *Beckmann–Sato neutral* (see Krelle [1969, p. 136] or Sato and Beckmann [1968, p. 63]; the reason for this name will become clear in Section 5.1).

1.10.24 **Theorem.** *Let inventions be Beckmann–Sato neutral and Hicks neutral at the same time. Let the underlying production function Φ satisfy (1.10.1), let $f := \phi_1/\phi_4$ be well defined, nondecreasing, and nonconstant for $t > 0$, and let ϕ_5 have the form described in (1.10.10). Then Φ is the (linearly homogeneous) Cobb–Douglas function with respect to K and L.*

Proof. By the hypotheses of the theorem,

$$\Phi_4(\phi_4(t)\,K,\ \phi_4(t)\,\phi_5(t)\,L) = \phi_1(t)\Phi_1(K, L). \tag{1.10.25}$$

Because of the linear homogeneity,

$$\Phi_4(K,\ \phi_5(t)\,L) = f(t)\Phi_1(K, L). \tag{1.10.26}$$

From here we conclude, as in the proof of Theorem 1.10.7, that

$$\Phi_1(K, \tau L) = \tau^\delta\Phi_1(K, L) \qquad (\delta \text{ a positive constant}). \tag{1.10.27}$$

Since

$$\Phi(K, L, t) = \phi_1(t)\,\Phi_1(K, L)$$

is linearly homogeneous with respect to K and L, we obtain, for all $K > 0$,

$$\Phi_1(K, L) = K\Phi_1(1, L/K) = K\cdot(L/K)^\delta\Phi_1(1, 1)$$

where the right-hand equality follows from (1.10.27). Since Φ_4 is nondecreasing by definition, (1.10.25) implies that Φ_1 is nondecreasing. But then

$$\Phi_1(K, L) = CK^{1-\delta}L^\delta$$

where $\delta \leqq 1$, $C = \Phi_1(1,1)$, and the theorem is proved. ■

2

Generalizations of Cauchy's Equations: Several Unknown Functions and Restricted Domains[1]

It is well known[2] that a linearly homogeneous production function[3] $\Phi: \mathbb{R}^2_{++} \to \mathbb{R}_+$ with CES (constant elasticity of substitution; see (2.3.3)), σ, is a CD (Cobb–Douglas [1928]) production function

$$\Phi(x_1, x_2) = Cx_1^{\alpha_1}x_2^{\alpha_2}, \qquad \begin{array}{l} C > 0, \quad \alpha_1 > 0, \quad \alpha_2 > 0 \\ \text{real constants}, \alpha_1 + \alpha_2 = 1 \end{array} \tag{2.0.1}$$

for $\sigma = 1$, or an ACMS (Arrow, Chenery, Minhas, Solow [1961]) production function

$$\Phi(x_1, x_2) = (\beta_1 x^{-\varrho} + \beta_2 x_2^{-\varrho})^{-1/\varrho} \qquad \begin{array}{l} \varrho > -1, \quad \varrho \neq 0, \\ \beta_1 > 0, \quad \beta_2 > 0 \text{ real const.} \end{array} \tag{2.0.2}$$

for $\sigma = 1/(1 + \varrho)$, $(x_1, x_2) \in \mathbb{R}^2_{++}$.

Note that in the case in which $C = 1$ the function value (2.0.1) is a mean value of order 1; in the case in which $\beta_1 + \beta_2 = 1$, the function value (2.0.2) is a mean value of order $-\varrho = 1 - 1/\sigma$ (see Hardy, Littlewood, Pólya [1934, p. 13]).

In what follows, let us call a function $\Phi: \mathbb{R}^n_{++} \to \mathbb{R}$ a *CD-type function* if

$$\Phi(x_1, x_2, \ldots, x_n) = Cx_1^{\alpha_1}x_2^{\alpha_2}\cdots x_n^{\alpha_n}, \qquad C > 0, \quad \alpha_1, \alpha_2, \ldots, \alpha_n \text{ real const.}$$
$$\text{with } \textstyle\sum \alpha_\nu = 1, \quad \alpha_1 \alpha_2 \cdots \alpha_n \neq 0, \tag{2.0.3}$$

---

[1] Sections 2.3–2.6 of this chapter contain essential parts of a paper by Stehling [1975]' while Sections 2.1, 2.2, and 2.7 are taken from a paper [1974b] by the author. Section 2.8 treats a functional equation that was solved by Bellman and Kalaba [1957].

[2] See, e.g., Allen [1967, pp. 51–53], Paroush [1964], or Schips [1970]).

[3] For the definitions of terms and symbols not defined in the context see Chapter 13.

Wolfgang Eichhorn, Functional Equations in Economics.

ISBN 0–201–01948–5/01949–3 PBK

and an *ACMS-type function* if

$$\Phi(x_1, x_2, \ldots, x_n) = (\beta_1 x_1^{-\varrho} + \beta_2 x_2^{-\varrho} + \cdots + \beta_n x_n^{-\varrho})^{-1/\varrho}, \ \beta_1 > 0, \ \beta_2 > 0, \ldots, \beta_n > 0, \ \varrho \neq 0 \text{ real const.} \tag{2.0.4}$$

Several characterizations of the CD-type functions, by means of functional equations, can be found in this book (see Sections 3.6, 7.1, 8.2, and 10.6).

Production functions of type (2.0.4) with $\varrho > -1$, $\beta_1 > 0$, $\beta_2 > 0$, ..., $\beta_n > 0$ have been characterized, via partial elasticities of substitution, by Uzawa [1962].

The purpose of this chapter is a *joint* characterization of the CD-type and ACMS-type functions by means of a property that differs completely from CES. This property is the so-called *quasilinearity* of (2.0.3) and (2.0.4) (see Section 2.1). In Section 2.2 it will be shown that (2.0.3) and (2.0.4) are the only systems of functions that are at the same time linearly homogeneous and quasilinear. As Stehling [1975] has shown, the same can be said if one replaces "linearly homogeneous" by "homogeneous of degree $\gamma \neq 0$" and "quasilinear" by "generalized quasilinear" (see Sections 2.3, 2.4). In Section 2.5 the consequences of weakening the homogeneity assumption to the assumption of homotheticity will be analyzed. In passing, it may be noted that differentiability assumptions are not needed in what follows.

Another joint characterization of the CD-type and ACMS-type functions, in terms of neutralities of technical progress, is due to Stehling [1974a, c]; see Chapter 5.

As we will see in what follows, our problem of determining all linearly homogeneous and quasilinear functions yields the problem of solving, under continuity or monotonicity assumptions, the following generalizations of Cauchy's functional equations:

$$\phi(v_1 + \cdots + v_n) = \psi(v_1) + \cdots + \psi_n(v_n) \tag{2.0.5}$$

where $\psi_i: I_i \to \mathbb{R}$ $(i = 1, \ldots, n)$, $(v_1, \ldots, v_n) \in I_1 \times \cdots \times I_n$, the I_i's being open and nonvoid intervals of the real axis,

$$\phi: I_0 \to \mathbb{R}, \qquad I_0 := I_1 + \cdots + I_n := \{y \mid y = v_1 + \cdots + v_n; \ v_1 \in I_1, \ldots, v_n \in I_n\},$$

$$f(\lambda x) = \alpha(\lambda) f(x) + \beta(\lambda) \tag{2.0.6}$$

where f, α, and β map $\mathbb{R}_{++}$ into $\mathbb{R}$, $(\lambda, x) \in \mathbb{R}^2_{++}$.

This will be done in Sections 2.6. and 2.7, respectively. The concluding section (2.8) treats a functional equation that determines the criterion functions for optimal wagering policies.

2.1 Quasilinear Functions

Let D be a domain in $\mathbb{R}^n$. According to Aczél [1966, p. 151], a function $\Phi: D \to \mathbb{R}$ is called *quasilinear* if there exist real constants $a_1, a_2, \ldots, a_n, b$ with $a_1 a_2 \cdots a_n \neq 0$ and a continuous and strictly monotonic function f with inverse f^{-1}, both with suitable domains, such that

$$\Phi(x_1, x_2, \ldots, x_n) = f^{-1}[a_1 f(x_1) + a_2 f(x_2) + \cdots + a_n f(x_n) + b]. \quad (2.1.1)$$

In the following let $D = \mathbb{R}^n_{++}$.

2.1.2 **Remark.** Since f is continuous and strictly monotonic, the set

$$I: = \{u \mid u = f(x), x \in \mathbb{R}_{++}\}$$

is an open nonvoid interval of the real axis.

If $b = 0$, $a_1 = a_2 = \cdots = a_n = 1$, (2.1.1) becomes the so-called *quasiaddition*

$$\Phi(x_1, x_2, \cdots, x_n) = f^{-1}[f(x_1) + f(x_2) + \cdots + f(x_n)].$$

If $b = 0$, $a_1 > 0$, $a_2 > 0, \ldots, a_n > 0$, $\sum a_\nu = 1$, (2.1.1) becomes the so-called *quasilinear mean.* If $f(x) = x$, the "quasi" can be cancelled in the preceding definitions.

2.1.3 **Remark.** Note that both the CD-type functions (2.0.3) and ACMS-type functions (2.0.4) are quasilinear: Φ with (2.0.3) is quasilinear since

$$\Phi(x_1, x_2, \ldots, x_n) = \exp(\alpha_1 \log x_1 + \alpha_2 \log x_2 + \ldots + \alpha_n \log x_n + \log C),$$

that is

$$f(x) = \log x, \qquad f^{-1}(y) = e^y \qquad (f: \mathbb{R}_{++} \to \mathbb{R});$$

Φ with (2.0.4) is quasilinear:

$$f(x) = x^{-\varrho}, \qquad f^{-1}(y) = y^{-1/\varrho} \qquad (f: \mathbb{R}_{++} \to \mathbb{R}).$$

Moreover, both the CD-type functions and ACMS-type functions are linearly homogeneous.

2.2 Characterization of the CD- and ACMS-type Functions by Quasilinearity and Linear Homogeneity

2.2.1 **Theorem.** *Let the function $\Phi: \mathbb{R}^n_{++} \to \mathbb{R}$ be linearly homogeneous. It is a CD-type function (see (2.0.3)) or an ACMS-type function (see (2.0.4)) if and only if it is quasilinear.*

Let us call, for the moment, $\Phi\colon \mathbb{R}^n_{++} \to \mathbb{R}$ a *production function* if

$$\Phi(x_1, \cdots, x_n) \geqq 0 \qquad \text{for all} \quad (x_1, \cdots, x_n) \in \mathbb{R}^n_{++} \tag{2.2.2}$$

and

$$\begin{aligned} &x_\nu \to \Phi(x_1, \cdots, x_n) \text{ is strictly concave} \\ &\text{for } x_\nu \text{ sufficiently large } (\nu = 1, \cdots, n), \end{aligned} \tag{2.2.3}$$

that is, if Φ satisfies the so-called law of diminishing returns.

Obviously Theorem 2.2.1 yields the following.

2.2.4 **Corollary.** *Let the function $\Phi\colon \mathbb{R}^2_{++} \to \mathbb{R}$ be a linearly homogeneous production function. It is a CD production function (see (2.0.1)) or an ACMS production function (see (2.0.2)) if and only if it is quasilinear.*

Proof of the theorem. Because of Remark2.1.3 it remains to prove that every quasilinear function Φ: $\mathbb{R}^n_{++} \to \mathbb{R}$ that is linearly homogeneous is given by (2.0.3) or (2.0.4). Let Φ be such a function. Then

$$\begin{gathered} \lambda f^{-1}[a_1 f(x_1) + \cdots + a_n f(x_n) + b] = f^{-1}[a_1 f(\lambda x_1) + \cdots + a_n f(\lambda x_n) + b], \\ \lambda > 0, \quad a_1, a_2, \cdots, a_n, b \text{ real constants with } a_1 a_2 \cdots a_n \neq 0. \end{gathered}$$

Write

$$\begin{aligned} &g(x) := f^{-1}(x), \qquad f_\lambda(x) := f(\lambda x), \\ &f(x_\nu) =: u_\nu \qquad (\nu = 1, 2, \cdots, n) \end{aligned} \tag{2.2.5}$$

Then, because of

$$f[g(x)] = x, \qquad g(u_\nu) = x_\nu \qquad (\nu = 1, 2, \ldots, n), \tag{2.2.6}$$

$$f_\lambda[g(a_1u_1 + \cdots + a_nu_n + b)] = a_1 f_\lambda[g(u_1)] + \cdots + a_n f_\lambda[g(u_n)] + b$$

or, with

$$f_\lambda[g(x)] =: h_\lambda(x), \tag{2.2.7}$$

$$\begin{gathered} h_\lambda(a_1u_1 + \cdots + a_nu_n + b) = a_1 h_\lambda(u_1) + \cdots + a_n h_\lambda(u_n) + b, \\ \lambda > 0, \quad a_1, a_2, \ldots, a_n, b \quad \text{real constants with} \quad a_1 a_2 \cdots a_n \neq 0. \end{gathered} \tag{2.2.8}$$

We do *not* care about the constant solutions of (2.2.8), since

$$h_{\lambda_0}(x) = c_0 \qquad \text{for some} \quad \lambda_0 > 0 \quad \text{and all} \quad x$$

excludes

$$f[g(x)] = h_1(x) = x \qquad \text{(cf. (2.2.5), 2.2.6))}.$$

Since $u_\nu = f(x_\nu)$ (see (2.2.5)), the function h_λ is not necessarily defined on all of $\mathbb{R}$. According to Remark 2.1.2 we know only that h_λ is defined on the open nonvoid set $I \cup I'$ where I is defined above (see Remark (2.1.2)) and

$$\begin{aligned} I' :&= (a_1 I + \cdots + a_n I + b) \\ :&= \{v \mid v = a_1u_1 + \cdots + a_nu_n + b,\ u_1 \in I, \ldots, u_n \in I\}. \end{aligned} \tag{2.2.9}$$

The function h_λ is continuous on $I \cup I'$ since both f and $g = f^{-1}$ are continuous.

Let us write

$$\left.\begin{aligned} a_1u_1 &= : v_1, \ldots, a_nu_n = : v_n, \\ h_\lambda(v_1 + \cdots + v_n + b) - b &= : \phi\lambda(v_1 + \cdots + v_n), \\ a_1h_\lambda(v_1/a_1) &= : \psi_\lambda^1(v_1), \ldots, a_nh_\lambda(v_n/a_n) = : \psi_\lambda^n(v_n). \end{aligned}\right\} \tag{2.2.10}$$

Then (2.2.8) becomes

$$\phi_\lambda(v_1 + \cdots + v_n) = \psi_\lambda^1(v_1) + \cdots + \psi_\lambda^n(v_n) \tag{2.2.11}$$

where

$$\left.\begin{aligned} v_i \in I_i : &= \{v_i \mid v_i = a_iu_i, \quad u_i \in I, \quad a_i \neq 0\} \qquad (i = 1, \ldots, n), \\ (v_1 + \cdots + v_n) \in I_0 : &= \{w \mid w = v_1 + \cdots + v_n, v_1 \in I_1, \cdots, v_n \in I_n\} \\ &= : I_1 + \cdots + I_n. \end{aligned}\right\} \tag{2.2.12}$$

For every fixed λ, Eq. (2.2.11) with (2.2.12) is a generalization of Cauchy's functional equation (1.0.1) with respect to both the number of unknown functions and the domain of definition. Note that the intervals $I_0, I_1, \ldots, I_n$ defined in (2.2.12) are open and nonvoid since the interval I is open and nonvoid according to (2.1.2). Hence, since h_λ, and thus $\phi_\lambda, \psi_\lambda^1, \ldots, \psi_\lambda^n$, are continuous and nonconstant, we can apply a theorem from Section 2.6 (see Theorem 2.6.3) stating that under these assumptions every solution of (2.2.11) with (2.2.12) can be written as

$$\begin{aligned} \phi_\lambda(t) &= \alpha_\lambda t + \gamma_\lambda \qquad (t \in I_0), \\ \psi_\lambda^i(v_i) &= \alpha_\lambda v_i + \gamma_\lambda^i \qquad (v_i \in I_i; i = 1, \ldots, n), \end{aligned} \tag{2.2.13}$$

where $\alpha_\lambda \neq 0, \gamma_\lambda, \gamma_\lambda^1, \ldots, \gamma_\lambda^n$ are suitably chosen real constants.

From here it is obvious that each nonconstant continuous solution h_λ of Eq. (2.2.8), defined on $I \cup I'$ (see (2.1.2), (2.2.9)), can be written as

$$h_\lambda(u) = \alpha_\lambda u + \begin{cases} \beta_\lambda & \text{for} \quad u \in I, \\ \beta'_\lambda & \text{for} \quad u \in I', \end{cases} \tag{2.2.14}$$

where $\alpha_\lambda \neq 0$, β_λ and β'_λ are suitably chosen real constants.

From (2.2.14) with

$$u = f(x) \quad \text{(see (2.2.5))}, \qquad \alpha_\lambda = : \alpha(\lambda), \qquad \beta_\lambda = : \beta(\lambda), \qquad \beta'_\lambda = : \beta'(\lambda)$$

we learn, because of (2.2.5) and (2.2.7), that in any case f must satisfy an equation like

$$f(\lambda x) = \alpha(\lambda) f(x) + \beta(\lambda) \qquad (\alpha(\lambda) \neq 0 \quad \text{for all } \lambda; \quad \lambda > 0). \tag{2.2.15}$$

Since we are interested in finding all linearly homogeneous functions that are *quasilinear* (see the beginning of Section 2.1), we have to solve Eq. (2.2.15) under the assumption that $f\colon \mathbb{R}_{++} \to \mathbb{R}$ is strictly monotonic.

As will be shown in Section 2.7, there exist exactly two systems of solutions of (2.2.15) with strictly monotonic $f\colon \mathbb{R}_{++} \to \mathbb{R}$, namely

$$f(x) = \gamma \log x + \delta, \qquad \alpha(\lambda) \equiv 1, \qquad \beta(\lambda) = \gamma \log \lambda \tag{2.2.16}$$

and

$$f(x) = \gamma x^{-\varrho} + \delta, \qquad \alpha(\lambda) = \lambda^{-\varrho}, \qquad \beta(\lambda) = \delta\cdot(1-\lambda^{-\varrho}), \tag{2.2.17}$$

where $\gamma \neq 0$, $\varrho \neq 0$, and δ are arbitrary real constants.

With

$$f(x) = \gamma \log x + \delta \qquad (\gamma \neq 0, \quad \delta \text{ real const.; see (2.2.16)})$$

formula (2.1.1) becomes

$$\Phi(x_1, x_2, \ldots, x_n) = x_1^{a_1}x_2^{a_2} \cdots x_n^{a_n}\, e^{(b + a_1\delta + \cdots + a_n\delta - \delta)/\gamma},$$

that is, in the case of linear homogeneity ($\sum a_\nu = 1$), a CD-type function (2.0.3) with $\alpha_1 = a_1, \ldots, \alpha_n = a_n$, $C = e^{b/\gamma}$.

Similarly,

$$f(x) = \gamma x^{-\varrho} + \delta \qquad (\gamma \neq 0, \quad \varrho \neq 0 \text{ real const.; see (2.2.17)})$$

gives rise to

$$\Phi(x_1, \ldots, x_n) = (a_1 x_1^{-\varrho} + \cdots + a_n x_n^{-\varrho} + (1/\gamma)(b + a_1\delta + \cdots + a_n\delta - \delta))^{-1/\varrho},$$

which is defined for all $\varrho \neq 0$, $x_1 > 0, \ldots, x_n > 0$ only if the a_ν's ($\neq 0$ by assumption) are positive. This Φ is linearly homogeneous if and only if $b + a_1\delta + \cdots + a_n\delta - \delta = 0$; that is, if Φ is an ACMS-type function (see (2.0.4) with $\beta_1 = a_1, \ldots, \beta_n = a_n$).

Our theorem is proved. ■

2.3 Generalized Quasilinear Functions

Stimulated by the author's [1974b] result (2.2.1), Stehling [1975] introduced the notion of generalized quasilinearity and solved the problem of determining all functions $F\colon \mathbb{R}^n_{++} \to \mathbb{R}$ that are generalized quasilinear and homogeneous of degree $r \neq 0$ (see (4.1.1)) at the same time.

Let $D = D_1 \times D_2 \times \ldots \times D_n \subseteq \mathbb{R}^n$. The function $F\colon D \to \mathbb{R}$ is called *generalized quasilinear* if there exist continuous and strictly monotonic functions $g_i\colon D_i \to \mathbb{R}$, with ranges $W_i \subseteq \mathbb{R}$ ($i = 1, \ldots, n$), and a continuous and strictly monotonic function $f\colon W_1 + \cdots + W_n \to \mathbb{R}$ such that

$$F(x_1, \ldots, x_n) = f(g_1(x_1) + \cdots + g_n(x_n)) \qquad \text{for all} \quad (x_1, \ldots, x_n) \in D. \tag{2.3.1}$$

Obviously all quasilinear functions are also generalized quasilinear. The converse is not true, as can be seen by simple examples.

Every generalized quasilinear function is strictly monotonic and continuous in each variable (the other variables fixed). A generalized quasilinear function is not necessarily differentiable. Let us assume, for the moment, that a production function $F\colon \mathbb{R}^n_+ \to \mathbb{R}_+$ is given that is both generalized quasilinear and differentiable. Let the functions $f, g_1, \ldots, g_n$ in the representation (2.3.1) of F also be differentiable. Then the generalized quasilinearity implies the following properties of F.

(i) *The marginal rate of substitution between inputs i and j*, that is,

$$\frac{\partial F(x_1, \ldots, x_n)}{\partial x_i} \Bigg/ \frac{\partial F(x_1, \ldots, x_n)}{\partial x_j} =: \frac{F_i(x_1, \ldots, x_n)}{F_j(x_1, \ldots, x_n)} \tag{2.3.2}$$

depends only on the quantities x_i and x_j of these inputs:

$$\frac{F_i(x_1, \ldots, x_n)}{F_j(x_1, \ldots, x_n)} = \frac{dg_i(x_i)}{dx_i} \Bigg/ \frac{dg_j(x_j)}{dx_j} =: \frac{g_i'(x_i)}{g_j'(x_j)}.$$

(ii) The quotient of the relative rate of returns from inputs i and j depends only on the quantities x_i and x_j of these inputs:

$$\frac{x_iF_i(x_1, \ldots, x_n)}{F(x_1, \ldots, x_n)} \Bigg/ \frac{x_jF_j(x_1, \ldots, x_n)}{F(x_1, \ldots, x_n)} = \frac{x_ig_i'(x_i)}{x_jg_j'(x_j)}.$$

(iii) *The elasticity of substitution between inputs i and j*, σ_{ij}, that is,

$$\sigma_{ij} := -\frac{F_iF_j}{x_ix_j} \cdot \frac{x_iF_i + x_jF_j}{F_{jj}F_i^2 - 2F_iF_jF_{ij} + F_{ii}F_j^2},[4] \tag{2.3.3}$$

depends only on the quantities x_i and x_j of these inputs:

$$\sigma_{ij} = -\frac{g_i(x_i)\, g_i'(x_j)\, [x_ig_i'(x_i) + x_jg_j'(x_j)]}{x_ix_j[g_j''(x_j)\, g_i'(x_i)^2 + g_i''(x_i)\, g_j'(x_j)^2]}.$$

Differentiability will be not assumed in what follows.

2.4 Characterization of the CD- and ACMS-type Functions by Generalized Quasilinearity and Homogeneity

2.4.1 **Theorem.** *A function $F\colon \mathbb{R}^n_{++} \to \mathbb{R}$ is homogeneous of degree $r \neq 0$ (see (4.1.1)) and generalized quasilinear if and only if it is a CD-type function*

---

[4] $F_i := \dfrac{\partial F(x_1, \ldots, x_n)}{\partial x_i}, \quad F_{ii} := \dfrac{\partial^2 F(x_1, \ldots, x_n)}{\partial x_i^2}, \quad F_{ij} := \dfrac{\partial^2 F(x_1, \ldots, x_n)}{\partial x_i\, \partial x_j}.$

(see (2.0.3)) with $\Sigma a_\nu = r$ or an ACMS-type function (see (2.0.4)) with r/ϱ instead of $1/\varrho$.

Proof. Since one direction of the proof is obvious it is sufficient to show that F has either the form (2.0.3) (with $\Sigma a_\nu = r$) or the form (2.0.4) (with r/ϱ instead of $1/\varrho$) if F is homogeneous of degree $r \neq 0$ and generalized quasi-linear.

Let F have these properties. Then

$$f(g_1(\lambda x_1) + \cdots + g_n(\lambda x_n)) = \lambda^r f(g_1(x_1) + \cdots + g_n(x_n)) \tag{2.4.2}$$

or, since f is strictly monotonic,

$$f^{-1}[\lambda^r f(g_1(x_1) + \cdots + g_n(x_n))] = g_1(\lambda x_1) + \cdots + g_n(\lambda x_n) \tag{2.4.3}$$

for $(\lambda, x_1, \ldots, x_n) \in \mathbb{R}_{++}^{n+1}$.

Taking into account that the g_i's are strictly monotonic, we write

$$\left.\begin{aligned} v_i &:= g_i(x_i) && (i = 1, \ldots, n), \\ g_{i,\lambda}^{-1}(v_i) &:= \lambda g_i^{-1}(v_i) := \lambda x_i && (i = 1, \ldots, n), \\ f_\lambda^{-1}(y) &:= f^{-1}(\lambda^r y). \end{aligned}\right\} \tag{2.4.4}$$

With this notation, (2.4.3) can be written as

$$f_\lambda^{-1}(f(v_1 + \cdots + v_n)) = g_1(g_{1,\lambda}^{-1}(v_1)) + \cdots + g_n(g_{n,\lambda}^{-1}(v_n))$$

or as

$$\phi_\lambda(v_1 + \cdots + v_n) = \psi_\lambda^1(v_1) + \cdots + \psi_\lambda^n(v_n) \tag{2.4.5}$$

where

$$\begin{aligned} \phi_\lambda(y) &:= f_\lambda^{-1}(f(y)), \\ \psi_\lambda^i(v) &:= g_i(g_{i,\lambda}^{-1}(v_i)) \qquad (i = 1, \ldots, n). \end{aligned} \tag{2.4.6}$$

Note that $W_1, \ldots, W_n$ and $W_0 := W_1 + \cdots + W_n$ (see Section 2.3), that is, the domains of $\psi_\lambda^1, \ldots, \psi_\lambda^n$ and ϕ_λ, respectively, are open and nonvoid because of the strict monotonicity of the g_i's on $\mathbb{R}_{++}$. Note further that, for every fixed λ, the ψ_λ^i's and ϕ_λ are continuous since the g_i's and f are assumed to be continuous.

Comparing Eq. (2.4.5) (defined for $v_i \in W_i$, $(v_1 + \ldots + v_n) \in W_0$) with Eq. (2.2.11) (defined for $v_i \in I_i$, $(v_1 + \ldots + v_n) \in I_0$), we see that the proof of Theorem 2.4.1 requires the solution of exactly the same functional equation as did the proof of Theorem 2.2.1. As we stated there and as will be proved in Section 2.6, every continuous solution of this equation is given by (2.2.13).

From here on the proof runs analogously to that of Theorem 2.2 1. ■

2.5 Determination of All Homothetic and Generalized Quasilinear Functions

According to Shephard [1953, p. 41], a function $F\colon D \subseteq \mathbb{R}^n \to \mathbb{R}$ is called *homothetic* if there exist both a linearly homogeneous function $\Phi\colon D \to \mathbb{R}$, with range W, and a continuous and strictly increasing function $G\colon W \to \mathbb{R}$ such that

$$F(x_1, \ldots, x_n) = G(\Phi(x_1, \ldots, x_n)). \tag{2.5.1}$$

2.5.2 **Theorem.** *A function $F\colon \mathbb{R}^n_{++} \to \mathbb{R}$ is both homothetic and generalized quasilinear if and only if it can be written as*

$$F(x_1, x_2, \ldots, x_n) = H(Cx_1^{\alpha_1}x_2^{\alpha_2} \cdots x_n^{\alpha_n}), \qquad \begin{array}{l} C > 0, \quad \alpha_1, \alpha_2, \ldots, \alpha_n \quad \text{real} \\ \text{const with } \alpha_1\alpha_2 \ldots \alpha_n \neq 0,\ \Sigma\alpha_i = 1, \end{array}$$

or as

$$F(x_1, \ldots, x_n) = \bar{H}[(\beta_1 x_1^{-\varrho} + \cdots + \beta_n x_n^{-\varrho})^{-1/\varrho}] \qquad \begin{array}{l} \beta_1 > 0, \ldots, \beta_n > 0, \varrho \neq 0 \\ \text{real const,} \end{array}$$

where H and $\bar{H}$ are continuous and strictly increasing functions.

Proof. As assumed,

$$F(x_1, \ldots, x_n) = G(\Phi(x_1, \ldots, x_n)) = f(g_1(x_1) + \cdots + g_n(x_n)),$$

where G is strictly increasing, ϕ is linearly homogeneous, and $f, g_1, \ldots, g_n$ are strictly monotonic. Hence

$$G(\lambda\Phi(x_1, \ldots, x_n)) = f(g_1(\lambda x_1) + \cdots + g_n(\lambda x_n))$$

or

$$\Phi(x_1, \ldots, x_n) = \frac{1}{\lambda} G^{-1}[f(g_1(\lambda x_1) + \cdots + g_n(\lambda x_n))],$$

whence

$$G[\Phi(x_1, \ldots, x_n)] = G\left(\frac{1}{\lambda} G^{-1}[f(g_1(\lambda x_1) + \cdots + g_n(\lambda x_n))]\right).$$

On the other hand,

$$G[\Phi(x_1, \ldots, x_n)] = f(g_1(x_1) + \cdots + g_n(x_n)),$$

such that

$$G^{-1}[f(g_1(\lambda x_1) + \cdots + g_n(\lambda x_n))] = \lambda G^{-1}[f(g_1(x_1) + \cdots + g_n(x_n))]. \tag{2.5.3}$$

With

$$\Gamma(\cdot) := G^{-1}[f(\cdot)]$$

Eq. (2.5.3) becomes

$$\Gamma(g_1(\lambda x_1) + \cdots + g_n(\lambda x_n)) = \lambda\Gamma(g_1(x_1) + \cdots + g_n(x_n)),$$

that is, a functional equation of type (2.4.2) (note that Γ is continuous and strictly monotonic, since the same is true for G and f). Therefore we obtain, as in Section 2.4,

$$\begin{aligned}\Phi(x_1, \ldots, x_n) &= G^{-1}[f(g_1(x_1) + \cdots + g_n(x_n))] \\ &= \Gamma(g_1(x_1) + \cdots + g_n(x_n)) \\ &= Cx_1^{\alpha_1} \cdots x_n^{\alpha_n} \qquad \begin{array}{l} C > 0, \quad \alpha_1, \ldots, \alpha_n \quad \text{real} \\ \text{const with} \quad \alpha_1 \ldots \alpha_n \neq 0, \quad \sum \alpha_i = 1, \end{array}\end{aligned}$$

or analogously,

$$\Phi(x_1, \ldots, x_n) = (\beta_1 x_1^{-\varrho} + \cdots + \beta_n x_n^{-\varrho})^{-1/\varrho} \qquad \begin{array}{l} \beta_1 > 0, \ldots, \beta_n > 0, \quad \varrho \neq 0 \\ \text{real const,} \end{array}$$

whence either

$$F(x_1, x_2, \ldots, x_n) = G(Cx_1^{\alpha_1}x_2^{\alpha_2}\cdots x_n^{\alpha_n})$$

or

$$F(x_1, \ldots, x_n) = G[(\beta_1 x_1^{-\varrho} + \cdots + \beta_n x_n^{-\varrho})^{-1/\varrho}],$$

which was to be proved. ■

2.6 The Equation $\phi(v_1 + \cdots + v_n) = \psi_1(v_1) + \cdots + \psi_n(v_n)$ with $(v_1, \cdots, v_n) \in I_1 \times \cdots \times I_n$, the I_i's Arbitrary Nondegenerate Intervals of $\mathbb{R}$

We still have to deal with Eqs. (2.0.5) ((2.2.11), (2.4.5)) and (2.0.6) ((2.2.15)). Let us first consider Eq. (2.0.5), that is

$$\phi(v_1 + \cdots + v_n) = \psi_1(v_1) + \cdots + \psi_n(v_n). \tag{2.6.1}$$

Being a little more general than was necessary in Sections 2.2 and 2.4, we assume

$$\begin{array}{l}(v_1, \ldots, v_n) \in I_1 \times \cdots \times I_n, \quad (v_1 + \cdots + v_n) \in (I_1 + \cdots + I_n), \\ I_1 \subseteq \mathbb{R}, \cdots, I_n \subseteq \mathbb{R} \text{ arbitrary nondegenerate intervals, that is,} \\ \text{arbitrary intervals with nonvoid interior.}\end{array} \tag{2.6.2}$$

2.6.3 **Theorem.** *Given any continuous or monotonic solution $\phi, \psi_1, \ldots, \psi_n$ of Eq. (2.6.1) with (2.6.2), there exist real constants $\alpha, \gamma_1, \ldots, \gamma_n$ such that*

$$\begin{aligned}\phi(v_1 + \cdots + v_n) &= \alpha\cdot(v_1 + \cdots + v_n) + \gamma_1 + \cdots + \gamma_n \\ \psi_i(v_i) &= \alpha v_i + \gamma_i \qquad (v_i \in I_i; \quad i = 1, \ldots, n).\end{aligned} \tag{2.6.4.}$$

Conversely, every system of functions $\phi, \psi_1, \ldots, \psi_n$ given by (2.6.4) satisfies Eq. (2.6.1).

Proof. The second assertion is obvious. To prove the first we choose, from the interior of any particular interval I_i, an arbitrary v_i^0, which will be fixed in the following. Then any $v_i \in I_i$ can be uniquely represented by

$$v_i = v_i^0 + w_i \qquad (i = 1, \ldots, n) \tag{2.6.5}$$

where w_i lies in a nondegenerate interval J_i containing 0.

Inserting (2.6.5) into (2.6.1) we obtain

$$\phi\left(\sum_{i=1}^{n} v_i^0 + \sum_{i=1}^{n} w^i\right) = \psi_1(v_1^0 + w_1) + \cdots + \psi_n(v_n^0 + w_n), \tag{2.6.6}$$

whence, successively putting $w_k = 0$ $(k = 1, \ldots, i-1, i+1, \ldots, n)$, we obtain

$$\psi_i(v_i^0 + w_i) = \phi\left(\sum_{j=1}^{n} v_j^0 + w_i\right) - \sum_{\substack{k=1 \\ k \neq i}}^{n} \gamma_k \qquad (i = 1, \ldots, n) \tag{2.6.7}$$

where

$$\gamma_j = \psi_j(v_j^0) \qquad (j = 1, \ldots, n).$$

With (2.6.7), Eq. (2.6.6) becomes

$$\phi\left(\sum_{i=1}^{n} v_i^0 + \sum_{i=1}^{n} w_i\right) = \phi\left(\sum_{i=1}^{n} v_i^0 + w_1\right) + \cdots + \phi\left(\sum_{i=1}^{n} v_i^0 + w_n\right) - (n-1)\sum_{i=1}^{n} \gamma_i$$

or, with

$$\chi(y) := \phi\left(\sum_{i=1}^{n} v_i^0 + y\right) - \sum_{i=1}^{n} \gamma_i,$$

$$\chi(w_1 + \cdots + w_n) = \chi(w_1) + \cdots + \chi(w_n). \tag{2.6.8}$$

Our theorem is proved if the following turns out to be true.

2.6.9 **Theorem.** *Every continuous or monotonic solution of Eq. (2.6.8) with $w_i \in J_i$, $0 \in J_i$ $(i = 1, \ldots, n)$ can be written as*

$$\chi\left(\sum_{i=1}^{n} w_i\right) = c \sum_{i=1}^{n} w_i, \qquad \chi(w_i) = cw_i \qquad (w_i \in J_i;\ \ i = 1, \ldots, n), \tag{2.6.10}$$

where c is an arbitrary real constant. Every function χ given by (2.6.10) is a solution of (2.6.8).

The following elegant proof of Theorem 2.6.9 was communicated to the author by Aczél.

Proof. Since the second assertion is obvious, we have to prove only the first one. Let

$$\begin{aligned}
&K_i := J_i \cap \mathbb{R}_+ && (i = 1, \ldots, n),\\
&K := K_k \quad \text{where} \quad K_k \supseteq K_i && (i = 1, \ldots, n),\\
&K' := K_l \quad \text{where} \quad K_l \supseteq K_j && (j = 1, \ldots, k-1, k+1, \ldots, n).
\end{aligned}$$

Obviously,

$$K' \subseteqq K \subset (K + K'): = \{x + y \mid x \in K, y \in K'\}.$$

Putting $w_1 = w_2 = \cdots = w_n = 0$ in Eq. (2.6.10), we obtain $\chi(0) = 0$, whence, putting $w_i = 0$ for all $i \neq k$, $i \neq l$,

$$\chi(x + y) = \chi(x) + \chi(y) \qquad \text{for all} \quad x \in K, \quad y \in K'. \tag{2.6.11}$$

From (2.6.11) follows by induction

$$\chi(nx) = n\chi(x) \qquad \text{whenever} \quad x \in K', \quad nx \in (K + K'). \tag{2.6.12}$$

We choose an arbitrary positive $b \in K'$. Then

$$\chi(b) = \chi(nb/n) = n\chi(b/n) \qquad (\text{since also } (b/n) \in K');$$

hence

$$\chi(b/n) = \chi(b)/n$$

and

$$\chi(m\,b/n) = m\chi(b/n) = (m/n)\,\chi(b) \qquad \text{whenever} \quad (m/n)\,b \in (K+K').$$

Since χ is assumed to be continuous or monotonic, we have

$$\chi(tb) = t\chi(b) \qquad \text{for all nonnegative } t \text{ with } tb \in (K+K'),$$

whence

$$\chi(w) = w\frac{\chi(b)}{b} = cw \quad \text{on} \quad K+K' \qquad \left(c : = \frac{\chi(b)}{b}\right).$$

But then $\chi(w) = cw$ is valid also on $K_1 + K_2 \cdots + K_n$, because of Eq. (2.6.10). The same arguments can be applied to the nonpositive parts of the intervals J_i. This completes the proof of Theorem 2.6.9 and, hence, of Theorem 2.6.3. ■

The *general* solution of Eq. (2.6.8) with $w_i \in I_i$, where the I_i's are arbitrary nondegenerate intervals, can be derived from Daróczy and Losonczi [1967].

2.7 The Equation $f(\lambda x) = \alpha(\lambda) f(x) + \beta(\lambda)$ with $(\lambda, x) \in \mathbb{R}^2_{++}$, f Strictly Monotonic

It remains to consider Eq. (2.0.6) ((2.2.15)); that is,

$$f(\lambda x) = \alpha(\lambda) f(x) + \beta(\lambda) \tag{2.7.1}$$

where

$$\begin{aligned} &f : \mathbb{R}_{++} \to \mathbb{R} \quad \text{is strictly monotonic,}^5 \\ &\alpha : \mathbb{R}_{++} \to \mathbb{R}, \quad \beta : \mathbb{R}_{++} \to \mathbb{R}, \quad (\lambda, x) \in \mathbb{R}^2_{++}. \end{aligned} \tag{2.7.2}$$

[5] This implies $\alpha(\lambda) \neq 0$ for all λ, for if there exists a λ^* such that $\alpha(\lambda^*) = 0$, then, from (2.7.1), $f(x) \equiv \text{const.}$

2.7.3 **Theorem.** *There exist exactly two systems of solutions of (2.7.1) with (2.7.2), namely,*

$$f(x) = \lambda \log x + \delta, \qquad \alpha(\lambda) \equiv 1, \quad \beta(\lambda) = \gamma \log \lambda, \tag{2.7.4}$$

and

$$f(x) = \gamma x^{-\varrho} + \delta, \qquad \alpha(\lambda) = \lambda^{-\varrho}, \quad \beta(\lambda) = \delta(1 - \lambda^{-\varrho}), \tag{2.7.5}$$

where $\gamma \neq 0$, $\varrho \neq 0$ *and* δ *are arbitrary real constants.*

Proof (analogous to Aczél's [1966, p. 149] proof of a similar theorem). In order to solve (2.7.1), we substitute $x = 1$ to obtain

$$f(\lambda) = \alpha(\lambda) f(1) + \beta(\lambda)$$

and subtract this equation from (2.7.1). With the notation

$$f(x) - f(1) = : \phi(x), \qquad f(x) = \phi(x) + \delta \qquad (\delta = f(1)), \tag{2.7.6}$$

this yields the functional equation

$$\phi(\lambda x) = \alpha(\lambda)\, \phi(x) + \phi(\lambda), \qquad \text{where} \quad \phi(1) = 0. \tag{2.7.8}$$

Interchanging the variables in (2.7.8), we obtain

$$\phi(\lambda x) = \alpha(x)\, \phi(\lambda) + \phi(x),$$

which, together with (2.7.8), leads to

$$\phi(x)\, [\alpha(\lambda) - 1] = \phi(\lambda)\, [\alpha(x) - 1]. \tag{2.7.9}$$

If $\alpha(\lambda) \equiv 1$, then (2.7.8) with $(\lambda, x) \in \mathbb{R}^2_{++}$ reduces to

$$\phi(\lambda x) = \phi(x) + \phi(\lambda) \qquad [(\lambda, x) \in \mathbb{R}^2_{++}]. \tag{2.7.10}$$

As we know from Theorem 1.7.1,

$$\phi(x) = \gamma \log x \qquad (\gamma \neq 0 \text{ an aribitrary real constant})$$

is the most general solution of (2.7.10) that is strictly monotonic. Hence, we obtain (2.7.4) as solution of (2.7.1).

If, however, there exists a λ_0 such that $\alpha(\lambda_0) \neq 1$, it follows from (2.7.9) that

$$\phi(x) = \frac{\phi(\lambda_0)}{\alpha(\lambda_0) - 1} [\alpha(x) - 1] = c[\alpha(x) - 1] \tag{2.7.11}$$

where c is a constant. By (2.7.6) $c = 0$ leads to $f(x) \equiv \delta$, which contradicts the strict monotonicity. Hence $c \neq 0$. Put (2.7.11) into (2.7.8),

$$c[\alpha(\lambda x) - 1] = c[\alpha(x) - 1]\, \alpha(\lambda) + c[\alpha(\lambda) - 1]$$

in order to get the Cauchy-type functional equation

$$\alpha(\lambda x) = \alpha(x)\, \alpha(\lambda).$$

Its most general solution on $\mathbb{R}^2_{++} \ni (\lambda, x)$ that is strictly monotonic[6] is

$$\alpha(\lambda) = \lambda^{-\varrho}$$

($\varrho \neq 0$ an arbitrary real constant; see Theorem 1.9.13). Hence we obtain (2.7.5). There are no other cases left and so we have proved the theorem. ∎

2.8 A Functional Equation Determining the Criterion Functions for Optimal Wagering Policies

In connection with problems posed by Kelly [1956], Bellman and Kalaba [1957] considered the following model.

A gambler starts with an initial holding $x \in \mathbb{R}_{++}$ and bets a nonnegative amount $y \leqq x$ on the outcome of each event so as to maximize his expected gains. The probability of winning the amount y is p, that of losing the amount y is $1-p$. The gambler wishes to pursue a policy that will prevent him from ever being ruined. He may therefore proceed to maximize the *expected value* of the logarithm of his capital at the end of N stages of play.

For the one-stage process, he is faced with the problem of maximizing

$$p \log(x + y) + (1 - p) \log(x - y) \tag{2.8.1}$$

over all y in $[0, x]$. It is easy to see that if $p > 1 - p$, we have, as the maximizing value of y,

$$y = (p - (1 - p))\, x = (2p - 1)\, x.$$

If $p \leqq 1 - p$, the maximum is at $y = 0$.

Kelly showed that if we consider N-stage processes, where we restrict ourselves to wagering policies that require the wagered amount to be a *fixed* proportion of the total capital at each stage, then the policy just described is optimal.

At this point the question arises whether the logarithm is the only nonlinear criterion function that yields an invariant policy at each stage. Bellman and Kalaba treated the following version of this problem.

Let $\phi : \mathbb{R}_+ \to \mathbb{R}$ be a strictly increasing concave function. Consider the one-stage process where we wish to maximize

$$E(y) = p\phi(x + y) + (1 - p)\, \phi(x - y) \tag{2.8.2}$$

(cf. (2.8.1)). The function $E : [0, x] \to \mathbb{R}$, $x \in \mathbb{R}_{++}$, is concave, and thus has a unique maximum, unless ϕ is linear and $p = \frac{1}{2}$. We dismiss the case of linear-

---

[6] Note that α is strictly monotonic since f is strictly monotonic (see (2.7.6), (2.7.11)).

ity by requiring strict concavity, $\phi''(\xi) < 0$, and take $p \in]\frac{1}{2}, 1[$. If $p = 1$, no problem has to be solved.

Let us assume that for all $x \in \mathbb{R}_{++}$ there is a solution of

$$\frac{dE(y)}{dy} = p\phi'(x + y) - (1 - p)\,\phi'(x - y) = 0 \tag{2.8.3}$$

having the form

$$y = r(p)\,x \tag{2.8.4}$$

where $r\colon]\frac{1}{2}, 1[\to]0, 1]$ has a continuous derivative. Then (2.8.3) is equivalent to the functional equation

$$\frac{p}{1-p}\,\phi'(x + r(p)\,x) = \phi'(x - r(p)\,x) \qquad \text{for} \quad (x, p) \in \mathbb{R}_{++} \times]\tfrac{1}{2}, 1[. \tag{2.8.5}$$

Bellman and Kalaba [1957] obtained the following result about Eq. (2.8.5).

2.8.6 **Theorem.** *Every solution*

$$\phi'\colon \mathbb{R}_{++} \to \mathbb{R}_{++}, \qquad r\colon]\tfrac{1}{2}, 1[\to]0, 1] \tag{2.8.7}$$

of functional equation (2.8.5), which is continuously differentiable and which satisfies $\phi''(\xi) < 0$ for all $\xi \in \mathbb{R}_{++}$, can be written in the form

$$\phi'(\xi) = a\xi^{-c} \qquad (\alpha \in \mathbb{R}_{++},\ c \in \mathbb{R}_{++} \quad const), \tag{2.8.8}$$

$$r(p) = \frac{p^{1/c} - (1-p)^{1/c}}{p^{1/c} + (1-p)^{1/c}}. \tag{2.8.9}$$

Conversely, every pair of functions (2.8.7) given by (2.8.8), (2.8.9) is a solution of functional equation (2.8.5).

Proof. The second assertion can be shown by substituting (2.8.8), (2.8.9) into (2.8.5). In order to prove the first one, we differentiate (2.8.5) with respect to x and p, obtaining

$$\frac{p}{1-p}\,\phi''(x + r(p)\,x)(1 + r(p)) = \phi''(x - r(p)\,x)(1 - r(p))$$

and

$$\frac{1}{(1-p)^2}\,\phi'(x + r(p)\,x) + \frac{p}{1-p}\,\phi''(x + r(p)\,x)\,xr'(p)$$
$$= -\,\phi''(x - r(p)\,x)\,xr'(p),$$

respectively. It follows from the second equation that if there exists p such that $r'(p) = 0$, then ϕ is constant, which has been excluded. Therefore we can assume $r'(p) \neq 0$ for all p in what follows.

Dividing the second equation by the first, we obtain

$$\frac{x\phi''(x + r(p)\,x)}{\phi'(x + r(p)\,x)} = \frac{r(p) - 1}{2p(1 - p)\,r'(p)}. \tag{2.8.10}$$

If there exists some p with $r(p) = 1$, then Eq. (2.8.10) yields the linearity of ϕ, which has been excluded.

In view of the assumptions $x > 0$, $\phi'(\xi) > 0$, $\phi''(\xi) < 0$, Eq. (2.8.10) implies

$$\frac{x\phi''(x + \alpha x)}{\phi'(x + \alpha x)} = -C \qquad (C \in \mathbb{R}_{++} \quad \text{a const}), \tag{2.8.11}$$

where $\alpha := r(p^*) \in]0, 1[$ for a fixed $p^* \in]\frac{1}{2}, 1[$ and

$$-C := \frac{r(p^*) - 1}{2p^*(1 - p^*)\,r'(p^*)}.$$

Let us write Eq. (2.8.11) in the form

$$\frac{\phi''(\xi)}{\phi'(\xi)} = -\frac{c}{\xi} \qquad (\xi := x + \alpha x, \quad c := (1 + \alpha)C),$$

which implies

$$\log \phi'(\xi) = -c \log \xi + b \qquad (b \in \mathbb{R} \quad \text{a constant}),$$

that is,

$$\phi'(\xi) = a\xi^{-c} \qquad (a := e^b \in \mathbb{R}_{++}).$$

Finally, if we substitute this result into (2.8.5), we see that $r(p)$ can only have the form (2.8.9). ∎

Without loss of generality, let us normalize, so that $\varphi'(1) = 1$. Then

$$\phi'(\xi) = \xi^{-c}.$$

If $c \neq 1$, we have

$$\phi(\xi) = \frac{\xi^{1-c}}{1 - c} + \beta \qquad (\beta \in \mathbb{R} \quad \text{a constant}).$$

If $c = 1$, we have

$$\phi(\xi) = \log \xi + \gamma \qquad (\gamma \in \mathbb{R} \quad \text{a constant}).$$

Finally, without loss of generality, we can let $\beta = \gamma = 0$.

We summarize the result of Bellman and Kalaba:

2.8.12 **Corollary.** *Up to additive and positive multiplicative constants, the nonlinear criterion functions of the model of optimal wagering policies just described are given by*

$$\phi(\xi) = \log \xi \qquad \textit{and} \qquad \phi(\xi) = \xi^{1-c}/(1 - c) \qquad (c \in \mathbb{R}_{++},\ c \neq 1).$$

It should be noted here that models and functional equations similar to those considered in this section play an important role in information theory. See, for instance, Bellman [1971], Fischer [1974, 1975], and Aczél and Daróczy [1975, pp. 118–120].

Part II

Functional Equations for Scalar-Valued Functions of Several Variables

3

Generalizations of Cauchy's Equations: Pexider's Functional Equations for Functions of Several Variables

The following generalizations of Cauchy's functional equations (1.0.1)-(1.0.5) can be regarded as Pexider's [1903] equations for functions of n non-negative or, in the case of (3.0.4), positive variables $(x_1, \ldots, x_n) =: \mathbf{x}$ or $(y_1, \ldots, y_n) =: \mathbf{y}$.

$$F_1(\mathbf{x} + \mathbf{y}) = F_2(\mathbf{x}) + F_3(\mathbf{y}), \quad \text{where} \quad (\mathbf{x}, \mathbf{y}) \in \mathbb{R}^{2n}, \quad F_j : \mathbb{R}^n \to \mathbb{R}, \tag{3.0.1}$$

$$G_1(\mathbf{x} + \mathbf{y}) = G_2(\mathbf{x}) + G_3(\mathbf{y}), \quad \text{where} \quad (\mathbf{x}, \mathbf{y}) \in \mathbb{R}^{2n}_{+}, \quad G_j : \mathbb{R}^n_{+} \to \mathbb{R}, \tag{3.0.2}$$

$$H_1(\mathbf{x} + \mathbf{y}) = H_2(\mathbf{x})\, H_3(\mathbf{y}) \quad \text{where} \quad (\mathbf{x}, \mathbf{y}) \in \mathbb{R}^{2n}_{+}, \quad H_j : \mathbb{R}^n_{+} \to \mathbb{R}, \tag{3.0.3}$$

$$L_1(x_1y_1, \ldots, x_ny_n) = L_2(\mathbf{x}) + L_3(\mathbf{y}) \quad \text{where} \quad (\mathbf{x}, \mathbf{y}) \in \mathbb{R}^{2n}_{++}, \quad L_j : \mathbb{R}^n_{++} \to \mathbb{R}, \tag{3.0.4}$$

$$M_1(x_1y_1, \ldots, x_ny_n) = M_2(\mathbf{x})\, M_3(\mathbf{y}) \quad \text{where} \quad (\mathbf{x}, \mathbf{y}) \in \mathbb{R}^{2n}_{+}, \quad M_j : \mathbb{R}^n_{+} \to \mathbb{R} \tag{3.0.5}$$

$(j = 1, 2, 3)$. Solutions of (3.0.1)-(3.0.5) are of interest here since the special cases of (3.0.1)-(3.0.5) that follow play a role in various fields of economics:

$$G_1(\mathbf{x} + \mathbf{y}) = G_1(\mathbf{x}) + G_2(\mathbf{y}) \qquad \text{(see Section 3.2)},$$
$$G(\mathbf{x} + \mathbf{y}) = G(\mathbf{x}) + G(\mathbf{y}) \qquad \text{(see Section 3.3)},$$
$$H_1(\mathbf{x} + \mathbf{y}) = H_1(\mathbf{x})\, H_2(\mathbf{y}) \qquad \text{(see Section 3.4)},$$
$$L_1(x_1y_1, \ldots, x_ny_n) = L_1(\mathbf{x}) + L_2(\mathbf{y}) \qquad \text{(see Section 3.5)},$$
$$M_1(x_1y_1, \ldots, x_ny_n) = M_1(\mathbf{x})\, M_2(\mathbf{y}) \qquad \text{(see Section 3.6)}.$$

ISBN 0-201-01948-5/01949-3 PBK

Wolfgang Eichhorn, Functional Equations in Economics.

Applications are made to price and advertising policies of firms, the theory of utility, cost and production functions, and the theory of index numbers.

3.1 The Equation $F_1(\mathbf{x} + \mathbf{y}) = F_2(\mathbf{x}) + F_3(\mathbf{y})$, $(\mathbf{x}, \mathbf{y}) \in \mathbb{R}^{2n}$, $F_j : \mathbb{R}^n \to \mathbb{R}$

3.1.1 **Theorem.** *Let*

$$\mathbf{x} = (x_1, \ldots, x_n) \in \mathbb{R}^n, \qquad \mathbf{y} = (y_1, \ldots, y_n) \in \mathbb{R}^n.$$

Let the three functions

$$F_j : \mathbb{R}^n \to \mathbb{R} \qquad (j = 1, 2, 3)$$

satisfy the functional equation

$$F_1(\mathbf{x} + \mathbf{y}) = F_2(\mathbf{x}) + F_3(\mathbf{y}). \tag{3.1.2}$$

Then there exist two real constants a, b and a function $F : \mathbb{R}^n \to \mathbb{R}$ such that

$$F_1(\mathbf{x}) = F(\mathbf{x}) + a + b, \qquad F_2(\mathbf{x}) = F(\mathbf{x}) + a, \qquad F_3(\mathbf{x}) = F(\mathbf{x}) + b, \tag{3.1.3}$$

where F satisfies the functional equation

$$F(\mathbf{x} + \mathbf{y}) = F(\mathbf{x}) + F(\mathbf{y}) \tag{3.1.4}$$

and $a = F_2(\mathbf{0})$, $b = F_3(\mathbf{0})$. Conversely, every triple (3.1.3) with (3.1.4) satisfies (3.1.2).

Proof. Setting $\mathbf{x} = \mathbf{0}$ in (3.1.2), we find

$$F_3(\mathbf{y}) = F_1(\mathbf{y}) - F_2(\mathbf{0}) = F_1(\mathbf{y}) - a \qquad (a = F_2(\mathbf{0})),$$

and setting $\mathbf{y} = \mathbf{0}$,

$$F_2(\mathbf{x}) = F_1(\mathbf{x}) - F_3(\mathbf{0}) = F_1(\mathbf{x}) - b \qquad (b = F_3(\mathbf{0})).$$

Upon substitution in (3.1.2), we obtain

$$F_1(\mathbf{x} + \mathbf{y}) = F_1(\mathbf{x}) + F_1(\mathbf{y}) - a - b.$$

By setting

$$F(\mathbf{x}) = F_1(\mathbf{x}) - a - b,$$

we get (3.1.4). The last assertion of the theorem is obvious. ■

To solve Eq. (3.1.4) we set

$$x_1 = \cdots = x_{\nu-1} = x_{\nu+1} = \cdots = x_n = y_1 = \cdots = y_{\nu-1} = y_{\nu+1} = \cdots = y_n = 0$$

and obtain

$$F(0, \ldots, 0, x_\nu + y_\nu, 0, \ldots, 0) = F(0, \ldots, 0, x_\nu, 0, \ldots, 0) + F(0, \ldots, 0, y_\nu, 0, \ldots, 0).$$

This is Cauchy's basic equation (1.0.1) for

$$f_\nu(x_\nu) := F(0, \ldots, 0, x_\nu, 0, \ldots, 0).$$

Since

$$\begin{aligned} F(\mathbf{x}) &= F(x_1 + 0, 0 + x_2, \ldots, 0 + x_n) = F(x_1, 0, \ldots, 0) + F(0, x_2, \ldots, x_n) \\ &= F(x_1, 0, \ldots, 0) + F(0 + 0, x_2 + 0, 0 + x_3, \ldots, 0 + x_n) \\ &= F(x_1, 0, \ldots, 0) + F(0, x_2, 0, \ldots, 0) + F(0, 0, x_3, \ldots, x_n) \\ &= F(x_1, 0, \ldots, 0) + F(0, x_2, 0, \ldots, 0) + \cdots + F(0, \ldots, 0, x_n) \\ &= f_1(x_1) + f_2(x_2) + \cdots + f_n(x_n), \end{aligned}$$

we have

3.1.5 **Theorem.** *Every solution of the functional equation*

$$F(\mathbf{x} + \mathbf{y}) = F(\mathbf{x}) + F(\mathbf{y}), \qquad (\mathbf{x}, \mathbf{y}) \in \mathbb{R}^{2n}, \quad F : \mathbb{R}^n \to \mathbb{R}, \tag{3.1.6}$$

can be written in the form

$$F(\mathbf{x}) = f_1(x_1) + f_2(x_2) + \cdots + f_n(x_n) \tag{3.1.7}$$

where the $f_\nu : \mathbb{R} \to \mathbb{R}$ *satisfy Cauchy's basic equation*

$$f(x + y) = f(x) + f(y), \qquad (x, y) \in \mathbb{R}^2, \quad f : \mathbb{R} \to \mathbb{R}. \tag{3.1.8}$$

Conversely, every function F of the form (3.1.7) where the f_ν*'s satisfy (3.1.8) is a solution of (3.1.6).*

If F in (3.1.6) is

(i) continuous at a single point or
(ii) monotonic in an arbitrarily small ε-neighborhood (see (13.2.14)) of a point,

then the same is true for the f_ν's. As a consequence of this and 1.2.10 we have

3.1.9 **Corollary.** *If a function* $F : \mathbb{R}^n \to \mathbb{R}$ *satisfies (3.1.6) and (i) or (ii), then*

$$F(\mathbf{x}) = c_1 x_1 + c_2 x_2 + \cdots + c_n x_n, \tag{3.1.10}$$

or briefly,

$$F(\mathbf{x}) = \mathbf{cx},$$

where the c_ν*'s are real constants. Conversely, every function F given by (3.1.10) with arbitrary real* c_ν*'s is a solution of Eq. (3.1.6).*

3.1.11 **Remark.** As can be easily seen from their proofs,

(a) Theorems 3.1.1 and 3.1.5 remain true if the domain $\mathbb{R}^n$ of the functions F_j and F is restricted to $\mathbb{R}^n_+$, and

(b) Theorem 3.1.5 is still valid when $\mathbb{R}^n$ is replaced by $\mathbb{R}^n_+ \setminus \{(0, \ldots, 0)\}$. In both cases, the domain of the f_ν's in Theorem 3.1.5 must be restricted correspondingly. Because of Corollary 1.3.7,

(c) Corollary 3.1.9 remains true upon replacing $\mathbb{R}^n$ by $\mathbb{R}^n_+$ or $\mathbb{R}^n_+ \setminus \{(0, \ldots, 0)\}$.

3.2 Application of Section 3.1 to the Theory of Cost and Utility Functions

Let $\mathbf{x} = (x_1, \ldots, x_n) \in \mathbb{R}^n_+$ be the output of a firm that produces n commodities. Let $K : \mathbb{R}^n_+ \to \mathbb{R}_+$ be its cost function assigning to each output vector $\mathbf{x}$ the (minimum) cost of producing $\mathbf{x}$, namely $K(\mathbf{x})$. We are interested in the class of all cost functions K that are additive in the following sense:

$$K(\mathbf{x} + \boldsymbol{\xi}) = K(\mathbf{x}) + L(\boldsymbol{\xi}), \qquad K : \mathbb{R}^n_+ \to \mathbb{R}_+, \quad L : \mathbb{R}^n_+ \to \mathbb{R}_+. \tag{3.2.1}$$

That is, the cost of the sum of the output $\mathbf{x} \geqq \mathbf{0}$ and the increment output $\boldsymbol{\xi} = (\xi_1, \ldots, \xi_n) \geqq \mathbf{0}$ equals the sum of the cost of the output $\mathbf{x}$ and a nonnegative real number depending on $\boldsymbol{\xi}$. For $n = 1$, that is, for the case of a single-product firm, (3.2.1) has been solved in Section 1.8.

3.2.2 **Theorem.** *If a function K (e.g., a cost function) satisfies (3.2.1), then there exist real constants $\alpha \geqq 0, \beta_1 \geqq 0, \ldots, \beta_n \geqq 0$ such that*

$$K(\mathbf{x}) = \alpha + \beta_1 x_1 + \cdots + \beta_n x_n = : \alpha + \boldsymbol{\beta}\mathbf{x}, \tag{3.2.3}$$

$$L(\boldsymbol{\xi}) = \beta_1 \xi_1 + \cdots + \beta_n \xi_n = \boldsymbol{\beta}\boldsymbol{\xi}. \tag{3.2.4}$$

Every pair (3.2.3), (3.2.4) satisfies (3.2.1). If $L(\boldsymbol{\xi}) > 0$ for every $\boldsymbol{\xi} \neq \mathbf{0}$ then $\beta_1 > 0, \ldots, \beta_n > 0$.

Note that in the case where K is a cost function, α is the *fixed cost* and β_ν is the *marginal cost with respect to the νth output* ($\nu \in \{1, \ldots, n\}$).

Proof of the theorem. From Theorem 3.1.1 with $F_1(\mathbf{x}) = F_2(\mathbf{x})$ it follows that

$$K(\boldsymbol{\xi}) = L(\boldsymbol{\xi}) + \alpha$$

where

$$L(\boldsymbol{\xi} + \boldsymbol{\eta}) = L(\boldsymbol{\xi}) + L(\boldsymbol{\eta}).$$

Since, by assumption, L is nonnegative-valued,

$$L(\boldsymbol{\xi} + \boldsymbol{\eta}) \geqq L(\boldsymbol{\xi}) \qquad \text{for all} \quad \boldsymbol{\xi} \geqq \mathbf{0}, \quad \boldsymbol{\eta} \geqq \mathbf{0};$$

that is, L is nondecreasing. Then, according to Remark 3.1.11c,

$$L(\boldsymbol{\xi}) = \boldsymbol{\beta}\boldsymbol{\xi}, \qquad K(\mathbf{x}) = \alpha + \boldsymbol{\beta}\mathbf{x}.$$

Since $K(\mathbf{x}) \in \mathbb{R}_+$ (see (3.2.1)), we have $K(\mathbf{0}) = \alpha \geqq 0$. The β's are nonnegative since L is nondecreasing. The last two assertions of the theorem are obvious. ■

Alternatively, if we interprete $K(\mathbf{x})$ as the *utility* of the commodity vector $\mathbf{x}$, then equation (3.2.1) can be regarded as the defining relation for a class of additive utility functions, namely the class given by (3.2.3). In this case, the β's are usually called *weights*. Note that in utility theory, a utility function $u : \mathbb{R}_+^n \to \mathbb{R}$ is called *additive* if there exist functions $v_\nu : \mathbb{R}_+^n \to \mathbb{R}$ such that for all $\mathbf{x} \in \mathbb{R}_+^n$,

$$u(\mathbf{x}) = \sum_{\nu=1}^{n} v_\nu(x_\nu).$$

The v_ν's need not be additive in the sense of satisfying Cauchy's equation (1.0.2). See, for instance, Katzner [1970, p. 28].

3.3 The Role of the Equation $G(\mathbf{x} + \mathbf{y}) = G(\mathbf{x}) + G(\mathbf{y})$, $(\mathbf{x}, \mathbf{y}) \in \mathbb{R}_+^{2n}$, $G : \mathbb{R}_+^n \to \mathbb{R}$ in Axiomatic Characterizations of Classical Indices[1]

Let $\mathbf{a} = (a_1, \ldots, a_m)$ and $\mathbf{b} = (b_1, \ldots, b_n)$ be two constant vectors with positive components; let $\mathbf{x} = (x_1, \ldots, x_n) \neq (0, \ldots, 0) =: \mathbf{0}$ and $\mathbf{u} = (u_1, \ldots, u_m)$ be two variable vectors with nonnegative components; and let

$$\mathbf{au} := a_1u_1 + \cdots + a_mu_m, \qquad \mathbf{bx} := b_1x_1 + \ldots + b_nx_n.$$

The function I, given by

$$I(\mathbf{x}, \mathbf{u}) = \mathbf{au} / \mathbf{bx}, \tag{3.3.1}$$

is often used to define indices in economics. If, for instance, $\mathbf{u}$ is an output vector which can be obtained from the input vector $\mathbf{x}$, and if $\mathbf{a}$ and $\mathbf{b}$ are the prices of $\mathbf{u}$ and $\mathbf{x}$, respectively, then (3.3.1) is called the *productivity (index)* of the *production process* $(\mathbf{x}, \mathbf{u})$. Other well-known examples of indices of the form (3.3.1) are the *price indices* of (i) Laspeyres [1871] ($m = n$, $\mathbf{a} = \mathbf{b} =$ quantities of the "*basket of goods*" of the base year), and (ii) Paasche [1874] ($m = n$, $\mathbf{a} = \mathbf{b} =$ quantities of the current "*basket of goods*"). Here $\mathbf{x}$ and $\mathbf{u}$ are the base year prices and the current prices, respectively.

As can easily be seen, an index given by (3.3.1) is *additive* in the following sense:

---

[1] The following consists of parts of two joint papers of the author with Aczél [1974a], [1974b]. An algebraic generalization of these two papers is due to Aczél [1975].

$$I(\mathbf{x}, \mathbf{u} + \mathbf{v}) = I(\mathbf{x}, \mathbf{u}) + I(\mathbf{x}, \mathbf{v}) \qquad \text{for all} \quad \mathbf{x} \geqslant \mathbf{0}, \mathbf{u} \geqq \mathbf{0}, \mathbf{v} \geqq \mathbf{0};^{2} \quad (3.3.2)$$

$$\frac{1}{I(\mathbf{x} + \mathbf{y}, \mathbf{u})} = \frac{1}{I(\mathbf{x}, \mathbf{u})} + \frac{1}{I(\mathbf{y}, \mathbf{u})} \qquad \text{for all} \quad \mathbf{x} \geqslant \mathbf{0}, \mathbf{y} \geqslant \mathbf{0}, \mathbf{u} \geqslant \mathbf{0}. \quad (3.3.3)$$

Note that a function

$$I : (\mathbb{R}_{+}^{n} \setminus \{\mathbf{0}\}) \times \mathbb{R}_{+}^{m} \to \mathbb{R}_{+} \qquad (3.3.4)$$

given by (3.3.1) with **a, b, x, u** as defined earlier satisfies

$$I(\mathbf{x}, \mathbf{u}) > 0 \qquad \text{for all} \quad \mathbf{x} \geqslant \mathbf{0}, \mathbf{u} \geqslant \mathbf{0}. \qquad (3.3.5)$$

Let us forget for the time being about the form (3.3.1) of I. In the following *we are interested in the general solution of functional equations (3.3.2), (3.3.3) with (3.3.4), (3.3.5), that is, in all indices (3.3.4) that satisfy (3.3.2), (3.3.3), and (3.3.5).*

By repeated application of (3.3.2) we obtain

$$I(\mathbf{x}, N\mathbf{v}) = NI(\mathbf{x}, \mathbf{v}) \qquad \text{for all positive integers } N$$

or, with

$$\mathbf{v} = \frac{M}{N}\mathbf{u}, \qquad (M \text{ also a positive integer}),$$

$$I\left(\mathbf{x}, \frac{M}{N}\mathbf{u}\right) = \frac{1}{N} I(\mathbf{x}, M\mathbf{u}) = \frac{M}{N} I(\mathbf{x}, \mathbf{u}),$$

that is,

$$I(\mathbf{x}, \lambda\mathbf{u}) = \lambda I(\mathbf{x}, \mathbf{u}) \qquad \text{for all positive rational } \lambda. \qquad (3.3.6)$$

Similarly, (3.3.3) implies

$$I(\lambda\mathbf{x}, \mathbf{u}) = (1/\lambda)\, I(\mathbf{x}, \mathbf{u}) \qquad \text{for all positive rational } \lambda. \qquad (3.3.7)$$

From (3.3.6) and (3.3.7) it follows that

$$I(\lambda\mathbf{x}, \lambda\mathbf{u}) = I(\mathbf{x}, \mathbf{u}) \qquad \text{for all positive rational } \lambda. \qquad (3.3.8)$$

Also, (3.3.7) follows from (3.3.6) and (3.3.8) (and (3.3.6) from (3.3.7) and (3.3.8).

As will become clear from Theorem 3.3.9, every solution of (3.3.2), (3.3.3) with (3.3.4), (3.3.5) is a solution of Eqs. (3.3.6)–(3.3.8) with arbitrary positive *real* λ. The converse is not true.

Note that properties (3.3.5), (3.3.6), and (3.3.8) make sense in index theory, especially in price index theory: (3.3.5) The price index is positive if there is at least one positive base year price and at least one positive current price. (3.3.6)

[2] For the definitions of $\geqslant$ and $\geqq$ see Chapter 13.

If the base year prices $\mathbf{x}$ remain unchanged, then a μ percent increase (decrease) of all current prices $\mathbf{u}$ yields a μ percent increase (decrease) of the price index. (3.3.8) If two economies are identical except for the definition of the unit of money, then the price indices are equal.

Properties (3.3.6)–(3.3.8) have been derived from functional equations (3.3.2), (3.3.3) without any knowledge about the general solution of these functional equations. In the following it will be demonstrated that there do not exist any solutions of (3.3.2), (3.3.3) with (3.3.4), (3.3.5) that are different from (3.3.1). In other words, *the indices given by (3.3.1) are characterized by (3.3.2)–(3.3.5).*

3.3.9 **Theorem.** *A function (3.3.4) satisfies (3.3.5) as well as functional equations (3.3.2) and (3.3.3) if and only if it has the form (3.3.1) with* $\mathbf{a} > \mathbf{0}$, $\mathbf{b} > \mathbf{0}$.

3.3.10 **Corollary.** *In the case where $m = n$, a function (3.3.4) satisfies (3.3.2), (3.3.3), (3.3.5), and*

$$I(\mathbf{x}, \mathbf{x}) = 1 \qquad \textit{for all } \mathbf{x} \quad (3.3.11)$$

[3]

if and only if it has the form

$$I(\mathbf{x}, \mathbf{u}) = \mathbf{au}/\mathbf{ax} \qquad \textit{with} \quad \mathbf{a} > \mathbf{0}. \quad (3.3.12)$$

Note that in neither the theorem nor its corollary are continuity or monotonicity assumptions made.

Proof of the corollary. Obviously (3.3.12) satisfies (3.3.2), (3.3.3), (3.3.5), (3.3.11). The theorem says that every solution of (3.3.2), (3.3.3), (3.3.5) with $m = n$ has the form

$$I(\mathbf{x}, \mathbf{u}) = \frac{\mathbf{au}}{\mathbf{bx}} = \frac{a_1u_1 + \cdots + a_nu_n}{b_1x_1 + \cdots + b_nx_n} \qquad \text{with} \quad \mathbf{a} > \mathbf{0},\ \mathbf{b} > \mathbf{0}.$$

Such a function satisfies (3.3.11); that is

$$(\mathbf{a} - \mathbf{b})\,\mathbf{x} = 0 \qquad \text{for all } \mathbf{x}$$

if and only if $\mathbf{a} = \mathbf{b}$. ■

Proof of the theorem. That (3.3.1) satisfies (3.3.2)–(3.3.5) is obvious. It remains to show the converse. From (3.3.3), (3.3.5) it follows that, for all $\mathbf{x} \geq \mathbf{0}, \mathbf{u} \geq \mathbf{0}$,

$$(1/I(\mathbf{x}, \mathbf{u})) = \mathbf{b}(\mathbf{u})\,\mathbf{x} \qquad [\mathbf{b}(\mathbf{u}) = (b_1(\mathbf{u}), \ldots, b_n(\mathbf{u})) > \mathbf{0}]; \quad (3.3.13)$$

---

[3] If I is a price index, then formula (3.3.11) describes the case where the prices $\mathbf{x}$ do not change.

see Remark 3.1.11c together with Corollary 1.3.7. Inserting (3.3.13) into (3.3.2), we obtain, for all $\mathbf{x} \geqq \mathbf{0}, \mathbf{u} \geq \mathbf{0}, \mathbf{v} \geq \mathbf{0}$,

$$\frac{1}{\mathbf{b}(\mathbf{u}+\mathbf{v})\,\mathbf{x}} = \frac{1}{\mathbf{b}(\mathbf{u})\,\mathbf{x}} + \frac{1}{\mathbf{b}(\mathbf{v})\,\mathbf{x}}.$$

Put here successively

$$\mathbf{x} = \mathbf{e}^1 := (1, 0, \ldots, 0), \ldots, \mathbf{x} = \mathbf{e}^n := (0, \ldots, 0, 1)$$

in order to get

$$\frac{1}{b_h(\mathbf{u}+\mathbf{v})} = \frac{1}{b_h(\mathbf{u})} + \frac{1}{b_h(\mathbf{v})} \qquad (h = 1, \ldots, n).$$

Taking into account that $b_h(u)$ is positive, we know from Remark 3.1.11c together with Corollary 1.3.7 that

$$\frac{1}{b_h(\mathbf{u})} = \mathbf{a}^h\mathbf{u} \qquad \text{where} \quad \mathbf{a}^h = (a_1^h, \ldots, a_m^h) > \mathbf{0};\ h = 1, \ldots, n,. \tag{3.3.14}$$

With (3.3.14), Eq. (3.3.13) becomes

$$\frac{1}{I(\mathbf{x}, \mathbf{u})} = \frac{x_1}{\mathbf{a}^1\mathbf{x}} + \cdots + \frac{x_n}{\mathbf{a}^n\mathbf{x}} \qquad (\mathbf{x} \geq \mathbf{0}, \mathbf{u} \geq \mathbf{0}, \mathbf{a}^h > \mathbf{0}). \tag{3.3.15}$$

From this formula it follows that

$$I(\mathbf{e}^1 + \cdots + \mathbf{e}^n, \mathbf{u}) = \left(\frac{1}{\mathbf{a}^1\mathbf{u}} + \cdots + \frac{1}{\mathbf{a}^n\mathbf{u}}\right)^{-1} \qquad (\mathbf{u} \geq \mathbf{0}, \mathbf{a}^h \geq \mathbf{0}). \tag{3.3.16}$$

But in view of (3.3.2),

$$I(\mathbf{e}^1 + \cdots + \mathbf{e}^n, \mathbf{u}+\mathbf{v}) = I(\mathbf{e}^1 + \cdots + \mathbf{e}^n, \mathbf{u}) + I(\mathbf{e}^1 + \cdots + \mathbf{e}^n, \mathbf{v})$$
$$(\mathbf{u} \geq \mathbf{0}, \mathbf{v} \geq \mathbf{0}),$$

whence, using (3.3.5) and Remark 3.1.11c with Corollary 1.3.7, we obtain

$$I(\mathbf{e}^1 + \cdots + \mathbf{e}^n, \mathbf{u}) = \mathbf{a}\mathbf{u} \qquad (\mathbf{a} > \mathbf{0}, \mathbf{u} \geq \mathbf{0}).$$

If we compare this with (3.3.16), we have

$$\left(\frac{1}{\mathbf{a}^1\mathbf{u}} + \cdots + \frac{1}{\mathbf{a}^n\mathbf{u}}\right)^{-1} = \mathbf{a}\mathbf{u},$$

that is,

$$\mathbf{a}^1\mathbf{u}\left(1 + \frac{\mathbf{a}^1\mathbf{u}}{\mathbf{a}^2\mathbf{u}} + \cdots + \frac{\mathbf{a}^1\mathbf{u}}{\mathbf{a}^n\mathbf{u}}\right)^{-1} = \mathbf{a}\mathbf{u}.$$

This can be written as

$$(\mathbf{a}^1 - \psi(\mathbf{u})\mathbf{a})\,\mathbf{u} = 0 \qquad \text{where} \quad \psi(\mathbf{u}) := 1 + \frac{\mathbf{a}^1\mathbf{u}}{\mathbf{a}^2\mathbf{u}} + \cdots + \frac{\mathbf{a}^1\mathbf{u}}{\mathbf{a}^n\mathbf{u}}. \tag{3.3.17}$$

Note that $\psi(\mathbf{u}) > 0$ for all $\mathbf{u} \geq \mathbf{0}$. If $\mathbf{a}^1 > \mathbf{0}$ and $\mathbf{a} > \mathbf{0}$ are linearly independent, (3.3.17) cannot be true for all $\mathbf{u} \geq \mathbf{0}$ (it is not valid for any $\mathbf{u}$ not perpendicular to the plane spanned by $\mathbf{a}^1$ and $\mathbf{a}$). Hence $\mathbf{a}^1 = \lambda_1 \mathbf{a}$ with $\lambda_1 > \mathbf{0}$. In the same way we conclude that $\mathbf{a}^2 = \lambda_2 \mathbf{a}, \ldots, \mathbf{a}^n = \lambda_n \mathbf{a}$ ($\lambda_2, \ldots, \lambda_n$ positive constants). With these $\mathbf{a}^h$'s formula (3.3.15) becomes

$$\frac{1}{I(\mathbf{x}, \mathbf{u})} = \frac{b_1 x_1 + \cdots + b_n x_n}{\mathbf{a}\mathbf{u}} \qquad \left(b_1 = \frac{1}{\lambda_1}, \ldots, b_n = \frac{1}{\lambda_n}\right),$$

and the theorem is proved for all $\mathbf{x} \geq \mathbf{0}, \mathbf{u} \geq \mathbf{0}$. For $\mathbf{u} = \mathbf{0}$, the theorem follows by putting $\mathbf{v} = \mathbf{0}$ into (3.3.2). ■

An alternative proceeds up to Eq. (3.3.15), then substitutes the following equivalent form of (3.3.15)

$$I(x_1 \mathbf{e}^1 + \cdots + x_n, \mathbf{e}^n, \mathbf{u}) = \left(\frac{x_1}{\mathbf{a}^1\mathbf{u}} + \cdots + \frac{x_n}{\mathbf{a}^n\mathbf{u}}\right)^{-1} \qquad (\mathbf{x} \geq \mathbf{0}, \mathbf{u} \geq \mathbf{0}, \mathbf{a}^h > \mathbf{0}), \tag{3.3.18}$$

into (3.3.2) in order to get

$$\left(\frac{x_1}{\mathbf{a}^1\,\mathbf{u} + \mathbf{a}^1\mathbf{v}} + \cdots + \frac{x_n}{\mathbf{a}^n\mathbf{u} + \mathbf{a}^n\mathbf{v}}\right)^{-1} = \left(\frac{x_1}{\mathbf{a}^1\mathbf{u}} + \cdots + \frac{x_n}{\mathbf{a}^n\mathbf{u}}\right)^{-1} + \left(\frac{x_1}{\mathbf{a}^1\mathbf{v}} + \cdots + \frac{x_n}{\mathbf{a}^n\mathbf{v}}\right)^{-1}.$$

Put into this equation $x_h = c_h > 0$ $(h = 1, \ldots, n)$ and

$$\sigma_h = \frac{\mathbf{a}^h\mathbf{u}}{c_h} > 0, \qquad \tau_h = \frac{\mathbf{a}^h\mathbf{v}}{c_h} > 0 \tag{3.3.19}$$

and get

$$[(\sigma_1 + \tau_1)^{-1} + \cdots + (\sigma_n + \tau_n)^{-1}]^{-1} = (\sigma_1^{-1} + \cdots + \sigma_n^{-1})^{-1} + (\tau_1^{-1} + \cdots + \tau_n^{-1})^{-1}.$$

But this is the equality case of the Minkowski inequality, which (see Hardy, Littlewood, and Pólya [1934, pp. 30–31]) can hold only if the sequences $\{\sigma_h\}$ and $\{\tau_h\}$ are proportional, that is,

$$\tau_h = \delta\sigma_h \qquad (h = 1, \ldots, n;\ \delta > 0 \text{ a scalar constant}).$$

Hence from (3.3.19),

$$\mathbf{a}^h\mathbf{v} = \delta(\mathbf{u}, \mathbf{v})\, \mathbf{a}^h\mathbf{u} \qquad (h = 1, \ldots, n)$$

(since δ may depend upon $\mathbf{u}$ and $\mathbf{v}$), in particular

$$\mathbf{a}^1\mathbf{v} = \delta(\mathbf{u}, \mathbf{v})\, \mathbf{a}^1\mathbf{u}.$$

Dividing the last two equations, we get

$$\frac{\mathbf{a}^1\mathbf{v}}{\mathbf{a}^h\mathbf{v}} = \frac{\mathbf{a}^1\mathbf{u}}{\mathbf{a}^h\mathbf{u}} = \varkappa_h > 0 \qquad (h = 1, \ldots, n;\ \varkappa_1 = 1)$$

(the scalars $\varkappa_h$ are independent of $\mathbf{u}$, $\mathbf{v}$), or

$$\mathbf{a}^h\mathbf{u} = \mathbf{a}^1\mathbf{u}/\varkappa_h \qquad (h = 1, \ldots, n;\ \varkappa_1 = 1).$$

Putting this into (3.3.18) we obtain

$$I(\mathbf{x}, \mathbf{u}) = \left(\frac{x_1}{\mathbf{a}^1\mathbf{u}} + \frac{\varkappa_2 x_2}{\mathbf{a}^1\mathbf{u}} + \cdots + \frac{\varkappa_n x_n}{\mathbf{a}^1\mathbf{u}}\right)^{-1} = \frac{\mathbf{au}}{\mathbf{bx}}, \qquad \mathbf{a} = \mathbf{a}^1 > \mathbf{0},$$

$$\mathbf{b} = \mathbf{e}^1 + \varkappa_2\mathbf{e}^2 + \cdots + \varkappa_n\mathbf{e}^n > \mathbf{0},$$

for all $\mathbf{x} \geq \mathbf{0}$, $\mathbf{u} \geq \mathbf{0}$. Since this satisfies (3.3.2) also for $\mathbf{u} = \mathbf{0}$, the theorem is proved again. ∎

3.4 Price Policy of the Firm: The Role of the Equation $H_1(\mathbf{x} + \mathbf{y}) = H_2(\mathbf{x})\,H_3(\mathbf{y})$, $(\mathbf{x}, \mathbf{y}) \in \mathbb{R}_+^{2n}$, $H_j : \mathbb{R}_+^n \to \mathbb{R}$

In this section we partly generalize the model of Section 1.6, where we considered a single-product firm whose sales S depended only on its own price and advertising policy. Now we consider a market with $n \geqq 2$ single-product firms and many consumers, and assume the following.

The ith firm has only one strategic variable, namely its price $p_i \geqq 0$ $(i = 1, \ldots, n)$. (3.4.1)

The sales function S_i of the ith firm depends on all n prices, namely on $\mathbf{p} := (p_1, \ldots, p_n)$. Hence $S_i : \mathbb{R}_+^n \to \mathbb{R}_+$. (3.4.2)

The mappings $p_j \to S_i(\mathbf{p})$ are monotonic for every $(n-1)$-tuple $(p_1, \ldots, p_{j-1}, p_{j+1}, \ldots, p_n)$ of prices $(i = 1, \ldots, n; j = 1, \ldots, n;\ i \neq j)$. (3.4.3)

The mappings $p_i \to S_i(\mathbf{p})$ are strictly monotonically decreasing for every $(n-1)$-tuple $(p_1, \ldots, p_{i-1}, p_{i+1}, \ldots, p_n)$ of prices $(i = 1, \ldots, n)$. (3.4.4)

Every sales function $S_i : \mathbb{R}_+^n \to \mathbb{R}_+$ satisfies a functional equation of the form $S_i(\mathbf{p} + \boldsymbol{\pi}) = \psi_i(\boldsymbol{\pi})\,S_i(\mathbf{p})$ where $(\mathbf{p}, \boldsymbol{\pi}) \in \mathbb{R}_+^{2n}$, $\psi_i : \mathbb{R}_+^n \to \mathbb{R}_+$, $\psi_i(\mathbf{0}) = 1$. (3.4.5)

The equation in (3.4.5) says that if the prices $\mathbf{p}$ are changed by adding an increment vector $\boldsymbol{\pi} \in \mathbb{R}_+$, then the sales of the ith firm are a certain percentage of its sales at prices $\mathbf{p}$, this percentage depending only on the increment vector $\boldsymbol{\pi}$.

3.4.6 **Theorem.** *Every function $S_i : \mathbb{R}^n_+ \to \mathbb{R}_+$ with properties (3.4.2)–(3.4.5) can be written as*

$$S_i(\mathbf{p}) = a_i e^{c_{i1}p_1 + \cdots + c_{in}p_n} =: a_i e^{\mathbf{c}_i \mathbf{p}} \tag{3.4.7}$$

where $a_i > 0$, $c_{ii} < 0$, $c_{i1}, \ldots, c_{i,i-1}, c_{i,i+1}, \ldots, c_{in}$ are arbitrary real constants.

Proof. See the arguments preceding Theorem 3.4.18 and Corollary 3.4.23, which contains Theorem 3.4.6 as a special case. ■

3.4.8 **Remark.** In the foregoing model, the ith firm faces the following *elasticity ε_{ij} of demand x_i* with respect to the jth price p_j:

$$\varepsilon_{ij}(x_i, \mathbf{p}) := -\frac{\partial x_i}{\partial p_j}\frac{p_j}{x_i} = -\frac{\partial S_i(\mathbf{p})}{\partial p_j}\frac{p_j}{S_i(\mathbf{p})} = -c_{ij}p. \tag{3.4.9}$$

In other words, the model implies that $\varepsilon_{ij}(x_i, \mathbf{p})$ depends only on the price p_j. Note that $\varepsilon_{ij}(x_i, \mathbf{p}) = -c_{ij}p_j > 0$ does *not* depend on the prices $p_1, \ldots, p_{j-1}, p_{j+1}, \ldots, p_n$ of the competitors.

3.4.10 **Theorem.** *In the foregoing model, let the cost function K_i: $\mathbb{R}_+ \to \mathbb{R}_+$ of the ith firm be additive in the sense of (1.8.17). Then there exists a unique price $p_i^* > 0$ that maximizes the profit of the firm, and this price p_i^* does not depend on the prices of the competitors.*

Proof. According to (1.8.18), the cost function K_i is given by

$$K_i(x_i) = \alpha_i + \beta_i x_i \tag{3.4.11}$$

where $\alpha_i = K_i(0) \geqq 0$ is the fixed cost and $\beta_i > 0$ is the marginal cost of the ith firm. Because of (3.4.7), (3.4.11) its profit function Π_i: $\mathbb{R}^n_+ \to \mathbb{R}$ can be written as

$$\Pi_i(\mathbf{p}) = x_i p_i - K_i(x_i) = a_i e^{\mathbf{c}_i \mathbf{p}} p_i - \alpha_i - \beta_i a_i e^{\mathbf{c}_i \mathbf{p}}. \tag{3.4.12}$$

From

$$\frac{\partial \Pi_i(\mathbf{p})}{\partial p_i} = a_i e^{\mathbf{c}_i \mathbf{p}}(1 + c_{ii}p_i - \beta_i c_{it}) = 0,$$

$$\frac{\partial^2 \Pi_i(\mathbf{p})}{p_i^2} = a_i c_{ii} e^{\mathbf{c}_i \mathbf{p}}(2 + c_{ii}p_i - \beta_i c_{ii})$$

it follows that the profit-maximizing price is

$$p_i^* = \beta_i - \frac{1}{c_{ii}} > 0 \qquad (\beta_i > 0,\ c_{ii} < 0 \text{ as assumed}),$$

which proves the theorem. ■

3.4.13 **Remark.** In the terminology of game theory, our result can be phrased as follows. The unique *Nash equilibrium point* (see (13.3.25)) of the game defined by the *strategy sets* $\Sigma_i := \{\sigma_i \mid \sigma_i = p_i \geqq 0\}$ and the *payoff functions* $\Pi_i : \Sigma_1 \times \Sigma_2 \times \cdots \times \Sigma_n \to \mathbb{R}$ given by (3.4.12) is the vector

$$(p_1^*, \ldots, p_n^*) = \left(\beta_1 - \frac{1}{c_{11}}, \ldots, \beta_n - \frac{1}{c_{nn}}\right).$$

It is due to the special form of (3.4.12) that it was not necessary to solve for a system of n equations like

$$f_i(p_1, \ldots, p_n) = 0 \quad (f_i \text{ not depending only on } p_i;\ i = 1, \ldots, n)$$

in order to determine the set of the Nash equilibrium points of the foregoing game.

We conclude this section by considering the equation

$$H_1(\mathbf{x} + \mathbf{y}) = H_2(\mathbf{x})\, H_3(\mathbf{y}), \qquad (\mathbf{x}, \mathbf{y}) \in \mathbb{R}_+^{2n}, \quad H_j : \mathbb{R}_+^n \to \mathbb{R}, \quad (3.4.14)$$

which contains Eq. (3.4.5) as a special case. We set first $\mathbf{x} = \mathbf{0}$, $\mathbf{y} = \mathbf{z}$, and then $\mathbf{x} = \mathbf{z}$, $\mathbf{y} = \mathbf{0}$:

$$H_1(\mathbf{z}) = H_2(\mathbf{0})\, H_3(\mathbf{z}), \qquad H_1(\mathbf{z}) = H_2(\mathbf{z})\, H_3(\mathbf{0}). \qquad (3.4.15)$$

If, for example, $H_3(\mathbf{0}) = 0$, then $H_1(\mathbf{z}) \equiv 0$ and either $H_2(\mathbf{x}) \equiv 0$ or $H_3(\mathbf{y}) \equiv 0$, and $H_3(\mathbf{y})$ or $H_2(\mathbf{x})$, respectively, can be arbitrary; we will exclude this trivial system of solutions in what follows. Then we can write (3.4.15) as

$$H_3(\mathbf{z}) = H_1(\mathbf{z})/a, \qquad \text{where} \quad a := H_2(\mathbf{0}) \neq 0,$$
$$H_2(\mathbf{z}) = H_1(\mathbf{z})/b \qquad \text{where} \quad b := H_3(\mathbf{0}) \neq 0.$$

Moreover, the function $H\colon \mathbb{R}_+^n \to \mathbb{R}$ defined by

$$H(\mathbf{z}) := H_1(\mathbf{z})/ab \qquad (ab \neq 0)$$

satisfies

$$H(\mathbf{x} + \mathbf{y}) = H(\mathbf{x})\, H(\mathbf{y}), \qquad (\mathbf{x}, \mathbf{y}) \in \mathbb{R}_+^{2n},\ H : \mathbb{R}_+^n \to \mathbb{R}. \qquad (3.4.16)$$

If H is zero at a single point $\mathbf{x}_0 \in \mathbb{R}_+^n$, then, using arguments similar to those in the proof of Lemma 1.4.4, we can show that either $H(\mathbf{z}) = 0$ and hence, $H_1(\mathbf{z}) = H_2(\mathbf{z}) = H_3(\mathbf{z}) = 0$ for all $\mathbf{z} \geqq \mathbf{0}$ (which was already excluded) or

$$H(\mathbf{z}) = \begin{cases} 0 & \text{for all} \quad \mathbf{z} \geq \mathbf{0}, \\ 1 & \text{for} \quad \mathbf{z} = \mathbf{0}; \end{cases}$$

that is,

$$H_1(\mathbf{z}) = H_2(\mathbf{z}) = H_3(\mathbf{z}) = 0 \qquad \text{for all} \quad \mathbf{z} \geq \mathbf{0},$$
$$H_1(\mathbf{0}) = ab \qquad H_2(\mathbf{0}) = a, \qquad H_3(\mathbf{0}) = b.$$

In what follows, we are not interested in these trivial solutions. From (3.4.16) with $\mathbf{x} = \mathbf{y} = \mathbf{z}/2$ we obtain

$$H(\mathbf{z}) = H(\mathbf{z}/2)^2 > 0$$

for any nontrivial H, that is, any nontrivial function satisfying (3.4.16) is positive valued. Taking the logarithm on both sides of (3.4.16), we get

$$\log H(\mathbf{x} + \mathbf{y}) = \log H(\mathbf{x}) + \log H(\mathbf{y}), \qquad (\mathbf{x}, \mathbf{y}) \in \mathbb{R}_+^{2n}.$$

With

$$F(\mathbf{x}) := \log H(\mathbf{x}) \tag{3.4.17}$$

this becomes

$$F(\mathbf{x} + \mathbf{y}) = F(\mathbf{x}) + F(\mathbf{y}), \qquad (\mathbf{x}, \mathbf{y}) \in \mathbb{R}_+^{2n}, \quad F : \mathbb{R}_+^n \to \mathbb{R}.$$

Since we know the general solution of this equation from (3.1.5), (3.1.11) and since (3.4.17) is equivalent to

$$H(\mathbf{x}) = e^{F(\mathbf{x})},$$

we can summarize:

3.4.18 **Theorem.** *The systems of functions*

$$\left.\begin{aligned} H_1(\mathbf{z}) &= ab\, e^{g_1(z_1) + g_2(z_2) + \cdots + g_n(z_n)}, \\ H_2(\mathbf{z}) &= a\, e^{g_1(z_1) + g_2(z_2) + \cdots + g_n(z_n)}, \\ H_3(\mathbf{z}) &= b\, e^{g_1(z_1) + g_2(z_2) + \cdots + g_n(z_n)}, \end{aligned}\right\} \tag{3.4.19}$$

where $g_1, g_2, \ldots, g_n$ are arbitrary solutions of Cauchy's functional equation (1.0.2), and $a \neq 0$, $b \neq 0$ are arbitrary constants and the trivial solutions

$$H_1(\mathbf{z}) \equiv H_2(\mathbf{z}) \equiv 0, \qquad H_3(\mathbf{z}) \ \textit{arbitrary}, \tag{3.4.20}$$

$$H_1(\mathbf{z}) \equiv H_3(\mathbf{z}) \equiv 0, \qquad H_2(\mathbf{z}) \ \textit{arbitrary}, \tag{3.4.21}$$

$$\begin{aligned} &H_1(\mathbf{z}) = H_2(\mathbf{z}) = H_3(\mathbf{z}) = 0 \quad \textit{for all} \quad \mathbf{z} \geq \mathbf{0}, \\ &H_1(\mathbf{0}) = ab, \qquad H_2(\mathbf{0}) = a, \qquad H_3(\mathbf{0}) = b, \end{aligned} \tag{3.4.22}$$

and only these satisfy functional equation (3.4.14).

Because of (3.4.3) and (3.4.4), we are interested in the case where, for a particular z_ν ($\nu \in \{1, 2, \ldots, n\}$), the mapping $z_\nu \to H_1(\mathbf{z})$ is strictly monotonic, whereas the mappings $z_\mu \to H_1(\mathbf{z})$ ($\mu = 1, \ldots, \nu - 1, \nu + 1, \ldots, n$) are monotonic. Then the trivial solutions (3.4.20)–(3.4.22) of (3.4.14) are excluded and, as a consequence of (1.3.7), we have

3.4.23 **Corollary.** *Let the functions H_1, H_2, H_3 satisfy functional equation (3.4.14). Let the mappings $z_1 \to H_1(\mathbf{z}), \ldots, z_n \to H_1(\mathbf{z})$ be monotonic. If at least one of these mappings is strictly monotonic, then there exist constants $a \neq 0$, $b \neq 0$, and a constant vector $\mathbf{c} = (c_1, c_2, \ldots, c_n) \neq \mathbf{0}$ such that H_1, H_2, H_3 can be written as (3.4.19) with*

$$g_1(z_1) = c_1 z_1, \qquad g_2(z_2) = c_2 z_2, \ldots, g_n(z_n) = c_n z_n. \tag{3.4.24}$$

Conversely, every system of functions given by (3.4.19) with (3.4.24) satisfies functional equation (3.4.14).

3.5 Advertising Policy of the Firm: The Role of the Equation $L_1(x_1y_1, \ldots, x_ny_n) = L_2(\mathbf{x}) + L_3(\mathbf{y}),\quad (\mathbf{x}, \mathbf{y}) \in \mathbb{R}^{2n}_{++},\quad L_j : \mathbb{R}^n_{++} \to \mathbb{R}$

Suppose a seller of a certain commodity has k markets that are more or less spatially distinct. Let $(p_1, p_2, \ldots, p_k) =: \mathbf{p}$ be the vector of the prices of the commodity at the different markets. Suppose that the distances between the markets are such that there is no advantage for the consumers currently buying in market i to change to market $j (j \neq i)$. Let the cost of transportation of one unit to the markets be $(\gamma_1, \gamma_2, \ldots, \gamma_k) := \boldsymbol{\gamma}$.

In the following we will consider the problem of determining an optimal advertising policy $w_0, w_1, \ldots, w_k$ for a sales period. Here the $w_1, \ldots, w_k$ are the advertising expenditures aimed at the single markets, whereas the advertising expenditures w_0 are those made for the markets as a whole. The problem will be solved within the framework of a model that consists of the following assumptions[4]:

(i) See the first paragraph of this section.

(ii) The cost of making the quantity x of the commodity available is $K(x)$. The cost function $K : \mathbb{R}_+ \to \mathbb{R}_+$ is additive in the sense of (1.8.17).

(iii) The sales vector $(x_1, x_2, \ldots, x_k) =: \mathbf{x}$, which is the vector of the quantities sold in the different markets, is a unique function of the advertising expenditures $w_0 > 0$, $w_1 > 0, \ldots, w_k > 0$. In other words, there exists a vector-valued sales function

$$\mathbf{S} : \mathbb{R}^{k+1}_{++} \to \mathbb{R}^k$$

that maps each vector $\mathbf{w} := (w_0, w_1, \ldots, w_k)$ of the advertising expenditures on the vector $\mathbf{x} = (x_1, x_2, \ldots, x_k)$ of those quantities which are (likely) to be sold in the different markets within the sales period considered, when $\mathbf{w}$ is applied.

(iv) The sales function $\mathbf{S}$ has the following two properties:

$$\mathbf{S}(\mathbf{w}) > \mathbf{0} \qquad \text{for} \quad \mathbf{w} \geqq (1, 1, \ldots, 1), \tag{3.5.1}$$

that is, there are positive sales in each market at least when each component of the vector of the advertising expenditures is $\geqq 1$;

$$\mathbf{S}(w_0v_0, w_1v_1, \ldots, w_kv_k) = \mathbf{S}(\mathbf{w}) + \mathbf{T}(\mathbf{v}) \tag{3.5.2}$$

for all $\mathbf{w} > \mathbf{0}$, $\mathbf{v} := (v_0, v_1, \ldots, v_k) > \mathbf{0}$, where

$$\mathbf{T} : \mathbb{R}^{k+1}_{++} \to \mathbb{R}^k, \qquad \mathbf{T}(1, 1, \ldots, 1) = \mathbf{0}, \tag{3.5.3}$$

is a fixed vector-valued function of $\mathbf{v}$.

---

[4] Similar models (m commodities but only one market; monopoly; oligopoly) have been developed in the author's paper [1972c]. See also the model considered in Section 1.8.

Assumption (3.5.2) says that a *multiplicative* change of the advertising expenditures $w_0 > 0, w_1 > 0, \ldots, w_k > 0$ yields an *additive* change in the sales, where the additive term $\mathbf{T}$ depends only on the multipliers.

We are interested in the general solution of the $\varkappa$th component of Eq. (3.5.2), namely

$$S_\varkappa(w_0v_0, w_1v_1, \ldots, w_kv_k) = S_\varkappa(\mathbf{w}) + T_\varkappa(\mathbf{v}), \tag{3.5.4}$$

since this is equivalent to solving for Eq. (3.5.2) itself.

3.5.5 **Theorem.** *Let*

$$\mathbf{x} = (x_1, \ldots, x_n) \in \mathbb{R}^n_{++}, \qquad \mathbf{y} = (y_1, \ldots, y_n) \in \mathbb{R}^n_{++}.$$

Let the three functions

$$L_j : \mathbb{R}^n_{++} \to \mathbb{R} \qquad (j = 1, 2, 3)$$

satisfy the functional equation

$$L_1(x_1y_1, \ldots, x_ny_n) = L_2(\mathbf{x}) + L_3(\mathbf{y}), \qquad (\mathbf{x}, \mathbf{y}) \in \mathbb{R}^{2n}_{++},\ L_j : \mathbb{R}^n_{++} \to \mathbb{R}. \tag{3.5.6}$$

Then there exist two real constants a, b, and n functions $f_\nu : \mathbb{R} \to \mathbb{R}$ ($\nu = 1, \ldots, n$), satisfying Cauchy's basic equation

$$f(\xi + \eta) = f(\xi) + f(\eta), \qquad (\xi, \eta) \in \mathbb{R}^2, \quad f: \mathbb{R} \to \mathbb{R}, \tag{3.5.7}$$

such that

$$\left.\begin{aligned} L_1(\mathbf{x}) &= f_1(\log x_1) + \cdots + f_n(\log x_n) + a + b, \\ L_2(\mathbf{x}) &= f_1(\log x_1) + \cdots + f_n(\log x_n) + a, \\ L_3(\mathbf{x}) &= f_1(\log x_1) + \cdots + f_n(\log x_n) + b. \end{aligned}\right\} \tag{3.5.8}$$

Conversely, every triple (3.5.8) satisfies (3.5.6) if the f_ν's satisfy (3.5.7).

Note that Eq. (3.5.4) is a special case of Eq. (3.5.6).

Proof of the theorem. Since both vectors $\mathbf{x}$ and $\mathbf{y}$ are positive, we can write Eq. (3.5.6) as

$$\begin{aligned} &L_1(e^{\log x_1 + \log y_1}, \ldots, e^{\log x_n + \log y_n}) \\ &\quad = L_2(e^{\log x_1}, \ldots, e^{\log x_n}) + L_3(e^{\log y_1}, \ldots, e^{\log y_n}). \end{aligned} \tag{3.5.9}$$

If we now write

$$L_j(e^{\log z_1}, \ldots, e^{\log z_n}) = : F_j(\log z_1, \ldots, \log z_n) \qquad (j = 1, 2, 3)$$

and

$$\log x_\nu = : \xi_\nu, \qquad \log y_\nu = : \eta_\nu \qquad (\nu = 1, \ldots, n),$$

Eq. (3.5.9) becomes

$$F_1(\xi_1 + \eta_1, \ldots, \xi_n + \eta_n) = F_2(\xi_1, \ldots, \xi_n) + F_3(\eta_1, \ldots, \eta_n),$$

that is, Eq. (3.1.2). Hence we can apply Theorems 3.1.1 and 3.1.5 in order to obtain Theorem 3.5.5. ■

If one of the L_j's in (3.5.6) is (a) continuous at a single point of $\mathbb{R}^n_{++}$ or (b) monotonic in an arbitrarily small ε-neighborhood of a point of $\mathbb{R}^n_{++}$, then the same is true for the f_ν's in (3.5.8). As a consequence of this and (1.2.10) we have

3.5.10 **Corollary.** *If the functions L_1, L_2, and L_3 satisfy (3.5.6) and if at least one of them has a property like (a) or (b), then they can be written as (3.5.8) with*

$$f_1(\log x_1) = c_1 \log x_1, \ldots, f_n(\log x_n) = c_n \log x_n, \tag{3.5.11}$$

where the real constants a, b, $c_1, \ldots, c_n$ are suitably chosen. Every triple (3.5.8) with (3.5.11) satisfies (3.5.6).

Since from (3.5.1), (3.5.2) it follows that the $S_\varkappa$'s are strictly increasing, we can apply Corollary 3.5.10 and Theorem 3.5.5 in order to get

3.5.12 **Corollary.** *Let*

$$\mathbf{S} : \mathbb{R}^{k+1}_{++} \to \mathbb{R}^k, \qquad \mathbf{T} : \mathbb{R}^{k+1}_{++} \to \mathbb{R}^k$$

be functions satisfying (3.5.1)–(3.5.3). Then there exist real constants

$$b_\varkappa > 0, \qquad c_{\varkappa 0} > 0, \qquad c_{\varkappa 1} > 0, \ldots, c_{\varkappa k} > 0 \qquad (\varkappa = 1, \ldots, k) \tag{3.5.13}$$

such that

$$\begin{aligned} S_\varkappa(w_0, w_1, \ldots, w_k) &= \sum_{\lambda=0}^{k} c_{\varkappa\lambda} \log w_\lambda + b_\varkappa \\ T_\varkappa(w_0, w_1, \ldots, w_k) &= \sum_{\lambda=0}^{k} c_{\varkappa\lambda} \log w_\lambda \end{aligned} \qquad (\varkappa = 1, \ldots, k). \tag{3.5.14}$$

Conversely, every pair of functions **S**, **T** *given by (3.5.14) with constants (3.5.13) satisfies (3.5.1)–(3.5.3).*

That the functions $S_\varkappa$ given by (3.5.14) represent a very useful class of sales functions can be emphasized by the same arguments as were made in Remark 1.8.13 (ii), (iii).

In our model (i)–(iv), the profit Π of the seller is given by

$$\Pi(\mathbf{w}) = (\mathbf{p} - \boldsymbol{\gamma})\,\mathbf{S}(\mathbf{w}) - K\left(\sum_{\varkappa=1}^{k} S_\varkappa(\mathbf{w})\right) - \sum_{\lambda=0}^{k} w_\lambda.$$

Since **S** is given by the first line of (3.5.14) and since K has, as a consequence of (ii), the form (1.8.18), namely

$$K(x) = \alpha + \beta x \ (\alpha \geqq 0 \text{ the fixed cost}, \beta > 0 \text{ the marginal cost}),$$

the profit can be written as

$$\begin{aligned} \Pi(\mathbf{w}) = &\sum_{\varkappa=1}^{k} (p_\varkappa - \gamma_\varkappa)\left(\sum_{\lambda=0}^{k} c_{\varkappa\lambda} \log w_\lambda + b_\varkappa\right) \\ &- \alpha - \beta\left(\sum_{\varkappa=1}^{k}\sum_{\lambda=0}^{k} c_{\varkappa\lambda} \log w_\lambda + b_\varkappa\right) - \sum_{\lambda=0}^{k} w_\lambda. \end{aligned} \tag{3.5.15}$$

For a positive vector $\mathbf{w}^*$ maximizing the profit we have

$$\frac{\partial \Pi(\mathbf{w}^*)}{\partial w_\mu} = \sum_{\nu=1}^{k} (p_\varkappa - \gamma_\varkappa)\, c_{\varkappa\mu} \frac{1}{w_\mu^*} - \beta \sum_{\varkappa=1}^{k} c_{\varkappa\mu} \frac{1}{w_\mu^*} - 1 = 0,$$

that is,

$$w_\mu^* = \sum_{\varkappa=1}^{k} c_{\varkappa\mu}(p_\varkappa - \gamma_\varkappa - \beta) \qquad (\mu = 0, 1, \ldots, k). \tag{3.5.16}$$

If, on the other hand, a vector $\mathbf{w}^*$ given by (3.5.16) is positive, then it gives rise to a local maximum of the profit Π because

$$\frac{\partial^2 \Pi(\mathbf{w}^*)}{\partial w_\mu^2} = -\left(\frac{1}{w_\mu^*}\right)^2 \sum_{\varkappa=1}^{k} c_{\varkappa\mu}(p_\varkappa - \gamma_\varkappa - \beta) < 0,$$

$$\frac{\partial^2 \Pi(\mathbf{w})}{\partial w_\mu \partial w_\nu} = 0 \qquad (\mu = 0, \ldots, k;\ \nu = 0, \ldots, k;\ \mu \neq \nu).$$

That this maximum is *global* follows easily from the shape of the profit function (3.5.15). We summarize:

3.5.17 **Theorem.** *In the model (i)–(iv), let $p_\varkappa - \gamma_\varkappa - \beta$, that is, the profit contribution per unit, be positive. Then there exists one and only one vector $\mathbf{w}^* > \mathbf{0}$ of advertising expenditures that maximizes the profit. The components of $\mathbf{w}^*$ are given by (3.5.16).*

3.5.18 **Remark.** Obviously, in our model, the optimum advertising expenditures made for the μth market, namely (3.5.16), depend neither on the advertising expenditures $w_1, \ldots, w_{\mu-1}, w_{\mu+1}, \ldots, w_k$ aimed at the other markets nor on those, w_0, made for the markets as a whole. As we learn from (3.5.16), the optimum advertising expenditures w_μ^* made for the μth market are strictly increasing with the prices in the different markets and strictly decreasing with both the marginal cost and the cost of transportation of the unit of the commodity to the different markets.

3.5.19 **Example.** We specialize our model to the case of only two markets. Let $\mathbf{p} = (11, 14)$ be the prices and $\boldsymbol{\gamma} = (1, 2)$ the transport cost per unit. If the sales function is given by

$$\begin{aligned} x_1 &= S_1(\mathbf{w}) = 1000 + 50 \log w_0 + 75 \log w_1 + 15 \log w_2, \\ x_2 &= S_2(\mathbf{w}) = 900 + 60 \log w_0 + 10 \log w_1 + 100 \log w_2, \end{aligned}$$

and the cost function by

$$K(x) = K(x_1 + x_2) = 5564 + 4(x_1 + x_2),$$

then we have for the optimum advertising expenditures

$$\mathbf{w}^* = (w_0^*, w_1^*, w_2^*) = (780, 530, 890);$$

for the optimum sales on the two markets

$$\mathbf{x}^* = (x_1^*, x_2^*) = (1905.4, 2041.4);$$

and for the maximum profit

$$\Pi(\mathbf{w}^*) = 20\,000.$$

If these same total advertising expenditures were distributed as

$$\tilde{\mathbf{w}} = (\tilde{w}_0, \tilde{w}_1, \tilde{w}_2) = (1000, 600, 600),$$

then the profit would be only

$$\Pi(\tilde{\mathbf{w}}) = 19\,908.$$

3.6 Production and Utility Theory: The Role of the Equation $M_1(x_1y_1, \cdots, x_ny_n) = M_2(\mathbf{x})\, M_3(\mathbf{y}),\ (\mathbf{x}, \mathbf{y}) \in \mathbb{R}_+^{2n},\ M_j\colon \mathbb{R}_+^n \to \mathbb{R}$

Let the function

$$\Phi : \mathbb{R}_+^n \to \mathbb{R}, \qquad \mathbf{x} \to \Phi(\mathbf{x}), \qquad \Phi(\mathbf{x}) \not\equiv 0 \qquad [\mathbf{x} = (x_1, \ldots, x_n)] \tag{3.6.1}$$

satisfy the functional equation

$$\begin{aligned} &\Phi(\lambda_1 x_1, \ldots, \lambda_n x_n) = \phi(\lambda_1, \ldots, \lambda_n)\Phi(x_1, \ldots, x_n) \qquad \text{with} \\ &(\boldsymbol{\lambda}, \mathbf{x}) \in \mathbb{R}_+^{2n}, \qquad \boldsymbol{\lambda} := (\lambda_1, \ldots, \lambda_n), \quad \mathbf{x} := (x_1, \ldots, x_n), \end{aligned} \tag{3.6.2}$$

where

$$\phi : \mathbb{R}_+^n \to \mathbb{R}, \quad \boldsymbol{\lambda} \to \phi(\boldsymbol{\lambda}), \qquad \phi(1, \ldots, 1) = 1, \tag{3.6.3}$$

is strictly increasing. We may consider Φ as a (scalar-valued) production function (see Remark 13.3.7) or as a utility function (see Remark 13.3.8). In the second case, Eq. (3.6.2) can be interpreted as follows: If the quantities $x_1, \ldots, x_n$ of n commodities will be multiplied by nonnegative real numbers $\lambda_1, \ldots, \lambda_n$, respectively, then the utility of the vector $(\lambda_1 x_1, \ldots, \lambda_n x_n)$ is equal to the utility of the vector $(x_1, \ldots, x_n) = \mathbf{x}$ multiplied by a real number that is strictly increasing with the multipliers $\lambda_1, \ldots, \lambda_n$. If Φ is considered a production function, the interpretation is similar.

3.6.4 **Theorem.** *Let a function (3.6.1) and a strictly increasing function (3.6.3) be given that satisfy functional equation (3.6.2). Then there exist positive constants* $C, \alpha_1, \alpha_2, \ldots, \alpha_n$ *such that*

$$\Phi(\mathbf{x}) = C x_1^{\alpha} x_2^{\alpha_2} \cdots x_n^{\alpha_n}, \qquad \phi(\boldsymbol{\lambda}) = \lambda_1^{\alpha} \lambda_2^{\alpha_2} \ldots \lambda_n^{\alpha_n}. \tag{3.6.5}$$

Conversely, every pair of functions Φ, ϕ *given by (3.6.5) satisfies Eq. (3.6.2).*

In other words, we have the following characterization of a well-known class of production or utility functions.

3.6.6 **Corollary.** *The strictly increasing CD-type functions (2.0.3) are characterized by property (3.6.2) with (3.6.1), (3.6.3), where* ϕ *is strictly increasing.*

Instead of showing this we prove the more general

3.6.7 **Theorem.** *Let three functions*

$$M_1 : \mathbb{R}_+^n \to \mathbb{R}, \qquad (z_1, \ldots, z_n) = \mathbf{z} \to M_1(\mathbf{z}), \quad M_1(\mathbf{z}) \not\equiv 0,$$
$$M_2 : \mathbb{R}_+^n \to \mathbb{R}, \qquad (x_1, \ldots, x_n) = \mathbf{x} \to M_2(\mathbf{x}),$$
$$M_3 : \mathbb{R}_+^n \to \mathbb{R}, \qquad (y_1, \ldots, y_n) = \mathbf{y} \to M_3(\mathbf{y}),$$

be given, where M_2 *or* M_3 *is strictly increasing. Let*

$$M_1(x_1 y_1, \ldots, x_n, y_n) = M_2(\mathbf{x})\, M_3(\mathbf{y}), \qquad (\mathbf{x}, \mathbf{y}) \in \mathbb{R}_+^{2n}. \tag{3.6.8}$$

Then there exist positive real constants $A, B, \alpha_1, \alpha_2, \ldots, \alpha_n$ *such that*

$$M_1(\mathbf{z}) = AB z_1^{\alpha_1} z_2^{\alpha} \cdots z_n^{\alpha_n}, \qquad M_2(\mathbf{x}) = A x_1^{\alpha} x_2^{\alpha_2} \cdots x_n^{\alpha_n},$$
$$M_3(\mathbf{y}) = B y_1^{\alpha} y_2^{\alpha_2} \cdots y_n^{\alpha_n}. \tag{3.6.9}$$

Conversely, every triple of functions M_1, M_2, M_3 *given by (3.6.9) satisfies Eq (3.6.8).*

Proof. Setting first $\mathbf{x} = (1, \ldots, 1)$, $\mathbf{y} = \mathbf{z}$, and then $\mathbf{y} = (1, \ldots, 1)$, $\mathbf{x} = \mathbf{z}$, we get from (3.6.8)

$$M_1(\mathbf{z}) = M_2(1, \ldots, 1)\, M_3(\mathbf{z}), \qquad M_1(\mathbf{z}) = M_2(\mathbf{z})\, M_3(1, \ldots, 1). \tag{3.6.10}$$

If, for example, $A: = M_2(1, \ldots, 1) = 0$, then $M_1(\mathbf{z}) \equiv 0$, contradicting our assumption $M_1(\mathbf{z}) \not\equiv 0$. Hence $A \neq 0$. In the same way it follows that $B: = = M_3(1, \ldots, 1) \neq 0$. Hence we can write (3.6.10) as

$$M_3(\mathbf{z}) = M_1(\mathbf{z})/A, \qquad M_2(\mathbf{z}) = M_1(\mathbf{z})/B.$$

The function $M: \mathbb{R}_+^n \to \mathbb{R}$ introduced by

$$M(\mathbf{z}) : = M_1(\mathbf{z})/AB$$

satisfies the functional equation

$$M(x_1y_1, \ldots, x_ny_n) = M(\mathbf{x})\, M(\mathbf{y}), \qquad (\mathbf{x}, \mathbf{y}) \in \mathbb{R}_+^{2n}, \quad M : \mathbb{R}_+^n \to \mathbb{R}, \tag{3.6.11}$$

since the functions M_1, M_2, M_3, given by

$$M_1(\mathbf{z}) = ABM(\mathbf{z}), \qquad M_2(\mathbf{z}) = AM(\mathbf{z}), \qquad M_3(\mathbf{z}) = BM(\mathbf{z}), \tag{3.6.12}$$

satisfy Eq. (3.6.8). Note that M is strictly increasing, since we assumed the same for M_2 or M_3.

In order to complete the proof we have to show, in view of (3.6.12) and (3.6.9), that the class of the strictly increasing solutions of Eq. (3.6.11) is given by

$$M(\mathbf{z}) = z_1^{\alpha} z_2^{\alpha} \cdots z_n^{\alpha_n} \qquad (\alpha_1 > 0,\ a_2 > 0, \ldots, \alpha_n > 0 \text{ real const}).$$

This is the case: Eq. (3.6.11) implies

$$M^\nu(x_\nu y_\nu) = M^\nu(x_\nu)\, M^\nu(y_\nu)$$
$$\text{for} \quad M^\nu(z_\nu) := M(1, \ldots, 1, z_\nu, 1, \ldots, 1) \qquad (\nu = 1, \ldots, n).$$

According to Theorem 1.9.13, the strictly increasing solutions of this equation can be written as

$$M^\nu(z_\nu) = z_\nu^{\alpha_\nu} \qquad (\alpha_\nu > 0 \text{ a real const}).$$

Since from Eq. (3.6.11) it follows that

$$M(\mathbf{z}) = M^1(z_1)\, M^2(z_2) \cdots M^n(z_n),$$

we have proved the theorem. ■

4

The Functional Equation of the Homogeneous Functions and the Functional Inequalities Defining Convexity, Concavity, and Quasiconcavity of Functions

Tintner [1948] showed, 30 years ago, that homogeneous functions play an important role in mathematical economics. Since then, this role has become even more important, in particular where production theory or utility theory is concerned.

In this chapter we consider the functional equation of the homogeneous functions (Sections 4.1–4.6) and some generalizations of it (Section 4.7).

The general solution of the equation will be determined without requiring any regularity condition, such as differentiability or continuity (Section 4.1). However, the main purposes of this chapter are

(a) to describe properties of the homogeneous functions that are of interest in economics, for instance: Euler's homogeneity relation (4.1); the possibility of generating homogeneous functions of n variables with the aid of functions of less than n variables (4.2); and the special form of the domains of substitution, isoquants, and expansion paths of homogeneous and homothetic production functions (4.5);

(b) to analyze the problem of compatibility of homogeneity, convexity on certain domains, and the law of diminishing returns (4.3, 4.4);

(c) to characterize the concave functions by homogeneity of a certain degree (or homotheticity), quasiconcavity, and some other properties of production or utility functions (4.6).

Parts of Sections 4.2–4.5 and 4.7 are based on the author's *Theorie der homogenen Produktionsfunktion* [1970]. Theorem 4.1.5 and Section 4.6 have benefited from Aczél [1966, p. 229] and Friedman [1973], respectively.

ISBN 0ffi201–01948–5/01949–3 PBK

4.1 Some Properties of the Homogeneous Functions of Several Real Variables

For the sake of completeness, we present in this section some well-known results on homogeneous functions of several real variables. Since we are interested here in homogeneous functions occurring in economics, the domain of these functions is in most cases $\mathbb{R}^n_+$.

Let $F : \mathbb{R}^n_+ \to \mathbb{R}$ be *homogeneous of degree* $r(r \in \mathbb{R})$; that is, let

$$F(\lambda \mathbf{x}) = \lambda^r F(\mathbf{x}) \tag{4.1.1}$$

for all $(\lambda, \mathbf{x}) \in \mathbb{R}_{++} \times \mathbb{R}^n_+$. Then, for all $x_1 \in \mathbb{R}_{++}$.

$$F(\mathbf{x}) = F\left(x_1 \frac{\mathbf{x}}{x_1}\right) = x_1^r F\left(1, \frac{x_2}{x_1}, \ldots, \frac{x_n}{x_1}\right),$$

and the functions given by

$$F(\mathbf{x}) = x_1^r \phi_1\left(\frac{x_2}{x_1}, \ldots, \frac{x_n}{x_1}\right) \qquad (x_1 \in \mathbb{R}_{++}) \tag{4.1.2}$$

where ϕ_1 is an arbitrary real-valued function, do in fact satisfy (4.1.1). This approach and representation (4.1.2) make no sense for $x_1 = 0$. Therefore we consider the case in which $x_1 = 0$, $x_2 \in \mathbb{R}_{++}$ and write

$$\begin{aligned} F(0, x_2, \ldots, x_n) &= F\left(x_2 \cdot 0, x_2 \cdot 1, x_2 \frac{x_3}{x_2}, \ldots, x_2 \frac{x_n}{x_2}\right) \\ &= x_2^r F\left(0, 1, \frac{x_3}{x_2}, \ldots, \frac{x_n}{x_2}\right) = x_2^r \phi_2\left(\frac{x_3}{x_2}, \ldots, \frac{x_n}{x_2}\right), \end{aligned}$$

which also satisfies (4.1.1) on the respective domain. We note that both this representation and representation (4.1.2) make no sense for $x_1 = x_2 = 0$. Proceeding in the same way, we finally obtain the formulas

$$F(0, \ldots, 0, x_n) = F(x_n \cdot 0, \ldots, x_n \cdot 0, x_n \cdot 1) = x_n^r F(0, \ldots, 0, 1) \tag{4.1.3}$$

where $x_n \in \mathbb{R}_{++}$, and

$$F(0, \ldots, 0) = F(\lambda \cdot 0, \ldots, \lambda \cdot 0) = \lambda^r F(0, \ldots, 0);$$

that is,

$$F(0, \ldots, 0) = \begin{cases} 0 & \text{for} \quad r \neq 0 \\ \text{arbitrary} & \text{for} \quad r = 0. \end{cases} \tag{4.1.4}$$

Note that (4.1.3) and (4.1.4) also satisfy (4.1.1) on the respective domains. We summarize:

4.1.5 **Theorem.** *The general solution of Eq. (4.1.1) is, for* $r \neq 0$

$$F(\mathbf{x}) = \begin{cases} x_1^r \phi_1(x_2/x_1, \ldots, x_n/x_1) & (x_1 \in \mathbb{R}_{++}) \\ x_2^r \phi_2(x_3/x_2, \ldots, x_n/x_2) & (x_1 = 0,\ x_2 \in \mathbb{R}_{++}) \\ \vdots & \vdots \\ x_n^r a & (x_1 = \cdots = x_{n-1} = 0,\ x_n \in \mathbb{R}_{++}) \\ 0 & (\mathbf{x} = \mathbf{0}), \end{cases}$$

and for $r = 0$

$$F(\mathbf{x}) = \begin{cases} \psi_1(x_2/x_1, \ldots, x_n/x_1) & (x_1 \in \mathbb{R}_{++}) \\ \psi_2(x_3/x_1, \ldots, x_n/x_2) & (x_1 = 0,\ x_2 \in \mathbb{R}_{++}) \\ \vdots & \vdots \\ b & (x_1 = \cdots = x_{n-1} = 0,\ x_n \in \mathbb{R}_{++}) \\ c & (\mathbf{x} = \mathbf{0}), \end{cases}$$

where $a \in \mathbb{R}$, $b \in \mathbb{R}$, *and* $c \in \mathbb{R}$ *are arbitrary constants and the* ϕ_i*'s and* ψ_i*'s are arbitrary real-valued functions.*

Note that both the ϕ_i's and the ψ_i's may be discontinuous; that is, *a homogeneous function F is not necessarily differentiable or continuous.* Nevertheless, differentiability is assumed for some of the following derivations.

4.1.6 **Theorem.** *Let*

$$F : D \to \mathbb{R} \qquad (D \subseteq \mathbb{R}^n \text{ an open and connected set}) \tag{4.1.7}$$

be homogeneous of degree r ($r \in \mathbb{R}$), *that is, let*

$$F(\lambda\mathbf{x}) = \lambda^r F(\mathbf{x}) \text{ for all } \lambda \in \mathbb{R}_{++} \text{ of a sufficiently small neighborhood of } 1. \tag{4.1.8}$$

Moreover, let F be differentiable on D. Then Euler's homogeneity relation is valid on D; that is,

$$\frac{\partial F(\mathbf{x})}{\partial x_1} x_1 + \cdots + \frac{\partial F(\mathbf{x})}{\partial x_n} x_n = rF(\mathbf{x}). \tag{4.1.9}$$

Proof. Let us write

$$G(\lambda, \mathbf{x}) := F(\lambda\mathbf{x}) - \lambda^r F(\mathbf{x}), \tag{4.1.10}$$

$$H(\mathbf{x}) := \frac{\partial F(\mathbf{x})}{\partial x_1} x_1 + \cdots + \frac{\partial F(\mathbf{x})}{\partial x_n} x_n - rF(\mathbf{x}). \tag{4.1.11}$$

By the Chain rule 13.2.60, we have

$$\begin{aligned} \frac{\partial G(\lambda, \mathbf{x})}{\partial \lambda} &= \frac{\partial F(\lambda\mathbf{x})}{\partial(\lambda x_1)} \frac{\partial(\lambda x_1)}{\partial \lambda} + \cdots + \frac{\partial F(\lambda\mathbf{x})}{\partial(\lambda x_n)} \frac{\partial(\lambda x_n)}{\partial \lambda} - r\lambda^{r-1} F(\mathbf{x}) \\ &= \frac{\partial F(\lambda\mathbf{x})}{\partial(\lambda x_1)} x_1 + \cdots + \frac{\partial F(\lambda\mathbf{x})}{\partial(\lambda x_n)} x_n - r\lambda^{r-1} F(\mathbf{x}). \end{aligned} \tag{4.1.12}$$

Multiplication by λ yields, in view of (4.1.8), (4.1.11),

$$\lambda \frac{\partial G(\lambda, \mathbf{x})}{\partial \lambda} = H(\lambda \mathbf{x}). \tag{4.1.13}$$

According to assumption, $G(\lambda, \mathbf{x}) \equiv 0$. Hence, $\partial G(\lambda, \mathbf{x})/\partial \lambda \equiv 0$, and from (4.1.13) for $\lambda = 1$ we have $H(\mathbf{x}) \equiv 0$, that is, (4.1.9). ■

The converse of Theorem 4.1.6 is also true.

4.1.14 **Theorem.** *Every differentiable function (4.1.7) satisfying Euler's homogeneity relation (4.1.9) on D is homogeneous of degree r on D.*

Proof. Multiplication of (4.1.12) by λ yields

$$\begin{aligned}\lambda \frac{\partial G(\lambda, \mathbf{x})}{\partial \lambda} &= \frac{\partial F(\lambda \mathbf{x})}{\partial(\lambda x_1)}(\lambda x_1) + \cdots + \frac{\partial F(\lambda \mathbf{x})}{\partial(\lambda x)}(\lambda x_n) - r\lambda^r F(\mathbf{x}) \\ &= H(\lambda \mathbf{x}) + r\cdot(F(\lambda \mathbf{x}) - \lambda F(\mathbf{x})) \qquad \text{(by 4.1.11)} \\ &= rG(\lambda, \mathbf{x}) \qquad \text{(by (4.1.10); } H(\mathbf{x}) \equiv 0 \text{ is assumed).}\end{aligned}$$

The general solution of this differential equation is given by

$$G(\lambda, \mathbf{x}) = c(\mathbf{x})\, \lambda^r$$

where c is a function of $\mathbf{x}$. By Definition 4.1.10, $G(1, \mathbf{x}) \equiv 0$, hence, $c(\mathbf{x}) \equiv 0$, that is, $G(\lambda, \mathbf{x}) \equiv 0$, that is, F is homogeneous of degree r. ■

4.1.15 **Remark.** In Theorem 4.1.6, let $D = \mathbb{R}^n_+$, $r = 1$. If F is supposed to be a (linearly homogeneous) production function, Euler's homogeneity relation (4.1.9) can be interpreted as follows: If the factors of production are paid according to their marginal productivity, then the output quantity is exactly exhausted by the payments. Obviously, under this condition, some output would remain in the case in which $r \in]0, 1[$. It should be mentioned, in this connection, that Euler's homogeneity relation plays an important role in the (neoclassical) theory of income distribution.

4.1.16 **Remark.** A generalization of Theorem 4.1.6 to the case of non-homogeneous functions

$$F : D \to \mathbb{R} \qquad (D \subseteqq \mathbb{R}^n \text{ an open and connected set})$$

is the so-called Wicksell–Johnson theorem, that is, the identity

$$\frac{\partial F(\mathbf{x})}{\partial x_1} x_1 + \cdots + \frac{\partial F(\mathbf{x})}{\partial x_n} x_n = \varepsilon(1, \mathbf{x})\, F(\mathbf{x}), \tag{4.1.17}$$

where $\varepsilon(1, \mathbf{x})$ is defined by

$$\varepsilon(\lambda, \mathbf{x}) := \frac{\partial F(\lambda \mathbf{x})}{\partial \lambda} \frac{\lambda}{F(\lambda \mathbf{x})} \qquad (F(\lambda \mathbf{x}) \neq 0, \lambda \in \mathbb{R}_{++}). \tag{4.1.18}$$

Expression (4.1.18) is the *scale elasticity of F at* $(\lambda, \mathbf{x})$. According to Chain rule 13.2.60, we have

$$\varepsilon(\lambda, \mathbf{x}) = \frac{\partial F(\lambda \mathbf{x})}{\partial \lambda} \frac{\lambda}{F(\lambda \mathbf{x})} = \sum_{j=1}^{n} \frac{\partial F(\lambda \mathbf{x})}{\partial(\lambda x_j)} \frac{\partial(\lambda x_j)}{\partial \lambda} \frac{\lambda}{F(\lambda \mathbf{x})} = \sum_{j=1}^{n} \frac{\partial F(\lambda \mathbf{x})}{\partial(\lambda x_j)} \frac{\lambda x_j}{F(\lambda \mathbf{x})}. \tag{4.1.19}$$

For $\lambda = 1$, this is identity (4.1.17). Let F be a production function. Then

$$\varepsilon_j(\mathbf{x}) := \frac{\partial F(\mathbf{x})}{\partial x_j} \frac{x_j}{F(\mathbf{x})} \qquad (F(\mathbf{x}) \neq 0) \tag{4.1.20}$$

is the *production elasticity of the factor j at* $\mathbf{x}$. With (4.1.20), identity (4.1.19) can be written in the nice form

$$\varepsilon(\lambda, \mathbf{x}) = \varepsilon_1(\lambda \mathbf{x}) + \cdots + \varepsilon_n(\lambda \mathbf{x}).$$

We return to homogeneous functions:

4.1.21 **Theorem.** *Let the partial derivative of the function*

$$F : D \to \mathbb{R} \qquad (D \subseteqq \mathbb{R}^n_+ \text{ an open and connected set})$$

with respect to some component of $\mathbf{x}$*, say* x_1*, exist on D. If F is homogeneous of degree r on D, then this partial derivative of F is homogeneous of degree* $r - 1$ *on* $D^* := \{\mathbf{x} \mid \mathbf{x} \in D, x_1 \in \mathbb{R}_{++}\}$.

Proof. By the homogeneity of F,

$$F(\mathbf{x}) = F(x_1(\mathbf{x}/x_1)) = x_1^r F(\mathbf{x}/x_1) \qquad \text{on } D^*,$$

whence

$$\frac{\partial F(\mathbf{x})}{\partial x_1} = r x_1^{r-1} F\left(\frac{\mathbf{x}}{x_1}\right) - x_1^{r-2}\left[\frac{\partial F(\mathbf{x}/x_1)}{\partial(x_2/x_1)} x_2 + \cdots + \frac{\partial F(\mathbf{x}/x_1)}{\partial(x_n/x_1)} x_n\right] \qquad \text{on } D^*.$$

Obviously, the right-hand side of this equation is homogeneous of degree $r - 1$ on D^*. ■

4.2 Generation of Homogeneous Functions of *n* Real Variables with the Aid of Functions of Less than *n* Real Variables

Let

$$\Phi : \mathbb{R}^2_+ \to \mathbb{R}_+, \qquad (x, y) \to \Phi(x, y)$$

be an arbitrary production function that is not necessarily continuous everywhere. Then the graphs of the functions

$$x \to \Phi(x, y) \qquad \text{and} \quad y \to \Phi(x, y)$$

represent so-called *total product curves* (or rather, pieces of such curves).

Now, let two arbitrary total product curves (or pieces thereof) be given:

$$\{(x, u) \mid x \in [0, a];\ a \in \mathbb{R}_{++},\ \text{fixed};\ u = f(x);\ f\colon [0, a] \to \mathbb{R}_+\}$$

and

$$\{(y, u) \mid y \in [0, b[;\ b \in \mathbb{R}_{++},\ \text{fixed};\ u = g(y);\ g : [0, b[\to \mathbb{R}_+\}.$$

Does there exist a homogeneous function

$$F : \mathbb{R}^2_+ \backslash \{\mathbf{0}\} \to \mathbb{R}_+, \qquad (x, y) \to F(x, y),$$

such that

$$F(x, b) = f(x) \qquad \text{for} \quad x \in [0, a] \tag{4.2.1}$$

and

$$F(a, y) = g(y) \qquad \text{for} \quad y \in [0, b[? \tag{4.2.2}$$

The solution of this problem is a special case of the following theorem. (An economically interesting case is illustrated by Fig. 4.2.3.)

4.2.4 **Theorem.** *Let $a \in \mathbb{R}_{++}$ and $b \in \mathbb{R}_{++}$ be arbitrary constants and let*

$$f\colon [0, a] \to \mathbb{R} \qquad \text{and} \quad g : [0, b[\to \mathbb{R}$$

be arbitrary functions. For any $r \in \mathbb{R}$ there exists exactly one function F : $\mathbb{R}^2_+ \setminus \{\mathbf{0}\} \to \mathbb{R}$ which is homogeneous of degree r on the one hand and satisfies both identities (4.2.1) and (4.2.2) on the other, namely, the function given by

$$F(x, y) = \begin{cases} \left(\dfrac{y}{b}\right)^r f\left(x\dfrac{b}{y}\right) & \text{for} \quad x\dfrac{b}{y} \in [0, a], \\ \left(\dfrac{x}{a}\right)^r g\left(y\dfrac{a}{x}\right) & \text{for} \quad y\dfrac{a}{x} \in [0, b[. \end{cases} \tag{4.2.5}$$

Every homogeneous function $F : \mathbb{R}^2_+ \setminus \{\mathbf{0}\} \to \mathbb{R}$ can be generated by choosing suitable functions f and g in (4.2.5).

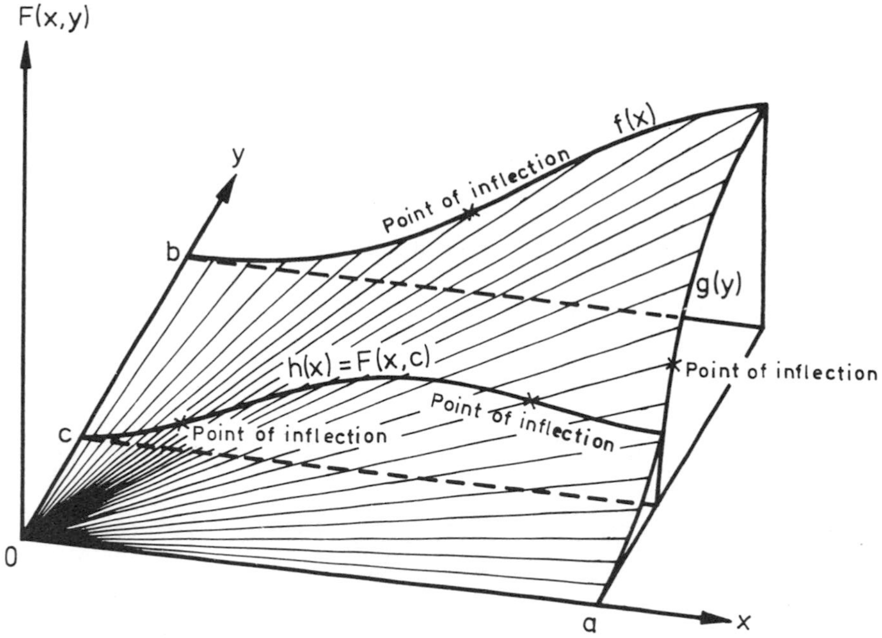

4.2.3 Figure. Product surface of a linearly homogeneous production function generated by two ∫-shaped total product curves.

Proof. The last assertion follows immediately from

$$F(x, y) = F\left(\frac{y}{b}x\frac{b}{y}, \frac{y}{b}b\right) = \left(\frac{y}{b}\right)^r F\left(x\frac{b}{y}, b\right)$$

and

$$F(x, y) = F\left(\frac{x}{a}a, \frac{x}{a}y\frac{a}{x}\right) = \left(\frac{x}{a}\right)^r F\left(a, y\frac{a}{x}\right).$$

Note that

$$\left(\frac{y}{b}\right)^r f\left(x\frac{b}{y}\right) \quad \text{is defined for all} \quad (x, y) \quad \text{with} \quad \frac{x}{y} \in \left[0, \frac{a}{b}\right]$$

and

$$\left(\frac{x}{a}\right)^r g\left(y\frac{a}{x}\right) \quad \text{is defined for all} \quad (x, y) \quad \text{with} \quad \frac{x}{y} \in \left]\frac{a}{b}, \infty\right[.$$

Hence, F given by (4.2.5) is defined on all of $\mathbb{R}^2_+ \setminus \{\mathbf{0}\}$. It is obvious that this F is homogeneous of degree r and that it satisfies (4.2.1) and (4.2.2). It remains to show that there does not exist any other function $G : \mathbb{R}_+^2 \setminus \{\mathbf{0}\} \to \mathbb{R}$, homogeneous of degree r and satisfying

$$G(x, b) = f(x) \qquad \text{for} \quad x \in [0, a] \tag{4.2.6}$$

and

$$G(a, y) = g(y) \qquad \text{for} \quad y \in [0, b[. \tag{4.2.7}$$

Let G be such a function. The homogeneity of degree r implies

$$G(x, y) = G\left(\frac{y}{b}x\frac{b}{y}, \frac{y}{b}b\right) = \left(\frac{y}{b}\right)^r G\left(x\frac{b}{y}, b\right) \qquad (y \in \mathbb{R}_{++}) \tag{4.2.8}$$

as well as

$$G(x, y) = G\left(\frac{x}{a}a, \frac{x}{a}y\frac{a}{x}\right) = \left(\frac{x}{a}\right)^r G\left(a, y\frac{a}{x}\right) \qquad (x \in \mathbb{R}_{++}). \tag{4.2.9}$$

Since G has properties (4.2.6) and (4.2.7), it follows from (4.2.8) and (4.2.9) that $G = F$, where F is defined by (4.2.5). ■

The following theorem considers the general case of functions of $n \geqq 2$ nonnegative real variables. Whereas in Theorem 4.2.4 a homogeneous function of two variables was generated by *two* functions on *bounded* intervals, in the following theorem a homogeneous function of n variables will be generated by a *single* function of $n - 1$ variables.

4.2.10 **Theorem.** *Let*

$$h : \mathbb{R}_+^{n-1} \to \mathbb{R}, \qquad (x_1, \ldots, x_{n-1}) \to h(x_1, \ldots, x_{n-1})$$

be an arbitrary function. Let the constants $r \in \mathbb{R}$ and $c \in \mathbb{R}_{++}$ be given. There exists exactly one function

$$H : \mathbb{R}_+^{n-1} \times \mathbb{R}_{++} \to \mathbb{R}, \qquad (x_1, \ldots, x_{n-1}, x_n) \to H(x_1, \ldots, x_{n-1}, x_n) \tag{4.2.11}$$

that satisfies

$$H(x_1, \ldots, x_{n-1}, c) = h(x_1, \ldots, x_{n-1}) \tag{4.2.12}$$

and is homogeneous of degree r as well, namely the function given by

$$H(x_1, \ldots, x_{n-1}, x_n) = \left(\frac{x_n}{c}\right)^r h\left(\frac{x_1}{x_n}c, \ldots, \frac{x_{n-1}}{x_n}c\right). \tag{4.2.13}$$

Conversely, every homogeneous function (4.2.11) can be generated by choosing a suitable function h in (4.2.13).

Proof. Obviously, H given by (4.2.13) satisfies (4.2.12). If H^* is another function, homogeneous of degree r, then

$$H^*(x_1, \ldots, x_{n-1}, x_n) = H^*\left(\frac{x_n}{c}\frac{x_1}{x_n}c, \ldots, \frac{x_n}{c}\frac{x_{n-1}}{x_n}c, \frac{x_n}{c}c\right)$$
$$= \left(\frac{x_n}{c}\right)^r H^*\left(\frac{x_1}{x_n}c, \ldots, \frac{x_{n-1}}{x_n}c, c\right).$$

In order that H^* satisfy (4.2.12), the last term has to be equal to the right-hand side of (4.2.13), that is, $H^* = H$. The last statement of the theorem is obvious: take h such that

$$h\left(\frac{x_1}{x_n}c, \ldots, \frac{x_{n-1}}{x_n}c\right) = H\left(\frac{x_1}{x_n}c, \ldots, \frac{x_{n-1}}{x_n}c, c\right). \quad \blacksquare$$

4.2.14 **Remark.** It follows easily from the foregoing reasoning that there exist infinitely many homogeneous functions (4.2.11) that satisfy

$$H(x_1, \ldots, x_{n-k}, c_1, \ldots, c_k) = h(x_1, \ldots, x_{n-k}) \qquad (2 \leqq k < n)$$

for any given $h : \mathbb{R}_+^{n-k} \to \mathbb{R}$ and $c_1 \in \mathbb{R}_+, \ldots, c_{k-1} \in \mathbb{R}_+, c_k \in \mathbb{R}_{++}$.

4.3 Linear Homogeneity, Convexity on Certain Input Domains, and the Law of Diminishing Returns

In many publications on production theory it is explicitly or implicitly assumed that the production functions under consideration are linearly homogeneous, that is, homogeneous of degree 1. Nevertheless there exist, particularly where practical applications are involved, production functions that most certainly are *not* linearly homogeneous. What, then, is the reason for the linear homogeneity assumption? Let us, in this connection, quote Krelle [1961, p. 60]:

> Ob wir mit homogenen Produktionsfunktionen von der 1. Ordnung, bei denen also eine Verdoppelung aller Faktoren eine Verdoppelung des Produkts hervorruft, rechnen oder nicht, ist im wesentlichen eine Frage der Betrachtungsweise. Wenn wir tatsächlich alle Faktoren, die für die Produktion eines Gutes von Bedeutung sind, explizit aufführen, so muß bei einem Gedankenexperiment, das alle diese Faktoren verdoppelt, auch das Produkt genau zu verdoppeln sein.

From this point of view every production function

$$\Phi : \mathbb{R}_+^n \to \mathbb{R}_+, \qquad (x_1, \ldots, x_n) \to \Phi(x_1, \ldots, x_n),$$

that is not linearly homogeneous can be interpreted as a "projection" of a linearly homogeneous production function

$$\Psi : \mathbb{R}_+^{n+m} \to \mathbb{R}_+, \qquad (x_1, \ldots, x_n, y_1, \ldots, y_m) \to \Psi(x_1, \ldots, x_n, y_1, \ldots, y_m),$$

whose input quantities $y_1, \ldots, y_m$ are fixed:

$$\Phi(x_1, \ldots, x_n) = \Psi(x_1, \ldots, x_n, c_1, \ldots, c_m).$$

As we saw in the preceding section (cf. Theorem 4.2.10 and Remark 4.2.14), this point of view can be justified. In this connection, we quote Samuelson [1948, p. 84, footnote 13]: "Any function whatsoever in n variables may be regarded as a subset of a larger function in more than n variables which is homogeneous of the first order...."

As a consequence of the foregoing reasoning, the assumption of linear homogeneity is justified in all those studies of production theory in which the list of factors employed in the production and specified as variables in the production function is complete or assumed to be complete.[1]

Another property of production functions that is discussed in many textbooks on economics is the following.

4.3.1 **Property.** Partial factor variation, or proportional variation of an incomplete factor complex,[2] yields a total product curve that is initially strictly increasing and convex and then strictly concave everywhere (see Fig. 4.3.2).

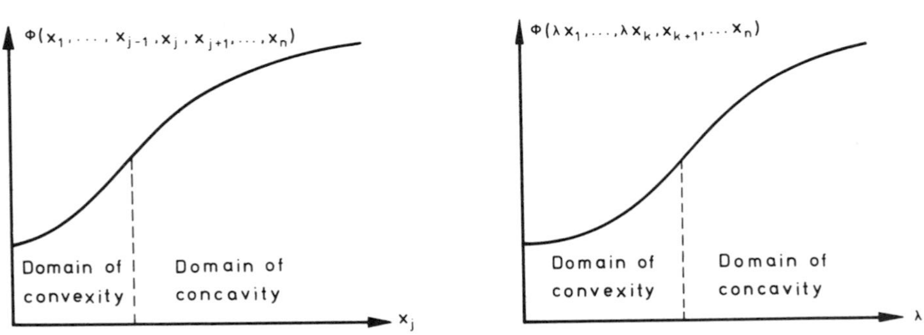

4.3.2 Figure. Total product curves as described under Property 4.3.1.

[1] The existence of such a (finite) list is taken for granted.

[2] An incomplete factor complex is a true subset of the set of factors.

The following problem now arises: Are the linear homogeneity assumption and assumption 4.3.1 compatible? There is a great deal of literature on this problem, for instance, that of Nutter [1963, 1964, 1965], Fontenay [1964], Liebhafsky [1964], Rowe [1964, 1965], Sato [1964], Schneider [1964], Moeseke [1965], Chattopadhyay [1966], Piron [1966], Eichhorn and Müller [1968], Eichhorn [1968b, c, 1970].

We will show, among other things, that linear homogeneity and Property 4.3.1 are *incompatible* in the following sense: If the function is linearly homogeneous and partial variation of a certain factor or proportional variation of a certain incomplete factor complex yields a total product curve as described in Property 4.3.1, then there exists another factor complex or factor such that proportional or partial variation yields a total product curve that is initially strictly concave and then convex everywhere. We point out here that a product curve of this kind contradicts the law of diminishing marginal returns as it is usually formulated in textbooks on economics.

4.3.3 **Definition.** A total product curve *satisfies the law of diminishing marginal returns* if there exists a point such that the curve becomes (and remains) strictly concave to the right of this point.

4.3.4 **Definition.** A production function $\Phi : \mathbb{R}^n_+ \to \mathbb{R}_+$ *satisfies the law of diminishing marginal returns* if *all* the total product curves generated by partial factor variation or by proportional variation of an incomplete factor complex satisfy this law.

Examples of linearly homogeneous production functions satisfying the law of diminishing marginal returns are the Cobb–Douglas functions given by (2.0.1) and the ACMS production functions given by (2.0.2). They are concave *everywhere*.

The function $F : \mathbb{R}^2_+ \to \mathbb{R}_+$ given by

$$F(x, y) = \frac{Ax^{1+\delta}y^{1+\varepsilon}}{Bx + Cy} \qquad (\delta \in]0, 1[, \ \varepsilon \in]0, 1[, \ A \in \mathbb{R}_{++}, \ B \in \mathbb{R}_{++}, \ C \in \mathbb{R}_{++}) \tag{4.3.5}$$

is *not* concave (the graphs of $x \to F(x, y)$ and $y \to F(x, y)$ are of the form drawn in Fig. 4.3.2), but nevertheless satisfies the law of diminishing marginal returns. Note that F is homogeneous of degree $1 + \delta + \varepsilon$, that is, not linearly homogeneous.

Let

$$\Phi : \mathbb{R}^n_+ \to \mathbb{R}_+, \qquad (\mathbf{x}, \mathbf{y}) \to \Phi(\mathbf{x}, \mathbf{y}), \qquad \mathbf{x} = (x_1, \ldots, x_l), \qquad \mathbf{y} = (y_1, \ldots, y_m) \qquad (l+m = n) \tag{4.3.6}$$

be a linearly homogeneous production function that is not necessarily differentiable. Let us assume that $\xi \to \Phi(\xi\mathbf{x}, \mathbf{y})$ is convex for all $\xi \in]0, C]$, where $C \in \mathbb{R}_{++}$ is a constant depending on $\mathbf{x}$ and $\mathbf{y}$, and is strictly concave for all $\xi \in]C, \infty[$.

The convexity of $\xi \to \Phi(\xi\mathbf{x}, \mathbf{y})$ for $\xi \in]0, C]$ can be expressed by the following functional inequality:

$$\Phi[(\mu\xi + \nu\eta)\mathbf{x}, \mathbf{y}] \leqq \mu\Phi(\xi\mathbf{x}, \mathbf{y}) + \nu\Phi(\eta\mathbf{x}, \mathbf{y}), \qquad \mu \in \mathbb{R}_{+}, \nu \in \mathbb{R}_{+}, \mu + \nu = 1,$$
$$\xi \in]0, C], \eta \in]0, C]. \tag{4.3.7}$$

On the other hand, the functional inequality

$$\Phi[(\mu\xi + \nu\eta)\,\mathbf{x}, \mathbf{y}] > \mu\Phi(\xi\mathbf{x}, \mathbf{y}) + \nu\Phi(\eta\mathbf{x}, \mathbf{y}), \qquad \mu \in \mathbb{R}_{++}, \nu \in \mathbb{R}_{++}, \mu + \nu = 1,$$
$$\xi \in]C, \infty[, \eta \in]C, \infty[, \xi \neq \eta, \tag{4.3.8}$$

says that $\xi \to \Phi(\xi\mathbf{x}, \mathbf{y})$ is strictly concave for all $\xi \in]C, \infty[$.

4.3.9 **Theorem.** *Under these assumptions, the convexity of $\xi \to \Phi(\xi\mathbf{x}, \mathbf{y})$ on $]0, C]$ implies the convexity of $\bar{\xi} \to \Phi(\mathbf{x}, \bar{\xi}\mathbf{y})$ on $[1/C, \infty[$, and the concavity of $\xi \to \Phi(\xi\mathbf{x}, \mathbf{y})$ on $]C, \infty[$ implies the concavity of $\bar{\xi} \to \Phi(\mathbf{x}, \bar{\xi}\mathbf{y})$ on $]0, 1/C[$.*

This result is illustrated by Fig. 4.3.11.

Proof. By the linear homogeneity of Φ and the convexity of $\xi \to \Phi(\xi\mathbf{x}, \mathbf{y})$ for $\xi \in]0, C]$,

$$\begin{aligned}
\Phi[\mathbf{x}, (\bar{\mu}\bar{\xi} + \bar{\nu}\bar{\eta})\mathbf{y}] &= (\bar{\mu}\bar{\xi} + \bar{\nu}\bar{\eta})\Phi\left(\frac{\mathbf{x}}{\bar{\mu}\bar{\xi} + \bar{\nu}\bar{\eta}}, \mathbf{y}\right) \\
&= (\bar{\mu}\bar{\xi} + \bar{\nu}\bar{\eta})\Phi\left[\left(\frac{\bar{\mu}\bar{\xi}}{\bar{\mu}\bar{\xi} + \bar{\nu}\bar{\eta}}\frac{1}{\bar{\xi}} + \frac{\bar{\nu}\bar{\eta}}{\bar{\mu}\bar{\xi} + \bar{\nu}\bar{\eta}}\frac{1}{\bar{\eta}}\right)\mathbf{x}, \mathbf{y}\right] \\
&\leqq \bar{\mu}\bar{\xi}\Phi\left(\frac{\mathbf{x}}{\bar{\xi}}, \mathbf{y}\right) + \bar{\nu}\bar{\eta}\Phi\left(\frac{\mathbf{x}}{\bar{\eta}}, \mathbf{y}\right) \\
&= \bar{\mu}\Phi(\mathbf{x}, \bar{\xi}\mathbf{y}) + \bar{\nu}\Phi(\mathbf{x}, \bar{\eta}\mathbf{y})
\end{aligned}$$
$$(\bar{\mu} \in \mathbb{R}_{++}, \bar{\nu} \in \mathbb{R}_{++}, \bar{\mu} + \bar{\nu} = 1, \bar{\xi} \in \mathbb{R}_{++}, \bar{\eta} \in \mathbb{R}_{++})$$

for all $(1/\bar{\xi}) \in]0, C]$, $(1/\bar{\eta}) \in]0, C]$; and by (4.3.8), similarly,

$$\Phi[\mathbf{x}, (\bar{\mu}\bar{\xi} + \bar{\nu}\bar{\eta})\,\mathbf{y}] > \bar{\mu}\Phi(\mathbf{x}, \bar{\xi}\mathbf{y}) + \bar{\nu}\Phi(\mathbf{x}, \bar{\eta}\mathbf{y})$$

for all $(1/\bar{\xi}) \in]C, \infty[$, $(1/\bar{\eta}) \in]C, \infty[$, $\bar{\xi} \neq \bar{\eta}$. Hence, $\bar{\xi} \to \Phi(\mathbf{x}, \bar{\xi}\mathbf{y})$ is strictly concave for all $\bar{\xi} \in]0, 1/C[$ and convex for all $\bar{\xi} \in [1/C, \infty[$. ■

An immediate consequence of Theorem 4.3.9 is

4.3.10 **Corollary.** *A linearly homogeneous production function $\Phi: \mathbb{R}^n_+ \to \mathbb{R}_+$ ($n \geqq 2$) does not satisfy the law of diminishing marginal returns if partial variation*

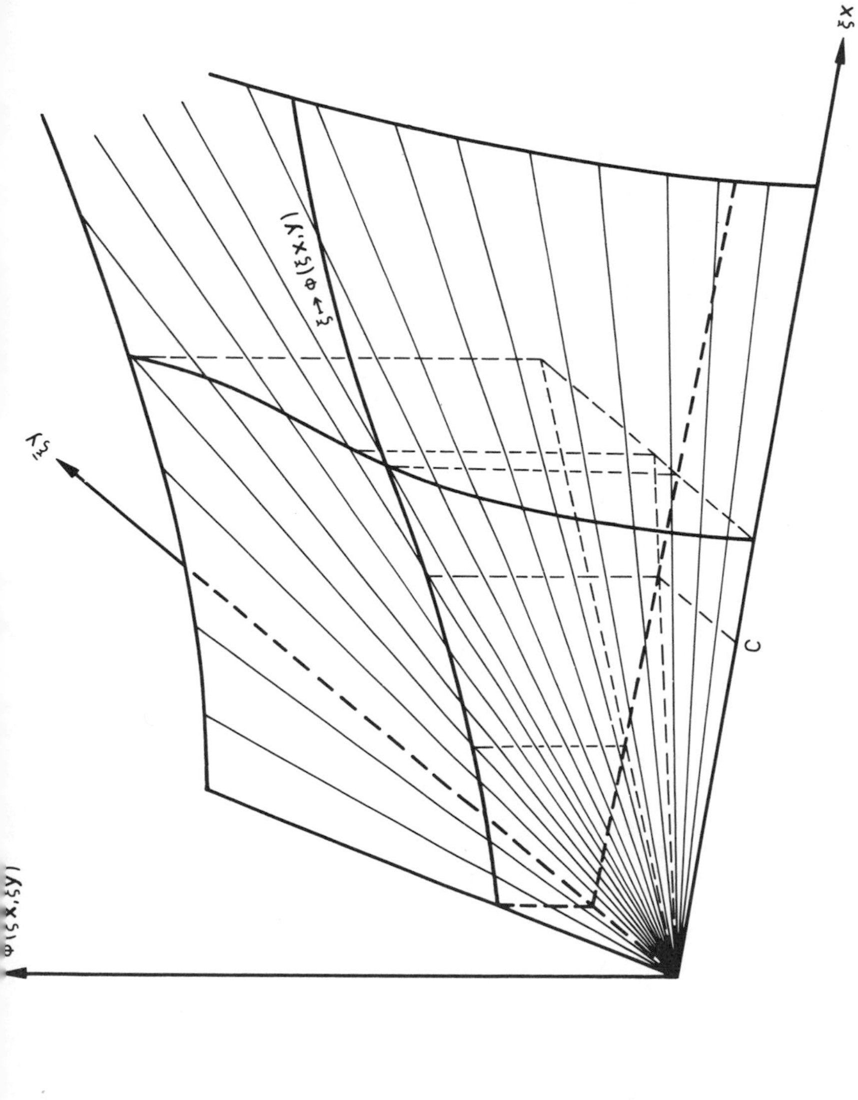

4.3.10 Figure. Output surface of a linearly homogeneous function that satisfies Property 4.3.1 with respect to the factor complex **x**.

of at least one factor or proportional variation of at least one incomplete factor complex yields a total product curve that is initially convex.

In other words, the total product curves derived from a linearly homogeneous production function Φ: $\mathbb{R}^n_+ \to \mathbb{R}_+$ $(n \geqq 2)$ by partial variation of any factor or by proportional variation of any incomplete factor complex satisfy

(i) the law of diminishing marginal returns, and
(ii) the condition that intervals of strict concavity are always unbounded to the right.

if and only if they are strictly concave everywhere.

We may conclude from this result that the law of diminishing marginal returns as usually formulated in textbooks on economics should not play as outstanding a role as it does in many of them.

Let us remark in this connection that there *do* exist linearly homogeneous functions F: $\mathbb{R}^n_+ \to \mathbb{R}_+$ having the following property:

4.3.12 **Property.** Partial variation of any variable as well as proportional variation of any incomplete complex of variables yields bell-shaped curves of the kind shown in Fig. 4.3.13 (see also Fig. 4.3.2).

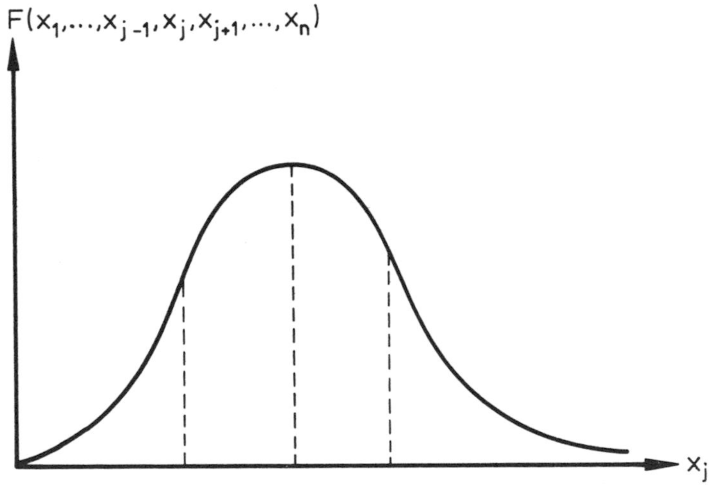

4.3.13 Figure. Example of a bell-shaped curve.

Examples of such functions F can easily be determined by the methods introduced in Section 4.2 (or in Eichhorn [1968b, 1970, pp. 21–33]). For instance,

F given by

$$F(x_1, x_2, \ldots, x_n) = \frac{Ax_1^{a_1}x_2^{a_2}\cdots x_n^{a_n}}{B_1x_1^b + B_2x_2^b + \cdots + B_nx_n^b}, \tag{4.3.14}$$

where A, a_i, B_i, b are positive real constants, $a_i > 1$, $\sum a_i - b = 1$, is such a function.

Although the above-mentioned bell-shaped curves are eventually strictly convex (contradicting the law of diminishing marginal returns), they are of a certain interest in production theory. For instance, the prototype of a twice continuously differentiable total product curve introduced by Frisch [1965, p. 90] looks something like the curve shown in Fig. 4.3.13.

It should, however, be mentioned that linearly homogeneous functions satisfying Property 4.3.12 are neither nondecreasing nor quasiconcave,[3] that is, do not satisfy two properties that are very often assumed in production theory. For instance, Shephard's [1967, 1970, p. 22] set of assumptions on production functions contains these two properties; see Section 13.3 ((13.3.1)–(13.3.6)).

As can be seen immediately from Fig. 4.3.11, the assumptions "linear homogeneity" and "bell shape of a single total product curve" do not necessarily imply that the other total product curves are bell-shaped.

Problems concerning the deduction of the laws of both diminishing marginal *and average* returns from axioms containing the linear homogeneity assumption have been treated by Menger [1936], and the author [1968c, 1970, pp. 51–65] and will be reconsidered in Chapter 10. At this point we already consider the so-called law of diminishing average returns.

Let $\Phi\colon \mathbb{R}_+^n \to \mathbb{R}_+$ be a production function. Then $\Phi(\mathbf{x})/x_j$ is called *average output rate or average return of the factor j at* $\mathbf{x}$. Correspondingly,

$$\Phi(\lambda x_1, \ldots, \lambda x_k, x_{k+1}, \ldots, x_n)/\lambda \qquad (\lambda \in \mathbb{R}_{++}, k \in \{2, \ldots, n-1\})$$

is called *average return in case of proportional variation of the factor complex* $(x_1, \ldots, x_k)$.

4.3.15 **Definition.** A production function $\Phi\colon \mathbb{R}_+^n \to \mathbb{R}_+$ *satisfies the law of diminishing average returns* if the functions defined by

$$x_j \to \Phi(\mathbf{x})/x_j \qquad (x_j \in \mathbb{R}_{++})$$

and

$$\lambda \to \Phi(\lambda x_1, \ldots, \lambda x_k, x_{k+1}, \ldots, x_n)/\lambda \qquad (\lambda \in \mathbb{R}_{++})$$

---

[3] A class of quasiconcave functions that are nondecreasing (i.e., "free disposal of inputs") will be considered in Section 4.6. See also Remark 4.5.13.

are eventually strictly decreasing (for all $j = 1, \ldots, n$; $k = 2, \ldots, n-1$; and for all other possible cases of proportional variation of an incomplete factor complex).

4.3.16 **Theorem.** *Let $\Phi\colon \mathbb{R}^n_+ \to \mathbb{R}_+$ be a production function that is homogeneous of degree r, where $r \in]0, 1]$. It satisfies the law of diminishing average returns if and only if the total product curves generated by partial factor variation or by variation of any incomplete factor complex are initially strictly increasing.*

Proof. The assertion follows easily from

$$\frac{\Phi(\mathbf{x})}{x_j} = \frac{x_j^r \Phi(\mathbf{x}/x_j)}{x_j} = x_j^{r-1}\Phi\left(\frac{x_1}{x_j}, \ldots, \frac{x_{j-1}}{x_j}, 1, \frac{x_{j+1}}{x_j}, \ldots, \frac{x_n}{x_j}\right) \qquad (x_j \in \mathbb{R}_{++})$$

and

$$\frac{\Phi(\lambda x_1, \ldots, \lambda x_k, x_{k+1}, \ldots, x_n)}{\lambda} = \lambda^{r-1}\Phi\left(x_1, \ldots, x_k, \frac{x_{k+1}}{\lambda}, \ldots, \frac{x_n}{\lambda}\right)$$
$$(\lambda \in \mathbb{R}_{++}). \quad \blacksquare$$

4.3.17 **Remark.** Theorem 4.3.16 is wrong when $r \in]0, 1]$ is replaced by $r \in \mathbb{R}_{++}$. For instance, the function Φ given by

$$\Phi(x, y) = x^{1+\varepsilon-\delta}y^{\delta} \qquad (\varepsilon \in \mathbb{R}_{++}, \delta \in \mathbb{R}_{++}, \varepsilon > \delta)$$

satisfies the assumptions of Theorem 4.3.16 with the exception of $r \in]0, 1]$. It is homogeneous of degree $1 + \varepsilon$. Whenever $y \in \mathbb{R}_{++}$, $x \to \Phi(x, y)/x$ is strictly increasing for all $x \in \mathbb{R}_{++}$.

4.4 Homogeneity of an Arbitrary Positive Degree, Convexity on Certain Input Domains, and the Law of Diminishing Returns

Example (4.3.5) shows that for every $r \in]1, 2[$ there exist functions Φ: $\mathbb{R}^2_+ \to \mathbb{R}_+$ that are homogeneous of degree r on one hand and that satisfy, on the other hand, Property 4.3.1 as well as the law of diminishing marginal returns (see Definition 4.3.4).

As we know from Theorem 4.3.9, there does not exist any function Φ: $\mathbb{R}^n_+ \to \mathbb{R}_+$ satisfying these properties when the degree r of homogeneity is equal to 1.

A similar nonexistence theorem can be proved when the degree r of homogeneity is smaller than 1.

4.4.1 **Theorem.** *There does not exist any twice continuously differentiable production function $\Phi\colon \mathbb{R}^n_+ \to \mathbb{R}_+$ that is homogeneous of degree r, where $r \in]0, 1]$,* *and that satisfies the following three properties simultaneously:*

The total product curves generated by partial factor variation satisfy the law of diminishing marginal returns (see Definition 4.3.3). (4.4.2)

$$\Phi(x_1, \ldots, x_{n-1}, 0) = \Phi(x_1, \ldots, x_{n-2}, 0, x_n) = \cdots = \Phi(0, x_2, \ldots, x_n) = 0. \tag{4.4.3}$$

There exist both an index $p \in \{1, \ldots, n\}$ *and a constant factor quantity* $x_p^* \in \mathbb{R}_{++}$ *such that for all* $(x_1, \ldots, x_{p-1}, x_{p+1}, \ldots, x_n) \in]0,\varepsilon[^{n-1}$ ($\varepsilon \in \mathbb{R}_{++}$ *a constant depending on* p *and* x_p^*) *the inequality*

$$\sum_{\substack{s,t=1 \\ s \neq p,\, t \neq p}}^{n} \frac{\partial^2 \Phi(x_1, \ldots, x_{p-1}, x_p^*, x_{p+1}, \ldots, x_n)}{\partial x_s\, \partial x_t} \xi_s \xi_t \geqq 0 \tag{4.4.4}$$

holds with arbitrary $\xi_s \in \mathbb{R}$, $\xi_t \in \mathbb{R}$ $(s \neq p,\ t \neq p)$.

Before we prove this theorem we make some comments and remarks.

According to Property 4.4.3 it is necessary to apply positive amounts of all input quantities in order to obtain positive output quantities. In other words, all inputs are *essential* for production.

Property 4.4.4 implies that the function given by

$$(x_1, \ldots, x_{p-1}, x_{p+1}, \ldots, x_n) \to \Phi\,(x_1, \ldots, x_{p-1}, x_p^*, x_{p+1}, \ldots, x_n)$$

is convex in the $(n-1)$-dimensional cube $]0, \varepsilon[^{n-1}$.

Note that the foregoing inequality yields

$$\frac{\partial^2 \Phi(x_1, \ldots, x_{p-1}, x_p^*, x_{p+1}, \ldots, x_n)}{\partial x_q^2} \geqq 0 \quad \text{for} \quad x_q \in]0, \varepsilon[,\ q \neq p;\ q = 1, \ldots, n,$$

that is, the functions

$$x_q \to \Phi(x_1, \ldots, x_{p-1}, x_p^*, x_{p+1}, \ldots, x_n)$$

are initially *convex*.

In the case in which $r = 1$, Theorem 4.4.1 remains true even without Property 4.4.3 (see Theorem 4.3.9). In the case in which $r \in]0, 1[$, none of Properties 4.4.2, 4.4.3, and 4.4.4 can be left out, as the following examples show.

The function Φ: $\mathbb{R}_+^2 \to \mathbb{R}_+$ given by

$$\Phi(x, y) = \frac{x^2 y^2}{x^{3+\varepsilon} + y^{3+\varepsilon}} \qquad (\varepsilon \in]0,1[)$$

satisfies Properties 4.4.3 and 4.4.4, but not 4.4.2.

The function Φ: $\mathbb{R}_+^2 \to \mathbb{R}_+$ given by

$$\Phi(x, y) = \frac{x^{2-\varepsilon}}{x + y} + y^{1-\varepsilon} \qquad (\varepsilon \in]0, 1[)$$

satisfies Properties 4.4.2 and 4.4.4, but not 4.4.3.

The function Φ: $\mathbb{R}_+^2 \to \mathbb{R}_+$ given by

$$\Phi(x, y) = (xy)^{1/3}$$

satisfies Properties 4.4.2 and 4.4.3, but not 4.4.4.

Proof of Theorem 4.4.1. Let Φ: $\mathbb{R}_+^n \to \mathbb{R}_+$ satisfy Property 4.4.4. Without loss of generality, choose $p = n$ and write x, c, and $\psi(x_1, \ldots, x_{n-1})$ for x_n, x_n^*, and $\Phi(x_1, \ldots, x_{n-1}, c)$, respectively. Then the inequality in 4.4.4 becomes

$$\sum_{j,k=1}^{n-1} \frac{\partial^2 \Psi(x_1, \ldots, x_{n-1})}{\partial x_j \, \partial x_k} \xi_j \xi_k \geqq 0 \qquad ((x_1, \ldots, x_{n-1}) \in]0, \varepsilon[^{n-1}). \quad (4.4.5)$$

Since Φ is assumed to be homogeneous of degree r,

$$\Phi(x_1, \ldots, x_{n-1}, x) = \left(\frac{x}{c}\right)^r \Psi\left(c\frac{x_1}{x}, \ldots, c\frac{x_{n-1}}{x}\right) \qquad (x \in \mathbb{R}_{++}, c \in \mathbb{R}_{++}). \quad (4.4.6)$$

We differentiate (4.4.6) twice with respect to x and write z_i for cx_i/x ($i = 1, \ldots, n-1$):

$$\begin{aligned} \frac{\partial^2 \Phi(x_1, \ldots, x_{n-1}, x)}{\partial x^2} &= r(r-1)\, c^{-r} x^{r-2}\, \Psi(z_1, \ldots, z_{n-1}) \\ &\quad - 2(r-1)\, c^{1-r} x^{r-3} \sum_{i=1}^{n-1} \frac{\partial \Psi(z_1, \ldots, z_{n-1})}{\partial z_i} x_i \qquad (4.4.7) \\ &\quad + c^{2-r} x^{r-4} \sum_{j,k=1}^{n-1} \frac{\partial^2 \Psi(z_1, \ldots, z_{n-1})}{\partial z_j \, \partial z_k} x_j x_k. \end{aligned}$$

We shall show that in the case where $r \in]0, 1]$, because of Properties 4.4.3, 4.4.4, expression (4.4.7) is greater than or equal to 0 for all $cx_i/x = z_i \in]0, \varepsilon[$, that is, for all $x > cx_i/\varepsilon$, which contradicts Property 4.4.2.

By assumption (4.4.4), that is, (4.4.5), the last term in (4.4.7) is greater than or equal to 0. Thus Theorem 4.4.1 is proved by showing that assumptions (4.4.3), (4.4.4), and $r \in]0, 1]$ yield the inequality

$$\begin{aligned} &r(r-1)\, c^{-r} x^{r-2}\, \Psi(z_1, \ldots, z_{n-1}) \\ &\quad - 2(r-1)\, c^{1-r} x^{r-3} \sum_{i=1}^{n-1} \frac{\partial \Psi(z_1, \ldots, z_{n-1})}{\partial z_i} x_i \geqq 0 \qquad (4.4.8) \end{aligned}$$

for all $(z_1, \ldots, z_{n-1}) \in]0, \varepsilon[^{n-1}$.

In order to prove this, consider the inequalities

$$\frac{r}{2}\frac{\Psi(z_1, \ldots, z_{n-1})}{z_i} - \frac{\partial\Psi(z_1, \ldots, z_{n-1})}{\partial z_i} \leqq 0 \qquad (i = 1, \ldots, n-1), \quad (4.4.9)$$

which hold true for all $(z_1, \ldots, z_{n-1}) \in]0, \varepsilon[^{n-1}$ because of both the convexity of Ψ on $[0, \varepsilon[^{n-1}$ and assumption (4.4.3); that is,

$$\Psi(z_1, \ldots, z_{i-1}, 0, z_{i+1}, \ldots, z_{n-1}) = 0 \qquad (i = 1, \ldots, n-1).$$

Multiplication of inequality (4.4.9) by the nonpositive expression $2(r - 1)\, c^{1-r}\, x^{r-3} x_i$ shows that inequality (4.4.8) is valid. This completes the proof of Theorem 4.4.1. ■

4.5 Domains of Substitution, Isoquants, and Expansion Paths of Homogeneous and Homothetic Production Functions

Let $\Phi\colon \mathbb{R}^n_+ \to \mathbb{R}_+$ be a production function. The *domain of substitution of* Φ is the set of all input vectors $\mathbf{x}$ satisfying

$$\Phi(x_1, \ldots, x_{j-1}, x_j + \xi_j, x_{j+1}, \ldots, x_n) > \Phi(\mathbf{x}) \qquad (4.5.1)$$

for all sufficiently small $\xi_j \in \mathbb{R}_{++}$, $j = 1, \ldots, n$.

In other words, an input vector $\mathbf{x}$ belongs to the domain of substitution of Φ if and only if every sufficiently small partial increase of any component of $\mathbf{x}$ yields an increase of the output quantity.

Now, let Φ be homogeneous of degree r ($r \in \mathbb{R}_{++}$), and multiply inequality (4.5.1) by λ^r ($\lambda \in \mathbb{R}_{++}$). We obtain

$$\Phi(\lambda x_1, \ldots, \lambda x_{j-1}, \lambda x_j + \lambda\xi_j, \lambda x_{j+1}, \ldots, \lambda x_n) > \Phi(\lambda\mathbf{x}),$$

that is, we have the following result.

4.5.2 **Theorem.** *If an input vector* $\mathbf{x}^*$ *belongs to the domain of substitution of an arbitrary homogeneous production function, then the whole input ray*

$$\{\mathbf{x} \mid \mathbf{x} = \lambda\mathbf{x}^*, \lambda \in \mathbb{R}_{++}\}$$

belongs to this domain. In other words, the domains of substitution of the homogeneous production functions consist of rays that run from the origin into the n-dimensional input space.

A generalization of the homogeneous production functions are the *homothetic* production functions Ψ (Shephard [1953]), which are given by

$$\Psi(\mathbf{x}) = g(F(\mathbf{x})) \qquad (4.5.3)$$

with linearly homogeneous $F : \mathbb{R}^n_+ \to \mathbb{R}_+$ and strictly increasing $g : \mathbb{R}_+ \to \mathbb{R}_+$ such that $g(0) = 0$ and $g(v) \to \infty$ for $v \to \infty$.

Note that Ψ satisfies

$$\Psi(x_1, \ldots, x_{j-1}, x_j + \xi_j, x_{j+1}, \ldots, x_n) > \Psi(\mathbf{x}),$$

whenever F of (4.5.3) satisfies (4.5.1), and that in this case

$$\begin{aligned}&\Psi(\lambda x_1, \ldots, \lambda x_{j-1}, \lambda x_j + \lambda\xi_j, \lambda x_{j+1}, \ldots, \lambda x_n)\\ &\quad = g(\lambda F(x_1, \ldots, x_{j-1}, x_j + \xi_j, x_{j+1}, \ldots, x_n)) > g(\lambda F(\mathbf{x})) = \Psi(\lambda\mathbf{x}),\end{aligned}$$

which gives rise to the

4.5.4 **Remark.** Theorem 4.5.2 remains valid if we replace "homogeneous" by "homothetic."

The *isoquant with respect to the output quantity* $u \in \mathbb{R}_+$ of a production function $\Phi : \mathbb{R}^n_+ \to \mathbb{R}_+$ is the set

$$\{\mathbf{x} \mid \Phi(\mathbf{x}) = u, u \in \mathbb{R}_+\},$$

that is, the set of all input vectors yielding exactly u.

It follows easily from the above-mentioned definition of a homothetic production function that, given an arbitrary homothetic production function Ψ, there always exists a linearly homogeneous function F such that both functions have the *same* set of isoquants.

4.5.5 **Remark.** In Section 12.2 it will be shown, among other things, that the homogeneous production functions yield so-called linear expansion paths. Since this property follows solely from the geometric properties of the set of isoquants of the respective functions, we can conclude, in view of the foregoing statement about homothetic functions, that the homothetic production functions yield linear expansion paths, too.

In what follows, let us consider the function $F : \mathbb{R}^2_+ \to \mathbb{R}_+$ given by

$$F(x_1, x_2) = \frac{x_1^{1.4}\, x_2^{1.6}}{x_1^2 + x_2^2}, \qquad F(0, 0) = 0, \tag{4.5.6}$$

Obviously, it has the following properties:

F is linearly homogeneous; (4.5.7)

$x_1 \to F(x_1, x_2)$ is both strictly increasing and strictly convex for all sufficiently small $x_1 \in \mathbb{R}_{++}$ ($x_2 \in \mathbb{R}_{++}$, fixed); (4.5.8)

$x_2 \to F(x_1, x_2)$ is both strictly increasing and strictly convex for all sufficiently small $x_2 \in \mathbb{R}_{++}$ ($x_1 \in \mathbb{R}_{++}$, fixed); (4.5.9)

$F(0, x_2) = 0$ for all $x_2 \in \mathbb{R}_+$; $F(x_1, 0) = 0$ for all $x_1 \in \mathbb{R}_+$. (4.5.10)

The geometric shape of the graph of F is represented by Fig. 4.2.3. As we see, F is *not* nondecreasing. Hence, if we consider F as a production function, this production function is not based on the assumption of free disposal of inputsl Furthermore, the mappings 4.5.8 and 4.5.9 are *not* strictly concave for al. sufficiently large x_1 or x_2, respectively; that is F does *not* satisfy the law of diminishing returns (see, in this connection, Corollary 4.3.10).

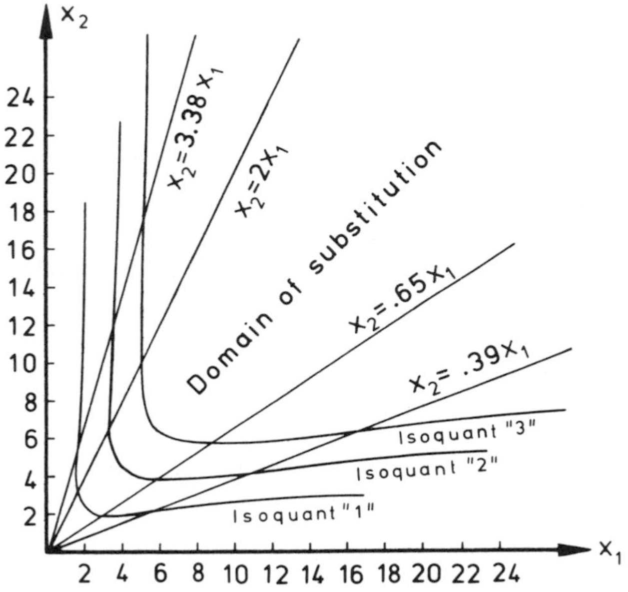

4.5.11 Figure. Three isoquants of the function F given by (4.5.6).

Figure 4.5.11 gives an impression of the set of isoquants of F. We notice that every isoquant has two points of inflection, one on the ray

$$\{(x_1, x_2) \mid x_2 = 0.39x_1, x_1 \in \mathbb{R}_+\},$$

and the other on the ray

$$\{(x_1, x_2) \mid x_2 = 3.38x_1, x_1 \in \mathbb{R}_+\}.$$

This turning point property implies that the so-called *level sets*

$$\mathscr{L}(u) := \{(x_1, x_2) \mid F(x_1, x_2) \geqq u, u \in \mathbb{R}_{++}, (x_1, x_2) \in \mathbb{R}^2_+\}, \quad (4.5.12)$$

that is, the sets of those input vectors which yield at least the positive output quantity u are *not* convex.

4.5.13 **Remark.** It can be shown that every twice continuously differentiable function $F : \mathbb{R}^2_+ \to \mathbb{R}_+$ that satisfies Properties 4.5.7–4.5.10 has isoquants of the form drawn in Figure 4.5.11. Each of these isoquants has two points of inflection, and the level sets (4.5.12) are *not* convex (see Eichhorn and Müller [1967] or Eichhorn [1970, Section 4.2]).

A function $F : \mathbb{R}^n_+ \to \mathbb{R}$ has convex level sets $\mathcal{L}(u)$ if and only if it is quasiconcave (see Theorem 4.6.2).

Since quasiconcavity is often assumed to be a property of production or utility functions, we will define and consider it in the following section.

4.6 Homogeneity, Homotheticity, and Quasiconcavity of Production or Utility Functions

Let $D \subseteqq \mathbb{R}^n$ be a convex set. A function $F : D \to \mathbb{R}$ satisfying the inequality

$$F(\theta \mathbf{x} + (1 - \theta)\,\mathbf{y}) \geqq \min\,\{F(\mathbf{x}), F(\mathbf{y})\} \tag{4.6.1}$$

for any two vectors $\mathbf{x} \in D$, $\mathbf{y} \in D$ and for all $\theta \in [0, 1]$ is called *quasiconcave* on D. It is called *strictly quasiconcave* on D if in 4.6.1 the $\geqq$ is replaced by $>$ for all $\theta \in \,]0, 1[$ and $\mathbf{x} \neq \mathbf{y}$.

The following theorem, which states the equivalence of the definitions of quasiconcavity and convexity of the level sets, is well known.

4.6.2 **Theorem.** *A function $F : D \to \mathbb{R}$ is quasiconcave on D if and only if the level sets*

$$\mathcal{L}(u) :\, = \{\mathbf{x} \mid F(\mathbf{x}) \geqq u, \mathbf{x} \in D\}$$

are convex for any $u \in \mathbb{R}$.

Proof. Suppose F is quasiconcave on D. Since the empty set $\emptyset$ is convex, we have only to show that $\mathcal{L}(u)$ is convex for all $u \in \mathbb{R}$ with $\mathcal{L}(u) \neq \emptyset$. Let $\mathbf{x}$ and $\mathbf{y}$ be any two points of such a level set $\mathcal{L}(u)$:

$$F(\mathbf{x}) \geqq u, \qquad F(\mathbf{y}) \geqq u.$$

It follows from the quasiconcavity of F on D that

$$F(\theta \mathbf{x} + (1 - \theta)\,\mathbf{y}) \geqq u \qquad \text{for all} \quad \theta \in [0, 1],$$

implying that $\theta \mathbf{x} + (1 - \theta)\,\mathbf{y}$ belongs to $\mathcal{L}(u)$ for all $\theta \in [0, 1]$. Hence, $\mathcal{L}(u)$ is convex for all $u \in \mathbb{R}$.

Next, suppose $\mathcal{L}(u)$ is convex for all $u \in \mathbb{R}$. Let $\mathbf{x}$ and $\mathbf{y}$ be any two points of D, and take $\varrho = \min\,\{F(\mathbf{x}), F(\mathbf{y})\}$. Then $\mathbf{x} \in \mathcal{L}(\varrho)$, $\mathbf{y} \in \mathcal{L}(\varrho)$ and, since $\mathcal{L}(\varrho)$ is convex,

$$(\theta\mathbf{x} + (1 - \theta)\,\mathbf{y}) \in \mathscr{L}(\varrho) \qquad \text{for all} \quad \theta \in [0, 1],$$

which implies

$$F(\theta\mathbf{x} + (1 - \theta)\,\mathbf{y}) \geqq \varrho = \min\{F(\mathbf{x}), F(\mathbf{y})\} \qquad \text{for all} \quad \theta \in [0, 1],$$

that is, F is quasiconcave on D. ■

A function $F : D \to \mathbb{R}$ is called *concave* on D if it satisfies the inequality

$$F(\theta\mathbf{x} + (1 - \theta)\,\mathbf{y}) \geqq \theta F(\mathbf{x}) + (1 - \theta)\,F(\mathbf{y}) \tag{4.6.3}$$

for any two vectors $\mathbf{x} \in D$, $\mathbf{y} \in D$ and all $\theta \in [0, 1]$. It is called *strictly concave* on D if in (4.6.3) the $\geqq$ is replaced by $>$ for all $\theta \in]0, 1[$ and $\mathbf{x} \neq \mathbf{y}$.

As Friedman [1973] has shown for functions $\Phi : \mathbb{R}^n_+ \to \mathbb{R}_+$, concavity is *not* implied by quasiconcavity and nonincreasing returns to scale. In order to obtain concavity it is necessary to add a third property of Φ. Friedman added homotheticity and showed that the three assumptions together yield concavity.

In what follows, we reproduce Friedman's very short and elementary proof of the preceding result. Moreover, we show that any two of the three assumptions do not yield concavity.

We consider the class of functions $\Phi : \mathbb{R}^n_+ \to \mathbb{R}$ that satisfy the following assumptions.

For any $\mathbf{x} \in \mathbb{R}^n_+$, $\mathbf{y} \in \mathbb{R}^n_+$ with $\mathbf{y} \geqq \mathbf{x}$ and for $\lambda \in \mathbb{R}_+$, $\lambda \to \Phi(\lambda\mathbf{x})$ is nondecreasing and concave, $\Phi(\lambda\mathbf{x}) \to 0$ for $\lambda \to 0$, $\Phi(\mathbf{x}) \to \Phi(x_1, \ldots, x_{j-1}, 0, x_{j+1}, \ldots, x_n)$ for $x_j \to 0$ (for all j), and $\Phi(\mathbf{y}) \geqq \Phi(\mathbf{x})$. (4.6.4)

For any $u \in \mathbb{R}_+$, the level set $\mathscr{L}(u) = \{\mathbf{x} \mid \Phi(\mathbf{x}) \geqq u,\ \mathbf{x} \in \mathbb{R}^n_+\}$ is convex. (4.6.5)

For any $\mathbf{x} \in \mathbb{R}^n_+$, $\mathbf{y} \in \mathbb{R}^n_+$ and $\mu \in \mathbb{R}_{++}$, $\Phi(\mathbf{x}) = \Phi(\mathbf{y})$ if and only if $\Phi(\mu\mathbf{x}) = \Phi(\mu\mathbf{y})$. (4.6.6)

Let us interpret this class of functions as a class of production (or utility) functions. Then, assumption (4.6.4) is nonincreasing returns to scale, free disposal, and continuity conditions at the boundary of $\mathbb{R}^n_+$; assumption (4.6.5) is quasiconcavity; and assumption (4.6.6) is homotheticity.

4.6.7 **Theorem.** *A function $\Phi : \mathbb{R}^n_+ \to \mathbb{R}_+$ that satisfies assumptions (4.6.4), (4.6.5), and (4.6.6) is concave on $\mathbb{R}^n_+$.*

Proof. Clearly Φ satisfies the concavity condition (4.6.3) when $\Phi(\mathbf{x}) = \Phi(\mathbf{y})$, and when $\mathbf{x} = \lambda\mathbf{y}$, $\lambda \in \mathbb{R}_+$, from assumptions (4.6.5) (see (4.6.1), Theorem 4.6.2) and (4.6.4), respectively. Let $\mathbf{x} \in \mathbb{R}^n_+$, $\mathbf{y} \in \mathbb{R}^n_+$ not satisfy eitherof these conditions. Say $\Phi(\mathbf{x}) < \Phi(\mathbf{y})$. Note that, by assumption (4.6.4), $\Phi(\mathbf{x}) > 0$

whenever $\mathbf{x} \neq 0$ and $\Phi(\mathbf{x}) \not\equiv 0$, which is what we assume from now on. Then by assumption (4.6.4) there is a unique $\mu \in \mathbb{R}_{++}$ such that $\Phi(\mathbf{x}) = \Phi(\mu\mathbf{y})$. By assumption (4.6.6), $\Phi(\mathbf{x}/\mu) = \Phi(\mathbf{y})$.

Now choose arbitrary $\theta \in [0, 1]$, determining

$$\mathbf{z}^\theta := \theta\mathbf{x} + (1 - \theta)\,\mathbf{y},$$

and let

$$\mathbf{x}^* = \frac{1 - \theta + \theta\mu}{\mu}\mathbf{x}, \qquad \mathbf{y}^* = (1 - \theta + \theta\mu)\,\mathbf{y}.$$

Then, by assumption (4.6.6), $\Phi(\mathbf{x}^*) = \Phi(\mathbf{y}^*)$ and

$$\begin{aligned}\mathbf{z}^\theta &= \frac{\theta\mu}{1 - \theta + \theta\mu}\mathbf{x}^* + \frac{1 - \theta}{1 - \theta + \theta\mu}\mathbf{y}^* \\ &= \omega\mathbf{x}^* + (1 - \omega)\,\mathbf{y}^* \qquad (\omega := \theta\mu/(1 - \theta + \theta\mu).\end{aligned}$$

By assumption (4.6.5)

$$\Phi(\mathbf{z}^\theta) \geqq \Phi(\mathbf{x}^*) = \Phi(\mathbf{y}^*)$$

and by assumption (4.6.4)

$$\begin{aligned}\Phi(\mathbf{y}^*) &= \Phi(\theta\mu\mathbf{y} + (1 - \theta)\mathbf{y}) \\ &\geqq \theta\Phi(\mu\mathbf{y}) + (1 - \theta)\,\Phi(\mathbf{y}) = \theta\Phi(\mathbf{x}) + (1 - \theta)\,\Phi(\mathbf{y});\end{aligned}$$

therefore Φ is concave on $\mathbb{R}^n_+$. ■

4.6.8 **Remark** As we easily see, *strict* concavity and, hence, the law of diminishing returns (see Definition 4.3.4) is implied by assumption (4.6.4) with strict concavity, assumption (4.6.5) with strict quasiconcavity, and assumption (4.6.6).

Let Φ: $\mathbb{R}^n_+ \to \mathbb{R}_+$ be homogeneous of degree r, where $r \in]0, 1]$. Then Φ satisfies assumption (4.6.6) (homotheticity) and, moreover, the assumptions

$\lambda \to \Phi(\lambda\mathbf{x})$ is nondecreasing and concave for any $\mathbf{x} \in \mathbb{R}^n_+$ and for $\lambda \in \mathbb{R}_+$ (nonincreasing returns to scale) (4.6.9)

and

$$\Phi(\lambda\mathbf{x}) \to 0 \qquad \text{for} \quad \lambda \to 0 \quad (\lambda \in \mathbb{R}_+) \tag{4.6.10}$$

from assumption (4.6.4). Thus we have the following well-known special case of Theorem 4.6.7 (see, e.g., Rader [1972]).

4.6.11 **Corollary.** *The following properties of a function* Φ: $\mathbb{R}^n_+ \to \mathbb{R}_+$ *(production or utility function, say) imply the concavity of* Φ:

(i) *homogeneity of degree r, where* $r \in]0, 1]$;
(ii) *quasiconcavity;*
(iii) *free disposal (see the last property of (4.6.4));*
(iv) $\Phi(\mathbf{x}) \to \Phi(x_1, \ldots, x_{j-1}, 0, x_{j+1}, \ldots, x_n)$ *for* $x_j \to 0$ *(for all j).*

It is interesting to determine whether any two of the assumptions (4.6.4), (4.6.5), and (4.6.6) are sufficient to yield concavity. The function $F\colon \mathbb{R}^2_+ \to \mathbb{R}_+$ given by (4.5.6) satisfies (4.6.4), (4.6.6) and is not concave; the function G: $\mathbb{R}^2_+ \to \mathbb{R}_+$ given by

$$G(x_1, x_2) = \frac{x_1^{1.1} x_2^{1.4}}{x_1 + x_2}, \qquad G(0, 0) = 0$$

satisfies (4.6.5), (4.6.6), and is not concave; and the function $H\colon \mathbb{R}^2_+ \to \mathbb{R}_+$ given by the graph in Fig. 4.6.12 satisfies (4.6.4), (4.6.5), and is not concave. The last example is due to Friedman [1973].

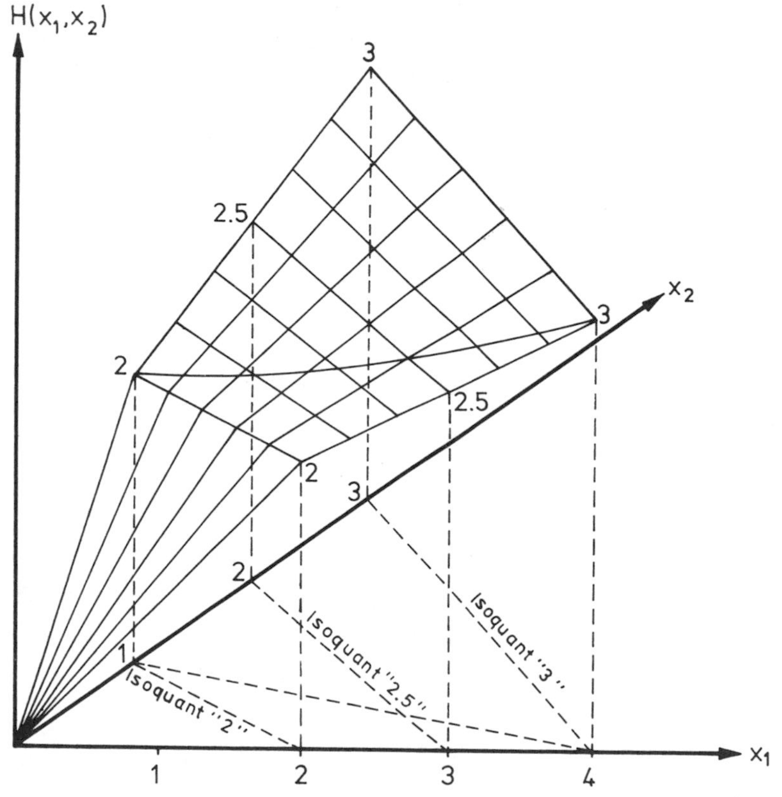

4.6.12 Figure. Example of a nonconcave output surface satisfying the assumptions of quasiconcavity and nonincreasing returns to scale.

We summarize:

4.6.13 **Theorem.** *Any two of the assumptions (4.6.4)–(4.6.6) do not yield concavity.*

4.7 Generalizations of the Functional Equation of the Homogeneous Functions

The properties of homogeneous functions expressed by Theorems 4.1.6, 4.3.9, 4.4.1, 4.5.2, Corollary 4.3.10, and Remarks 4.5.5, 4.5.13 indicate that the class of the homogeneous functions is perhaps too narrow for many purposes of production theory (or utility theory, in the respective interpretation).

There exist some attempts to extend the class of homogeneous functions $F\colon \mathbb{R}_+^n \to \mathbb{R}$. Shephard [1953] introduced the notion of a *homothetic production function* (see (4.5.3)), which is considerably more general than the notion of a homogeneous production function and which has given rise to many valuable applications. Nevertheless, as we pointed out in Section 4.5, given an arbitrary homothetic production function, there always exists a linearly homogeneous function such that both functions have the *same* set of isoquants. This yields several common properties of homogeneous and homothetic functions (see Remarks 4.5.4, 4.5.5).

For this and other reasons, another generalization of the concept of a homogeneous production function was made by Eichhorn [1969; 1970, pp. 103–111]; it is described next.

Instead of the equation of the homogeneous production functions,

$$\begin{aligned} &\Phi(\lambda \mathbf{x}) = \lambda^r \Phi(\mathbf{x}) \qquad \text{for all} \quad (\lambda, \mathbf{x}) \in \mathbb{R}_{++} \times \mathbb{R}_+^n \\ &\text{where } \Phi\colon \mathbb{R}_+^n \to \mathbb{R}_+ \quad \text{and} \quad r \in \mathbb{R}_{++}, \end{aligned} \tag{4.7.1}$$

we may first consider the equation

$$\begin{aligned} &\Phi(\lambda \mathbf{x}) = \psi(\lambda, \mathbf{x})\Phi(\mathbf{x}) \qquad \text{for all} \quad (\lambda, \mathbf{x}) \in \mathbb{R}_{++} \times \mathbb{R}_+^n \quad \text{where} \\ &\Phi\colon \mathbb{R}_+^n \to \mathbb{R}_+, \ \psi\colon \mathbb{R}_{++} \times \mathbb{R}_+^n \to \mathbb{R}_{++}, \ \psi(1, \mathbf{x}) = \psi(\lambda, \mathbf{0}) = 1. \end{aligned} \tag{4.7.2}$$

This equation is too general. It admits *every* function $\Phi\colon \mathbb{R}_+^n \to \mathbb{R}_+$ as a solution as can be easily seen by choosing ψ in the form

$$\psi(\lambda, \mathbf{x}) := \begin{cases} \Phi(\lambda \mathbf{x})/\Phi(\mathbf{x}) & \text{for all } \mathbf{x} \text{ with } \Phi(\mathbf{x}) > 0, \ \lambda \in \mathbb{R}_{++}, \\ 1 & \text{for all } \mathbf{x} \text{ satisfying } \Phi(\mathbf{x}) = 0, \ \lambda \in \mathbb{R}_{++}. \end{cases}$$

Consequently, we specialize Eq. (4.7.2) a little by specializing ψ as follows:

$$\psi(\lambda, \mathbf{x}) = \begin{cases} m(\lambda, \mathbf{x}/|\mathbf{x}|) \in \mathbb{R}_{++} & \text{for all} \quad \mathbf{x} \geq \mathbf{0}, \quad \lambda \in \mathbb{R}_{++}, \\ 1 & \text{for} \quad \mathbf{x} = \mathbf{0}, \quad \lambda \in \mathbb{R}_{++}. \end{cases} \tag{4.7.3}$$

By Corollary 1.9.32 and Remark 1.9.23, we know that a function $\Phi\colon \mathbb{R}_+^n \to \mathbb{R}_+$ with properties (1.9.1)–(1.9.3) (e.g., a production function) satisfies functional equation (4.7.2) in conjunction with (4.7.3) if and only if it satisfies, for all $\mathbf{x} \geq \mathbf{0}$, the functional equation

$$\Phi(\lambda\mathbf{x}) = \lambda^{g(\mathbf{x}/|\mathbf{x}|)}\Phi(\mathbf{x}) \tag{4.7.4}$$

where

$$\mathbf{x} \geq \mathbf{0}, \qquad g(\mathbf{x}/|\mathbf{x}|) \in \mathbb{R}_{++}, \qquad \lambda \in \mathbb{R}_{++}. \tag{4.7.5}$$

Let us call functions $\Phi\colon \mathbb{R}_+^n \to \mathbb{R}_+$ satisfying Eq. (4.7.4) with (4.7.5) *semihomogeneous*, in accordance with Shephard [1974a], who uses this term for production correspondences satisfying (4.7.4) with (4.7.5); see also Section 12.4.

4.7.6 **Theorem.** *Let $\Phi\colon \mathbb{R}_+^n \to \mathbb{R}_+$ be an arbitrary semihomogeneous function. Then there exists a function*

$$\Psi\colon \{\mathbf{y} \mid \mathbf{y} = \mathbf{x}/|\mathbf{x}|, \mathbf{x} \in \mathbb{R}_+^n, \mathbf{x} \neq \mathbf{0}\} \to \mathbb{R}_+$$

such that

$$\Phi(\mathbf{x}) = |\mathbf{x}|^{g(\mathbf{x}/|\mathbf{x}|)}\,\Psi(\mathbf{x}/|\mathbf{x}|). \tag{4.7.7}$$

Conversely, every function $\Phi\colon \mathbb{R}_+^n \to \mathbb{R}_+$ given by (4.7.7) with arbitrary Ψ is semihomogeneous.

Proof. The first assertion follows from the fact that, for $\mathbf{x} \geq \mathbf{0}$, every solution Φ of Eq. (4.7.4) can be written as

$$\Phi(\mathbf{x}) = \Phi(|\mathbf{x}|\mathbf{x}/|\mathbf{x}|) = |\mathbf{x}|^{g(\mathbf{x}/|\mathbf{x}|)}\Phi(\mathbf{x}/|\mathbf{x}|).$$

The second assertion can be proved by inserting (4.7.7) into (4.7.4). ■

4.7.8 **Remark.** Since a semihomogeneous function is homogeneous of a fixed degree along a given ray

$$\{\lambda\mathbf{x} \mid \mathbf{x} \in \mathbb{R}_+^n, \mathbf{x} \neq \mathbf{0}, \lambda \in \mathbb{R}_{++}\},$$

we may also call it *ray homogeneous*.

Goldman and Shephard [1972] have shown that ray homogeneity together with monotonicity (i. e., free disposal in case of a production function) imply homogeneity:

4.7.9 **Theorem.** *For (4.7.4) to hold with (4.7.5) and with*

$$\Phi(\tilde{\mathbf{x}}) \geqq \Phi(\mathbf{x}) \text{ for all } \tilde{\mathbf{x}} \in \mathbb{R}_+^n, \mathbf{x} \in \mathbb{R}_+^n \text{ satisfying } \tilde{\mathbf{x}} \geqq \mathbf{x} \tag{4.7.10}$$

it is necessary that the exponent $g(\mathbf{x}/|\mathbf{x}|)$ be a positive constant for all $\mathbf{x}$ such that $\Phi(\lambda\mathbf{x}) > 0$ for some $\lambda \in \mathbb{R}_{++}$.

Proof (Goldman and Shephard [1972, pp. 216–217]). Let $\mathbf{x} \geq \mathbf{0}$, $\mathbf{y} \geq \mathbf{0}$ be two arbitrary vectors such that $\Phi(\lambda\mathbf{x}) > 0$ for some $\lambda \in \mathbb{R}_{++}$ and $\Phi(\mu\mathbf{y}) > 0$

for some $\mu \in \mathbb{R}_{++}$. Assume (4.7.4) holds. Then there exist $\lambda_0 \in \mathbb{R}_{++}$ and $\mu_0 \in \mathbb{R}_{++}$ such that

$$\Phi(\lambda_0 \mathbf{x}) = \Phi(\mu_0 \mathbf{y}) = \bar{u} > 0.$$

Define $\bar{\mathbf{x}} = \lambda_0 \mathbf{x}$, $\bar{\mathbf{y}} = \mu_0 \mathbf{y}$. Note that

$$g(\bar{\mathbf{x}}/|\bar{\mathbf{x}}|) = g(\mathbf{x}/|\mathbf{x}|), \qquad g(\bar{\mathbf{y}}/|\bar{\mathbf{y}}|) = g(\mathbf{y}/|\mathbf{y}|).$$

Consider variations $\theta\bar{u}$, $\theta \in \mathbb{R}_{++}$. The corresponding vectors $\boldsymbol{\xi}(\theta) = \varrho\bar{\mathbf{x}}$, $\varrho \in \mathbb{R}_+$, and $\boldsymbol{\eta}(\theta) = \sigma\bar{\mathbf{y}}$, $\sigma \in \mathbb{R}_+$, belonging to the isoquant

$$\{\mathbf{x} \,|\, \Phi(\mathbf{x}) = \theta\bar{u},\ \bar{u} \in \mathbb{R}_{++},\ \theta \in \mathbb{R}_{++},\ \mathbf{x} \in \mathbb{R}^n_+\} \tag{4.7.11}$$

are

$$\boldsymbol{\xi}(\theta) = \theta^{g(\mathbf{x}/|\mathbf{x}|)^{-1}}\bar{\mathbf{x}}, \qquad \boldsymbol{\eta}(\theta) = \theta^{g(\mathbf{y}/|\mathbf{y}|)^{-1}}\bar{\mathbf{y}}.$$

Suppose $g(\mathbf{x}/|\mathbf{x}|) = g(\bar{\mathbf{x}}/|\bar{\mathbf{x}}|) > g(\bar{\mathbf{y}}/|\bar{\mathbf{y}}|) = g(\mathbf{y}/|\mathbf{y}|)$ and, to start with, let $\mathbf{x}$ and $\mathbf{y}$ be strictly positive. Let α denote the subscript of the component of $\bar{\mathbf{x}}$ and $\bar{\mathbf{y}}$ for which $r_i := (\bar{y}_i/\bar{x}_i)$, $i \in \{1, 2, \ldots, n\}$, takes on the smallest value. Then

$$r_\alpha(\theta) = \frac{\eta_\alpha(\theta)}{\xi_\alpha(\theta)} = \left(\frac{\bar{y}_\alpha}{\bar{x}_\alpha}\right)\theta^{(g(\bar{\mathbf{y}}/|\bar{\mathbf{y}}|)^{-1} - g(\bar{\mathbf{x}}/|\bar{\mathbf{x}}|)^{-1})},$$

and there exists a real number

$$\bar{\theta} := \left(\frac{\bar{x}_\alpha}{\bar{y}_\alpha}\right)^{(g(\bar{\mathbf{y}}/|\bar{\mathbf{y}}|)^{-1} - g(\bar{\mathbf{x}}/|\bar{\mathbf{x}}|)^{-1})^{-1}} > 0$$

such that $r_\alpha(\theta) > 1$ for $\theta > \bar{\theta}$ and $r_i(\theta) > 1$ for all $i \in \{1, 2, \ldots, n\}$, implying $\boldsymbol{\eta}(\theta) > \boldsymbol{\xi}(\theta)$ for $\theta > \bar{\theta}$. Consequently, if (4.7.4) holds, there exists $\varepsilon \in \mathbb{R}_{++}$ such that for $\theta > \bar{\theta}$

$$\begin{aligned} &\boldsymbol{\xi}(\theta) \in \text{isoquant (4.7.11)}, && \boldsymbol{\eta}(\theta) \in \text{isoquant (4.7.11)}, \\ &(1-\varepsilon)\,\boldsymbol{\eta}(\theta) \notin \{\mathbf{x} \,|\, \Phi(\mathbf{x}) \geqq \theta\bar{u}\}, && (1-\varepsilon)\,\boldsymbol{\eta}(\theta) > \boldsymbol{\xi}(\theta), \end{aligned}$$

contradicting (4.7.10). Hence, if $\mathbf{x} > \mathbf{0}$ and $\mathbf{y} > \mathbf{0}$,

$$g(\mathbf{x}/|\mathbf{x}|) = g(\bar{\mathbf{x}}/|\bar{\mathbf{x}}|) \leqq g(\bar{\mathbf{y}}/|\bar{\mathbf{y}}|) = g(\mathbf{y}/|\mathbf{y}|).$$

Next, for $\mathbf{x} > \mathbf{0}$ and $\mathbf{y} > \mathbf{0}$, suppose $g(\bar{\mathbf{y}}/|\bar{\mathbf{y}}|) > g(\bar{\mathbf{x}}/|\bar{\mathbf{x}}|)$. Then

$$r_\alpha(\theta)^{-1} = \frac{\xi_\alpha(\theta)}{\eta_\alpha(\theta)} = \left(\frac{\bar{x}_\alpha}{\bar{y}_\alpha}\right)\theta^{(g(\bar{\mathbf{x}}/|\bar{\mathbf{x}}|)^{-1} - g(\bar{\mathbf{y}}/|\bar{\mathbf{y}}|)^{-1})},$$

and there exists a scalar

$$\hat{\theta} := \left(\frac{\bar{y}_\alpha}{\bar{x}_\alpha}\right)^{(g(\bar{\mathbf{x}}/|\bar{\mathbf{x}}|)^{-1} - g(\bar{\mathbf{y}}/|\bar{\mathbf{y}}|)^{-1})^{-1}} > 0$$

such that $r_\alpha(\theta)^{-1} < 1$ for $\theta \in]0, \hat{\theta}[$ and $r_i(\theta)^{-1} < 1$ for all $\theta \in]0, \hat{\theta}[$ and $i \in \{1, 2, \ldots, n\}$, implying $\boldsymbol{\eta}(\theta) > \boldsymbol{\xi}(\theta)$ for $\theta \in]0, \hat{\theta}[$. Consequently, if (4.7.4) holds, there exists $\varepsilon \in \mathbb{R}_{++}$ such that for $\theta \in]0, \hat{\theta}[$

$$\boldsymbol{\xi}(\theta) \in \text{isoquant (4.7.11)}, \qquad \boldsymbol{\eta}(\theta) \in \text{isoquant (4.7.11)},$$
$$(1 - \varepsilon)\,\boldsymbol{\eta}(\theta) \notin \{\mathbf{x} \mid \Phi(\mathbf{x}) \geqq \theta\bar{u}\}, \qquad (1 - \varepsilon)\,\boldsymbol{\eta}(\theta) > \boldsymbol{\xi}(\theta),$$

contradicting (4.7.10). Accordingly, for $\mathbf{x} > \mathbf{0}$, $\mathbf{y} > \mathbf{0}$,

$$g(\mathbf{y}/|\mathbf{y}|) = g(\bar{\mathbf{y}}/|\bar{\mathbf{y}}|) = g(\bar{\mathbf{x}}/|\bar{\mathbf{x}}|) = g(\mathbf{x}/|\mathbf{x}|). \tag{4.7.12}$$

Now let $\mathbf{x} \geq \mathbf{0}$ and $\mathbf{y} > \mathbf{0}$. The foregoing argument to show (4.7.12) applies by merely deleting those subscripts $i \in \{1, 2, \ldots, n\}$ for which $\bar{x}_i = 0$, thus obtaining $\boldsymbol{\eta}(\theta) > \boldsymbol{\xi}(\theta)$ for $\theta > \bar{\theta}$ and $\theta \in [0, \hat{\theta}[$ in the two cases discussed, leading to similar contradictions of (4.7.10). ■

By similar arguments, Goldman and Shephard [1972] have also proved:

4.7.13 **Theorem.** *In order that (4.7.4) hold for (4.7.5) with quasiconcavity satisfied on* $\mathbb{R}^n_+$ *it is necessary that the exponent* $g(\mathbf{x}/|\mathbf{x}|)$ *be a positive constant for all* $\mathbf{x}$ *such that* $\Phi(\lambda\mathbf{x}) > 0$ *for some* $\lambda \in \mathbb{R}_{++}$.

4.7.14 **Remark.** Whereas semihomogeneous functions are homogeneous of a fixed degree along a given ray the following generalization of the homogeneous functions by Eichhorn and Oettli [1969] and Eichhorn [1970, pp. 100–102] does not necessarily give rise to a parabola along a given ray. A function $\Phi: \mathbb{R}^n_+ \to \mathbb{R}_+$ (a production or utility function, say) that satisfies a functional equation of the form

$$\begin{aligned} &\Phi(\mathbf{x}) = f(|\mathbf{x}|)\,\Phi(\mathbf{x}/|\mathbf{x}|), \qquad \text{where} \quad \mathbf{x} \geq \mathbf{0} \text{ and} \\ &f: \mathbb{R}_{++} \to \mathbb{R}_{++} \text{ is monotonically increasing, } f(1) = 1, \end{aligned} \tag{4.7.15}$$

is called *quasihomogeneous*. Quasihomogeneous production correspondences will be introduced in Section 12.4.

5

The Generalized Distributivity and Associativity Equation

FRANK STEHLING, University of Karlsruhe

In Section 1.10 it was shown that some problems in the theory of technical progress yield functional equations of the Cauchy type. In Sections 5.1–5.3 a systematic treatment of the most important concepts of technical progress is given; this exposition provides motivations and generalizations of the notions of neutral technical progress introduced in Section 1.10. The problem of compatibility of different kinds of generalized technical progress will yield the *generalized associativity equation*

$$\psi^1(\phi^1(x, y), z) = \psi^2(x, \phi^2(y, z)) \tag{5.0.1}$$

where $(x, y, z) \in \mathbb{R}^3_{++}$ and $\psi^1, \phi^1, \psi^2, \phi^2$ are functions mapping $\mathbb{R}^2_{++}$ into $\mathbb{R}_+$, and the *generalized distributivity equation*

$$\psi^1(\phi^1(x, y), z) = \psi^3(\phi^3(x, z), \phi^4(y, z)) \tag{5.0.2}$$

where $(x, y, z) \in \mathbb{R}^3_{++}$ and again $\psi^1, \phi^1, \psi^3, \phi^3, \phi^4$ are functions mapping $\mathbb{R}^2_{++}$ into $\mathbb{R}_+$.

5.1 Special Kinds of Neutral Technical Progress: Definitions

Let $F : \mathbb{R}^3_+ \to \mathbb{R}_+$ or $F : \mathbb{R}^2_{++} \times \mathbb{R}_+ \to \mathbb{R}_+$ be a macroeconomical production function. $F(K, L, t)$ is the maximum quantity of output (usually measured as gross national product) attainable with capital $K > 0$ and labor input $L > 0$ at time t. Alternatively, t can be interpreted as an index of the state of technology. It is well known that only a special kind of technical progress

ISBN 0-201-01948-5/01949-3 PBK

(so-called autonomous technical progress) can be described in this way (see Kalmbach [1972, p. 64]).

A priori, the dependence of the production function on technical progress can be arbitrary. But some hypotheses have been introduced in production theory that assert the invariance of certain relations between economic variables under the impact of technical progress. According to the variables whose relations remain invariant, we speak of a certain type of *neutral technical progress*.

5.1.1 **Definition.** A production function $F : \mathbb{R}^3_{++} \to \mathbb{R}_+$ or $F : \mathbb{R}^2_{++} \times \mathbb{R}_+ \to \mathbb{R}_+$ is called *neoclassical* if F possesses continuous first and second partial derivatives with respect to K and L with

$$F_K(K, L, t) := \frac{\partial F}{\partial K}(K, L, t) > 0, \qquad F_L(K, L, t) := \frac{\partial F}{\partial L}(K, L, t) > 0,$$

$$F_{KK}(K, L, t) := \frac{\partial^2 F}{\partial K^2}(K, L, t) < 0, \quad F_{LL}(K, L, t) := \frac{\partial^2 F}{\partial L^2}(K, L, t) < 0$$

for $(K, L, t) \in \mathbb{R}^3_{++}$.

5.1.2 **Definition.** The neoclassical production function $F : \mathbb{R}^3_{++} \to \mathbb{R}_+$ or $F: \mathbb{R}^2_{++} \times \mathbb{R}_+ \to \mathbb{R}_+$ represents

(i) *Hicks neutral technical progress* if F is linearly homogeneous with respect to K and L and a function $G^1 : \mathbb{R}_{++} \to \mathbb{R}_+$ exists with

$$s_{KL} := \frac{F_K(K, L, t)}{F_L(K, L, t)} = G^1\left(\frac{K}{L}\right) \quad \text{for} \quad (K, L, t) \in \mathbb{R}^3_{++}; \tag{5.1.3}$$

(ii) *Harrod neutral technical progress* if F is linearly homogeneous with respect to K and L and a function $G^2 : \mathbb{R}_+ \to \mathbb{R}_{++}$ exists with

$$F_K(K, L, t) = G^2\left(\frac{F(K, L, t)}{K}\right) \quad \text{for} \quad (K, L, t) \in {}^3_{++}; \tag{5.1.4}$$

(iii) *Solow neutral technical progress* if F is linearly homogeneous with respect to K and L and a function $G^3 : \mathbb{R}_+ \to \mathbb{R}_{++}$ exists with

$$F_L(K, L, t) = G^3\left(\frac{F(K, L, t)}{L}\right) \quad \text{for} \quad (K, L, t) \in \mathbb{R}^3_{++}, \tag{5.1.5}$$

(iv) *Beckmann–Sato neutral technical progress* if F is linearly homogeneous with respect to K and L and if there exists a function $G^4 : \mathbb{R}_+ \to \mathbb{R}$ with

$$\sigma_{KL} := \frac{F_K(K, L, t) \cdot F_L(K, L, t)}{F(K, L, t) \cdot F_{KL}(K, L, t)} = G^4\left(\frac{L \cdot F\ (K, L, t)}{F(K, L, t)}\right)$$

$$\text{for} \quad (K, L, t) \in \mathbb{R}^3_{++}. \tag{5.1.6}$$

By definition, in an economy with constant returns to scale, Hicks neutral technical progress prevails if the *marginal rate of substitution* (s_{KL}) *between capital and labor* is an invariant function (G^1) of the capital intensity; Harrod (Solow) neutral technical progress prevails if the *marginal product of capital* F_K (labor F_L) is an invariant function of capital (labor) productivity $F(K, L, t)/K$ ($F(K, L, t)/L$); Beckmann–Sato neutral technical progress prevails if the *elasticity* σ_{KL} *of substitution between K and L* is an invariant function of the share of labor.

It is well known that a certain type of neutral technical progress implies a special form of the production function representing this type (see, e.g. Uzawa [1961]; Sato and Beckmann [1968]):

The neoclassical production function F represents

(i) Hicks neutral technical progress if and only if F is of the form

$$F(K, L, t) = \phi^1(t) \cdot \psi^1(K, L) \qquad \text{for} \quad (K, L, t) \in \mathbb{R}^3_{++} \tag{5.1.7}$$

with a linearly homogeneous function ψ^1;

(ii) Harrod neutral technical progress if and only if F is of the form

$$F(K, L, t) = \psi^2(K, \varphi^2(t) \cdot L) \qquad \text{for} \quad (K, L, t) \in \mathbb{R}^3_{++} \tag{5.1.8}$$

with a linearly homogeneous function ψ^2;

(iii) Solow neutral technical progress if and only if F is of the form

$$F(K, L, t) = \psi^3(\varphi^3(t) \cdot K, L) \qquad \text{for} \quad (K, L, t) \in \mathbb{R}^3_{++} \tag{5.1.9}$$

with a linearly homogeneous function ψ^3;

(iv) Beckmann–Sato neutral technical progress only if F is of the form

$$F(K, L, t) = \psi^4(\phi^4(t) \cdot K, \phi^5(t) \cdot L) \qquad \text{for} \quad (K, L, t) \in \mathbb{R}^3_{++} \tag{5.1.10}$$

with a linearly homogeneous function ψ^4;
where the functions ψ^1, ψ^2, ψ^3, ψ^4, ϕ^1, ϕ^2, ϕ^3, ϕ^4, and ϕ^5 satisfy certain positivity and differentiability conditions.

Note that these results show the connection between the original neutrality concepts and those used in Section 1.10.

Since it cannot be expected that in every economy only constant returns to scale prevail, the types of neutral technical progress have been generalized in the following way (see Beckmann [1974]; Stehling [1974c, pp. 4–5]):

5.1.11 **Definition.** The neoclassical production function $F : \mathbb{R}^3_{++} \to \mathbb{R}_+$ or $F : \mathbb{R}^2_{++} \times \mathbb{R}_+ \to \mathbb{R}_+$ represents

(i) *generalized Hicks neutral technical progress* if a function $G^1 : \mathbb{R}_{++} \to \to \mathbb{R}_{++}$ exists with (5.1.3),

(ii) *generalized Harrod neutral technical progress* if a function $G^2 : \mathbb{R}_{+} \to \to \mathbb{R}_{++}$ exists with (5.1.4),

(iii) *generalized Solow neutral technical progress* if a function $G^3 : \mathbb{R}_{+} \to \to \mathbb{R}_{++}$ exists with (5.1.5).

According to the results for linearly homogeneous production functions, it can be shown (see Beckmann [1974]; Stehling [1974, pp. 5–7]) that a certain type of generalized technical progress implies a special form of the production function representing this type:

The neoclassical production function F represents

(i) generalized Hicks neutral technical progress if and only if F is of the form

$$F(K, L, t) = \psi^1(\phi^1(K, L), t) \qquad \text{for} \quad (K, L, t) \in \mathbb{R}^3_{++} \qquad (5.1.12)$$

with a linearly homogeneous function ϕ^1;

(ii) generalized Harrod neutral technical progress if and only if F is of the form

$$F(K, L, t) = \psi^2(K, \phi^2(L, t)) \qquad \text{for} \quad (K, L\ t) \in \mathbb{R}^3_{++} \qquad (5.1.13)$$

with a linearly homogeneous function ψ^2;

(iii) generalized Solow neutral technical progress if and only if F is of the form

$$F(K, L, t) = \psi^3(\phi^3(K, t), L) \qquad \text{for} \quad (K, L, t) \in \mathbb{R}^3_{++} \qquad (5.1.14)$$

with a linearly homogeneous function ψ^3;
where the functions ψ^1, ψ^2, ψ^3, ϕ^1, ϕ^2, and ϕ^3 again satisfy certain positivity and differentiability conditions.

In view of these results and (5.1.10), the following generalization suggests itself.

5.1.15 **Definition.** The neoclassical production function $F : \mathbb{R}^3_{++} \to \mathbb{R}_+$ or $F : \mathbb{R}^2_{++} \times \mathbb{R}_+ \to \mathbb{R}_+$ represents *generalized Beckmann–Sato neutral technical progress* if F is of the form

$$F(K, L, t) = \psi^4(\phi^4(K, t), \phi^5(L, t)) \qquad \text{for} \quad (K, L, t) \in \mathbb{R}^3_{++}$$

with a linearly homogeneous, twice continuously differentiable function ψ^4 and with positive-valued functions ϕ^4 and ϕ^5 with continuous first and second derivatives with respect to the first argument.

Definitions of the different types of generalized neutral technical progress can be extended to production processes with more than two factors of production; see Stehling [1974c, p. 50; 1977] and Gehrig [1976, pp. 12–31].

By (5.1.7)–(5.1.10) and (5.1.12)–(5.1.15), the question of the compatibility of different kinds of (generalized) neutral technical progress leads to the problem of solving certain functional equations. In Section 1.10 the compatibility of certain kinds of (nongeneralized) neutral technical progress was explored; in the following the more general case of the compatibility of different kinds of generalized neutral technical progress is treated. For a similar analysis of the compatibility of different kinds of neutral technical progress in the case of production with an arbitrary (but finite) number of production factors, see Stehling [1974c, pp. 49–77; 1977] and Gehrig [1976].

5.2 The Generalized Distributivity Equation: Generalized Hicks and Beckmann–Sato Neutral Technical Progress

Let $F : \mathbb{R}^2_{++} \times \mathbb{R}_+ \times \mathbb{R}_+$ be a production function depending on the arguments K, L, and t. Our purpose is to determine the structure of F if F represents both generalized Hicks and generalized Beckmann–Sato neutral technical progress. The assumptions on F are the following.

F is neoclassical. (5.2.1)

F represents generalized Hicks neutral technical progress in the sense that

$$F(K, L, t) = \psi^1(\phi^1(K, L), t) \qquad \text{for} \quad (K, L) \in \mathbb{R}^2_{++}, t \in \mathbb{R}_+ \tag{5.2.2}$$

where ψ^1 possesses continuous first and second partial derivatives with respect to the first argument and ϕ^1 is linearly homogeneous and positive valued with continuous first and second partial derivatives with respect to both arguments.

F represents generalized Beckmann–Sato neutral technical progress in the sense that

$$F(K, L, t) = \psi^4(\phi^4(K, t), \phi^5(L, t)) \qquad \text{for} \quad (K, L) \in \mathbb{R}^2_{++}, t \in \mathbb{R}_+ \tag{5.2.3}$$

with a linearly homogeneous, twice continuously differentiable function ψ^4 and positive-valued functions ϕ^4 and ϕ^5 with continuous first and second derivatives with respect to the first argument (for all $t \geqq 0$).

(i) There exists a $t^* > 0$ such that

$$\{\phi^4(K, t^*) \mid 0 < K < \infty\} = \mathbb{R}_{++} = \{\phi^5(L, t^*) \mid 0 < L < \infty\}.$$

(ii) $F(K, L, 0) = F_0 =$ constant for all $(K, L) \in \mathbb{R}^2_{++}$.
(iii) $t \to \phi^4(K, t)$ and $t \to \phi^5(L, t)$ are continuous at $t = 0$ for all $(K, L) \in \mathbb{R}^2_{++}$. (5.2.4)

Property (5.2.4i) means that both the capital–technology index ϕ^4 and the labor-technology index ϕ^5 by which the production function is representable run through all positive real numbers and that there exists a special state $t^* > 0$ of the technology where every amount of output is obtainable that can be produced sometime with a certain capital stock and labor input. Condition (5.2.4ii) says that output at $t = 0$ is independent of the input quantities. This may be justified if $t = 0$ is interpreted as an index that represents a very low level of technology in which capital and labor cannot be used effectively. Condition (5.2.4iii) is a technical assumption and does not restrict generality essentially.

In order to determine all production functions that satisfy assumptions (5.2.1)–(5.2.4), we have to solve the *generalized distributivity equation*

$$\psi^1(\phi^1(K, L), t) = \psi^4(\phi^4(K, t), \phi^5(L, t)) \tag{5.2.5}$$

for $(K, L) \in \mathbb{R}^2_{++}$ and $t \in \mathbb{R}_+$ under the additional assumptions made in (5.2.1)–(5.2.4).

First some implications of (5.2.1)–(5.2.4) are listed that can be proved very easily. Denoting by ψ^1_1 the first partial derivative of ψ^1 with respect to the first argument, by ϕ^1_K the first partial derivative of ϕ^1 with respect to K, and similarly for the other functions and their arguments, we have

$$\begin{array}{llll} \psi^1_1(x, t) \neq 0, & \phi^1_K(K, L) \neq 0, & \phi^1_L(K, L) \neq 0, & \\ \psi^4_1(y, z) \neq 0, & \phi^4_K(K, t) \neq 0, & \phi^4_2(L, t) \neq 0, & \phi^5_L(L, t) \neq 0, \end{array} \tag{5.2.6}$$

for all $x, y, K, L, t \in \mathbb{R}_{++}$. This shows that ψ^4 is strictly monotonic in both arguments, which implies, in view of (5.2.4ii) and the positivity of ϕ^4 and ϕ^5, that

$$\varphi^4(K, 0) = \text{const.} =: a > 0, \qquad \phi^5(L, 0) = \text{const.} =: b > 0 \tag{5.2.7}$$

for all $K, L \in \mathbb{R}_{++}$. Moreover, from (5.2.4i) with (5.2.6) it follows that the equations

$$\phi^4(K, t^*) = y \qquad \text{and} \qquad \phi^5(L, t^*) = z$$

are uniquely solvable for K and L for every $y \in \mathbb{R}_{++}$ and $z \in \mathbb{R}_{++}$, respectively. Denoting the inverses by θ and $\bar{\theta}$, respectively, such that

$$K = \theta(y) \quad \text{and} \quad L = \bar{\theta}(z) \qquad \text{for} \quad y, z \in \mathbb{R}_{++}, \tag{5.2.8}$$

we see that θ and $\bar{\theta}$ are continuously differentiable and strictly monotonic, by virtue of the same properties of ϕ^4 and ϕ^5 with respect to the first argument for $t = t^* > 0$.

5.2.9 **Theorem.** *Assume (5.2.1)–(5.2.4). Then the solutions of the generalized distributivity equation (5.2.5) are given by*

$$\psi^1(x, t) = h(f(t)\, g^{-1}(x) + \alpha(t) + \beta(t)) \quad \textit{for} \quad x > 0, \quad t \geqq 0, \tag{5.2.10}$$

$$\phi^1(K, L) = g(k(K) + 1(L)) \quad \textit{for} \quad K > 0, \quad L > 0, \tag{5.2.11}$$

$$\psi^4(y, z) = h(m(y) + n(z)) \quad \textit{for} \quad y > 0, \quad z > 0, \tag{5.2.12}$$

$$\phi^4(K, t) = m^{-1}(f(t)\, k(K) + \alpha(t)) \quad \textit{for} \quad K > 0, \quad t \geqq 0, \tag{5.2.13}$$

$$\phi^5(L, t) = n^{-1}(f(t)\, l(L) + \beta(t)) \quad \textit{for} \quad L > 0, \quad t \geqq 0, \tag{5.2.14}$$

with certain continuously differentiable and strictly monotonic functions g, h, k, l, m, n and certain functions α, β, f with f(0) = 0.

Proof. We follow essentially the proof of Hosszú (see Aczél [1966, pp. 333 ff.]), who determined local solutions of (5.2.5). By differentiation of (5.2.5),

$$\psi_1^1(\phi^1(K, L), t) \cdot \phi_K^1(K, L) = \psi_1^4(\phi^4(K, t), \phi^5(L, t)) \cdot \phi_K^4(K, t),$$
$$\psi_1^1(\phi^1(K, L), t) \cdot \phi_L^1(K, L) = \psi_2^4(\phi^4(K, t), \phi^5(L, t)) \cdot \phi_L^5(L, t).$$

Because of (5.2.6), the first of these equations can be divided by the second:

$$\frac{\phi_K^1(K, L)}{\phi_L^1(K, L)} = \frac{\psi_1^4(\phi^4(K, t), \phi^5(L, t))}{\psi_2^4(\phi^4(K, t), \phi^5(L, t))} \cdot \frac{\phi_K^4(K, t)}{\phi_L^5(L, t)};$$

and hence

$$\frac{\dfrac{\phi_K^1(K, L)}{\phi_L^1(K, L)} \cdot \dfrac{\phi_K^1(U, V)}{\phi_L^1(U, V)}}{\dfrac{\phi_K^1(K, V)}{\phi_L^1(K, V)} \cdot \dfrac{\phi_K^1(U, L)}{\phi_L^1(U, L)}} = \frac{\dfrac{\phi_1^4(\phi^4(K, t), \phi^5(L, t))}{\psi_2^4(\phi^4(K, t), \phi^5(L, t))} \cdot \dfrac{\psi_1^4(\phi^4(U, t), \phi^5(V, t))}{\psi_2^4(\phi^4(U, t), \phi^5(V, t))}}{\dfrac{\psi_1^4(\phi^4(K, t), \phi^5(V, t))}{\psi_2^4(\phi^4(K, t), \phi^5(V, t))} \cdot \dfrac{\psi_1^4(\phi^4(U, t), \phi^5(L, t))}{\psi_2^4(\phi^4(K, t), \phi^5(L, t))}}$$

for all $K, L, U, V, t \in \mathbb{R}_{++}$. Since ϕ^4 and ϕ^5 are continuous in t at $t = 0$ and ψ_1^4 and ψ_2^4 are continuous in both arguments, the last equation is valid even for $t = 0$. But for $t = 0$ the right-hand side of this equation is equal to 1. Setting $U = c =$ constant and $V = d =$ constant, we have

$$\phi_K^1(K, L) = \frac{k'(K)}{l'(L)}\, \phi_L^1(K, L) \tag{5.2.15}$$

where the functions k and l are defined respectively by

$$k(K) := \phi_L^1(c, d) \int \frac{\phi_K^1(K', d)}{\phi_L^1(K', d)}\, dK', \tag{5.2.16}$$

$$l(L) := \phi_K^1(c, d) \int \frac{\phi_L^1(c, L')}{\phi_K^1(c, L')}\, dL'. \tag{5.2.17}$$

For constant $\phi^1(K, L)$, the partial differential equation (5.2.15) is equivalent to

$$\frac{dK(L)}{dL} = -\frac{l'(L)}{k'(K(L))}$$

where $dK(L)/dL$ is the slope of the isoquant $\{(K, L) \mid \phi^1(K, L) = \text{const}\}$ at the point L. The last equation implies

$$k(K) = -l(L) + a$$

where a, the constant of integration, depends on the fixed $\phi^1(K, L)$; hence we write $a = A(\phi^1(K, L))$ and have

$$A(\phi^1(K, L)) = k(K) + l(L).$$

We show that A is a strictly monotonic function of φ^1. For this, assume that $\hat{\phi}^1 > \bar{\phi}^1$. Since ϕ^1_K and ϕ^1_L must be simultaneously either positive or negative valued (an implication of $F_K(K, L, t) > 0 < F_L(K, L, t)$), the functions k and l must be simultaneously strictly increasing or strictly decreasing. At first, assume k and l to have the first property. Then,

$$\hat{\phi}^1 = \phi^1(K_1, L_1) > \bar{\phi}^1 = \phi^1(K_2, L_2) \quad \text{with} \quad K_1 > K_2, L_1 > L_2.$$

Therefore,

$$\begin{aligned} A(\hat{\phi}^1) &= A(\phi^1(K_1, L_1)) = k(K_1) + l(L_1) > k(K_2) + l(L_2) \\ &= A(\phi^1(K_2, L_2)) = A(\bar{\phi}^1), \end{aligned}$$

which shows that in this case A is strictly increasing. Similarly, if k and l are both strictly decreasing, A is strictly decreasing, too. Hence, in each case A^{-1} exists, is continuously differentiable and strictly monotonic, and

$$\phi^1(K, L) = g(k(K) + l(L))$$

with $g = A^{-1}$. This proves (5.2.11).

By inserting (5.2.11) into (5.2.5) we get for $t = t^* > 0$

$$\psi^1\big(g(k(K) + l(L)), t^*\big) = \psi^4(\phi^4(K, t^*), \phi^5(L, t^*)) \tag{5.2.18}$$

for $(K, L) \in \mathbb{R}^2_{++}$. With (5.2.8) and the definitions

$$\left.\begin{aligned} m(y) &:= k(\theta(y)) && \text{for} \quad y \in \mathbb{R}_{++}, \\ n(z) &:= l(\bar{\theta}(z)) && \text{for} \quad z \in \mathbb{R}_{++}, \\ h(w) &:= \psi^1(g(w), t^*) && \text{for} \quad w \in D \subseteq \mathbb{R}, \end{aligned}\right\} \tag{5.2.19}$$

Eq. (5.2.18) implies

$$\psi^4(y, z) = h(m(y) + n(z)) \quad \text{for} \quad (y, z) \in \mathbb{R}^2_{++}.$$

Here, m, n, and h are strictly monotonic, continuously differentiable functions, because of the same properties of k, θ, l, $\bar{\theta}$, ψ^1, and g, which proves (5.2.12).

Substitution of (5.2.11) and (5.2.12) in (5.2.5) yields

$$\psi^1\big(g(k(K) + l(L)), t\big) = h\big(m(\phi^4(K, t)) + n(\phi^5(L, t)\big). \qquad (5.2.20)$$

Let us denote briefly

$$\begin{aligned} u :&= k(K), \qquad v := l(L), \\ P(w, t) :&= h^{-1}\left(\psi^1(g(w), t)\right), \\ M(u, t) :&= m\big(\phi^4(k^{-1}(u), t)\big), \\ N(v, t) :&= n\big(\phi^5(k^{-1}(v), t)\big). \end{aligned} \qquad (5.2.21)$$

The functions $P, M,$ and N are continuous with respect to the first argument, and (5.2.20) can be rewritten as

$$P(u + v, t) = M(u, t) + N(v, t) \qquad \text{for } t \geqq 0 \qquad (5.2.22)$$

where

$$\begin{aligned} u \in I_1 :&= \{\bar{u} \mid \exists\, K > 0 \text{ with } \bar{u} = k(K)\}, \\ v \in I_2 :&= \{\bar{v} \mid \exists\, L > 0 \text{ with } \bar{v} = l(L)\}. \end{aligned}$$

By virtue of the continuity and strict monotonicity of k and l, I_1 and I_2 are open intervals. We know from Theorem 2.6.3 that in this case every solution of (5.2.22) that is continuous with respect to the first argument can be written as

$$\left.\begin{aligned} P(u + v, t) &= f(t)\cdot(u + v) + \alpha(t) + \beta(t) && \text{for } t \geqq 0,\ u \in I_1,\ v \in I_2 \\ M(u, t) &= f(t)\, u + \alpha(t) && \text{for } t \geqq 0,\ u \in I_1, \\ N(v, t) &= f(t)\, v + \beta(t) && \text{for } t \geqq 0,\ v \in I_2 \end{aligned}\right\} \qquad (5.2.23)$$

with certain functions f, α, and β. By resubstitution of (5.2.21) we obtain from (5.2.23)

$$\psi^1(x, t) = h\big(P(g^{-1}(x), t)\big) = h(f(t)\, g^{-1}(x) + \alpha(t) + \beta(t)), \qquad (5.2.24)$$

$$\phi^4(K, t) = m^{-1}\big(M(k(K), t)\big) = m^{-1}(f(t)\, k(K) + \alpha(t)), \qquad (5.2.25)$$

$$\phi^5(L, t) = n^{-1}\big(N(l(L), t)\big) = n^{-1}(f(t)\, l(L) + \beta(t)) \qquad (5.2.26)$$

for all $t \geqq 0$.

Formula (5.2.24) is valid for all $x > 0$ since, for $u \in I_1$ and $v \in I_2$,

$$\psi^1(g(u + v), t) = h(P(u + v, t)) = h(f(t)\,(u + v) + \alpha(t) + \beta(t))$$

and

$$\begin{aligned} &\{x \mid \exists\, u \in I_1,\ v \in I_2 \text{ with } x = g(u + v)\} \\ &= \big\{x \mid \exists\, (K, L) \in \mathbb{R}^2_{++} \text{ with } x = g(k(K) + l(L))\big\} \\ &= \{x \mid \exists\, (K, L) \in \mathbb{R}^2_{++} \text{ with } x = \phi^1(K, L)\} = \mathbb{R}_{++}, \end{aligned}$$

since ϕ^1 is positive valued and linearly homogeneous. Formulas (5.2.25) and (5.2.26) are valid for $K > 0$ and $L > 0$ since

$$\{K \mid \exists\, u \in I_1 \text{ with } u = k(K)\} = \{L \mid \exists\, v \in I_2 \text{ with } v = l(L)\} = \mathbb{R}_{++},$$

by definition of the intervals I_1 and I_2. Hence, (5.2.10), (5.2.13), and (5.2.14) are proved. Finally, because of (5.2.7) and (5.2.25), we have

$$\phi^4(K, 0) = m^{-1}(f(0)\,k(K) + \alpha(0)) = \text{const} = a > 0$$

for all $K > 0$, which is possible, in view of the strict monotonicity of k and m, if and only if $f(0) = 0$. This completes the proof of the theorem. ■

An immediate consequence of Theorem 5.2.9 is

5.2.27 **Corollary.** *Every production function* $F\colon \mathbb{R}^2_{++} + \mathbb{R}_+ \to \mathbb{R}_+$ *satisfying 5.2.1–5.2.4 is of the form*

$$F(K, L, t) = h(f(t)\,k(K) + f(t)\,l(L) + \xi(t)) \tag{5.2.28}$$

with strictly monotonic, continuously differentiable functions h, k, and l and certain functions f and ξ with $f(0) = 0$.

Proof. By Theorem 5.2.9, for all $K > 0$, $L > 0$, $t \geqq 0$

$$\begin{aligned} F(K, L, t) = \psi^1(\phi^1(K, L), t) &= h\big(f(t)\,g^{-1}[g(k(K) + l(L))] + \alpha(t) + \beta(t)\big) \\ &= h(f(t)\,k(K) + f(t)\,l(L) + \xi(t)) \end{aligned}$$

with $\xi(t) := \alpha(t) + \beta(t)$, where the functions h, k, l, and f have the asserted properties. ■

In order to determine the unknown functions h, k, and l in (5.2.28), we will make use of the additional information that ϕ^1 and ψ^4, given by (5.2.11) and (5.2.12), are linearly homogeneous.

5.2.29 **Theorem.** *If a production function F satisfies (5.2.1)–(5.2.4), the functions h, k, and l by which F is representable according to Corollary 5.2.27 are given by*

$$k(K) = \gamma \log K + \delta \quad \textit{and} \quad l(L) = \gamma' \log L + \delta' \tag{5.2.30a}$$

or

$$k(K) = \varepsilon K^{-\varrho} + \sigma \quad \textit{and} \quad l(L) = \varepsilon' L^{-\varrho} + \sigma', \tag{5.2.30b}$$

$$h(x) = \bar{c}\, e^{x/(\bar{\gamma} + \bar{\gamma}')} \tag{5.2.31a}$$

or

$$h(x) = \bar{c}\cdot\left(\frac{x - \bar{\sigma} - \bar{\sigma}'}{\bar{\varepsilon} + \bar{\varepsilon}'}\right)^{-1/\bar{\varrho}} \quad \begin{cases} \textit{for} \ \ \bar{\varepsilon} > 0 \ \ \textit{and} \ \ x \geqq \bar{\sigma} + \bar{\sigma}', \\ \textit{for} \ \ \bar{\varepsilon} < 0 \ \ \textit{and} \ \ x \leqq \bar{\sigma} + \bar{\sigma}', \end{cases} \tag{5.2.31b}$$

where γ, δ, γ', δ', ε, ϱ, σ, ε', σ', $\bar{c}$, $\bar{\gamma}$, $\bar{\gamma}'$, $\bar{\sigma}$, $\bar{\sigma}'$, $\bar{\varepsilon}$, $\bar{\varepsilon}'$, $\bar{\varrho}$ are real constants, *γ, γ', ε, ϱ, ε', $\bar{\gamma}$, $\bar{\gamma}'$, $\bar{\varepsilon}$, $\bar{\varepsilon}'$, $\bar{\varrho}$ being different from 0 and $\bar{c} > 0$ with*

$$\operatorname{sgn}\gamma = \operatorname{sgn}\gamma', \quad \operatorname{sgn}\varepsilon = \operatorname{sgn}\varepsilon', \quad \operatorname{sgn}\bar{\gamma} = \operatorname{sgn}\bar{\gamma}', \quad \operatorname{sgn}\bar{\varepsilon} = \operatorname{sgn}\bar{\varepsilon}'.$$

Proof. By assumption (5.2.2) and Theorem 5.2.9, we know that $F(K, L, t) = \psi^1(\phi^1(K, L), t)$ where

$$\phi^1(K, L) = g(k(K) + l(L)) \qquad \text{for} \quad (K, L) \in \mathbb{R}^2_{++},$$

and ϕ^1 is linearly homogeneous. Hence, ϕ^1 is a so-called generalized quasilinear function. Such functions were considered in Chapter 2, but here the structure of ϕ^1 is not of interest; what have to be determined are the functions k and l (and h). We start in the same way as in the proof of Theorem 2.4.1 in order to get

$$d_\lambda(u + v) = e_\lambda(u) + n_\lambda(v) \tag{5.2.32}$$

where

$$\left.\begin{aligned} u :&= k(K), \qquad v := l(L),\\ d_\lambda(x) :&= g_\lambda^{-1}(g(x)),\\ e_\lambda(u) :&= k(k_\lambda^{-1}(u)),\\ n_\lambda(v) :&= l(l_\lambda^{-1}(v)),\\ g_\lambda^{-1}(x) :&= g^{-1}(\lambda x),\\ k_\lambda^{-1}(u) :&= \lambda k^{-1}(u) = \lambda K,\\ l_\lambda^{-1}(v) :&= \lambda l^{-1}(v) = \lambda L. \end{aligned}\right\} \tag{5.2.33}$$

The functions d_λ, l_λ, and n_λ are continuous because of the same property of all other functions defined in (5.2.33). Functional equation (5.2.32) is valid for

$$u \in I_1 := \{\bar{u} \mid \exists\, K > 0 \quad \text{with} \quad \bar{u} = k(K)\},$$
$$v \in I_2 := \{\bar{v} \mid \exists\, L > 0 \quad \text{with} \quad \bar{v} = l(L)\}.$$

By Theorem 2.3.6, the continuous solutions of (5.2.32) are

$$\begin{aligned} d_\lambda(u + v) &= c(\lambda)\cdot(u + v) + a(\lambda) + \bar{a}(\lambda),\\ e_\lambda(u) &= c(\lambda)\cdot u + a(\lambda),\\ n_\lambda(v) &= c(\lambda)\cdot v + \bar{a}(\lambda). \end{aligned}$$

Using definitions (5.2.33), we get

$$\begin{aligned} c(\lambda)\, k(K) + a(\lambda) &= k(\lambda K),\\ c(\lambda)\, l(L) + \bar{a}(\lambda) &= l(\lambda L). \end{aligned}$$

The solutions of the last two functional equations were determined in Section 2.7. Taking into account that k is strictly monotonic, we get from Theorem 2.7.3

$$k(K) = \gamma \log K + \delta \qquad \text{and} \qquad l(L) = \gamma' \log L + \delta' \tag{5.2.34}$$

or

$$k(K) = \varepsilon K^{-\varrho} + \sigma \qquad \text{and} \qquad l(L) = \varepsilon' L^{-\varrho} + \sigma' \tag{5.2.35}$$

where (5.2.34) belongs to the case in which $c(\lambda) \equiv 1$ and (5.2.35) to the case in which $c(\lambda) \not\equiv 1$. Here, $\gamma, \delta, \gamma', \delta', \varepsilon, \varrho, \sigma, \varepsilon', \sigma'$ are real constants; moreover, $\gamma, \gamma', \varepsilon, \varrho$, and ε' are different from 0. The strict monotonicity of g, k, and l implies

$$\operatorname{sgn} \gamma = \operatorname{sgn} \gamma', \qquad \operatorname{sgn} \varepsilon = \operatorname{sgn} \varepsilon'.$$

In order to determine the function h in (5.2.28) we use the linear homogeneity and special form of ψ^4 given by (5.2.12):

$$\psi^4(y, z) = h(m(y) + n(z)) \qquad \text{for} \quad (y, z) \in \mathbb{R}^2_{++}.$$

By exactly the same arguments as before we get

$$m(y) = \bar{\gamma} \log y + \bar{\delta} \qquad \text{and} \qquad n(z) = \bar{\gamma}' \log z + \bar{\delta}' \tag{5.2.36}$$

or

$$m(y) = \bar{\varepsilon} y^{-\bar{\varrho}} + \bar{\sigma} \qquad \text{and} \qquad n(z) = \bar{\varepsilon}' z^{-\bar{\varrho}} + \bar{\sigma}', \tag{5.2.37}$$

where $\bar{\gamma}, \bar{\delta}, \bar{\gamma}', \bar{\delta}', \bar{\varepsilon}, \bar{\varrho}, \bar{\sigma}, \bar{\varepsilon}', \bar{\sigma}'$ are real constants, $\bar{\gamma}, \bar{\gamma}', \bar{\varepsilon}, \bar{\varrho}$, and $\bar{\varepsilon}'$ being different from 0 and satisfying

$$\operatorname{sgn} \bar{\gamma} = \operatorname{sgn} \bar{\gamma}', \qquad \operatorname{sgn} \bar{\varepsilon} = \operatorname{sgn} \bar{\varepsilon}'.$$

By the linear homogeneity of ψ^4, it follows that

$$\lambda h(m(y) + n(z)) = h(m(\lambda y) + n(\lambda z))$$

for $(\lambda, y, z) \in \mathbb{R}^3_{++}$. Inserting (5.2.36) into this equation, we easily obtain

$$h(x) = \bar{c}\, e^{x/(\bar{\gamma} + \bar{\gamma}')},$$

whereas (5.2.37) yields

$$h(x) = \bar{c} \cdot \left(\frac{x - \bar{\sigma} - \bar{\sigma}'}{\bar{\varepsilon} + \bar{\varepsilon}'} \right)^{-1/\bar{\varrho}} \qquad \begin{array}{l} \text{for} \quad \bar{\varepsilon} > 0 \quad \text{and} \quad x \geqq \bar{\sigma} + \bar{\sigma}', \\ \text{for} \quad \bar{\varepsilon} > 0 \quad \text{and} \quad x \leqq \bar{\sigma} + \bar{\sigma}', \end{array}$$

which proves the theorem. ■

We are now able to prove the main theorem:

5.2.38 **Theorem.** *(i) Every production function $F : \mathbb{R}^2_{++} \times \mathbb{R}_+ \to \mathbb{R}_+$ satisfying (5.2.1)–(5.2.4) is either of the form*

$$F(K, L, t) = r(t) K^{a_1 f(t)} \cdot L^{a_2 f(t)} \tag{5.2.39}$$

or of the form

$$F(K, L, t) = (d_1 f(t)\, K^{-\varrho} + d_2 f(t)\, L^{-\varrho} + r(t))^{-1/\bar{\varrho}} \tag{5.2.40}$$

where $f(0) = 0$ and, in the case of (5.2.39), $r(t) > 0$ for $t \geqq 0$, $0 < a_1 f(t) < 1$, $0 < a_2 f(t) < 1$ for $t > 0$; and in the case of (5.2.40), $d_1 f(t) > 0 < d_2 f(t)$ for $t > 0$, $r(t) \geqq 0$ for $t \geqq 0$ and either $-1 < \varrho$ and $0 < \varrho/\bar{\varrho} \leqq 1$ or $-1 = \varrho$ and $0 < \varrho/\bar{\varrho} < 1$.

(ii) Conversely, every production function of the form (5.2.39) or (5.2.40) with the properties listed in (i) satisfies assumptions (5.2.1)–(5.2.4), if, additionally, r and f are continuous at $t = 0$, $r(0) > 0$ *and if in the case of (5.2.40)* $r(t^*) = 0$.

Proof. (i) Because of Theorem 5.2.29 we have four possible forms of the production function, which are implied by the four possible combinations of (5.2.30a, b) and (5.2.31a, b):

(a) Combination of (5.2.30a) with (5.2.31a) leads to

$$F(K, L, t) = h(f(t)\,k(K) + f(t)\,l(L) + \xi(t)) = r(t)\,K^{a_1 f(t)} \cdot L^{a_2 f(t)} \quad (5.2.41)$$

where

$$r(t) : = \bar{c} \exp\left(\frac{1}{\bar{\gamma} + \bar{\gamma}'}[f(t)(\delta + \delta') + \xi(t)]\right) > 0,$$

$$a_1 : = \frac{\gamma}{\bar{\gamma} + \bar{\gamma}'} \neq 0, \qquad a_2 : = \frac{\gamma'}{\bar{\gamma} + \bar{\gamma}'} \neq 0.$$

(b) Combination of (5.2.30a) with (5.2.31b) leads to

$$F(K, L, t) = (b_1 f(t) \log K + b_2 f(t) \log L + r(t))^{-1/\bar{\varrho}} \quad (5.2.42)$$

where

$$b_1 : = \bar{c}^{-\bar{\varrho}} \cdot \frac{\gamma}{\bar{\varepsilon} + \bar{\varepsilon}'} \neq 0, \qquad b_2 : = \bar{c}^{-\bar{\varrho}} \cdot \frac{\gamma'}{\bar{\varepsilon} + \bar{\varepsilon}'} \neq 0,$$

$$r(t) : = \bar{c}^{-\bar{\varrho}} \cdot \frac{1}{\bar{\varepsilon} + \bar{\varepsilon}'}(f(t)(\delta + \delta') + \xi(t) - \bar{\sigma} - \bar{\sigma}')\cdot$$

Since $\{x \mid \exists\, K > 0 \text{ with } x = \log K\} = \mathbb{R}$, the function F defined by (5.2.42) does not map $\mathbb{R}^2_{++} \times \mathbb{R}_+$ into $\mathbb{R}_+$ and, therefore, cannot be a solution of our problem.

(c) Combination of (5.2.30b) with (5.2.31a) leads to

$$F(K, L, t) = r(t) \exp(c_1 f(t)\,K^{-\varrho}) \exp(c_2 f(t)\,L^{-\varrho}) \quad (5.2.43)$$

where

$$c_1 : = \frac{\varepsilon}{\bar{\gamma} + \bar{\gamma}'} \neq 0, \qquad c_2 : = \frac{\varepsilon'}{\bar{\gamma} + \bar{\gamma}'} \neq 0,$$

$$r(t) : = \bar{c} \exp\left(\frac{1}{\bar{\gamma} + \bar{\gamma}'}[f(t)(\sigma + \sigma') + \xi(t)]\right).$$

By simple calculating, it can be seen that the function F defined by (5.2.43) does not satisfy $F_{KK}(K, L, t) < 0$ and $F_K(K, L, t) > 0$ simultaneously for all $K > 0$ and fixed $L > 0$, $t > 0$; hence F is not neoclassical.

(d) Combination of (5.2.30b) with (5.2.31b) leads to

$$F(K, L, t) = (d_1 f(t)\,K^{-\varrho} + d_2 f(t)\,L^{-\varrho} + r(t))^{-1/\bar{\varrho}} \quad (5.2.44)$$

where

$$d_1 := \bar{c}^{-\bar{\varrho}} \cdot \frac{\varepsilon}{\bar{\varepsilon} + \bar{\varepsilon}'} \neq 0, \qquad d_2 := \bar{c}^{-\bar{\varrho}} \cdot \frac{\varepsilon'}{\bar{\varepsilon} + \bar{\varepsilon}'} \neq 0,$$

$$r(t) := \bar{c}^{-\bar{\varrho}} \cdot \frac{1}{\bar{\varepsilon} + \bar{\varepsilon}'} (f(t)(\sigma + \sigma') - \bar{\sigma} - \bar{\sigma}' + \xi(t)).$$

Hence we have shown that the only functions that satisfy 5.2.1–5.2.4 have to be of the form of (5.2.41) and (5.2.44), that is, of the form of (5.2.39) and (5.2.40). In the case of (5.2.39) the properties of r, a_1, a_2, and f are easy consequences of (5.2.1)–(5.2.4). In the case of (5.2.40), we must have $d_1 f(t) > 0 < d_2 f(t)$ for $t > 0$ and $r(t) \geqq 0$ for $t \geqq 0$; otherwise F is not defined for all $(K, L) \in \mathbb{R}^2_{++}$ or does not satisfy $F_K(K, L, t) > 0 < F_L(K, L, t)$. Moreover, since

$$F_K(K, L, t) = (\varrho/\bar{\varrho})\, d_1 f(t)(d_1 f(t)\, K^{-\varrho} + d_2 f(t)\, L^{-\varrho} + r(t))^{-1/\bar{\varrho}-1} \cdot K^{-\varrho-1}$$

and

$$F_{KK}(K, L, t) = (\varrho/\bar{\varrho})\, d_1 f(t)(d_1 f(t)\, K^{-\varrho} + d_2 f(t)\, L^{-\varrho} + r(t))^{-1/\bar{\varrho}-2} \cdot K^{-\varrho-2}$$
$$\cdot \big(((\varrho/\bar{\varrho}) - 1)\, d_1 f(t)\, K^{-\varrho} + (-\varrho - 1)(d_2 f(t)\, L^{-\varrho} + r(t))\big),$$

we conclude that $\varrho/\bar{\varrho} > 0$ from $F_K(K, L, t) > 0$ and hence $\varrho > -1$ and $\varrho/\bar{\varrho} \leqq 1$ or $\varrho = -1$ and $\varrho/\bar{\varrho} < 1$ from $F_{KK}(K, L, t) < 0$. In any case, $f(0) = 0$ is implied by $F_K(K, L, 0) = 0$. This proves the first part of the theorem.

(ii) Now we have to show that every function of the form of (5.2.39) and (5.2.40), with the assumed properties of f and r and of the constants a_1, a_2, d_1, d_2, ϱ, and $\bar{\varrho}$, satisfies (5.2.1)–(5.2.4.) That (5.2.39) is neoclassical follows immediately.

If we set

$$\phi^1(K, L) = K^{a_1/(a_1 + a_2)} L^{a_2/(a_1 + a_2)}, \qquad \psi^1(x, t) = r(t) \cdot x^{(a_1 + a_2) f(t)},$$
$$\phi^4(K, t) = K^{(a_1 + a_2) f(t)} \cdot r(t), \qquad \phi^5(L, t) = L^{(a_1 + a_2) f(t)} \cdot r(t),$$
$$\psi^4(y, z) = y^{a_1/(a_1 + a_2)} z^{a_2/(a_1 + a_2)},$$

the functions ϕ^1, ψ^1, ϕ^4, ϕ^5, and ψ^4 satisfy all assumptions and we have for $(K, L) \in \mathbb{R}^2_{++}$, $t \geqq 0$,

$$F(K, L, t) = \psi^1(\phi^1(K, L), t) = \psi^4(\phi^4(K, t), \phi^5(L, t)).$$

That (5.2.40) is neoclassical is a consequence of the properties of r and f and of the constants ϱ, $\bar{\varrho}$, d_1, and d_2. If we set

$$\phi^1(K, L) = (d_1 K^{-\varrho} + d_2 L^{-\varrho})^{-1/\varrho}, \qquad \psi^1(x, t) = (f(t)\, x^{-\varrho} + r(t))^{-1/\bar{\varrho}},$$
$$\phi^4(K, t) = (d_1 f(t)\, K^{-\varrho} + \tfrac{1}{2} r(t))^{-1/\bar{\varrho}}, \qquad \phi^5(L, t) = (d_1 f(t)\, L^{-\varrho} + \tfrac{1}{2} r(t))^{-1/\bar{\varrho}}$$
$$\psi^4(y, z) = (y^{-\bar{\varrho}} + z^{-\bar{\varrho}})^{-1/\bar{\varrho}},$$

the functions ϕ^1, ψ^1, ϕ^4, ϕ^5, and ψ^4 satisfy all assumptions and we have for $(K, L) \in \mathbb{R}^2_{++}$, $t \geqq 0$,

$$F(K, L, t) = \psi^1(\phi^1(K, L), t) = \psi^4((\phi^4(K, t), \phi^5(L, t)),$$

which completes the proof of the theorem. ■

5.3 The Generalized Associativity Equation: Generalized Hicks and Harrod Neutral Technical Progress

Let $F\colon \mathbb{R}^3_{++} \to \mathbb{R}_+$ again be a production function depending on the arguments K, L, and t. The purpose now is to determine the structure of F if F represents both generalized Hicks and generalized Harrod neutral technical progress. The assumptions are explicitly

$F\colon \mathbb{R}^3_{++} \to \mathbb{R}_+$ is neoclassical. (5.3.1)

F represents generalized Hicks neutral technical progress in the sense of definition 5.1.11(i). (5.3.2)

F represents generalized Harrod neutral technical progress in the sense of definition 5.1.11(ii). (5.3.3)

(i) There exists $(\hat{K}, \hat{L}) \in \mathbb{R}^2_{++}$ such that $t \to F(\hat{K}, \hat{L}, t)$ is strictly monotonic and continuous and

$$\{F(\hat{K}, \hat{L}, t) \mid 0 < t < \infty\} = \mathbb{R}_{++};$$

(ii) there exists $(L^*, t^*) \in \mathbb{R}^2_{++}$ such that

$$\{F(K, L^*, t^*) \mid 0 < K < \infty\} = \mathbb{R}_{++}. \tag{5.3.4}$$

The second part of (5.3.4i) means that every output quantity can be produced with a fixed (and suitably chosen) input of capital and labor at a certain time or state of technology; the interpretation of (5.3.4ii) is analogous.

As we know from (5.1.12), assumption (5.3.2) is equivalent to the existence of functions ψ^1 and ϕ^1 with

$$F(K, L, t) = \psi^1(\phi^1(K, L)\, t) \qquad \text{for} \quad (K, L, t) \in \mathbb{R}^3_{++} \tag{5.3.2$'$}$$

where ψ^1 is continuously differentiable with respect to the first argument and ϕ^1 is linearly homogeneous, positive valued, and continuously differentiable with respect to both arguments.

Similarly, because of (5.1.13), assumption 5.3.3 is equivalent to the existence of functions ψ^2 and ϕ^2 with

$$F(K, L, t) = \psi^2(K, \phi^2(L, t)) \qquad \text{for} \quad (K, L, t) \in \mathbb{R}^3_{++} \tag{5.3.3$'$}$$

where ψ^2 is continuously differentiable with respect to both arguments and linearly homogeneous, and ϕ^2 is positive valued and continuously differentiable with respect to the first argument. Hence we have to solve the generalized associativity equation

$$\psi^1(\phi^1(K, L), t) = \psi^2(K, \phi^2(L, t)) \tag{5.3.5}$$

using the properties of ψ^1, ϕ^1, ψ^2, and ϕ^2 and the additional assumptions (5.3.1) and (5.3.4).

Immediate consequences of (5.3.1) and the linear homogeneity and positivity of ϕ^1 are

$$\begin{aligned} &\phi^1_K(K, L) \neq 0 \neq \psi^1_1(x, t) \\ &\phi^1_L(K, L) \neq 0 \neq \phi^2_L(L, t) \end{aligned} \quad \text{for} \quad (K, L, x, t) \in \mathbb{R}^4_{++}, \tag{5.3.6}$$

$$\begin{aligned} &\psi^2_1(K, y) \neq 0 \\ &\psi^2_2(K, y) \neq 0 \end{aligned} \quad \text{for} \quad y \in \{\phi^2(L, t) \mid (L, t) \in \mathbb{R}^2_{++}\}, \quad K > 0, \tag{5.3.7)$'$}$$

where we use the notation introduced in Section 5.2.

The following two lemmata are needed to prove the main theorem:

5.3.8 **Lemma** *Under (5.3.1)–(5.3.4) the function ϕ^1 of (5.3.5) satisfies*

$$\{x \in \mathbb{R}_{++} \mid \exists K > 0 \quad \textit{with} \quad x = \phi^1(K, L^*)\} = \mathbb{R}_{++}.$$

Proof. Since ϕ^1 is positive valued and strictly monotonic (see (5.3.6)), the existence of $\lim_{K\to 0} \phi^1(K, L^*) \geqq 0$ and $\lim_{K\to\infty} \phi^1(K, L^*) \geqq 0$ is assured; exactly one of the two limits may be $+\infty$. We distinguish the following cases.

Case. 1 ϕ^1 is strictly increasing in the first argument.

(a) Assume $\lim_{K\to 0} \phi^1(K, L^*) = : a > 0$. Since ϕ^1 is linearly homogeneous and positive valued, we have $\{x \in \mathbb{R}_{++} \mid \exists\, (K, L) \in \mathbb{R}^2_{++} \text{ with } x = \phi^1(K, L)\} = \mathbb{R}_{++}$. Hence, there exists $(K_0, L_0) \in \mathbb{R}^2_{++}$ with $a = \phi^1(K_0, L_0)$, and from the strict monotonicity of F in the first and second argument we conclude from $t^* > 0$ and $F(K, L, t^*) \geqq 0$

$$F(K_0, L_0, t^*) = \psi^1(\phi^1(K_0, L_0), t^*) = \psi^1(a, t^*) = : F_0 > 0.$$

By (5.3.4ii), we can choose $K_1 > 0$ small enough such that

$$F(K_1, L^*, t^*) < F(K_0, L_0, t^*) = F_0.$$

By assumption,

$$\phi^1(K_1, L^*) > \lim_{K\to 0} \phi^1(K, L^*) = a.$$

Since F and ϕ^1 are strictly increasing, ψ^1 has the same property; therefore,

$$F_0 = F(K_0, L_0, t^*) > F(K_1, L^*, t^*) = \psi^1(\phi^1(K_1, L^*), t^*) > \psi^1(a, t^*) = F_0,$$

q.e. a.; hence, $\lim_{K \to 0} \phi^1(K, L^*) = 0$.

(b) Assume $\lim_{K \to \infty} \varphi^1(K, L^*) =: b < \infty$. Again, there would exist $(K_0, L_0) \in \mathbb{R}^2_{++}$ with $\phi^1(K_0, L_0) = b$ and

$$+\infty > F(K_0, L_0, t^*) = \psi^1(\phi^1(K_0, L_0), t^*) = \psi^1(b, t^*) =: F_0 > 0.$$

By (5.3.4ii), we can choose $K_1 > 0$ large enough such that

$$F(K_1, L^*, t^*) > F(K_0, L_0, t^*) = F_0.$$

By assumption,

$$\phi^1(K_1, L^*) < \lim_{K \to \infty} \phi^1(K, L^*) = b.$$

But then,

$$F_0 = F(K_0, L_0, t^*) < F(K_1, L^*, t^*) = \psi^1(\phi^1(K_1, L^*), t^*) < \psi^1(b, t^*) = F_0,$$

q.e.a.; hence, we must have $\lim_{K \to \infty} \phi^1(K, L^*) = +\infty$.

Case 2. ϕ^1 is strictly decreasing in the first argument.

In the same way as in the first case, it can be shown that the assumptions $\lim_{K \to 0} \phi^1(K, L^*) = a < \infty$ and $\lim_{K \to \infty} \phi^1(K, L^*) = b > 0$ lead to contradictions, which completes the proof. ■

5.3.9 **Lemma** *Under (5.3.1)–(5.3.4) the function ϕ^2 of (5.3.5) satisfies*

(i) $t \to \phi^2(\hat{L}, t)$ *is strictly monotonic;*

(ii) $\{y \in \mathbb{R}_{++} \mid \exists\, t > 0$ *with* $y = \phi^2(\hat{L}, t)\} = \mathbb{R}_{++}$.

Proof. 1. Strict monotonicity of $t \to \phi^2(\hat{L}, t)$. Because of (5.3.2) and (5.3.4i) the mapping

$$t \to F(\hat{K}, \hat{L}, t) = \psi^2(\hat{K}, \phi^2(\hat{L}, t))$$

is strictly monotonic and continuous in t. We have to distinguish four cases according to the four possibilities that $t \to \psi^2(\hat{K}, \phi^2(\hat{L}, t))$ is strictly increasing or strictly decreasing and ψ^2 is strictly increasing or strictly decreasing in the second argument. We give the proof for only one case; the proofs of the other cases are very similar. Assume that $t \to \psi^2(\hat{K}, \phi^2(\hat{L}, t))$ is strictly increasing and ψ^2 is strictly increasing in the second argument. Let $t_1, t_2 \in \mathbb{R}_{++}$ and $t_1 < t_2$; then,

$$\psi^2(\hat{K}, \phi^2(\hat{L}, t_1)) < \psi^2(\hat{K}, \phi^2(\hat{L}, t_2));$$

therefore, $\phi^2(\hat{L}, t_1) < \phi^2(\hat{L}, t_2)$, which shows that ϕ^2 is in this case strictly increasing in t.

2. Continuity of $t \to \phi^2(\hat{L}, t)$. Assume that $t \to \phi^2(\hat{L}, t)$ is *not* continuous in $t_0 > 0$. Then, there exist both an $\varepsilon > 0$ and a sequence $\{t_n\}$ with $t_n \to t_0\ (n \to \infty)$ and $t_n > 0\ (n = 1, 2, \ldots)$ such that

$$|\phi^2(\hat{L}, t_n) - \phi^2(\hat{L}, t_0)| \geqq \varepsilon \qquad (n = 1, 2, \ldots).$$

We distinguish two cases:

(a) There exists a subsequence of $\{t_n\}$ that converges to t_0, which we denote again by $\{t_n\}$, such that

$$\phi^2(\hat{L}, t_n) \geqq \phi^2(\hat{L}, t_0) + \varepsilon \qquad (n = 1, 2, \ldots).$$

Now, if ψ^2 is strictly increasing in the second argument, we would have

$$\psi^2(\hat{K}, \phi^2(\hat{L}, t_n)) - \psi^2(\hat{K}, \phi^2(\hat{L}, t_0)) \geqq \psi^2(\hat{K}, \phi^2(\hat{L}, t_0) + \varepsilon) - \psi^2(\hat{K}, \phi^2(\hat{L}, t_0))$$
$$=: M > 0,$$

where M is a constant independent from n; but this is a contradiction to the continuity of $t \to \psi^2(\hat{K}, \phi^2(\hat{L}, t))$, assured by (5.3.4i).

On the other hand, if ψ^2 is strictly decreasing in the second argument, we would have

$$\psi^2(\hat{K}, \phi^2(\hat{L}, t_0)) - \psi^2(\hat{K}, \phi^2(\hat{L}, t_n)) \geqq \psi^2(\hat{K}, \phi^2(\hat{L}, t_0)) - \psi^2(\hat{K}, \phi^2(\hat{L}, t_0) + \varepsilon)$$
$$=: M > 0,$$

which again is a contradiction to the continuity of $t \to \psi^2(\hat{K}, \phi^2(\hat{L}, t))$.

(b) There exists a subsequence of $\{t_n\}$ that converges to t_0, which we denote again by $\{t_n\}$, such that

$$\phi^2(\hat{L}, t_n) \leqq \phi^2(\hat{L}, t_0) - \varepsilon \qquad (n = 1, 2, \ldots).$$

This case can be treated in exactly the same way as in case (a).

3. Proof of (ii). Again we have to distinguish four cases.

(a) $t \to \phi^2(\hat{L}, t)$ and $t \to F(\hat{K}, \hat{L}, t)$ are strictly increasing. Then ψ^2 is strictly increasing in the second argument, too. Assume that $\lim_{t \to 0} \phi^2(\hat{L}, t) = {}$ $=: a > 0$. From (5.3.4i) and the continuity of ψ^2 in the second argument it follows that

$$0 = \lim_{t \to 0} F(\hat{K}, \hat{L}, t) = \lim_{t \to 0} \psi^2(\hat{K}, \phi^2(\hat{L}, t)) = \psi^2(\hat{K}, \lim_{t \to 0} \phi^2(\hat{L}, t)) = \psi^2(\hat{K}, a).$$

Because of the linear homogeneity and strict monotonicity of ψ^2 the last equation would imply

$$0 = 2\psi^2(\hat{K}, a) = \psi^2(2\hat{K}, 2a) > \psi^2(\hat{K}, 2a) > \psi^2(\hat{K}, a) = 0,$$

q.e.a.; hence, $\lim_{t \to 0} \phi^2(\hat{L}, t) = 0$.

Assume that $\lim_{t\to\infty} \phi^2(\hat{L}, t) =: b < \infty$. From (5.3.4i) and the continuity of ψ^2 in the second argument it follows that

$$+\infty = \lim_{t\to\infty} F(\hat{K}, \hat{L}, t) = \lim_{t\to\infty} \psi^2(\hat{K}, \phi^2(\hat{L}, t)) = \psi^2(\hat{K}, \lim_{t\to\infty} \phi^2(\hat{L}, t)) = \psi^2(\hat{K}, b),$$

but this is not possible since ψ^2 is linearly homogeneous and, for every positive first argument and for at least certain positive second arguments, positive valued and hence bounded. Therefore, $\lim_{t\to\infty} \phi^2(\hat{L}, t) = \infty$ in this case. The other three cases:

(b) $t \to \phi^2(\hat{L}, t)$ is strictly increasing, $t \to F(\hat{K}, \hat{L}, t)$ is strictly decreasing;

(c) $t \to \phi^2(\hat{L}, t)$ is strictly decreasing, $t \to F(\hat{K}, \hat{L}, t)$ is strictly increasing;

(d) $t \to \phi^2(\hat{L}, t)$ and $t \to F(\hat{K}, \hat{L}, t)$ are strictly decreasing;

can be treated in a very similar way. ■

An immediate consequence is

5.3.10 **Corollary.** *Under (5.3.1)–(5.3.4) we have, for the functions ϕ^1 and ϕ^2 of (5.3.5):*

(i) *The equations*

$$x = \phi^1(K, L^*) \qquad \textit{and} \quad y = \phi^2(\hat{L}, t) \tag{5.3.11}$$

can be solved uniquely with respect to K and t for every $x > 0$ and $y > 0$.

(ii) *The solutions θ^1 and θ^2 of (5.3.11) that satisfy*

$$K = \theta^1(x) \qquad \textit{and} \qquad t = \theta^2(y)$$

identically for $x > 0$ and $y > 0$, are continuous and strictly monotonic. Moreover, θ^1 is continuously differentiable.

Proof. $\phi^1_K(K, L^*) \neq 0$ for all $K > 0$ and $\{x \in \mathbb{R}_{++} \mid \exists\, K > 0$ with $x = \phi^1(K, L^*)\} = \mathbb{R}_{++}$ imply that $x = \phi^1(K, L^*)$ is uniquely solvable with respect to K for all $x \in \mathbb{R}_{++}$, and because of the continuous differentiability of ϕ^1 in the first argument, the solution θ^1 is continuously differentiable as well. The strict monotonicity of ϕ^1 in the first argument implies the same property of θ^1.

The solvability of $y = \phi^2(\hat{L}, t)$ and the asserted properties of θ^2 follow from the statements of Lemma 5.3.9, which completes the proof. ■

Now we are able to determine the explicit form of the production functions F satisfying (5.3.1)–(5.3.4). At first, we will show that F can be expressed by four unknown functions of one variable. Second, three of these four functions will be determined with the aid of the linear homogeneity of ϕ^1 and ψ^2.

5.3.12 **Theorem.** *The solutions of the generalized associativity equation (5.3.5) under assumptions (5.3.1)–(5.3.4) are given by*

$$\psi^1(x, t) = h(f(x) + g(t)) \quad \textit{for} \quad (x, t) \in \mathbb{R}^2_{++}, \tag{5.3.13}$$
$$\phi^1(K, L) = f^{-1}(k(K) + l(L)) \quad \textit{for} \quad (K, L) \in \mathbb{R}^2_{++}, \tag{5.3.14}$$
$$\psi^2(K, y) = h(k(K) + m(y)) \quad \textit{for} \quad (K, y) \in \mathbb{R}^2_{++}, \tag{5.3.15}$$
$$\phi^2(L, t) = m^{-1}(l(L)) + g(t)) \quad \textit{for} \quad (L, t) \in \mathbb{R}^2_{++}, \tag{5.3.16}$$

where h, f, k, l, and m are strictly monotonic, continuously differentiable functions and g is a strictly monotonic continuous function.

Proof. We follow essentially Aczél [1966, pp. 327ff.]. Differentiation of (5.3.5) with respect to K and L leads to

$$\psi_1^1(\phi^1(K, L), t) \cdot \phi_K^1(K, L) = \psi_1^2(K, \phi^2(L, t)),$$
$$\psi_1^1(\phi^1(K, L), t) \cdot \phi_L^1(K, L) = \psi_2^2(K, \phi^2(L, t))\, \phi_L^2(L, t),$$

and by division, which is possible because of (5.3.6), for $L = \hat{L}$

$$\frac{\psi_1^2(K, \phi^2(\hat{L}, t))}{\psi_2^2(K, \phi^2(\hat{L}, t))} = \frac{\phi_K^1(K, \hat{L})}{\phi_L^1(K, \hat{L})} \cdot \phi_L^2(\hat{L}, t). \tag{5.3.17}$$

From Corollary 5.3.10 we know that $y = \phi^2(\hat{L}, t)$ is uniquely solvable for $y \in \mathbb{R}_{++}$, such that $t = \theta^2(y)$ with continuous, strictly monotonic θ^2. Defining the functions m and k by

$$m(y) := \int \frac{dy'}{\phi_L^2(\hat{L}, \theta^2(y'))}, \qquad k(K) := \int \frac{\phi_K^1(K', \hat{L})}{\phi_L^1(K', \hat{L})}\, dK' \tag{5.3.18}$$

we see that m and k are continuously differentiable and strictly monotonic for $(y, K) \in \mathbb{R}^2_{++}$; moreover, since ϕ_K^1 and ϕ_L^1 are of the same sign, k is strictly increasing. Identities (5.3.17) and (5.3.18) imply

$$\frac{\psi_1^2(K, y)}{\psi_2^2(K, y)} = \frac{k'(K)}{m'(y)}. \tag{5.3.19}$$

For constant $\psi^2(K, y)$, Eq. (5.3.19) is equivalent to

$$-\frac{dK(y)}{dy} = \frac{m'(y)}{k'(K(y))} \tag{5.3.20}$$

where $dK(y)/dy$ is the slope of the isoquant $\{(K, y) \mid \psi^2(K, y) = \text{const}\}$ at the point y. Equation (5.3.20) implies

$$k(K) = -m(y) + a$$

where a, the constant of integration, depends on the fixed $\psi^2(K, y)$; hence, we write $a = A(\psi^2(K, y))$ and have

$$A(\psi^2(K, y)) = k(K) + m(y). \tag{5.3.21}$$

In the same way as in Section 5.2 it can be shown that A is strictly increasing. Hence, $A^{-1} = :h$ exists and is continuously differentiable and strictly monotonic, such that from (5.3.21) it follows that

$$\psi^2(K, y) = h(k(K) + m(y))$$

with $h: = A^{-1}$. Because of (5.3.21), it can easily be seen that A, and therefore h, is continuously differentiable, which proves (5.3.15). If we substitute (5.3.15) into (5.3.5) we get

$$\psi^1(\phi^1(K, L), t) = \psi^2(K, \phi^2(L, t)) = h(k(K) + m(\phi^2(L, t))),$$

or, by setting $L = L^*$ and $x = \phi^1(K, L^*)$,

$$\psi^1(x, t) = h(f(x) + g(t)),$$

where

$$f(x) : = k(\theta^1(x)) \qquad \text{for} \quad x \in \mathbb{R}_{++},$$
$$g(t) : = m(\phi^2(L^*, t)) \qquad \text{for} \quad t \in \mathbb{R}_{++}.$$

By definition and Corollary 5.3.10(ii), f is a continuously differentiable and strictly monotonic function, g is a continuous and strictly monotonic function; hence (5.3.13) is proved. If we now substitute (5.3.13) and (5.3.15) into (5.3.5) we get

$$h(f(\phi^1(K, L)) + g(t)) = h(k(K) + m(\phi^2(L, t))),$$

which leads, in view of the strict monotonicity of h and f, to

$$\phi^1(K, L) = f^{-1}(k(K) + m(\phi^2(L, t)) - g(t)) \qquad \text{for} \quad (K, L, t) \in \mathbb{R}^3_{++}.$$

Here, the left-hand side does not depend on t; therefore, if we set $t = t^* > 0$ and

$$l(L) : = m(\phi^2(L, t^*)) - g(t^*) \qquad \text{for} \quad L \in \mathbb{R}_{++},$$

it follows that

$$\phi^1(K, L) = f^{-1}(k(K) + l(L))$$

with a strictly monotonic continuously differentiable function l, which proves (5.3.14). Finally, if we substitute (5.3.15) into (5.3.5) and make use of the strict monotonicity of h and m, we obtain

$$\phi^2(L, t) = m^{-1}(f(\phi^1(K, L)) + g(t) - k(K)) = m^{-1}(l(L) + g(t)),$$

which completes the proof of the theorem. ■

5.3.22 **Corollary.** *Every production function satisfying (5.3.1)–(5.3.4) is of the form*

$$F(K, L, t) = h(k(K) + l(L) + g(t)) \qquad \text{for} \quad (K, L, t) \in \mathbb{R}^3_{++}$$

where h, k, and l are strictly monotonic and continuously differentiable and g is strictly monotonic and continuous.

Proof. Property (5.3.3) and Theorem 5.3.12 imply

$$\begin{aligned} F(K, L, t) &= \psi^2(K, \phi^2(L, t)) = h\big(k(K) + m(m^{-1}[l(L) + g(t)])\big) \\ &= h(k(K) + l(L) + g(t)). \quad \blacksquare \end{aligned}$$

Analogously to Theorem 5.2.29 we prove the following theorem, which gives us complete information about the form of the unknown functions h, k, and l:

5.3.23 **Theorem.** *If F satisfies (5.3.1)–(5.3.4), the functions h, k, and l, by which F is representable according to Corollary 5.3.22, are given by*

$$\left.\begin{aligned} &k(K) = \gamma \log K + \delta, \quad l(L) = \gamma' \log L + \delta' && \text{for} \quad (K, L) \in \mathbb{R}^2_{++}, \\ &h(K) = \bar{c} \exp[x(\gamma + \gamma'')^{-1}] && \text{for} \quad x \in \mathbb{R}, \end{aligned}\right. \tag{5.3.24}$$

or by

$$\left.\begin{aligned} &k(K) = \varepsilon K^{-\varrho} + \sigma, \quad l(L) = \varepsilon' L^{-\varrho} = +\sigma' && \text{for} \quad (K, L) \in \mathbb{R}^2_{++}, \\ &h(x) = \bar{c} \cdot \left(\frac{x - \sigma - \sigma''}{\varepsilon + \varepsilon''}\right)^{-1/\varrho} && \begin{cases} \text{for} & \varepsilon > 0, \ x \geqq \sigma + \sigma'', \\ \text{for} & \varepsilon < 0, \ x \leqq \sigma + \sigma'', \end{cases} \end{aligned}\right. \tag{5.3.25}$$

where $\gamma, \delta, \gamma', \delta', \varepsilon, \varrho, \sigma, \varepsilon', \sigma', \bar{c}, \sigma'', \varepsilon''$ *are real constants* $\gamma, \gamma', \gamma'', \varepsilon, \varepsilon', \varepsilon'', \varrho$ *being different from* 0 *and* $\bar{c} > 0$ *with*

$$\operatorname{sgn} \gamma = \operatorname{sgn} \gamma' = \operatorname{sgn} \gamma'', \qquad \operatorname{sgn} \varepsilon = \operatorname{sgn} \varepsilon' = \operatorname{sgn} \varepsilon''.$$

Proof. From Theorem 5.3.12 and (5.3.2′) we know that

$$\phi^1(K, L) = f^{-1}(k(K) + l(L)) \qquad \text{for} \quad (K, L) \in \mathbb{R}^2_{++}, \tag{5.3.14}$$

and from (5.3.3′) that

$$\psi^2(K, y) = h(k(K) + m(y)) \qquad \text{for} \quad (K, y) \in \mathbb{R}^2_{++}, \tag{5.3.15}$$

where ϕ^1 and ψ^2 are linearly homogeneous. This shows that ϕ^1 and ψ^2 are generalized quasilinear functions and we can proceed as in the proof of Theorem 5.2.29 in order to obtain either

$$\left.\begin{aligned} &k(K) = \gamma \log K + \delta, \quad l(L)) = \gamma' \log L + \delta' && \text{for} \quad (K, L) \in \mathbb{R}^2_{++}, \\ &f^{-1}(x) = c \exp[x(\gamma + \gamma')^{-1}] && \text{for} \quad x \in \mathbb{R}, \end{aligned}\right. \tag{5.3.26}$$

or

$$k(K) = \varepsilon K^{-\varrho} + \sigma, \qquad l(L) = \varepsilon' L^{-\varrho} + \sigma' \qquad \text{for} \quad (K, L) \in \mathbb{R}^2_{++},$$
$$f^{-1}(x) = c \cdot \left(\frac{x - \sigma - \sigma'}{\varepsilon + \varepsilon'}\right)^{-1/\varrho} \qquad \begin{cases} \text{for} \quad \varepsilon > 0 \quad \text{and} \quad x \geqq \sigma + \sigma', \\ \text{for} \quad \varepsilon < 0 \quad \text{and} \quad x \leqq \sigma + \sigma', \end{cases} \tag{5.3.27}$$

and similarly for (5.3.15) either

$$k(K) = \gamma \log K + \delta, \qquad m(y) = \gamma'' \log y + \delta'' \qquad \text{for} \quad (K, y) \in \mathbb{R}^2_{++},$$
$$h(x) = \bar{c} \exp\,[x(\gamma + \gamma'')^{-1}] \qquad \text{for} \quad x \in \mathbb{R}, \tag{5.3.28}$$

or

$$k(K) = \varepsilon K^{-\varrho} + \sigma, \qquad m(y) = \varepsilon'' y^{-\varrho} + \sigma'' \qquad \text{for} \quad (K, y) \in \mathbb{R}^2_{++},$$
$$h(x) = \bar{c} \cdot \left(\frac{x - \sigma - \sigma''}{\varepsilon + \varepsilon''}\right)^{-1/\varrho} \qquad \begin{cases} \text{for} \quad \varepsilon > 0, \quad x \geqq \sigma + \sigma'', \\ \text{for} \quad \varepsilon < 0, \quad x \leqq \sigma + \sigma'', \end{cases} \tag{5.3.29}$$

where the constants γ, γ', γ'', ε, ε', ε'', δ, δ', δ'', ϱ, c, $\bar{c}$ have the asserted property. ■

The main result now easily follows:

5.3.30 **Theorem.** (i) *Every production function satisfying (5.3.1)–(5.3.4) is necessarily of the CD (Cobb and Douglas [1928]) type*

$$F(K, L, t) = c(t)\, K^a L^b \qquad \textit{for} \quad (K, L, t) \in \mathbb{R}^3_{++}, \tag{5.3.31}$$

where a, b are real constants with $0 < a < 1$, $0 < b < 1$ and c is a strictly monotonic, continuous function with

$$\lim_{t \to 0} c(t) = 0 \qquad \textit{and} \qquad \lim_{t \to \infty} c(t) = \infty$$

or

$$\lim_{t \to 0} c(t) = \infty \qquad \textit{and} \qquad \lim_{t \to \infty} c(t) = 0.$$

(ii) *Conversely, every function of the form (5.3.31) satisfies (5.3.1)–(5.3.4) if the constants a and b and the function have the properties stated in (i).*

Proof. Since (ii) is obvious, it remains to prove (i). By Theorem 5.3.23, the functions h, k and l by which F can be expressed according to Corollary 5.3.22, are given either by the triple (5.3.24) or by (5.3.25). If we insert (5.3.24) into

$$F(K, L, t) = h(k(K) + l(L) + g(t)), \tag{5.3.32}$$

we get exactly (5.3.31) with $c(t) := \bar{c} \exp\left[(\delta + \delta' + g(t)) \,/\, (\gamma + \gamma'')\right]$, $a := \gamma/(\gamma + \gamma'')$, $b := \gamma' \,/\, (\gamma + \gamma'')$. Because of (5.3.1), we must have $0 < a < 1$, $0 < b < 1$, and because of (5.3.4), c must have the asserted properties.

If we insert (5.3.25) into (5.3.32) we obtain

$$F(K, L, t) = \bar{c} \cdot (c_1 K^{-\varrho} + c_2 L^{-\varrho} + r(t)^{-1/\varrho} \tag{5.3.33}$$

with $r(t) := (g(t) + \sigma' - \sigma'') / (\varepsilon + \varepsilon'')$, $c_1 := \varepsilon / (\varepsilon + \varepsilon'') > 0$, $c_2 := \varepsilon' / (\varepsilon + \varepsilon'') > 0$, where necessarily r must be positive valued because of (5.3.4i) and since otherwise F is not defined for all $(K, L) \in \mathbb{R}^2_{++}$ or takes on negative values (for certain $(K, L) \in \mathbb{R}^2_{++}$). But if $r(t) > 0$ for $t > 0$, assumption 5.3.4(ii) cannot be satisfied. Hence, the functions (5.3.33) are no solutions of our problem; this proves the theorem. ■

If we assume, instead of (5.3.3) (generalized Harrod neutrality of technical progress), that F represents generalized Solow neutral technical progress, we have, because of the complete symmetry of definitions (5.1.11ii) and (5.1.11iii) in K and L (implying the symmetry of (5.1.13) and (5.1.14) in K and L):

5.3.34 **Theorem.** *Every production function satisfying (5.3.1), (5.3.2), (5.3.4) and representing generalized Solow neutral technical progress is necessarily of the CD type (5.3.31).*

5.3.35 **Remark.** It is easy to show that the functions (5.3.33) represent both generalized Hicks and Harrod neutral technical progress and are neoclassical as well as CD-type functions. Only the additional assumptions (5.3.4), which we essentially need for our proof, are not satisfied by them. It is an open problem to determine all neoclassical production functions representing generalized Hicks and Harrod (or Solow) neutral technical progress without any additional regularity conditions like (5.3.4).

6

The Functional Equation of Aggregation

FRITZ POKROPP, University of Hamburg

In economics the problem of aggregation is a systematic link between microeconomics and macroeconomics: macroeconomic quantities and their relations must be consistent with microeconomic facts. Discussion of this topic has been carried out to a large extent in the context of macroeconomic production theory and utility theory.

Suppose that in the economy there are n firms, each of which provides one product. Suppose that each firm uses m production factors (inputs). Let

$$x_{ij} = j\text{th input quantity in the } i\text{th firm.}$$

Let $f^1, \ldots, f^n$ be the n production functions of the n firms and let y be (the index for) total output. Under what conditions is it possible to find a macroeconomic production function F which clearly must be defined as a function of macroeconomic production factors $g^1, \ldots, g^m$? Formally, this problem means that we have to solve the following *functional equation of aggregation:*

$$\begin{aligned} &y(f^1(x_{11}, \ldots, x_{1m}), \ldots, f^n(x_{n1}, \ldots, x_{nm})) \\ &= F(g^1(x_{11}, \ldots, x_{n1}), \ldots, g^m(x_{1m}, \ldots, x_{nm})). \end{aligned} \tag{6.0.1}$$

If we consider each side of (6.0.1) as a function of the $n \cdot m$ variables $x_{11}, \ldots, x_{nm}$, say

$$G(x_{11}, \ldots, x_{1m}, x_{21}, \ldots, x_{2m}, \ldots, x_{n1}, \ldots x_{nm}),$$

we may look at aggregation as a "grouping of variables" problem. The special grouping (6.0.1) is called *Klein–Nataf aggregation.* It has been dealt with by Klein [1946a, b] and Nataf [1948] under differentiability assumptions. The monograph by Green [1964] gives a good summary on aggregation problems

Wolfgang Eichhorn, Functional Equations in Economics.

ISBN 0-201-01948-5/01949-3 PBK

(in particular of (6.0.1)) if all the functions involved are differentiable. Special aggregation problems for a large variety of well-known microeconomic production functions that in general are differentiable have been investigated by Sato [1975].

Continuous solutions of (6.0.1) were given by Gorman [1968]. In Section 6.3 we shall give a somewhat sketchy account of results and proofs for differentiable and continuous solutions of (6.0.1). A treatment of (6.0.1) without continuity and differentiability assumptions can be found in Pokropp [1972a, b]. The monograph ([1972b]; see it for further references) served as a basic text for this chapter. In Section 6.1 some fundamental concepts and notations are introduced. Section 6.2 contains the main results concerning the existence and structure of solutions of (6.0.1). In particular, (6.0.1) is reduced to a functional equation for only two functions. Section 6.4 determines solutions of (6.0.1) if in a certain sense each factor (resp. firm) may be replaced by any other factor (resp. firm).

Although the economic interpretation of definitions, theorems, and other statements is made in terms of production theory, we emphasize that applications to other areas are possible as well. In particular, utility theory has played a decisive part in posing problems and formulating results in aggregation theory. In fact, some methods of treating aggregation problems have been induced by utility theory more than by anything else (see, e.g., Debreu [1960]; Gorman [1968]). The particular aggregation problem (6.0.1), however, has been dealt with mainly in the context of production theory.

There is a last introductory remark we wish to make. In (6.0.1) no reference is made to distribution patterns of production factors among firms. That means that whatever the distribution of factors may be ("efficient," not efficient, or anything else), F (resp. y) will give total output as a function of *suitably defined* "aggregated production factors" (resp. of single outputs). In what way aggregates (including total output!) are to be constructed (defined!) is not predetermined by the famous deus-ex-machina "homogeneity" or the equally famous diabolus-ex-machina "inhomogeneity."

6.1 The Klein–Nataf Aggregation Problem

For any pair (i, j), $i = 1, \ldots, n$, $j = 1, \ldots, m$, let

$$X_{ij} \subseteqq \mathbb{R}_+, \quad \text{nonempty}$$

be (or represent) the set of possible input quantities of the jth factor in the

ith firm. For Cartesian products we introduce the abbreviations

$$X_{i.} := X_{i1} \times \cdots \times X_{im}, \qquad x_{i.} := (x_{i1}, \ldots, x_{im}) \in X_{i.},$$
$$X_{.j} := X_{1j} \times \cdots \times X_{nj}, \qquad x_{.j} := (x_{1j}, \ldots, x_{nj}) \in X_{.j},$$
$$X_{..} := X_{1.} \times \cdots \times X_{n.}, \qquad x_{..} := (x_{1.}, \ldots, x_{n.}) \in X_{..},$$
$$X^{*}_{..} := X_{.1} \times \cdots \times X_{.m}, \qquad x^{*}_{..} := (x_{.1}, \ldots, x_{.m}) \in X^{*}_{..}.$$

The production function of the ith firm is defined on $X_{i.}$ as a function into $\mathbb{R}_+$ that is monotonically increasing (not necessarily strictly) in each variable; symbolically, we have

$$f^i : X_{i.} \to \mathbb{R}_+ \text{ is a } \uparrow\text{-function.} \tag{6.1.1}$$

We do not try to justify assumption (6.1.1) here; however, we note that (6.1.1) is in accordance with production function axioms given by Shephard [1970].

The index function for total output is defined as a function of the single outputs $w_i = f^i(x_{i.})$, strictly increasing in each variable; symbolically,

$$y: W_1 \times \cdots \times W_n \to \mathbb{R}_+ \text{ is a } \updownarrow\text{-function} \tag{6.1.2}$$

where

$$W_i = f^i(X_{i.}) = \{f^i(x_{i.}) \mid x_{i.} \in X_{i.}\}. \tag{6.1.3}$$

Total output as a function of all $n \cdot m$ microeconomic input quantities is then given by

$$G(x_{..}) = y(f^1(x_{1.}), \ldots, f^n(x_{n.})) \qquad (x_{..} \in X_{..}). \tag{6.1.4}$$

Clearly,

$$G: X_{..} \to \mathbb{R}_+ \text{ is a } \uparrow\text{-function.} \tag{6.1.5}$$

Conversely, we may start with an arbitrary function G satisfying (6.1.5) and try to construct functions (6.1.1), (6.1.2) (with (6.1.3)) such that (6.1.4) holds.

We now focus our attention on the macroeconomic production function. In the first place we have to define index functions for macroeconomic production factors. We decide (perhaps with good economic reasons) that the n inputs (in the n firms) with fixed number j are "of the same type." There are then m "types" of production factors in the economy and each firm uses each type. The total quantity of the jth type is given by the index function g^j, which must depend on $x_{1j}, \ldots, x_{nj}$ only:

$$g^j : X_{.j} \to \mathbb{R}_+ \text{ is a } \uparrow\text{-function.} \tag{6.1.6}$$

The macroeconomic production function F is to be defined on the Cartesian product of the sets

$$Z_j = g^j(X_{.j}); \tag{6.1.7}$$

$$F: Z_1 \times \cdots \times Z_m \to \mathbb{R}_+ \text{ is a } \updownarrow\text{-function.} \tag{6.1.8}$$

By means of (6.1.6), (6.1.8) we obtain the second representation of total output as a function of the microeconomic input quantities x_{ij}:

$$G^*(x^*_{\cdot\cdot}) = F(g^1(x_{\cdot 1}), \ldots, g^m(x_{\cdot m})) \qquad (x^*_{\cdot\cdot} \in X^*_{\cdot\cdot}). \tag{6.1.9}$$

Clearly,

$$G^* : X^*_{\cdot\cdot} \to \mathbb{R}_+ \text{ is a } \uparrow\text{-function.} \tag{6.1.10}$$

Conversely, we can start with G^*, which might be given by G from (6.1.4) in the following way:

$$G^*(x^*_{\cdot\cdot}) = G(x_{\cdot\cdot}) \qquad \text{where} \quad (x^*_{\cdot\cdot})_{ji} = (x_{\cdot\cdot})_{ij} = x_{ij}. \tag{6.1.11}$$

We then have to find functions (6.1.6), (6.1.8) (with (6.1.7)) such that (6.1.9) holds.

6.1.12 **Definition.** Let G be given as in (6.1.5), $f^1, \ldots, f^n$ as in (6.1.1), y as in (6.1.2), (6.1.3). We call $(y; f^1, \ldots, f^n)$ *an aggregate solution for* G if (6.1.4) holds. Let G^* be given as in (6.1.10); $g^1, \ldots, g^m$ as in (6.1.6); F as in (6.1.8), (6.1.7). We call $(F; g^1, \ldots, g^m)$ an *aggregate solution for* G^* if (6.1.9) holds.

Let G, G^* be given as in (6.1.5), (6.1.10), respectively. We call (G, G^*) a *dual pair* (or G^* the *dual* of G, or vice versa) if (6.1.11) holds. $(y; f^1, \ldots, f^n/F; g^1, \ldots, g^m)$ is called an *aggregate solution for* (G, G^*) if (G, G^*) is a dual pair and $(y; f^1, \ldots, f^n)$ is an aggregate solution for G and $(F; g^1, \ldots, g^m)$ is an aggregate solution for G^*.

Our aim is to determine all solutions of (6.0.1); that is to determine all functions that may occur in aggregate solutions for dual pairs. It will turn out (see Section 6.2, Theorems 6.2.1 and 6.2.9) that our problem is to determine all dual pairs that possess aggregate solutions.

The concept of (functional) separability as defined in 6.1.13 will play a decisive part. The essential idea goes back to Leontief [1947].

6.1.13 **Definition.** Let G, G^* be given as in (6.1.5), (6.1.10), respectively. G is called *$(i\cdot)$-separable* if

$$\left.\begin{array}{l} G(x_{1\cdot}, \ldots, x_{i\cdot}, \ldots, x_{n\cdot}) \leqq G(x_{1\cdot}, \ldots, x'_{1\cdot}, \ldots, x_{n\cdot}). \\ \text{implies} \\ G(x'_{1\cdot}, \ldots, x_{i\cdot}, \ldots, x'_{n\cdot}). \leqq G(x'_{1\cdot}, \ldots, x'_{i}, \ldots x'_{n\cdot}) \\ \text{for all } x_{\cdot\cdot}, x'_{\cdot\cdot} \in X_{\cdot\cdot}. \end{array}\right\} \tag{6.1.14}$$

G^* is called *$(\cdot j)$-separable* if

$$\left.\begin{array}{l} G^*(x_{\cdot 1}, \ldots, x_{\cdot j}, \ldots, x_{\cdot m}) \leqq G^*(x_{\cdot 1}, \ldots, x'_{\cdot j}, \ldots, x_{\cdot m}) \\ \text{implies} \\ G^*(x'_{\cdot 1}, \ldots, x_{\cdot j}, \ldots, x'_{\cdot m}) \leqq G^*(x'_{\cdot 1}, \ldots, x'_{\cdot j}, \ldots, x'_{\cdot m}) \\ \text{for all } x^*_{\cdot\cdot}, x^{*\prime}_{\cdot\cdot} \in X^*_{\cdot\cdot}. \end{array}\right\} \tag{6.1.15}$$

6.1.16 **Lemma.** *Let G be $(i\cdot)$-separable (G^* be $(\cdot j)$-separable). Then valid implications are obtained if in (6.1.14) (in (6.1.15)) $\leqq$ is replaced by $=$ or $\leqq$ is replaced by $<$.*

The proof is left to the reader.

6.2 Existence and Structure of Aggregate Solutions

6.2.1 **Theorem** *(Existence). Let G (resp. G^*) be a function as in (6.1.5) (resp. (6.1.10)). There exists an aggregate solution for G if and only if G is $(i\cdot)$-separable for all $i = 1, \ldots, n$. There exists an aggregate solution for G^* if and only if G^* is $(\cdot j)$-separable for all $j = 1, \ldots, m$. There exists an aggregate solution for a dual pair (G, G^*) if and only if G is $(i\cdot)$-separable and G^* is $(\cdot j)$-separable for all i, j.*

Proof. It is sufficient to prove the first part only. Suppose that we are given an aggregate solution $(y; f^1, \ldots, f^n)$ for G. Since y is a $\uparrow$-function we have, for all i,

$$y(w_1, \ldots, w_i, \ldots, w_n) \leqq y(w_1, \ldots, w_i', \ldots, w_n) \quad \text{if and only if} \quad w_i \leqq w_i',$$
$$y(w_1', \ldots, w_i, \ldots, w_n') \leqq y(w_1, \ldots, w_1', \ldots, w_n') \quad \text{if and only if} \quad w_i \leqq w_i'.$$

Replace w_t by $f^t(x_{t\cdot})$, w_t' by $f^t(x_{t\cdot})$ for $t = 1, \ldots, i, \ldots, n$ and obtain (6.1.14) from (6.1.4).

Conversely, let G be $(i\cdot)$-separable for all i. Let

$$x_{\cdot\cdot}^0 = (x_{1\cdot}^0, \ldots, x_{n\cdot}^0) \in X_{\cdot\cdot}$$

be an arbitrary but fixed point. Define $\uparrow$-functions f_0^i from $X_{i\cdot}$ into $\mathbb{R}_+$ by

$$f_0^i(x_{i\cdot}) := G(x_{1\cdot}^0, \ldots, x_{i\cdot}, \ldots, x_{n\cdot}^0). \tag{6.2.2}$$

Define a $\updownarrow$-function y_0 from $f_0^1(X_{1\cdot}) \times \cdots \times f_0^n(X_{n\cdot})$ into $\mathbb{R}_+$ by means of representatives:

$$y_0(w_1, \ldots, w_n) := G(x_{1\cdot}, \ldots, x_{n\cdot}) \tag{6.2.3}$$

where $(x_{1\cdot}, \ldots, x_{n\cdot}) \in X_{\cdot\cdot}$ is chosen in such a way that

$$w_i = f_0^i(x_{i\cdot}) \quad \text{for all } i. \tag{6.2.4}$$

We have to show that y_0 is well-defined, that is, that y_0 is a function of $w_1, \ldots, w_n$ only. Take a second set of representatives $x_{1\cdot}', \ldots, x_{n\cdot}'$ (for $w_1, \ldots, w_n$), which according to (6.2.4) must satisfy

$$f_0^i(x_{i\cdot}) = w_i = f_0^i(x_{i\cdot}') \quad \text{for all } i.$$

From (6.2.2) we then obtain

$$G(x_{1\cdot}^0, \ldots, x_{i\cdot}, \ldots, x_{n\cdot}^0) = G(x_{1\cdot}^0, \ldots, x_i', \ldots, x_{n\cdot}^0) \quad \text{for all } i.$$

By means of Lemma 6.1.16 we conclude that

$$\begin{aligned} &G(x_{1\cdot}, \ldots x_{(i-1)\cdot}, \ldots, x_{i\cdot})\, x_{i\cdot}, x'_{(i+1)\cdot}, \ldots, x'_{n\cdot}) \\ &\quad = G(x_{1\cdot}, \ldots, x_{(i-1)\cdot}, x'_{i\cdot}, x'_{(i+1)\cdot}, \ldots, x'_{n\cdot}) \end{aligned}$$

for all $i = 1, \ldots, n$ with obvious modifications for $i = 1$ and $i = n$. These n equations together yield $G(x_{\cdot\cdot}) = G(x'_{\cdot\cdot})$. This proves y_0 in (6.2.3) to be well defined.

In order to show that y_0 is a $\updownarrow$-function, we consider (for fixed i)

$$w_i = f^i_0(x_{i\cdot}) < w'_i = f^i_0(x'_{i\cdot}).$$

By (6.2.2) we obtain

$$G(x^0_{1\cdot}, \ldots, x_{i\cdot}, \ldots, x^0_{n\cdot}) < G(x^0_{1\cdot}, \ldots, x'_{i\cdot}, \ldots, x^0_{n\cdot}).$$

Lemma 6.1.16 states that the $x^0_{\iota.}$ can be replaced by arbitrary $x_{\iota\cdot}$. Then (6.2.3) yields

$$y_0(w_1, \ldots, w_i, \ldots, w_n) < y_0(w_1, \ldots, w'_i, \ldots, w_n).$$

Finally, we have to show that $(y_0; f^1_0, \ldots, f^n_0)$ is an aggregate solution of G. Replace w_i in (6.2.3) by $f^i_0(x_{i\cdot})$ from (6.2.4). Then (6.1.4) follows. ■

The construction of an aggregate solution for G^* analogous to the construction in the preceding proof is given as follows:

$$g^j_0(x_{\cdot j}) := G^*(x^0_{\cdot 1}, \ldots, x_{\cdot j}, \ldots, x^0_{\cdot m}), \tag{6.2.5}$$

$$F_0(z_1, \ldots, z_m) := G^*(x_{\cdot 1}, \ldots, x_{\cdot m}) \quad \text{for} \quad z_j \in g^j_0(X_{\cdot j}) \tag{6.2.6}$$

where the $x_{\cdot j}$ are chosen in such a way that

$$z_j = g^j_0(x_{\cdot j}). \tag{6.2.7}$$

The point $x^{*0}_{\cdot\cdot} = (x^0_{\cdot 1}, \ldots, x^0_{\cdot m}) \in X^*_{\cdot\cdot}$ in (6.2.5) is arbitrary but fixed.

6.2.8 **Definition.** The aggregate solution for G given by (6.2.2)–(6.2.4) is called *normed by* $x^0_{\cdot\cdot}$. The aggregate solution for G^* given by (6.2.5)–(6.2.7) is called *normed by* $x^{*0}_{\cdot\cdot}$. The aggregate solution for a dual pair (G, G^*) given by (6.2.2)–(6.2.7) is called *normed by* $x^0_{\cdot\cdot}$ if $x^{*0}_{\cdot\cdot} = (x^0_{\cdot\cdot})^*$ (i.e., if $(x^{*0}_{\cdot\cdot})_{ji} = (x^0_{\cdot\cdot})_{ij} = x^0_{ij}$).

The following theorem states that we need to investigate only normed solutions, since any other solution can be obtained from a normed solution in a simple way:

6.2.9 **Theorem.** *Let* $(y; f^1, \ldots, f^n)$ *and* $(\bar{y}; \bar{f}^1, \ldots, \bar{f}^n)$ *be aggregate solutions for* G. *Then there exist*

$$\varkappa^i : f^i(X_{i\cdot}) \xrightarrow{\text{onto}} \bar{f}^i(X_{i\cdot}), \quad \updownarrow\text{-functions},$$

such that

$$\bar{y}(\alpha^1(w_1), \ldots, \alpha^n(w_n)) = y(w_1, \ldots, w_n) \qquad \textit{for all} \quad w_i \in f^i(X_{i\cdot}). \quad (6.2.10)$$

Proof. For $w_i \in f^i(X_{i\cdot})$ define α^i by means of representatives:

$$\alpha^i(w_i) := \bar{f}^i(x_{i\cdot}) \qquad \text{with } x_{i\cdot} \text{ such that } \ f^i(x_{i\cdot}) = w_i. \qquad (6.2.11)$$

We have to show that α^i is well defined. Let $x'_{i\cdot}$ also be a representative of w_i. We then have

$$f^i(x_{i\cdot}) = w_i = f^i(x'_{i\cdot}).$$

For fixed i and arbitrary $x_{t\cdot}$ $(t \neq i)$ we obtain from (6.1.4)

$$G(x_{1\cdot}, \ldots, x_{i\cdot}, \ldots, x_{n\cdot}) = G(x_{1\cdot}, \ldots, x'_{i\cdot}, \ldots, x_{n\cdot}).$$

However, (6.1.4) also holds for $(\bar{y}; \bar{f}^1, \ldots, \bar{f}^n)$ by assumption. The preceding equality thus leads to

$$\bar{y}(\bar{f}^1(x_{1\cdot}), \ldots, \bar{f}^i(x_{i\cdot}), \ldots, \bar{f}^n(x_{n\cdot})) = \bar{y}(\bar{f}^1(x_{1\cdot}), \ldots, \bar{f}^i(x'_{i\cdot}), \ldots, \bar{f}^n(x_{n\cdot})).$$

The $\updownarrow$-property of $\bar{y}$ now shows that $\bar{f}^i(x_{i\cdot}) = \bar{f}^i(x'_{i\cdot})$. Thus α^i in (6.2.11) is well defined and, clearly, "onto."

If $w_i < w'_i$, then $f^i(x_{i\cdot}) = w_i < w'_i = f^i(x'_{i\cdot})$. Use (6.1.4) with arbitrary $x_{t\cdot}$ for $t \neq i$) to show that then $\bar{f}^i(x_{i\cdot}) < \bar{f}^i(x'_{i\cdot})$ also holds. Definition (6.2.11) yields $\alpha^i(w_i) < \alpha^i(w'_i)$. Finally, (6.2.10) follows from (6.2.11) and the fact that (6.1.4) holds for both $(y; f^1, \ldots, f^n)$ and $(\bar{y}; \bar{f}^1, \ldots, \bar{f}^n)$. ■

From the proof of Theorem 6.2.1 we know how to construct normed solutions. From Theorem 6.2.9 we know how to construct arbitrary aggregate solutions. With obvious modifications, Theorem 6.2.9 holds for aggregate solutions for G^* and for dual pairs (G, G^*). The structure of normed aggregate solutions for dual pairs is given in the following theorem.

6.2.12 **Theorem** *(Structure). Let* $\{y_0; f_0^1, \ldots, f_0^n/F_0; g_0^1, \ldots, g_0^m\}$ *be an aggregate solution for* (G, G^*) *normed by* $x^0_{\cdot\cdot}$. *Then there exist*

$$k_0^{ij} : X_{ij} \to \mathbb{R}_+, \quad \uparrow\textit{-functions}, \qquad (6.2.13)$$

such that

$$f_0^i(x_{i\cdot}) = F_0(a_{i\cdot}), \qquad g_0^j(x_{\cdot j}) = y_0(a_{\cdot j}) \qquad (6.2.14)$$

for all i, j and all

$$a_{ij} = k_0^{ij}(x_{ij}) \in A_{ij} = k_0^{ij}(X_{ij}). \qquad (6.2.15)$$

Furthermore, y_0 *and* F_0 *satisfy the functional equation*

$$y_0(F_0(a_{1\cdot}), \ldots, F_0(a_{n\cdot})) = F_0(y_0(a_{\cdot 1}), \ldots, y_0(a_{\cdot m})) \qquad (6.2.16)$$

for all $a_{ij} \in A_{ij}$ *(with* A_{ij} *from (6.2.15)). Ultimately, we have, for*

$$e = G(x^0_{..}) = G^*(x^{*0}_{..}) = k^{ij}_0(x^0_{ij}) = f^i_0(x^0_{i.}) = g^j_0(x^0_{.j})$$

$$y_0(e, \ldots, w_i, \ldots, e) = w_i, \qquad F_0(e, \ldots, z_j, \ldots, e) = z_j \qquad (6.2.17)$$

for all i, j *and all* $w_i \in F_0(A_{i.})$, $z_j \in y_0(A_{.j})$.

Conversely, if we start with given $\updownarrow$*-functions* y_0, F_0 *satisfying (6.2.16) for given sets* A_{ij}*; if furthermore we are given* $\uparrow$*-functions (6.2.13) onto* A_{ij}*, we may define* f^i_0 *and* g^j_0 *for* $x_{ij} \in (k^{ij}_0)^{-1}(A_{ij})$ *by (6.2.14) to obtain the aggregate solution* $(y_0; f^1_0, \ldots, f^n_0/F_0; g^1_0, \ldots, g^m_0)$ *for* (G, G^*)*, where* G *is given by the left-hand side of (6.2.16) if* a_{ij} *is replaced by* $k^{ij}_0(x_{ij})$.

Proof. Define the $\uparrow$-functions in (6.2.13) by

$$k^{ij}_0(x_{ij}) = G(x^0_{1.}, \ldots, x^0_{i1}, \ldots, x_{ij}, \ldots, x^0_{im}, \ldots, x^0_{n.}). \qquad (6.2.18$$

From (6.2.2), (6.2.5), and (6.2.18) we obtain

$$f^i_0(x^0_{i1}, \ldots, x_{ij}, \ldots, x^0_{im}) = k^{ij}_0(x_{ij}) = g^j_0(x^0_{1j}, \ldots, x_{ij}, \ldots, x^0_{nj}). \qquad (6.2.19)$$

From (6.2.2) and (6.1.11) we conclude that

$$f^i_0(x_{i.}) = G^*(x^0_{11}, \ldots, x_{i1}, \ldots, x^0_{n1}, \ldots, x^0_{1m}, \ldots, x_{im}, \ldots, x^0_{nm}).$$

This implies (using (6.1.9), (6.2.6), (6.2.5))

$$f^i_0(x_{i.}) = F_0(g_0(x^0_{11}, \ldots, x_{i1}, \ldots, x^0_{n1}), \ldots, g^m_0(x^0_{1m}, \ldots, x_{im}, \ldots, x^0_{nm})).$$

Equation (6.2.19) leads to the first part of (6.2.14). The second part is shown analogously. Now (6.2.16) becomes a trivial consequence of (6.0.1) and (6.2.14).

To check (6.2.17) let $w_i = F_0(a_i)$ (according to (6.2.14) and (6.2.15)). From (6.2.16) we obtain

$$\begin{aligned} y_0(e, \ldots, w_i, \ldots, e) &= y_0(F_0(e, \ldots, e), \ldots, F_0(a_i), \ldots, F_0(e, \ldots, e)) \\ &= F_0(y_0(e, \ldots, a_{i1}, \ldots, e), \ldots, y_0(e, \ldots, a_{im}, \ldots, e)) \end{aligned}$$

since by definition of e we have $e = F_0(e, \ldots, e)$. Identities (6.2.14), (6.2.15), and (6.2.19) show that $y_0(e, \ldots, a_{ij}, \ldots, e) = a_{ij}$. We obtain

$$y_0(e, \ldots, w_i, \ldots, e) = F_0(a_{i1}, \ldots, a_{im}) = F_0(a_{i.}) = w_i.$$

The rest of (6.2.17) is shown analogously.

The rest of the proof is trivial. ■

There are three aspects of Theorem 6.2.12 we wish to point out:

First, in the sense of (6.2.14) all microeconomic production functions must be "of the same kind" as the macroeconomic production function; all index functions (for production factors and for total output) must be "of the same kind." Note, however, that the k^{ij}_0 give some freedom, at least.

Second, we have to solve functional equation (6.2.16) (involving only two functions) rather than (6.0.1) (involving $2 + n + m$ functions).

Third, since the f^i (and hence the f_0^i) need not be strictly increasing, it makes sense to pose the following question: is aggregation possible if some of the f^i are of the Walras–Leontief type? The answer is no! (For a proof see Pokropp [1972b].) An intuitive argument might be drawn from (6.2.14): the ↑-functions f_0^i and the ↟-function F_0 must not be "too different." If they are "too different," the distribution of production factors becomes a constitutive part in the construction of a macroeconomic production function, which then cannot satisfy (6.0.1) for *all* x_{ij}.

The rest of this chapter deals with methods for solving Eq. (6.2.16).

6.3 Differentiable Solutions; Continuous Solutions

Consider the functional equation for ↟-functions

$$y_0(F_0(a_{1\cdot}), \ldots, F_0(a_{n\cdot})) = F_0(y_0(a_{\cdot 1}), \ldots, y_0(a_{\cdot m})) \tag{6.3.1}$$

for $a_{ij} \in A_{ij}$ = given sets of $\mathbb{R}_+$. Let $e_{\cdot\cdot} := (e, \ldots, e)$ (with $e \in A_{ij}$ for all i, j) be a "neutral element" satisfying

$$y_0(e, \ldots, w_i, \ldots, e) = w_i, \qquad F_0(e, \ldots, z_j, e) = z_j \tag{6.3.2}$$

or all i, j and for all

$$w_i \in W_i = F_0(A_{i\cdot}), \qquad z_j \in Z_j = y_0(A_{\cdot j}). \tag{6.3.3}$$

Each side in (6.3.1) can be considered a function of the a_{ij}:

$$\begin{aligned} G_0(a_{\cdot\cdot}) &= y_0(F_0(a_{1\cdot}), \ldots, F_0(a_{n\cdot})), \\ G_0^*(a_{\cdot\cdot}^*) &= F_0(y_0(a_{\cdot 1}), \ldots, y_0(a_{\cdot m})). \end{aligned} \tag{6.3.4}$$

Clearly, $(y_0; F_0, \ldots, F_0/F_0; y_0, \ldots, y_0)$ is an aggregate solution for (G_0, G_0^*) normed by $e_{\cdot\cdot}$.

All assumptions so far are justified by Theorem 6.2.12. We now assume in this section that A_{ij}, W_i, and Z_j from (6.3.3) are open intervals for all i, j.

6.3.5 **Theorem.** *(Nataf [1948]). Let the above-mentioned assumptions be satisfied. If y_0 and F_0 satisfying (6.3.1) have (positive) partial derivatives everywhere, then there exists a function h and constants c, d such that*

$$\begin{aligned} y_0(w_1, \ldots, w_n) &= h\left(\sum_i h^{-1}(w_i) + c\right), \\ F_0(z_1, \ldots, z_m) &= h\left(\sum_j h^{-1}(z_j) + d\right). \end{aligned} \tag{6.3.6}$$

6.3.7 **Remark.** If y and F in an aggregate solution are differentiable, then so are y_0 and F_0 and vice versa. (This follows from (6.2.10) and the fact that by (6.2.17) the α^i in (6.2.10) are differentiable if y or y_0 is.) Thus the analytical properties of the microproduction functions and of the index functions for production factors (f^i and g^j) are totally irrelevant for aggregation problem (6.0.1).

Proof (for details see Green [1964]). We differentiate (6.3.1) in order to obtain

$$\frac{\partial y_0}{\partial w_i}\,\frac{\partial F_0(a_{i\cdot})}{\partial a_{ij}} = \frac{\partial F_0}{\partial z_j}\,\frac{\partial y_0(a_{\cdot j})}{\partial a_{ij}}$$

and hence

$$\frac{\partial y_0/\partial w_i}{\partial F_0/\partial z_j} = \frac{\partial y_0(a_{\cdot j})/\partial a_{ij}}{\partial F_0(a_{i\cdot})/\partial a_{ij}}\,. \tag{6.3.8}$$

The right-hand side of (6.3.8) is a function of $a_{i\cdot}$ and $a_{\cdot j}$ only. Since the left-hand side of (6.3.8) is a function of $w_1, \ldots, w_n, z_1, \ldots, z_m$, it must be possible to write

$$\frac{\partial y_0/\partial w_i}{\partial F_0/\partial z_j} = \frac{u^i(w_i)}{v^j(z_j)} \quad \text{or} \quad \frac{\partial y_0}{\partial w_i} = u^i(w_i)\cdot\frac{\partial F_0/\partial z_j}{v^j(z_j)}\,. \tag{6.3.9}$$

Since (6.3.9) holds for all i, j, it must be possible to find a function $D : \mathbb{R}^n_+ \to \mathbb{R}_+$ (independent of i, j) such that

$$\partial y_0/\partial w_i = u^i(w_i)\, D(w_1, \ldots, w_n) \qquad \text{for} \quad i = 1, \ldots, n.$$

The solution of this system is known to be

$$y_0(w_1, \ldots, w_n) = h\left(\sum_i h^i(w_i)\right).$$

From (6.3.2) we obtain $h^i(w_i) = h^{-1}(w_i) + c$. This proves the first part of (6.3.6). In the same way we obtain

$$F_0(z_1, \ldots, z_m) = k\left(\sum_j k^{-1}(z_j) + d\right).$$

It is possible to take $k = h$ without loss of generality. ■

6.3.10 **Theorem** *(Gorman [1968]). Theorem 6.3.5 remains valid if the differentiability assumption is replaced by the assumption that y_0 and F_0 are continuous everywhere.*

Remark. Continuity of the microproduction functions f^i and of the index functions g^j for production factors in an aggregate solution is irrelevant. (See Remark 6.3.7.)

Proof (for details see Gorman [1968]). Consider the special case in which $i = 1, j = 1$. Write

$$a_{*1} := (a_{21}, \ldots, a_{n1}), \qquad a_{1*} := (a_{12}, \ldots, a_{1m}), \qquad a^{11}_{**} := (a_{22}, \ldots, a_{nm}).$$

Define the function K_{11} as

$$K_{11}(a_{11}, a_{1*}, a_{1*}, a^{11}_{**}) := G_0(a_1, \ldots, a_{n\cdot}). \tag{6.3.11}$$

With obvious modifications we may, for any fixed pair (i, j), define

$$K_{ij}(a_{ij}, a_{*i}, a_{*j}, a^{ij}_{**}) := G_0(a_{i\cdot}, \ldots, a_{n\cdot}).$$

Show then that there exist functions h, r, s, t such that

$$K_{11}(a_{11}, a_{1*}, a_{*1}, a^{11}_{**}) = h(r(a_{11}) + s(a_{1*}) + t(a_{*1}), a^{11}_{**}). \tag{6.3.12}$$

Then G_0 will be of the form

$$G_0(a_{1\cdot}, \ldots, a_{n\cdot}) = h\left(\sum_{i,j} k_{ij}(a_{ij})\right),$$

and then (6.3.6) follows from (6.3.2) and (6.3.4).

The first step in proving (6.3.12) is to show that there exist functions $\phi = \phi_{11}$, $q = q_{11}$ such that

$$F_0(a_{11}, a_{1*}) = q(\phi(a_{1*}), a_{11}). \tag{6.3.13}$$

According to Theorem 6.2.1 and Definition 6.1.13, (6.3.13) is equivalent to

$$F_0(a_{11}, a_{1*}) \leqq F(a_{11}, a'_{0*}) \quad \text{implies} \quad F_0(a'_{11}, a_{1*}) \leqq F_0(a'_{11}, a'_{1*}) \tag{6.3.14}$$
$$\text{for all } a_{11}, a'_{11}, a'_{1*}), a_{1*}.$$

Suppose that $F_0(a_{11}, a_{1*}) \leqq F_0(a_{11}, a'_{1*})$. Then for arbitrary but fixed (suitably chosen in (6.3.15)) $a^0_{21}, \ldots, a^0_{n1}$ we have

$$y_0(F_0(a_{11}, a_{1*}), a^0_{21}, a_{1*} \ldots, a^0_{n1}) \leqq y_0(F_0(a_{11}, a'_{1*}), a^0_{21}, \ldots, a^0_{n1}).$$

Then (6.3.1) implies

$$F_0(y_0(a_{11}, a^0_{*1}), a_{12}, \ldots, a_{1m}) \leqq F_0(y_0(a_{11}, a^0_{*1}), a'_{12}, \ldots, a'_{1n}).$$

If for given a_{11}, a'_{11} there always exist a^0_{*1}, a^{00}_{*1} such that

$$y_0(a_{11}, a^0_{*1}) = y_0(a'_{11}, a^{00}_{*1}), \tag{6.3.15}$$

we can apply the steps preceding (6.3.15) in reverse to obtain

$$y_0(F_0(a'_{11}, a_{1*}), a^{00}_{21}, \ldots, a^{00}_{n1}) \leqq y_0(F_0(a'_{11}, a'_{1*}), a^{00}_{21}, \ldots, a^{00}_{n1}).$$

The $\updownarrow$-property of y_0 then yields $F_0(a'_{11}, a_{1*}) \leqq F_0(a'_{11}, a'_{1*})$. Thus in order to show (6.3.13), we have to show (6.3.15) with suitably chosen a^0_{*1}, a^{00}_{*1}.

Analogously we have to show that, given a_{11}, a'_{11}, there always exist a^0_{1*}, a^{00}_{1*} such that

$$F_0(a_{11}, a^0_{1*}) = F_0(a'_{11}, a^{00}_{1*}). \tag{6.3.16}$$

Clearly, (6.3.16) will yield the separability of y_0 analogously to (6.3.14) and hence to (6.3.13). There exist functions $\eta = \eta_{11}$, $p = p_{11}$ such that

$$y_0(a_{11}, a_{*1}) = p(a_{11}, \eta(a_{*1})). \tag{6.3.17}$$

Before we proceed with (6.3.17) and (6.3.13) we indicate how (6.3.15) (and (6.3.16)) can be obtained: Define an equivalence relation on A_{11} as follows: $a_{11} \sim a'_{11}$ if and only if there exist a^0_{*1}, a^{00}_{*1} such that (6.3.15) holds.

The following statements heavily rely upon continuity:

All equivalence classes are intervals. Suppose there are at least two different classes. Then let a^0_{11} be a common boundary point of two neighboring classes, I_1 and I_2, say. There are points in I_1 and I_2 that are arbitrarily close to a^0_{11}. But then there must exist $a_{11} \in I_1$, a^0_{*1}, a^{00}_{*1} such that $y_0(a^0_{11}, a^0_{1*}) = y(a_{11}, a^{00}_{*1})$ or $a^0_{11} \sim a_{11}$. In the same way there must exist $a'_{11} \in I_2$ such that $a^0_{11} \sim a'_{11}$. This means that $I_1 \cap I_2 \neq \emptyset$, a contradiction. Thus A_{11} is the only equivalence class of $\sim$; Eqs. (6.3.15) and, analogously, (6.3.16) hold.

From (6.3.13), (6.3.17), and (6.3.1) we conclude that K_{11} in (6.3.11) can be written in two different ways: there exist $\updownarrow$-functions $L = L_{11}$, $M = M_{11}$ such that

$$L\big(\phi(a_{1*}), p(a_{11}, \eta(a_{*1})), a^{11}_{**}\big) = K_{11} = M\big(q(\phi(a_{1*}), a_{11}), \eta(a_{*1}), a^{11}_{**}\big). \tag{6.3.18}$$

Since y_0, F_0 are continuous $\updownarrow$-functions, all functions in (6.3.18) are continuous $\updownarrow$-functions. But then without loss of generality we may assume (perhaps after suitable continuous $\updownarrow$-transformations) that for fixed a^{11}_{**}

$$\begin{gathered} \phi(A_{1*}) = A_{11} = \eta(A_{*1}), \qquad p(A_{11}, A_{11}) = A_{11} = q(A_{11}, A_{11}), \\ L(A_{11}, A_{11}, a^{11}_{**}) = A_{11} = M(A_{11}, A_{11}, a^{11}_{**}). \end{gathered} \tag{6.3.19}$$

Under condition (6.3.19) the solution of (6.3.18) is known. All functions in (6.3.18)—apart from ϕ and η—are generalized quasilinear (see definition (2.3.1)); there are continuous $\updownarrow$-functions f, g, k, m, α, β such that

$$\begin{aligned} L(x, y) &= \beta[k(x) + \alpha(y)], \qquad & M(x, y) &= \beta[f(x) + g(y)], \\ p(x, y) &= \alpha^{-1}[m(x) + g(y)], \qquad & q(x, y) &= f^{-1}[k(x) + m(y)]. \end{aligned} \tag{6.3.20}$$

We omit the somewhat lengthy proof of (6.3.20) and refer to Aczél [1966, Corollary 1, p. 312]. Clearly, (6.3.20) and (6.3.18) imply that we can write (for fixed a^{11}_{**}):

$$K_{11} = \beta(k[\phi(a_{1*})] + m[a_{11}] + g[\eta(a_{*1})]). \tag{6.3.21}$$

It must be possible to choose k, m, g independently of a^{11}_{**}(p and q in (6.3.20) are independent of a^{11}_{**}, as is seen from (6.3.13), (6.3.17); for a detailed proof see Gorman [1968]). Thus we in fact obtain (6.3.12) from (6.3.21). ■

Remark. Apparently, (6.3.18) is again the generalized associativity equation (5.0.1). The assumptions under which (6.3.18) was to be solved here are given by (6.3.19) and the fact that L, M, p, q are continuous $\updownarrow$-functions. In Chapter 5, differentiability was available, and the treatment there cannot be applied to (6.3.18).

6.4 Substitutional Solutions

In this section we treat the functional equation for $\uparrow$-functions

$$y_0(F_0(a_{1.}), \ldots, F_0(a_{n.})) = F_0(y_0(a_{.1}), \ldots, y_0(a_{.m})) \tag{6.4.1}$$

with $a_{ij} \in A_{ij}$ (given) and with given neutral element $e \in A_{ij}$:

$$y_0(e, \ldots, w_i, \ldots, e) = w_i, \qquad F_0(e, \ldots, z_j, \ldots, e) = z_j \tag{6.4.2}$$

for $w_i \in W_i$, $z_j \in Z_j$ (see (6.3.3)) under the additional assumption that all A_{ij} are equal:

$$A_{ij} = A \quad \text{for all} \quad i = 1, \ldots, n, \quad \text{all} \quad j = 1, \ldots, m. \tag{6.4.3}$$

What is the economic meaning of (6.4.3)? If we consider (6.2.15) and (6.2.19), we can write, with $f^i := f^i_0$, $g^j := g^j_0$,

$$f^i(x^0_{i1}, \ldots, X_{ij}, \ldots, x^0_{im}) = f^i(x^0_{i1}, \ldots, X_{is}, \ldots, x^0_{im}), \tag{6.4.4}$$

$$g^j(x^0_{1j}, \ldots, X_{ij}, \ldots, x^0_{nj}) = g^j(x^0_{1j}, \ldots, X_{tj}, \ldots, x^0_{nj}) \tag{6.4.5}$$

for all $i, t = 1, \ldots, n$ and all $j, s = 1, \ldots, m$. Clearly, Theorem 6.2.9 assures that then (6.4.4) and (6.4.5) hold for f^i, g^j in any aggregate solution (not necessarily normed by $x^0_{..}$).

Equations (6.4.4) and (6.4.5) suggest the following economic interpretation of (6.4.3). If we start with a given factor combination $x^0_{i.}$, then changes of output caused by changes of one factor input (the jth, say) may also be obtained by changes of any other factor (the sth, say). Analogously, starting from the "distribution" $x^0_{.j}$ of the jth factor type among the n firms, any change in the aggregated jth factor caused by one firm might have been caused by any other firm.

6.4.6 **Definition.** f^i is called *(j, s)-substitutional (in $x^0_{i.}$)* if (6.4.4) holds. g^j is called *(i, t)-substitutional (in $x^0_{.j}$)* if (6.4.5) holds. An aggregate solution $(y; f^1, \ldots, f^n/F; g^1, \ldots, g^m)$ is called *substitutional (in $x^0_{..}$)* if (6.4.4) and (6.4.5) hold for all $i, t = 1, \ldots, n$, all $j, s = 1, \ldots, m$ (if (6.4.3) holds for all i, j with A_{ij} from (6.2.15), (6.2.19)).

6.4.7 **Theorem.** *Under (6.4.3), (6.4.2) the ‡-functions y_0 and F_0 in (6.4.1) are symmetric; that is,*

$$\begin{aligned} F_0(z_1, \ldots, z_j, \ldots, z_s, \ldots, z_m) &= F_0(z_1, \ldots, z_j' = z_s, \ldots, z_s' = z_j, \ldots, z_m), \\ y_0(w_1, \ldots, w_i, \ldots, w_t, \ldots, w_n) &= y_0(w_1, \ldots, w_i' = w_t, \ldots, w_t' = w_i, \ldots, w_n) \end{aligned} \tag{6.4.8}$$

for all $w_1, \ldots, w_n$, *all* $z_1, \ldots, z_m$, *all* $i, t = 1, \ldots, n$, *and all* $j, s = 1, \ldots, m$.

Proof. We prove only the first part of (6.4.8). Let $z_r = y_0(a_{.r})$ for $r = 1, \ldots, m$. Let j, s be fixed. Then

$$\begin{aligned} &F_0(z_1, \ldots, z_j, \ldots, z_s, \ldots, z_m) \\ &\quad = y_0(F_0(a_{11}, \ldots, a_{1j}, \ldots, a_{1s}, \ldots, a_{1m}), \ldots, F_0(a_{n1}, \ldots, a_{nj}, \ldots, a_{ns}, \ldots, a_{nm})), \end{aligned}$$

by (6.4.1). It is thus sufficient to show that F_0 is symmetric on $A^m = A \times \times \cdots \times A$ (m times). Let $a_1 \in A, \ldots, a_m \in A$. Then from (6.4.2) and (6.4.1) we obtain

$$\begin{aligned} &F_0(a_1, \ldots, a_j, \ldots, a_s, \ldots, a_m) \\ &= F_0(y_0(a_1, e, \ldots), \ldots, y_0(e, a_j, e, \ldots), \ldots, y_0(e, a_s, e, \ldots), \ldots, y_0(a_m, e, \ldots)) \\ &= y_0(F_0(a_1, \ldots, e_j = e, \ldots, e_s = e, \ldots, a_m), F_0(e, \ldots, a_j, \ldots, a_s, \ldots, e), \\ &e, \ldots, e). \end{aligned}$$

It is thus sufficient to show that

$$F_0(e, \ldots, a_j, \ldots, a_s, \ldots, e) = F_0(e, \ldots, a_j' = a_s, \ldots, a_s' = a_j, \ldots, e)$$

for all $a_j, a_s \in A$. At first we note that

$$\begin{aligned} &F_0(e, \ldots, a_j, \ldots, a_s, \ldots, e) \\ &\quad = F_0(e, \ldots, y_0(a_j, e, \ldots), \ldots, y_0(e, a_s, e, \ldots), \ldots, e) \\ &\quad = y_0(F_0(a_j, e, \ldots), F_0(e, a_s, e, \ldots), e, \ldots, e) = F_0(a_j, a_s, e, \ldots, e) \end{aligned}$$

(use (6.4.1) and (6.4.2)). But we also have (again use, (6.4.1), (6.4.2))

$$\begin{aligned} F_0(a_j, a_s, e, \ldots, e) &= y_0(F_0(e, a_j, e, \ldots, e), F_0(a_s, e, \ldots, e), e, \ldots, e) \\ &= F_0(a_s, a_j, e, \ldots, e). \end{aligned}$$

This completes the proof. ■

6.4.9 **Theorem.** *Under (6.4.1)–(6.4.3) the ‡-functions y_0 and F_0 are generated on A^n and A^m, respectively, in the following way: There exists a ‡-function of two variables only,*

$$H : (F_0(A^m) \cup y_0(A^n)) \times (F_0(A^m) \cup y_0(A_u)) \to \mathbb{R},$$

such that for all $i < n, j < m$

$$\begin{aligned} y_0(a_1, \ldots, a_i, a_{i+1}, e, \ldots, e) &= H(a_{i+1}, y_0(a_1, \ldots, a_i, e, \ldots, e)), \\ F_0(a_1, \ldots, a_j, a_{j+1}, e, \ldots, e) &= H(a_{j+1}, F_0(a_1, \ldots, a_j, e, \ldots, e)), \end{aligned} \tag{6.4.10}$$

$$H(u, e) = u = H(e, u) \tag{6.4.11}$$

(H a symmetric $\updownarrow$-function). Furthermore,

$$\left.\begin{aligned} &y_0(a_1, \ldots, a_i, a_{i+1}, \ldots, a_n) \\ &\qquad = H(y_0(a_1, \ldots, a_i, e, \ldots, e), y_0(e, \ldots, e, a_{i+1}, \ldots, a_n)), \\ &F_0(a_1, \ldots, a_j, a_{j+1}, \ldots, a_m) \\ &\qquad = H(F_0(a_1, \ldots, a_j, e, \ldots, e), F_0(e, \ldots, e, a_{j+1}, \ldots, a_m)) \end{aligned}\right\} \quad (6.4.12)$$

for all i, j. H satisfies the associativity law

$$H(a, H(b, c)) = H(H(a, b), c) \qquad \text{for all} \quad a, b, c \in A. \qquad (6.4.13)$$

Proof. We first show that

$$W \subseteqq Z \quad \text{for} \quad m \leqq n, \qquad Z \subset W \quad \text{for} \quad n \leqq m \quad \text{with} \quad W = F_0(A^m), \quad Z = y_0(A^n). \qquad (6.4.14)$$

Indeed, (6.4.7) implies that $G_0 = G_0^*$, where G_0, G_0^* are given by (6.3.4). Since

$$\begin{aligned} F_0(A^m) &= G_0(A, \ldots, A_m = A, e, \ldots, e) \subseteqq G_0^*(A, \ldots, A_n = A, e, \ldots, e) \\ &= y_0(A, \ldots, A_n = A, e, \ldots, e) \end{aligned}$$

for $m \leqq n$ (by (6.4.2), (6.4.3) with $y_0(e, \ldots, e) = e = F_0(e, \ldots, e)$), we may conclude that $W \subseteqq Z$. The second part of (6.4.14) follows in the same way.

By a similar argument we obtain

$$\begin{aligned} F_0(w_1, \ldots, w_m) &= y_0(w_1, \ldots, w_m, e, \ldots, e) \quad &&\text{for} \quad m \leqq n, \quad w_j \in W, \\ y_0(z_1, \ldots, z_n) &= F_0(z_1, \ldots, z_n, e, \ldots, e) \quad &&\text{for} \quad n \leqq m, \quad z_i \in Z. \end{aligned} \qquad (6.4.15)$$

(Note first that (6.4.15) holds for all w_j, $z_i \in A$, then deduce (6.4.15) for all w_j, z_i.)

We now have to define the $\uparrow$-function $H : [W \cup Z] \times [W \cup Z] \to \mathbb{R}$:

$$\begin{aligned} H(u, v) &:= F_0(u, v, e, \ldots, e) \quad &&\text{for} \quad m \leqq n, \quad W \cup Z = Z, \\ H(u, v) &:= y_0(u, v, e, \ldots, e) \quad &&\text{for} \quad n \leqq m, \quad W \cup Z = W. \end{aligned} \qquad (6.4.16)$$

(Note that (6.4.15) excludes contradictions in (6.4.16)).

Property (6.4.11) follows from (6.4.16), (6.4.2), (6.4.7). In order to show (6.4.10) it is sufficient to show (6.4.12). We show the first part of (6.4.12) only. From (6.4.2), (6.4.1) we obtain

$$\begin{aligned} &y_0(a_1, \ldots, a_n) \\ &\quad = y_0(F_0(a_1, e, \ldots, e), \ldots, F_0(a_i, e, \ldots, e), \\ &\qquad\qquad F_0(e, a_{i+1}, e, \ldots, e), \ldots, F_0(e, a_n, e, \ldots, e)) \\ &\quad = F_0(y_0(a_1, \ldots, a_i, e, \ldots, e), y_0(e, \ldots, e, a_{i+1}, \ldots, a_n), e, \ldots, e). \end{aligned}$$

The first equation of (6.4.12) follows now from (6.4.16).

Finally, (6.4.13) is a consequence of

$$H(H(a, d), H(b, c)) = H(H(a, b), H(d, c)), \qquad a, b, c, d \in A, \quad (6.4.17)$$

if in (6.4.17) we set $d = e$ and observe (6.4.11). Equation (6.4.17) is nothing but a special version of (6.4.1) with $a_{ij} = e$ for $i > 2$ or $j > 2$ and with (6.4.16).

Theorem 6.4.9 has drastically reduced the aggregation problem and thus the problem of solving (6.4.1). All we have to do is determine the structure of H. In particular, we have to solve (6.4.13) and/or (6.4.17). This does not seem possible without further assumptions. For instance, we have not yet said whether $H(a, b) \in A$ for $a, b \in A$ or not. Before we introduce further assumptions (see (6.4.23) and (6.4.26)), we look at the economic meaning of (6.4.10) and (6.4.12).

From (6.4.12) and (6.4.11) we conclude that y_0 on A^n and F_0 on A^m are separable in the sense of (6.1.13) with respect to any collection of variables. y_0 on A^n and F_0 on A^m may be written as functions of arbitrary "subaggregates" (Theorem 6.2.1). If in particular we pay attention to (6.4.10), we see, for instance, that from (6.2.14), (6.2.15) and Theorem 6.2.9 we obtain

$$\begin{aligned} f^i(x_{i1}, \ldots, x_{i,j-1}, x_{ij}, x^0_{i,j+1}, \ldots, x^0_{im}) \\ = \alpha^i H(k_0^{ij}(x_{ij}), \alpha^{-i} f^i(x_{i1}, \ldots, x_{i,j-1}, x^0_{ij}, \ldots, x^0_{im})) \end{aligned} \qquad (6.4.18)$$

for all $i = 1, \ldots, n$, where α^i (with inverse α^{-i}) is the $\updownarrow$-transformation defined by $f^i = \alpha^i f^i_0$ according to (6.2.9).

To formula (6.4.18) we give the following economic interpretation: The production process in the ith firm (described by f^i) is generated by a production process with only two inputs, as described by the "production function" $\alpha^i H$ if inputs are suitably measured. As for (6.4.18), we may deduce an "elementary process" $\beta^j H$ (where $g^j = \beta^j g^j_0$) to generate the index function g^j.

6.4.19 **Definition.** The function H defined by (6.4.16) is called the *elementary process of* (G_0, G_0^*) *normed by* e. H is also called the *elementary process of* (G, G^*) *normed by* $x^0_{..}$ (where $G(x^0_{..}) = e$).

In order to determine the structure of the elementary process, we restrict our attention to production functions and index functions that are in a certain sense "unlimited." Shephard [1970, p. 22] states the following axiom (his A.4) for a production function Φ.

$$\Phi(\mu \cdot x_{..}) \to \infty \quad \text{as} \quad \mu \to \infty \qquad \text{for any} \quad x_{..} > 0. \qquad (6.4.20)$$

Analogously to (6.4.20) we want to express that with a fixed quantity $a \in A$ with $a > e$ (clearly, e must take the role of the neutral element 0 in (6.4.20)) we may exceed every possible output if sufficiently large multiples of quantity a are used as inputs. However, an "ordinary" multiple $r \cdot a$ might not belong to A. To realize "r times a" as an input quantity we therefore apply a "successive" procedure: the elementary process H is carried out r times such that at stage $m (m \leqq r)$ the product quantity of stage $m-1$ and quantity a are used as input quantities. This successive procedure can be made possible (see (6.4.21)) by the following postulate: Aggregate solutions of (G, G^*) are substitutional in each $x_{..}$.

6.4.21 **Theorem.** *An aggregate solution for* (G, G^*) *is substitutional in every point* $x_{..} \in X_{..}$ *if and only if the elementary process* H *of* (G, G^*) *normed by an arbitrary but fixed point* $x^0_{..}$ *satisfies*

$$H(a, A) = A \qquad \textit{for all} \quad a \in A. \tag{6.4.22}$$

Proof. As can easily be seen from (6.4.10), (6.4.22) is equivalent to

$$\begin{aligned} F_0(a_1, \ldots, A_j = A, \ldots, a_m) &= A \qquad \text{for all} \quad a_1, \ldots, a_m \in A, \quad \text{all } j, \\ y_0(a_1, \ldots, A_i = A, \ldots, a_n) &= A \qquad \text{for all} \quad a_1, \ldots, a_n \in A, \quad \text{all } i. \end{aligned} \tag{6.4.23}$$

Observe that (6.4.23) together with (6.2.14) makes (6.4.21) trivial. (Consider, e. g., (6.4.4) with $s = j+1$ and with $(x^0_{i1}, \ldots, x^0_{i,j-1}, x^0_{ij}, x_{i,j+2}, \ldots, x^0_{i\cdot})$ instead of $x^0_{\cdot\cdot}$). ■

For the rest of this chapter the validity of (6.4.22) will be assumed. We can then introduce the notation

$$0 * a = e \quad \text{and} \quad r * a = H(a, (r-1) * a) \qquad \text{for} \quad r = 1, 2, 3, \ldots, \tag{6.4.24}$$

which defines "r times a" $= r * a$ for all $a \in A$ and all $r = 0, 1, 2, \ldots$. The "product" $r * a$ represents that quantity that is produced by the process if a is used r times as additional input. In accordance with (6.4.20) we suggest

(6.4.25) **Definition.** The elementary process is called *unlimited* if for any $a \in A$, $b \in A$, $a > e$, $b > e$ there exists a natural number r such that $r * a > b$ (where $*$ is defined by (6.4.24)).

Note that, according to (6.4.23), A is also the set of all possible outputs of F_0 and hence of f^i_0.

6.4.26 **Theorem.** *Let* (G, G^*) *have an aggregate solution that is substitutional in every point. Let the elementary process* H *of* (G, G^*) *normed by an arbitrary but fixed point* $x^0_{..}$ *be unlimited. Then there exists a* $\updownarrow$*-function* h *such that*

$$H(a, b) = h(h^{-1}(a) + h^{-1}(b)) \qquad \textit{for all} \quad a, b \in A. \tag{6.4.27}$$

Equivalently we may say that G (resp. G^*) is of the form

$$G(x_{1\cdot}, \ldots, x_{n\cdot}) = h\Big(\sum_{i,j} k^{ij}(x_{ij})\Big) = G^*(x_{\cdot 1}, \ldots, x_{\cdot m}).$$

Proof. From (6.4.22), (6.4.13), (6.4.11) we conclude that with

$$a \oplus b := H(a, b) \qquad \text{for} \quad a, b \in A \tag{6.4.28}$$

we define a fully ordered Abelian group on A, denoted by $A(\oplus)$. Unlimitedness, according to (6.4.25), makes the order Archimedean. It is known that fully ordered Archimedean groups are order isomorphic to an additive subgroup of the real numbers (see Fuchs [1963, p. 45]). Thus there exists a ⥉-function $h^{-1}: A \to \mathbb{R}$ such that

$$h^{-1}(a \oplus b) = h^{-1}(a) + h^{-1}(b) \qquad \text{for all} \quad a, b \in A.$$

Formula (6.4.27) now follows from (6.4.28). The rest of Theorem 6.4.26 is trivial. ■

The foregoing proof shows that if the assumption of unlimitedness is dropped, $A(\oplus)$ may not be Archimedean. All we can say about H then is that it is given by an Abelian group operation according to (6.4.28).

Keeping in mind (6.4.10), we can state the following results about the solutions of functional equation (6.4.1).

6.4.29 **Theorem.** *Let y_0, F_0 satisfy (6.4.1) and (6.4.2). Let further (6.4.3) and (6.4.23) hold. Let y_0 and F_0 be ⥉-functions. Then on A we can find an operation $\oplus$ such that $A(\oplus)$ is a fully ordered Abelian group and*

$$y_0(a_1, \ldots, a_n) = a_1 \oplus a_2 \oplus \cdots \oplus a_n,$$
$$F_0(a_1, \ldots, a_m) = a_1 \oplus a_2 \oplus \cdots \oplus a_m.$$

If $\oplus$ is unlimited in the sense of (6.4.25) with $r * a = a \oplus \cdots \oplus a$ (r times), then $A(\oplus)$ is Archimedean and we have

$$y_0(a_1, \ldots, a_n) = h\left(\sum_i h^{-1}(a_i)\right), \qquad F_0(a_1, \ldots, a_m) = h\left(\sum_j h^{-1}(a_j)\right)$$

with a suitable function h.

7

Functional Equations in the Theory of Price Level and Quantity Level

This chapter (which contains results presented in lecture notes by Eichhorn and Voeller [1976]) is concerned with some functional equations that play an important role in the theory of price level and quantity level. For illustrative purposes we consider Fisher's [1911] famous equation of exchange; this equation leads to several functional equations for which no solutions exist. We shall formulate theorems stating the nonexistence of price and quantity levels of a desirable kind.

The reason for these rather disappointing results lies in the fact that the equations considered impose too strong conditions on the respective (classes of) price levels or quantity levels. A price level is defined as a function that "aggregates" a vector of commodity prices into the nonegative real numbers. Analogously, a quantity level is defined as a function that "aggregates" the commodity vector into the nonnegative real numbers.

Similar nonexistence theorems can be shown very often in connection with problems of aggregation. Compare, for example, the results on the functional equation of aggregation in the preceding chapter, or the results on systems of functional equations in the theory of the price index in Chapter 8.

In certain cases we succeed in finding or characterizing important classes of functions that aggregate vectors of economic data by imposing several structural conditions on them; see Chapters 8 and 9, where the structural conditions have in most cases the form of functional equations.

ISBN 0-201-01948-5/01949-3 PBK

7.1 Price Levels and Quantity Levels

We denote by $\mathbf{p} = (p_1, \ldots, p_n) \in \mathbb{R}^n_+$ the vector of prices of n commodities, and by $\mathbf{q} = (q_1, \ldots, q_n) \in \mathbb{R}^n_+$ the vector of quantities of the commodities.

A *price level P depending only on the (vector of) prices*[1] $\mathbf{p}$ is defined to be a function

$$P : \mathbb{R}^n_+ \to \mathbb{R}_+, \qquad \mathbf{p} \to P(\mathbf{p})$$

that satisfies the following two properties, called axioms:

7.1.1 *Monotonicity Axiom.* The function P is *strictly increasing*, that is, for every pair $\mathbf{p} \in \mathbb{R}^n_+$, $\bar{\mathbf{p}} \in \mathbb{R}^n_+$ with $\mathbf{p} \geq \bar{\mathbf{p}}$ we have $P(\mathbf{p}) > P(\bar{\mathbf{p}})$.

7.1.2 *Linear Homogeneity Axiom.* The function P is *linearly homogeneous* (homogeneous of degree 1), that is, for all $\mathbf{p} \in \mathbb{R}^n_+$, $\lambda \in \mathbb{R}_+$ we have

$$P(\lambda \mathbf{p}) = \lambda P(\mathbf{p}).$$

The value $P(\mathbf{p})$ of the function P is called *value of the price level at prices* $\mathbf{p}$.

Examples of such price levels are given by (7.1.8)–(7.1.10). Important classes of such price levels can be characterized by the following properties, which we call tests:

7.1.3 *Additivity Test.* A price level P is called *additive* if every additive change of the prices from $\mathbf{p}$ to $\mathbf{p} + \mathbf{p}^*$ yields an additive change of the value of the price level from $P(\mathbf{p})$ to $P(\mathbf{p}) + P(\mathbf{p}^*)$ that is, if for all pairs of price vectors $\mathbf{p} \in \mathbb{R}^n_+$, $\mathbf{p}^* \in \mathbb{R}^n_+$

$$P(\mathbf{p} + \mathbf{p}^*) = P(\mathbf{p}) + P(\mathbf{p}^*).$$

7.1.4 *Homogeneity in all $(n - 1)$-tuples of Prices Test.* A price level P is called *homogeneous of positive degree in every $(n - 1)$-tuple of prices* if for all $\mathbf{p} \in \mathbb{R}^n_+$, $\lambda \in \mathbb{R}_+$, $j = 1, \ldots, n$, there is an $r_j > 0$ such that

$$P(\lambda p_1, \ldots, \lambda p_{j-1}, p_j, \lambda p_{j+1}, \ldots, \lambda p_n) = \lambda^{r_j} P(\mathbf{p}).$$

7.1.5 *Multiplicativity Test.* A price level P is called *multiplicative* if the value of the price level at prices $\lambda_1 p_1, \ldots, \lambda_n p_n$, where $\lambda_1, \ldots, \lambda_n$ are arbitrary nonnegative real numbers, is equal to the value of the price level at $\mathbf{p} = (p_1, \ldots, p_n)$ times a nonnegative real number that depends only on the λ_i's; that is, if for all $\mathbf{p} \in \mathbb{R}^n_+$ and $(\lambda_1, \ldots, \lambda_n) \in \mathbb{R}^n_+$ there is a $\phi(\lambda_1, \ldots, \lambda_n) \in \mathbb{R}_+$ such that

$$P(\lambda_1 p_1, \ldots, \lambda_n p_n) = \phi(\lambda_1, \ldots, \lambda_n) P(\mathbf{p}).$$

---

[1] Price levels that depend on both prices and quantities will be introduced later.

7.1.6. *Quasilinearity Test.* A price level P is called *quasilinear* if there exist real constants $a_1, a_2, \ldots, a_n, b$ with $a_1 a_2 \ldots a_n \neq 0$ and a continuous and strictly monotonic function $f\colon \mathbb{R}_{++} \to \mathbb{R}$ with inverse f^{-1} such that we have, for the restriction of P to $\mathbb{R}^n_{++}$,

$$P(\mathbf{p}) = f^{-1}[a_1 f(p_1) + a_2 f(p_2) + \cdots + a_n f(p_n) + b]$$

(see 2.1.1)) for all $\mathbf{p} \in \mathbb{R}^n_{++}$.

We shall now present a theorem that establishes the classes of price levels for the previously listed tests:

7.1.7 **Theorem.** *The class of the price levels $P\colon \mathbb{R}^n_+ \to \mathbb{R}_+$ which:*

(i) *satisfies Additivity Test 7.1.3 is given by*

$$P(\mathbf{p}) = c_1 p_1 + \cdots + c_n p_n \tag{7.1.8.}$$

where $c_1 > 0, \ldots, c_n > 0$ are arbitrary real constants;

(ii) *satisfies Homogeneity Test 7.1.4 is given by*

$$P(\mathbf{p}) = C p_1^{\alpha_1} p_2^{\alpha_n} \cdots p_n^{\alpha_n} \tag{7.1.9}$$

where $C > 0, \alpha_1 > 0, \ldots, \alpha_n > 0$ are arbitrary real constants, and $\Sigma\alpha_\nu = 1$;

(iii) *satisfies Multiplicativity Test 7.1.5 is given by (7.1.9);*

(iv) *satisfies Quasilinearity Test 7.1.6 is given by (7.1.9) and by*

$$P(\mathbf{p}) = (\beta_1 p_1^{-\varrho} + \cdots + \beta_n p_n^{-\varrho})^{-1/\varrho} \tag{7.1.10}$$

where $\beta_1 > 0, \ldots, \beta_n > 0$, and $\varrho \neq 0$ are arbitrary real constants.

Proof. In view of Axioms 7.1.1 and 7.1.2, assertion (i) follows from Corollary 3.1.9 and Remark 3.1.11c, (ii) from Theorem 9.6.1, (iii) from Theorem 3.6.4, and (iv) from Theorem 2.2.1. ■

A *quantity level T depending only on the vector of quantities*[2] $\mathbf{q}$ is defined to be a function

$$T\colon \mathbb{R}^n_+ \to \mathbb{R}_+, \qquad \mathbf{q} \to T(\mathbf{q}), \tag{7.1.11}$$

which also satisfies Axioms 7.1.1 and 7.1.2. The value $T(\mathbf{q})$ of the function T is called the *value of the quantity level at quantities* $\mathbf{q}$.

Classes of quantity levels can be defined in analogy to the classes of price indices introduced earlier.

[2] Quantity levels that depend on both the quantities and the prices will be introduced later.

7.2 Fisher's Equation of Exchange

As an example of the relevance of price levels and quantitiy levels in economics, we shall discuss Fisher's [1911, pp. 21ff] famous equation of exchange, namely

$$MV = p_1q_1 + \cdots + p_nq_n. \tag{7.2.1}$$

Here M denotes the "average amount of money in circulation in the community during the year" and V is called the *velocity of circulation* and represents "the average rate of turnover of money in its exchange for goods."

We do *not* consider the question whether Eq. (7.2.1) is only a relation in order to define V (= $\mathbf{pq}/M$). Instead, our aim here is to analyze the possibility of simplifying the right-hand side of (7.2.1) as proposed by Fisher, whom we quote on this point: "We may, if we wish, further simplify the right side by writing it in the form PT where P is a weighted average of all the p's, and T is the sum of all the q's. P then represents in one magnitude the level of prices, and T represents in one magnitude the volume of trade" [1911, p. 21].

This "simplification" has been utilized in most of the relevant economic literature without ever questioning the validity of the underlying assumptions.

Fisher's proposed "simplification" of Eq. (7.2.1) leads to the well-known (see, e.g., Lipsey [1975, p. 619]) equation

$$MV = PT, \tag{7.2.2}$$

which is correct in view of Eq. (7.2.1) if and only if

$$PT = p_1q_1 + \cdots + p_nq_n \tag{7.2.3}$$

holds identically for all permissible quantities and prices.

In the next section we shall illustrate that Eqs. (7.2.1) and (7.2.2) are *not* equivalent. There does not exist a price level P depending only on the prices and a quantity level T depending only on the quantities such thas (7.2.3) holds for all $\mathbf{p} = (p_1, \ldots, p_n) \in \mathbb{R}_+^n$ and all $\mathbf{q} = (q_1, \ldots, q_n) \in \mathbb{R}_+^n$.

As a consequence of this, conclusions made from the "simplified" version (7.2.2) are not necessarily correct with respect to the original version (7.2.1) of the equation of exchange. For instance, from (7.2.2) it follows that the price level P increases with the average amount M of money if the velocity V of cicrculation and the volume T of trade are constant. But if V and the quantities $q_1, \ldots, q_n$ of trade are constant in (7.2.1), then an increase of M does not necessarily imply an increase of all prices $p_1, \ldots, p_n$; some of them may decrease, so that a suitably chosen price level P does *not* increase.

Many economists (e.g., most authors of textbooks) are apparently not aware of this fact, although a cue was indicated in Reed [1942, p. 144] or Warburton [1953].

7.3 Nonexistence of Price Levels and Quantity Levels in the Context of Fisher's Equation of Exchange

We shall now verify our claim, made in the preceding section, about the nonexistence of a price level P depending only on prices $\mathbf{p}$ and a quantity level T depending only on quantities $\mathbf{q}$, within the context of the equation of exchange. Eq. (7.2.3) reduces in this case to

$$P(\mathbf{p})\,T(\mathbf{q}) = p_1q_1 + \cdots + p_nq_n \qquad (\mathbf{p} \in \mathbb{R}_+^n, \mathbf{q} \in \mathbb{R}_+^n). \tag{7.3.1}$$

Let us denote

$$P(1, \ldots, 1) =: a, \qquad T(1, \ldots, 1) =: b.$$

The constants a and b are positive because of the strict monotonicity of both functions $P\colon \mathbb{R}_+^n \to \mathbb{R}_+$ and $T\colon \mathbb{R}_+^n \to \mathbb{R}_+$. Put $\mathbf{q} = (1, \ldots, 1)$ in (7.3.1) in order to get

$$P(\mathbf{p}) = (p_1 + \cdots + p_n)/b.$$

Analogously we obtain

$$T(\mathbf{q}) = (q_1 + \cdots + q_n)/a.$$

By inserting these two expressions into (7.3.1), we obtain

$$(1/ab)(p_1 + \cdots + p_n)(q_1 + \cdots + q_n) = p_1q_1 + \cdots + p_nq_n.$$

However, for $n \geqq 2$, this equation cannot be valid for all $\mathbf{p}$, $\mathbf{q}$; this proves

7.3.2 **Theorem.** *If $n \geqq 2$, there does not exist any pair of functions $P\colon \mathbb{R}_+^n \to \mathbb{R}_+$, $T\colon \mathbb{R}_+^n \to \mathbb{R}_+$ satisfying the functional equation (7.3.1).*

7.3.3 **Corollary.** *Let the price level P and quantity level T be defined as in Section 7.1. Then Fisher's equation of exchange (7.2.1) is not equivalent to its "simplified form", (7.2.2).*

This result suggests considering the price level P as a function of both prices *and* quantities; that is, we define a price level by

$$P : \mathbb{R}_+^{2n} \to \mathbb{R}_+, \qquad (\mathbf{q}, \mathbf{p}) \to P(\mathbf{q}, \mathbf{p}). \tag{7.3.4}$$

This price level should satisfy the following three axioms.

7.3.5 *Monotonicity Axiom*

$$P(\mathbf{q}, \mathbf{p}) > P(\mathbf{q}, \bar{\mathbf{p}}) \qquad \text{for all} \quad \mathbf{q} \in \mathbb{R}_{++}^n, \quad \mathbf{p} \in \mathbb{R}_+^n, \bar{\mathbf{p}} \in \mathbb{R}_+^n \qquad \text{with} \quad \mathbf{p} \geq \bar{\mathbf{p}}.$$

7.3.6 *Linear Homogeneity Axiom*

$$P(\mathbf{q}, \lambda\mathbf{p}) = \lambda P(\mathbf{q}, \mathbf{p}) \qquad \text{for all} \quad \mathbf{q} \in \mathbb{R}_+^n, \mathbf{p} \in \mathbb{R}_+^n, \lambda \in \mathbb{R}_+.$$

7.3.7 *Commensurability Axiom*

$$P\left(\frac{q_1}{\lambda_1}, \ldots, \frac{q_n}{\lambda_n}, \lambda_1 p_1, \ldots, \lambda_n p_n\right) = P(\mathbf{q}, \mathbf{p}) \qquad \text{for all} \quad (\mathbf{q}, \mathbf{p}) \in \mathbb{R}_+^{2n}, \boldsymbol{\lambda} \in \mathbb{R}_{++}^n;$$

that is, changing the units of measurement of the commodities leaves the value of the price level unchanged.

Eq. (7.2.3) becomes, by using price level (7.3.4),

$$P(\mathbf{q}, \mathbf{p})\, T(\mathbf{q}) = p_1 q_1 + \cdots + p_n q_n \qquad (\mathbf{p} \in \mathbb{R}_+^n, \mathbf{q} \in \mathbb{R}_+^n). \tag{7.3.8}$$

We shall, in addition, consider the quantity level T as a function of both the quantities and prices; that is, we define a quantity level by

$$T : \mathbb{R}_+^{2n} \to \mathbb{R}_+, \qquad (\mathbf{q}, \mathbf{p}) \to T(\mathbf{q}, \mathbf{p}). \tag{7.3.9}$$

This quantity level is required to satisfy Axioms 7.3.5–7.3.7, redefined in this case for function (7.3.9).

Equation (7.2.3) specializes, with price level (7.3.4) and quantity level (7.3.9), to

$$P(\mathbf{q}, \mathbf{p})\, T(\mathbf{q}, \mathbf{p}) = p_1 q_1 + \cdots + p_n q_n \qquad (\mathbf{p} \in \mathbb{R}_+^n, \mathbf{q} \in \mathbb{R}_+^n). \tag{7.3.10}$$

Consider now an arbitrary quantity level of either the form (7.1.11), namely T: $\mathbb{R}_+^n \to \mathbb{R}_+$, or the form (7.3.9), namely T : $\mathbb{R}_+^{2n} \to \mathbb{R}_+$. There will always exist functions P: $\mathbb{R}_+^{2n} \to \mathbb{R}_+$ such that (7.3.8) or (7.3.10) is valid, namely

$$P(\mathbf{q}, \mathbf{p}) = \begin{cases} \dfrac{p_1 q_1 + \cdots + p_n q_n}{T(\mathbf{q})} & \text{for } \mathbf{q} \geq \mathbf{0},^3 \\ 0 \quad \text{for } \mathbf{q} = \mathbf{0}, \end{cases} \tag{7.3.11}$$

$$P(\mathbf{q}, \mathbf{p}) = \begin{cases} \dfrac{p_1 q_1 + \cdots + p_n q_n}{T(\mathbf{q}, \mathbf{p})} & \text{for } \mathbf{pq} > 0,^4 \\ 0 \quad \text{for } \mathbf{pq} = 0, \end{cases} \tag{7.3.12}$$

respectively. But these functions cannot be considered price levels, since both do not satisfy Commensurability Axiom 7.3.7. For the function given by (7.3.11) this follows, even in the case in which $\lambda_1 = \cdots = \lambda_n =: \lambda$, from the linear homogeneity of T:

$$P\left(\frac{\mathbf{q}}{\lambda}, \lambda \mathbf{p}\right) = \frac{\lambda \mathbf{p}(\mathbf{q}/\lambda)}{T(\mathbf{q}/\lambda)} = \lambda P(\mathbf{q}, \mathbf{p}) \not\equiv P(\mathbf{q}, \mathbf{p}).$$

---

[3] Since T: $\mathbb{R}_+^n \to \mathbb{R}_+$ is strictly increasing, $T(\mathbf{q}) > 0$ for $\mathbf{q} \geq \mathbf{0}$.

[4] According to (7.3.10), $T(\mathbf{q}, \mathbf{p}) > 0$ if $p_1 q_1 + \cdots + p_n q_n = : \mathbf{pq} > 0$.

For the function given by (7.3.12) we have, by linear homogeneity of P with respect to $\mathbf{p}$,

$$\lambda(\mathbf{pq}/T(\mathbf{q}, \mathbf{p})) = \lambda P(\mathbf{q}, \mathbf{p}) = P(\mathbf{q}, \lambda\mathbf{p}) = (\lambda\mathbf{qp}/T(\mathbf{q}, \lambda\mathbf{p})).$$

Thus, it follows that

$$T(\mathbf{q}, \lambda\mathbf{p}) = T(\mathbf{q}, \mathbf{p})$$

must hold. However, by linear homogeneity of T with respect to $\mathbf{q}$, it then follows that

$$P\left(\frac{\mathbf{q}}{\lambda}, \lambda\mathbf{p}\right) = \frac{\lambda\mathbf{p}(\mathbf{q}/\lambda)}{T(\mathbf{q}/\lambda, \lambda\mathbf{p})} = \frac{\mathbf{qp}}{(1/\lambda)T(\mathbf{q}, \lambda\mathbf{p})} = \lambda\frac{\mathbf{qp}}{T(\mathbf{q}, \mathbf{p})} = \lambda P(\mathbf{q}, \mathbf{p}),$$

which violates Axiom 7.3.7. This proves

7.3.13 **Theorem.** *Let P: $\mathbb{R}_+^{2n} \to \mathbb{R}_+$, where $n \geqq 2$, be a function satisfying the axioms 7.3.5–7.3.7, that is, a price level. Also, let the functions T: $\mathbb{R}_+^n \to \mathbb{R}_+$ or T: $\mathbb{R}_+^{2n} \to \mathbb{R}_+$ be quantity levels as defined in (7.1.11) or (7.3.9), respectively. Then P and T cannot be solutions of functional equations (7.3.8) or (7.3.10), respectively.*

7.4 Price Levels and Quantity Levels under Optimizing Behavior

The result indicated in Theorem 7.3.13 is again nonaffirmative for the existence of price levels and quantity levels. Therefore, let us consider a third interpretation of Eq. (7.2.3): Given a quantity level $T: \mathbb{R}_+^n \to \mathbb{R}_+$, find a price level P: $\mathbb{R}_+^n \to \mathbb{R}_+$ such that for every price vector $\mathbf{p}$ there exists (at least) one quantity vector $\mathbf{q} = \mathbf{q}(\mathbf{p})$ that satisfies

$$P(\mathbf{p})\,T(\mathbf{q}(\mathbf{p})) = p_1q_1(\mathbf{p}) + \cdots + p_nq_n(\mathbf{p}), \tag{7.4.1}$$

whereas for all $\mathbf{q} \in \mathbb{R}_+^n$ the inequality

$$P(\mathbf{p})\,T(\mathbf{q}) \leqq p_1q_1 + \cdots + p_nq_n \tag{7.4.2}$$

is valid. The question asked is now the following: Do there exist pairs P, T of price and quantity levels satisfying (7.4.1), (7.4.2)? If T is a continuous quantity level, then

$$P(\mathbf{p}) = \begin{cases} \min\limits_{\substack{\mathbf{q} \in \mathbb{R}_+^n \\ \mathbf{q} \neq \mathbf{0}}} (\mathbf{pq}/T(\mathbf{q})) = \min\limits_{\substack{\mathbf{q} \in \mathbb{R}_+^n \\ |\mathbf{q}| = 1}} (\mathbf{pq}/T(\mathbf{q})) & \text{for } \mathbf{p} \geq \mathbf{0},^5 \\ 0 \quad \text{for } \mathbf{p} = \mathbf{0} \end{cases} \tag{7.4.3}$$

[5] The minima are equal because of the linear homogeneity of T, and they exist since $\mathbf{pq}/T(\mathbf{q})$ is continuous on the compact (i.e., closed and bounded) set $\{\mathbf{q} \mid \mathbf{q} \in \mathbb{R}_+^n, |\mathbf{q}| = 1\}$. Note that $T(\mathbf{q}) > 0$ for $\mathbf{q} \geq \mathbf{0}$, since $T: \mathbb{R}_+^n \to \mathbb{R}_+$ is strictly increasing.

is a (continuous and linearly homogeneous) function that satisfies, together with T, the inequality (7.4.2), and together with T and

$$\mathbf{q}(\mathbf{p}) \in \begin{cases} \{\mathbf{q} \mid (\mathbf{pq}/T(\mathbf{q})) \to \min, \mathbf{q} \in \mathbb{R}^n_+, \mathbf{q} \neq \mathbf{0}\} & \text{for} \quad \mathbf{p} \geq \mathbf{0}, \\ \mathbb{R}^n_+ \quad \text{for} \quad \mathbf{p} = \mathbf{0}, \end{cases}$$

Eq. (7.4.1). The function P given by (7.4.3) is called the *dual*[6] of the given quantity level T (see, for instance, Samuelson and Swamy [1974, p. 569]). Samuelson and Swamy consider it a price level if T "has been defined as a homogeneous first-degree numerical indicator of homothetic preferences, unique up to an arbitrary scale or dimensionality constant."

7.4.4 **Theorem.** *There do exist quantity levels T such that their duals P cannot be considered price levels.*

Proof. The function T given by $T(\mathbf{q}) = a_1q_1 + \ldots + a_nq_n$ ($a_1 > 0, \ldots, a_n > 0$ arbitrary real constants) is a quantity level and its dual P is given by

$$P(\mathbf{p}) = \min_{\substack{\mathbf{q} \in \mathbb{R}^n_+ \\ |\mathbf{q}| = 1}} \frac{\mathbf{pq}}{a_1q_1 + \cdots + a_nq_n} = \min\left\{\frac{p_1}{a_1}, \ldots, \frac{p_n}{a_n}\right\}. \tag{7.4.5}$$

However, this function P is *not* strictly increasing, as required by Monotonicity Axiom 7.1.1.

Can we solve this dilemma by weakening the Monotonicity Axiom? We do not believe so, since (7.4.5) has the following property: If, for instance,

$$\frac{p_1}{a_1} < \frac{p_\nu}{a_\nu} \qquad (\nu = 2, \ldots, n), \qquad p_1 = \bar{p}_1 = \text{const},$$

then $P(\mathbf{p}) = \bar{p}_1/a_1 =$ constant for *arbitrarily increasing* prices $p_2, \ldots, p_n$. We cannot accept such a P as a price level.

7.5 A Functional Equation Involving the Prices, the Price Level, and the Return of a Firm

Most work on oligopoly theory assumes, for simplicity, that each competitor has only one strategic variable, namely a single price. In Section 3.4 we assumed the same.[7] This simplification would not restrict generality

---

[6] A duality theory of cost and production structures from which the wording above stems is due to Shephard [1953, 1970].

[7] Contributions to oligopoly theory, where each oligopolist supplies several commodities, have been made by Selten [1970] and the author [1971, 1972d, 1973a]; see also Section 11.3 of this book.

(i) if the strategic variable could be considered a price *level*

$$P : \mathbb{R}_+^k \to \mathbb{R}_+, \qquad (p_1, \ldots, p_k) = : \mathbf{p} \to P(\mathbf{p}) \tag{7.5.1}$$

(see 7.1.1, 7.1.2) where the $p_\varkappa$'s are the prices of the k commodities sold by the respective firm; and

(ii) if, given any system of sales functions $f_1 : \mathbb{R}_+^k \to \mathbb{R}_+, \ldots, f_k : \mathbb{R}_+^k \to \mathbb{R}_+$, there would always exist both a price level (7.5.1) and a "sales level" $F : \mathbb{R}_+ \to$ $\to \mathbb{R}_+$ (depending on P) such that the "equation of return"

$$P(\mathbf{p})\, F(P(\mathbf{p})) = p_1 f_1(\mathbf{p}) + \cdots + p_k f_k(\mathbf{p}) \tag{7.5.2}$$

is valid for all $\mathbf{p} \in \mathbb{R}_+^n$.

The following example shows that there do exist solutions of Eq. (7.5.2) that make economic sense:

$$f_\varkappa(\mathbf{p}) = \frac{\beta_\varkappa p_1^{\alpha_{\varkappa 1}} p_2^{\alpha_{\varkappa 2}} \cdots p_k^{\alpha_{\varkappa k}}}{p_\varkappa}, \qquad \begin{cases} \varkappa = 1, 2, \ldots, k; \quad \beta_\varkappa > 0, \\ \alpha_{\varkappa\lambda} > 0 \,\text{const}, \ \sum\limits_{\lambda=1}^{k} \alpha_{\varkappa\lambda} = \dfrac{1}{2}, \end{cases} \tag{7.5.3}$$

$$F(P) = 1/\sqrt{P},$$

$$P(\mathbf{p}) = (\beta_1 p_1^{\alpha_{11}} p_2^{\alpha_{12}} \cdots p_k^{\alpha_{1k}} + \cdots + \beta_k p_1^{\alpha_{k1}} p_2^{\alpha_{k2}} \cdots p_k^{\alpha_{kk}})^2.$$

However, this example cannot serve as an illustration of a more general case. Instead, we present

7.5.4 **Theorem.** *There exist sales functions $f_1, \ldots, f_k$ for which it is impossible to find both a price level P and a "sales level" F such that functional equation (7.5.2) is satisfied for all $\mathbf{p} \in \mathbb{R}_+^n$.*

Proof. Let the $f_\varkappa$'s be given as in (7.5.3) with the exception that

$$\sum_{\lambda=1}^{\alpha} \alpha_{\varkappa\lambda} = \gamma_\varkappa, \qquad \begin{matrix} 0 < \gamma_\varkappa < 1; \quad \varkappa = 1, 2, \ldots, k; \\ \text{not all } \gamma_\varkappa\text{'s equal.} \end{matrix} \tag{7.5.5}$$

Then the functions $f_\varkappa$ can be considered, as in (7.5.3), sales functions for goods that are substitutes. Let us write $F(P(\mathbf{p}))\,P(\mathbf{p}) = : G(P(\mathbf{p}))$. Equation (7.5.2) then becomes

$$G(P(\mathbf{p})) = \beta_1 p_1^{\alpha_{11}} p_2^{\alpha_{12}} \cdots p_k^{\alpha_{1k}} + \cdots + \beta_k p_1^{\alpha_{k1}} p_2^{\alpha_{k2}} \cdots p_k^{\alpha_{kk}}. \tag{7.5.6}$$

We note that the right-hand side of (7.5.6) is strictly increasing and that the same is true for P because of Monotonicity Axiom 7.1.1. It follows that G is strictly increasing, and the inverse of G, namely G^{-1}, exists. Therefore, (7.5.6) can be written as

$$P(\mathbf{p}) = G^{-1}(\beta_1 p_1^{\alpha_{11}} p_2^{\alpha_{12}} \cdots p_k^{\alpha_{1k}} + \cdots + \beta_k p_1^{\alpha_{k1}} p_2^{\alpha_{k2}} \cdots p_k^{\alpha_{kk}}).$$

Due to the conditions specified in (7.5.5), this P is *not* linearly homogeneous, as required by Axiom 7.1.2, and thus cannot be considered a price level. ■

Part III

Systems of Three or More Functional Equations for a Single Scalar-Valued Function of Several Variables

8

Systems of Functional Equations in the Theory of the Price Index

The theory presented in this chapter considers a price index as a positive-valued function:

(i) of the prices of n commodities of a base year and of the current year (see Sections 8.1, 8.2); or

(ii) of both the prices *and* quantities of n commodities of a base year and of the current year (see Sections 8.3–8.6).

In the spirit of Fisher [1922], Frisch [1930], Swamy [1965], and most statistical bureaus that are concerned with the actual calculation of price indices, we treat prices and quantities as independent variables. In other words, we are interested in the "statistical" (so called by Allen [1975, p. 47]) or "mechanistic" (so called by Samuelson and Swamy [1974, p. 567]) approach to the price index. That is, we do *not* consider the so-called economic—theoretic approach, where the utility function of an individual consumer (or consumer group) is involved in such a way that the prices and quantities constituting the price index become functions of each other (see, e.g., Afriat [1967, 1972], Banerjee [1975], Blackorby and Russell [1978], Diewert [1976], Fisher and Shell [1972], Frisch [1936, 1954], Hasenkamp [1978], Klein and Rubin [1948], Muellbauer [1975], Phlips [1974], Phlips and Sanz-Ferrer [1975], Pollak [1971, 1975], Samuelson and Swamy [1974], Ulmer [1949], Voeller [1974], and Wald [1937, 1939]).

We define the price indices by four (see Section 8.1) or five (see Section 8.3) natural properties that we call axioms. One of these axioms says that a price index is a *strictly* increasing function of the prices. This condition can be called natural here, since we are interested in the *statistical* approach, which implies

ISBN 0-201-01948-5/01949-3 PBK

Wolfgang Eichhorn, Functional Equations in Economics.

that a price index is sensitive to any change of the prices. Most of the axioms are given in the form of a functional equation. The independence of these axioms will be shown, and an impression of the class of functions (i.e., price indices) that satisfy the axioms simultaneously will be given.

After we have characterized some special classes of price indices (see Section 8.2) and deduced some important consequences of the axioms (see Sections 8.1, 8.3), we will consider Fisher's [1922] famous system of tests for price indices (see Section 8.4). Implications of subsets of Fisher's tests will be considered, and uniqueness and inconsistency theorems will be proved (see Section 8.5). In the concluding section (8.6), Fisher's system of tests is weakened considerably; without any regularity assumption (such as differentiability or continuity) we will show that every subset of the system of weakened tests is consistent, whereas the whole system is inconsistent. The question how far the whole system must be weakened in order to obtain a consistent set of tests is also considered.

For technical reasons, we will always consider the *positive* orthant as the domain of price indices. If the *nonnegative* orthant is considered as the domain, then even classical price indices, such as Laspeyres' index (8.3.7) or Paasche's index (8.3.8) are not (and cannot appropriately be) defined for certain points of this orthant. In this connection, it should be remarked that there exists a test expressing the behavior of a price index as any scalar argument (price or quantity) tends to zero, namely, Fisher's Determinateness Test (see Test T.3 in Section 8.4).

This chapter contains results presented in lecture notes by Eichhorn and Voeller [1976].

8.1 Price Indices Π Depending only on Prices: Definition, Axioms, Examples

Let

$$\mathbf{p}^0 = (p_1^0, \ldots, p_n^0) \in \mathbb{R}^n_{++}, \qquad \mathbf{p} = (p_1, \ldots, p_n) \in \mathbb{R}^n_{++} \tag{8.1.0}$$

be the vectors of the prices of n commodities of a base year and of the current year, respectively.

By a *price index depending only on the (vectors of) prices* (8.1.0) we understand a function

$$\Pi : \mathbb{R}^{2n}_{++} \to \mathbb{R}_{++}, \qquad (\mathbf{p}^0, \mathbf{p}) \to \Pi(\mathbf{p}^0, \mathbf{p})$$

satisfying the following four properties, which we call axioms. The value $\Pi(\mathbf{p}^0, \mathbf{p})$ is called the *value of the price index at the price situation* $(\mathbf{p}^0, \mathbf{p})$.

8.1.1 *Monotonicity Axiom.* The function Π is *strictly increasing with respect to* $\mathbf{p}$ and *strictly decreasing with respect to* $\mathbf{p}^0$; that is, for every quadruple $\mathbf{p}^0, \bar{\mathbf{p}}^0, \mathbf{p}, \bar{\mathbf{p}}$ of vectors of $\mathbb{R}^n_{++}$ we have

$$\Pi(\mathbf{p}^0, \mathbf{p}) > \Pi(\mathbf{p}^0, \bar{\mathbf{p}}) \qquad \text{if} \quad \mathbf{p} \geq \bar{\mathbf{p}}$$

and

$$\Pi(\mathbf{p}^0, \mathbf{p}) < \Pi\bar{\mathbf{p}}^0, \mathbf{p}) \qquad \text{if} \quad \mathbf{p}^0 \geq \bar{\mathbf{p}}^0,$$

respectively.

8.1.2 *Linear Homogeneity Axiom.* The function Π is *linearly homogeneous with respect to* $\mathbf{p}$; that is, for all $\mathbf{p}^0 \in \mathbb{R}^n_{++}, \mathbf{p} \in \mathbb{R}^n_{++}, \lambda \in \mathbb{R}_{++}$ we have

$$\Pi(\mathbf{p}^0, \lambda\mathbf{p}) = \lambda\Pi(\mathbf{p}^0, \mathbf{p}).$$

At this point it is instructive to compare Axioms 8.1.1, 8.1.2 with Axioms 7.1.1, 7.1.2, respectively.

8.1.3 *Identity Axiom.* For all $\mathbf{p}^0 \in \mathbb{R}^n_{++}, \Pi(\mathbf{p}^0, \mathbf{p}^0) = 1$. In other words, if the prices of the base year do not change, the value of the price index is equal to 1.

8.1.4 *Dimensionality Axiom.* For all $\mathbf{p}^0 \in \mathbb{R}^n_{++}$, $\mathbf{p} \in \mathbb{R}^n_{++}$, $\lambda \in \mathbb{R}_{++}$,

$$\Pi(\lambda\mathbf{p}^0, \lambda\mathbf{p}) = \Pi(\mathbf{p}^0, \mathbf{p}).$$

In other words, if two economies are identical except for the definition of the unit of money, then the respective values of the price indices are equal.

8.1.5 **Theorem.** *Axioms 8.1.1–8.1.4 are independent in the following sense: Any three of them can be satisfied by a function* $F\colon \mathbb{R}^{2n}_{++} \to \mathbb{R}_{++}$ *that does not fulfill the remaining axiom.*

Proof. The function F given by

$$F(\mathbf{p}^0, \mathbf{p}) = \left(\frac{p_1}{p_1^0}\right)^{\alpha_1}\left(\frac{p_2}{p_2^0}\right)^{\alpha_2} \cdots \left(\frac{p_n}{p_n^0}\right)^{\alpha_n}, \qquad \begin{cases} \alpha_1 < 0, \alpha_2 > 0, \cdots, \alpha_n > 0 \\ \text{real const, } \sum \alpha_\nu = 1, \end{cases}$$

satisfies 8.1.2–8.1.4, but not 8.1.1 (since $\alpha_1 < 0$). The function F given by

$$F(\mathbf{p}^0, \mathbf{p}) = (\mathbf{ap}/\mathbf{ap}^0)^{1/2} \qquad \text{with notation (8.1.11)}$$

satisfies 8.1.1, 8.1.3, and 8.1.4, but not 8.1.2. The function F given by

$$F(\mathbf{p}^0, \mathbf{p}) = \mathbf{ap}/\mathbf{bp}^0 \qquad \text{with (8.1.11)} \quad (\mathbf{a} \neq \mathbf{b})$$

satisfies 8.1.1, 8.1.2, and 8.1.4, but not 8.1.3. Finally, the function F given by[1]

$$F(\mathbf{p}^0, \mathbf{p}) = \frac{\sum p_\nu^0}{\sum p_\nu^0 + 1}\,\frac{1}{n}\sum \frac{p_\nu}{p_\nu^0} + \frac{1}{\sum p_\nu^0 + 1}\max\left\{\frac{p_1}{p_1^0}, \ldots, \frac{p_n}{p_n^0}\right\}$$

satisfies 8.1.1–8.1.3, but not 8.1.4. ■

---

[1] This example is due to Helmut Funke.

Thus, none of these functions F can be regarded as a price index Π. Examples of price indices Π are given by

$$\Pi(\mathbf{p}^0, \mathbf{p}) = \frac{c_1 p_1 + \cdots + c_n p_n}{c_1 p_1^0 + \cdots + c_n p_n^0} \qquad (c_1 > 0, \ldots, c_n > 0 \quad \text{real const}); \tag{8.1.6}$$

$$\Pi(\mathbf{p}^0, \mathbf{p}) = \frac{[\beta_1 p_1^{-\varrho} + \cdots + \beta_n p_n^{-\varrho}]^{-1/\varrho}}{[\beta_1 (p_1^0)^{-\varrho} + \cdots + \beta_n (p_n^0)^{-\varrho}]^{-1/\varrho}}, \qquad \begin{array}{l} \varrho \neq 0, \beta_1 > 0, \ldots, \beta_n > 0 \\ \text{real const}, \sum \beta_\nu = 1; \end{array} \tag{8.1.7}$$

$$\Pi(\mathbf{p}^0, \mathbf{p}) = [\beta_1 (p_1/p_1^0)^{-\varrho} + \cdots + \beta_n (p_n/p_n^0)^{-\varrho}]^{-1/\varrho}, \tag{8.1.8}$$

$$\Pi(\mathbf{p}^0, \mathbf{p}) = (p_1/p_1^0)^{\alpha_1} (p_2/p_2^0)^{\alpha_2} \cdots (p_n/p_n^0)^{\alpha_n}, \qquad \begin{array}{l} \alpha_1 > 0, \alpha_2 > 0, \ldots, \alpha_n > 0 \\ \text{real const}, \sum \alpha_\nu = 1; \end{array} \tag{8.1.9}$$

$$\Pi(\mathbf{p}^0, \mathbf{p}) = [(\mathbf{ap}/\mathbf{ap}^0)(\mathbf{bp}/\mathbf{bp}^0)]^{1/2}; \tag{8.1.10}$$

where

$$\left.\begin{array}{l} \mathbf{a} = (a_1, \ldots, a_n) > \mathbf{0}, \ \mathbf{b} = (b_1, \ldots, b_n) > \mathbf{0} \quad \text{are vectors of real const,} \\ \mathbf{ap} := a_1 p_1 + \cdots + a_n p_n, \qquad \mathbf{bp} := b_1 p_1 + \cdots + b_n p_n, \quad \text{and so on.} \end{array}\right\} \tag{8.1.11}$$

Let $P\colon \mathbb{R}_+^n \to \mathbb{R}_+$ be a price level as defined in Section 7.1. Then

$$\Pi(\mathbf{p}^0, \mathbf{p}) = P(\mathbf{p})/P(\mathbf{p}^0), \qquad (\mathbf{p}^0, \mathbf{p}) \in \mathbb{R}_{++}^{2n} \tag{8.1.12}$$

gives a price index Π, since Axioms 7.1.1 and 7.1.2 for P imply that (8.1.12) satisfies axioms 8.1.1–8.1.4.

At this point we note that there exist price indices Π that cannot be written as the ratio of a price level P at $\mathbf{p}$ and $\mathbf{p}^0$, for instance, the price index Π given by (8.1.8),

8.1.13 **Remark.** As can easily be seen, the following is true. *If $\Pi_1, \ldots, \Pi_k$ are an arbitrary number k of price indices Π, then*

$$F := (\beta_1 \Pi_1^\delta + \cdots + \beta_k \Pi_k^\delta)^{1/\delta}, \qquad \begin{array}{l} \delta \neq 0, \quad \beta_1 \geqq 0, \ldots, \beta_k \geqq 0 \\ \textit{real const}, \sum \beta_\varkappa = 1, \end{array} \tag{8.1.14}$$

and

$$G := \Pi_1^{\delta_1} \Pi_2^{\delta_1} \cdots \Pi_k^{\delta_k}, \quad \delta_1 \geqq 0, \delta_2 \geqq 0, \ldots, \delta_k \geqq 0 \, \textit{real const}, \sum \delta_\varkappa = 1, \tag{8.1.15}$$

are also price indices Π. Here Π^δ is defined by

$$(\mathbf{p}^0, \mathbf{p}) \to [\Pi(\mathbf{p}^0, \mathbf{p})]^\delta.$$

We note that (8.1.15) with $\delta_\varkappa = \beta_\varkappa$ follows from (8.1.14) for $\delta \to 0$.

8.1.16 **Remark.** As we see from (8.1.14) or (8.1.15), the set of all price indices is a convex set. The problem of determining this set seems to be difficult. In order to solve this problem, a theorem of Krein and Milman [1940] on convex sets may be useful.

Axioms 8.1.1–8.1.4 imply many interesting properties of a price index. For instance, from Axioms 8.1.2 and 8.1.3 it follows that every price index Π satisfies the so-called

8.1.17 *Proportionality Test.* For all $\mathbf{p}^0 \in \mathbb{R}^n_{++}$, $\lambda \in \mathbb{R}_{++}$,

$$\Pi(\mathbf{p}^0, \lambda\mathbf{p}^0) = \lambda.$$

From 8.1.2, 8.1.4 it follows that every price index Π also satisfies

8.1.18 *Homogeneity of Degree Minus One Test.* For all $\mathbf{p}^0 \in \mathbb{R}^n_{++}$, $\mathbf{p} \in \mathbb{R}^n_{++}$, $\lambda \in \mathbb{R}_{++}$,

$$\Pi(\lambda\mathbf{p}^0, \mathbf{p}) = \frac{1}{\lambda}\Pi(\mathbf{p}^0, \mathbf{p}).$$

On the other hand, properties 8.1.2 and 8.1.18 imply 8.1.4, and 8.1.2 follows from 8.1.4 and 8.1.18.

It suggests itself that a price index Π should also satisfy the following test, which we call the

8.1.19 *Mean Value Test.* For all $\mathbf{p}^0 \in \mathbb{R}^n_{++}$, $\mathbf{p} \in \mathbb{R}^n_{++}$,

$$\min\left\{\frac{p_1}{p_1^0}, \ldots, \frac{p_n}{p_n^0}\right\} \leqq \Pi(\mathbf{p}^0, \mathbf{p}) \leqq \max\left\{\frac{p_1}{p_1^0}, \ldots, \frac{p_n}{p_n^0}\right\}.$$

In other words, the value of the price index Π is a mean value between the minimum and the maximum of the ratios of the corresponding prices of the two periods under consideration.

8.1.20 **Theorem.** *The Mean Value Test is a consequence of Axioms 8.1.1–8.1.3 in the following sense: Every function $F : \mathbb{R}^{2n}_{++} \to \mathbb{R}_{++}$ that satisfies 8.1.1–8.1.3, that is, the Monotonicity Axiom, Linear Homogeneity Axiom, and Identity Axiom, also satisfies the Mean Value Test.*

8.1.21 **Corollary.** *Every price index Π satisfies the Mean Value Test.*

Proof[2] *of the theorem.* By definition,

$$\min\left\{\frac{p_1}{p_1^0}, \ldots, \frac{p_n}{p_n^0}\right\}\mathbf{p}^0 \leqq \mathbf{p} \leqq \max\left\{\frac{p_1}{p_1^0}, \ldots, \frac{p_n}{p_1^0}\right\}\mathbf{p}^0. \qquad (8.1.22)$$

Now, on the one hand,

$$\begin{aligned} \min\left\{\frac{p_1}{p_1^0}, \ldots, \frac{p_n}{p_n^0}\right\} &=: \mu(\mathbf{p}^0, \mathbf{p}) \\ &= \mu(\mathbf{p}^0, \mathbf{p})\, F(\mathbf{p}^0, \mathbf{p}^0) && \text{(by 8.1.3)}, \\ &= F(\mathbf{p}^0, \mu(\mathbf{p}^0, \mathbf{p})\mathbf{p}^0) && \text{(by 8.1.2)}, \\ &\leqq F(\mathbf{p}^0, \mathbf{p}) && \text{(by 8.1.1 and (8.1.22))}; \end{aligned}$$

[2] I am indebted to Helmut Funke for the idea of this proof.

and on the other hand,

$$\max\left\{\frac{p_1}{p_1^0}, \ldots, \frac{p_n}{p_n^0}\right\} = : M(\mathbf{p}^0, \mathbf{p})$$
$$= M(\mathbf{p}^0, \mathbf{p})F(\mathbf{p}^0, \mathbf{p}^0) \qquad \text{(by 8.1.3)},$$
$$= F(\mathbf{p}^0, M(\mathbf{p}^0, \mathbf{p})\mathbf{p}^0) \qquad \text{(by 8.1.2)},$$
$$\geqq F(\mathbf{p}^0, \mathbf{p}) \qquad \text{(by 8.1.1 and (8.1.22)},$$

which completes the proof. ■

8.2 Characterizations of Some Classes of Price Indices Π

In this section we shall characterize classes of price indices by "tests" that —on intuitive grounds—a price index should satisfy.

Let the price index $\Pi : \mathbb{R}^{2n}_{++} \to \mathbb{R}_{++}$ be given by

$$\Pi(\mathbf{p}^0, \mathbf{p}) = P(\mathbf{p})/P(\mathbf{p}^0), \qquad (\mathbf{p}^0, \mathbf{p}) \in \mathbb{R}^{2n}_{++}, \tag{8.2.1}$$

where $P : \mathbb{R}^n_+ \to \mathbb{R}_+$ is a price level depending only on prices (see Section 7.1). Then this price index satisfies the so-called

8.2.2 *Circular Test.* If all prices change from $\mathbf{p}^0$ to $\mathbf{p}^1$ and then further to $\mathbf{p}$, then the price index for the whole change is the product of the two individual price indices for the two sequential changes:

$$\Pi(\mathbf{p}^0, \mathbf{p}^1)\,\Pi(\mathbf{p}^1, \mathbf{p}) = \Pi(\mathbf{p}^0, \mathbf{p}) \qquad \text{for all} \quad \mathbf{p}^0 \in \mathbb{R}^n_{++}, \quad \mathbf{p}^1 \in \mathbb{R}^n_{++}, \quad \mathbf{p} \in \mathbb{R}^n_{++}. \tag{8.2.3}$$

The following properties are straightforward consequences of (8.2.3):

$$\Pi(\mathbf{p}^0, \mathbf{p}^0) = 1 \qquad \text{(i.e., Identity Axiom 8.1.3)}. \tag{8.2.4}$$

$$\Pi(\mathbf{p}^0, \mathbf{p})\,\Pi(\mathbf{p}, \mathbf{p}^0) = 1 \qquad \text{(Time Reversal Test)}. \tag{8.2.5}$$

$$\Pi(\mathbf{p}^0, \mathbf{p}^1)\,\Pi(\mathbf{p}^1, \mathbf{p})\,\Pi(\mathbf{p}, \mathbf{p}^0) = 1. \tag{8.2.6}$$

Identity (8.2.6) is the reason for the name "Circular Test."

8.2.7 **Theorem.** *The class of price indices that satisfy Circular Test 8.2.2 is equal to the class of price indices given by (8.2.1), where $P : \mathbb{R}^n_+ \to \mathbb{R}_+$ is a price level depending only on prices.*

Proof. Since we know already that every price index given by (8.2.1) satisfies (8.2.3), we have only to show that every price index satisfying (8.2.3) can be written in the form (8.2.1), where P is a price level. This is the case: Writing (8.2.3) as

$$\Pi(\mathbf{p}^1, \mathbf{p}) = \Pi(\mathbf{p}^0, \mathbf{p})/\Pi(\mathbf{p}^0, \mathbf{p}^1) \qquad \text{for all} \quad \mathbf{p}^0 \in \mathbb{R}^n_{++}, \quad \mathbf{p}^1 \in \mathbb{R}^n_{++}, \quad \mathbf{p} \in \mathbb{R}^n_{++},$$

we see that the left-hand side and, consequently, the right-hand side, is independent of $\mathbf{p}^0$. Hence we may write this as

$$\Pi(\mathbf{p}^1, \mathbf{p}) = \frac{\Pi(1, \ldots, 1, \mathbf{p})}{\Pi(1, \ldots, 1, \mathbf{p}^1)} =: \frac{P(\mathbf{p})}{P(\mathbf{p}^1)},$$

and P satisfies, in consequence of Monotonicity Axiom 8.1.1 and Linear Homogeneity Axiom 8.1.2, the Axioms 7.1.1 and 7.1.2. ■

8.2.8 **Theorem.** *Every function $F: \mathbb{R}^{2n}_{++} \to \mathbb{R}_{++}$ satisfying Identity Axiom 8.1.3 and the properties*

$$F(\mathbf{p}^0, \mathbf{p} + \bar{\mathbf{p}}) = F(\mathbf{p}^0, \mathbf{p}) + F(\mathbf{p}^0, \bar{\mathbf{p}}) \qquad (\textit{see (3.3.3)}) \tag{8.2.9}$$

and

$$\frac{1}{F(\mathbf{p}^0 + \bar{\mathbf{p}}^0, \mathbf{p})} = \frac{1}{F(\mathbf{p}^0, \mathbf{p})} + \frac{1}{F(\bar{\mathbf{p}}^0, \mathbf{p})} \qquad (\textit{see (3.3.3)}) \tag{8.2.10}$$

can be written in the form

$$F(\mathbf{p}^0, \mathbf{p}) = \frac{c_1 p_1 + \cdots + c_n p_n}{c_1 p_1^0 + \cdots + c_n p_n^0}, \qquad c_1 > 0, \ldots, c_n > 0 \textit{ real const; see (8.1.6)}, \tag{8.2.11}$$

that is, can be regarded as a price index Π.[3] *Conversely, every function F given by (8.2.11) satisfies axiom 8.1.3 and (8.2.9), (8.2.10).*

Proof. See the proofs of Theorem 3.3.9 and Corollary 3.3.10. ■

8.2.12 **Theorem.** *Every function $F: \mathbb{R}^{2n}_{++} \to \mathbb{R}_{++}$ that satisfies both Linear Homogeneity Axiom 8.1.2 and Dimensionality Axiom 8.1.4 can be written in the form*

$$F(\mathbf{p}^0, \mathbf{p}) = \frac{\mathbf{ap}}{\mathbf{bp}^0}\,\Phi\left(\frac{\mathbf{p}^0}{\mathbf{bp}^0}, \frac{\mathbf{p}}{\mathbf{ap}}\right) \tag{8.2.13}$$

(cf. notation (8.1.11)), where $\Phi: \mathbb{R}^{2n}_{++} \to \mathbb{R}_{++}$ is an arbitrary function. Every function F given by (8.2.13) with arbitrary $\Phi: \mathbb{R}^{2n}_{++} \to \mathbb{R}_{++}$ satisfies Axioms 8.1.2 and 8.1.4.

Proof. With notation (8.1.11) we can write

$$F(\mathbf{p}^0, \mathbf{p}) = F\left(\mathbf{bp}^0 \frac{\mathbf{p}^0}{\mathbf{bp}^0}, \mathbf{ap}\frac{\mathbf{p}}{\mathbf{ap}}\right).$$

---

[3] Hence, properties (8.2.9), (8.2.10) and Identity Axiom 8.1.3 yield the Monotonicity Axiom 8.1.1, Linear Homogeneity Axiom 8.1.2, Dimensionality Axiom 8.1.4, Proportionality Test 8.1.17, Homogeneity of Degree Minus One Test 8.1.18, Mean Value Test 8.1.19, and Circular Test 8.2.2.

We know already that Test 8.1.18 follows from Axioms 8.1.2 and 8.1.4. Because of 8.1.2 and 8.1.18, the right-hand side is equal to

$$\frac{\mathbf{ap}}{\mathbf{bp}^0} F\left(\frac{\mathbf{p}^0}{\mathbf{bp}^0}, \frac{\mathbf{p}}{\mathbf{ap}}\right).$$

The second assertion of the theorem follows easily by inserting (8.2.13) into Axioms 8.1.2 and 8.1.4. ■

For a function F as defined by (8.2.13) to be interpreted as a price index Π, it also has to satisfy both Identity Axiom 8.1.3, implying

$$\Phi\left(\frac{\mathbf{p}^0}{\mathbf{bp}^0}, \frac{\mathbf{p}^0}{\mathbf{ap}^0}\right) = \frac{\mathbf{bp}^0}{\mathbf{ap}^0} \qquad \text{for all} \quad \mathbf{p}^0 \in \mathbb{R}^n_{++},$$

and Monotonicity Axiom 8.1.1.

We note that (8.2.13) with either

$$\Phi(\mathbf{r}, \mathbf{s}) \equiv 1, \qquad \mathbf{a} = \mathbf{b} =: \mathbf{c} = (c_1, \ldots, c_n),$$

or

$$\Phi(\mathbf{r}, \mathbf{s}) = (s_1/r_1)^{\alpha_1} (s_2/r_2)^{\alpha_2} \cdots (s_n/r_n)^{\alpha_n} \qquad \alpha_1 > 0, \ \alpha_2 > 0, \cdots, a_n > 0 \ \text{real const}, \ \textstyle\sum \alpha_\nu = 1,$$

or

$$\Phi(\mathbf{r}, \mathbf{s}) = (\mathbf{bs}/\mathbf{ar})^{1/2} \qquad (\mathbf{a}, \mathbf{b} \text{ as in (8.1.11)})$$

becomes (8.1.6), (8.1.9), or (8.1.10), respectively.

8.2.14 **Theorem.** *Let $F\colon \mathbb{R}^{2n}_{++} \to \mathbb{R}_{++}$ be an arbitrary function satisfying the Monotonicity Axiom 8.1.1, Linear Homogeneity Axiom 8.1.2, Identity Axiom 8.1.3 and the functional equation*[4]

$$F(\varkappa_1 p_1^0, \ldots, \varkappa_n p_n^0, \lambda_1 p_1, \ldots, \lambda_n p_n) = \phi(\varkappa_1, \ldots, \varkappa_n, \lambda_1, \ldots, \lambda_n) F(\mathbf{p}^0, \mathbf{p}), \quad (8.2.15)$$

where $\phi : \mathbb{R}^{2n}_{++} \to \mathbb{R}_{++}$, $\phi(1, \ldots, 1, 1, \ldots, 1) = 1$. Then there exist n positive real constants $\alpha_1, \alpha_2, \ldots, \alpha_n$ satisfying $\alpha_1 + \alpha_2 + \cdots + \alpha_n = 1$, such that

$$F(\mathbf{p}^0, \mathbf{p}) = \left(\frac{p_1}{p_1^0}\right)^{\alpha_1} \left(\frac{p_2}{p_2^0}\right)^{\alpha_2} \cdots \left(\frac{p_n}{p_n^0}\right)^{\alpha_n} \qquad (\textit{see (8.1.9)}), \qquad (8.2.16)$$

that is, F can be regarded as a price index Π.[5] *Conversely, every function F*

[4] If F is regarded as a price index, then the interpretation of (8.2.15) follows along lines similar to the one given in Test 7.1.5.

[5] Hence, Axioms 8.1.1–8.1.3 and functional equation (8.2.15) restrict a function F to the extent that it satisfies Dimensionality Axiom 8.1.4 as well as all the tests formulated in this and the preceding section.

given by (8.2.16) with the foregoing properties of the α_ν*'s satisfies Axioms 8.1.1–8.1.3 and functional equation (8.2.15).*

Proof. If we write

$$p_\nu^0 =: 1/x_\nu, \qquad \varkappa_\nu =: 1/\mu_\nu \qquad (\nu = 1, \ldots, n),$$

then (8.2.15) becomes

$$G(\mu_1 x_1, \ldots, \mu_n x_n, \lambda_1 p_1, \ldots, \lambda_n p_n) = \psi(\mu_1, \ldots, \mu_n, \lambda_1, \ldots, \lambda_n)\, G(\mathbf{x}, \mathbf{p}) \quad (8.2.17)$$

where

$$G(\mathbf{x}, \mathbf{p}) := F\left(\frac{1}{x_1}, \ldots, \frac{1}{x_n}, \mathbf{p}\right),$$

$$\psi(\mu_1, \ldots, \mu_n, \lambda_1, \ldots, \lambda_n) := \phi\left(\frac{1}{\mu_1}, \ldots, \frac{1}{\mu_n}, \lambda_1, \ldots, \lambda_n\right).$$

Because of 8.1.1, $G: \mathbb{R}_{++}^{2n} \to \mathbb{R}_{++}$ is strictly increasing. Hence, $\psi: \mathbb{R}_{++}^{2n} \to \mathbb{R}_{++}$ is strictly increasing. Since all values in (8.2.17) are positive, we can rewrite Eq. (8.2.17) as

$$\log G(\mu_1 x_1, \ldots, \mu_n x_n, \lambda_1 p_1, \ldots, \lambda_n p_n) = \log \psi(\mu_1, \ldots, \mu_n, \lambda_1, \ldots, \lambda_n) + \log G(\mathbf{x}, \mathbf{p})$$

or, with $\log G =: H$, $\log \psi =: \chi$,

$$H(\mu_1 x_1, \ldots, \mu_n x_n, \lambda_1 p_1, \ldots, \lambda_n p_n) = \chi(\mu_1, \ldots, \mu_n, \lambda_1, \ldots, \lambda_n) + H(\mathbf{x}, \mathbf{p}). \quad (8.2.18)$$

We note that both functions H and χ are strictly increasing. According to Theorem 3.5.5 and Corollary 3.5.10, it follows that the set of the solutions of (8.2.18) is given by

$$H(\mathbf{x}, \mathbf{p}) = \gamma_1 \log x_1 + \cdots + \gamma_n \log x_n + \gamma_{n+1} \log p_1 + \cdots + \gamma_{2n} \log p_n + b,$$
$$\chi(\mathbf{x}, \mathbf{p}) = H(\mathbf{x}, \mathbf{p}) - b,$$

where the real constants b and $\gamma_1 > 0, \ldots, \gamma_{2n} > 0$ are arbitrary. Hence

$$G(\mathbf{x}, \mathbf{p}) = e^{\log G(\mathbf{x}, \mathbf{p})} = e^{H(\mathbf{x}, \mathbf{p})} = e^b x_1^{\gamma_1} \cdots x_n^{\gamma_n} p_1^{\gamma_{n+1}} \cdots p_n^{\gamma_{2n}}$$

and

$$F(\mathbf{p}^0, \mathbf{p}) = e^b \frac{p_1^{\gamma_{n+1}}}{(p_1^0)^{\gamma_1}} \cdots \frac{p_n^{\gamma_{2n}}}{(p_n^0)^{\gamma_n}}.$$

This F satisfies both Linear Homogeneity Axiom 8.1.2 and Identity Test 8.1.3 if and only if $b = 0$, $\gamma_{n+1} = \gamma_1 =: \alpha_1, \ldots, \gamma_{2n} = \gamma_n =: \alpha_n$, $\alpha_1 + \cdots + \alpha_n = 1$, which was to be proved. The second assertion of the theorem is obvious. ■

Let

$$\mathbf{q}^0 = (q_1^0, \ldots, q_n^0) \in \mathbb{R}_{++}^n, \qquad \mathbf{q} = (q_1, \ldots, q_n) \in \mathbb{R}_{++}^n \quad (8.2.19)$$

denote the vectors of the quantities of n commodities of a base year and of the current year, respectively, and let

$$Q : \mathbb{R}^{2n}_{++} \to \mathbb{R}_{++}, \qquad (\mathbf{q}^0, \mathbf{q}) \to Q(\mathbf{q}^0, \mathbf{q}) \tag{8.2.20}$$

be a *quantity index* that satisfies axioms analogous to those satisfied by a price index Π.

For reasons similar to those formulated in Section 7.1, the following test is of interest.

8.2.21 *Product Test.* A price index Π is said to *satisfy the Product Test* if there exists a quantity index (8.2.20) such that the product of the two indices is a ratio of the values $\mathbf{qp}$ and $\mathbf{q}^0\mathbf{p}^0$; that is,

$$\Pi(\mathbf{p}^0, \mathbf{p})\, Q(\mathbf{q}^0, \mathbf{p}) = (\mathbf{qp}/\mathbf{q}^0\mathbf{p}^0) \qquad \text{for all} \quad \mathbf{p}^0, \mathbf{q}^0, \mathbf{p}, \mathbf{q}. \tag{8.2.22}$$

With the arguments presented in Section 7.1 we can prove

8.2.23. **Theorem.** *If $n \geqq 2$, there does not exist any pair of functions Π, Q that satisfy functional equation (8.2.22).*

In particular, there does not exist any price index Π satisfying the Product Test. This disappointing result fades away if we consider a price index (and a quantity index) as a function of *both* the prices (8.1.0) *and* the quantities (8.2.19). This leads us to the following sections.

8.3 Price Indices $\mathcal{P}$ Depending on Prices and Quantities; Definition, Axioms, Examples

In the following a *price index* will be understood to be a function

$$\mathcal{P} : \mathbb{R}^{4n}_{++} \to \mathbb{R}_{++}, \qquad (\mathbf{q}^0, \mathbf{p}^0, \mathbf{q}, \mathbf{p}) \to \mathcal{P}(\mathbf{q}^0, \mathbf{p}^0, \mathbf{q}, \mathbf{p}), \tag{8.3.0}$$

that depends on both the prices (8.1.0) and the quantities (8.2.19), and which, in addition, satisfies the following five properties, called axioms:[6]

8.3.1 *Monotonicity Axiom*

$$\mathcal{P}(\mathbf{q}^0, \mathbf{p}^0, \mathbf{q}, \mathbf{p}) > \mathcal{P}(\mathbf{q}^0, \mathbf{p}^0, \mathbf{q}, \bar{\mathbf{p}}) \quad \text{for all} \quad \mathbf{q}^0, \mathbf{p}^0, \mathbf{q}, \mathbf{p}, \bar{\mathbf{p}} \quad \text{with} \quad \mathbf{p} \geq \bar{\mathbf{p}},$$
$$\mathcal{P}(\mathbf{q}^0, \mathbf{p}^0, \mathbf{q}, \mathbf{p}) < \mathcal{P}(\mathbf{q}^0, \bar{\mathbf{p}}^0, \mathbf{q}, \mathbf{p}) \quad \text{for all} \quad \mathbf{q}^0, \mathbf{p}^0, \bar{\mathbf{p}}^0, \mathbf{q}, \mathbf{p} \quad \text{with} \quad \mathbf{p}^0 \geq \bar{\mathbf{p}}^0.$$

8.3.2 *Linear Homogeneity Axiom*

$$\mathcal{P}(\mathbf{q}^0, \mathbf{p}^0, \mathbf{q}, \lambda\mathbf{p}) = \lambda\mathcal{P}(\mathbf{q}^0, \mathbf{p}^0, \mathbf{q}, \mathbf{p}) \qquad \text{for all} \quad \lambda \in \mathbb{R}_{++}, \mathbf{q}^0, \mathbf{p}^0, \mathbf{q}, \mathbf{p}.$$

---

[6] Compare with Axioms 8.1.1–8.1.4.

8.3.3 *Identity Axiom*

$$\mathcal{P}(\mathbf{q}^0, \mathbf{p}^0, \mathbf{q}, \mathbf{p}^0) = 1 \qquad \text{for all} \quad \mathbf{q}^0, \mathbf{p}^0, \mathbf{q}.$$

8.3.4 *Dimensionality Axiom*

$$\mathcal{P}(\mathbf{q}^0, \lambda\mathbf{p}^0, \mathbf{q}, \lambda\mathbf{p}) = \mathcal{P}(\mathbf{q}^0, \mathbf{p}^0, \mathbf{q}, \mathbf{p}) \qquad \text{for all} \quad \lambda \in \mathbb{R}_{++}, \mathbf{q}^0, \mathbf{p}^0, \mathbf{q}, \mathbf{p}.$$

8.3.5 *Commensurability Axiom.* A price index $\mathcal{P}$ must be independent of the units of measurement of the quantities

$$\mathcal{P}\left(\frac{q_1^0}{\lambda_1}, \ldots, \frac{q_n^0}{\lambda_n}, \lambda_1 p_1^0, \ldots, \lambda_n p_n^0, \frac{q_1}{\lambda_1}, \ldots, \frac{q_n}{\lambda_n}, \lambda_1 p_1, \ldots, \lambda_n p_n\right)$$
$$= \mathcal{P}(\mathbf{q}^0, \mathbf{p}^0, \mathbf{q}, \mathbf{p}) \qquad \text{for all} \quad \lambda_1 \in \mathbb{R}_{++}, \ldots, \lambda_n \in \mathbb{R}_{++}, \mathbf{q}^0, \mathbf{p}^0, \mathbf{q}, \mathbf{p}.^7$$

8.3.6 **Theorem.** *Axioms 8.3.1–8.3.5 are independent: Any four of them can be satisfied by a function $G : \mathbb{R}_{++}^{4n} \to \mathbb{R}_{++}$ that does not fulfill the remaining axiom.*

Proof. The function G given by

$$G(\mathbf{q}^0, \mathbf{p}^0, \mathbf{q}, \mathbf{p}) = \left(\frac{p_1}{p_1^0}\right)^{\alpha_1}\left(\frac{p_2}{p_2^0}\right)^{\alpha_2}\cdots\left(\frac{p_n}{p_n^0}\right)^{\alpha_n}, \qquad \begin{array}{l}\alpha_1 < 0, \alpha_2 > 0, \ldots, \alpha_n > 0\\ \text{real const}, \sum \alpha_\nu = 1,\end{array}$$

satisfies Axioms 8.3.2–8.3.5, but not 8.3.1. The function G given by

$$G(\mathbf{q}^0, \mathbf{p}^0, \mathbf{q}, \mathbf{p}) = (\mathbf{q}^0\mathbf{p}/\mathbf{q}^0\mathbf{p}^0)^{1/2}$$

where

$$\mathbf{q}^0\mathbf{p} = q_1^0 p_1 + \cdots + q_n^0 p_n, \qquad \mathbf{q}^0\mathbf{p}^0 = q_1^0 p_1^0 + \cdots + q_n^0 p_n^0,$$

statisfies Axioms 8.3.1 and 8.3.3–8.3.5, but not 8.3.2. The function G given by

$$G(\mathbf{q}^0, \mathbf{p}^0, \mathbf{q}, \mathbf{p}) = \mathbf{q}\mathbf{p}/\mathbf{q}^0\mathbf{p} \quad \text{with } \mathbf{q} \neq \mathbf{q}^0$$

satisfies Axioms 8.3.1, 8.3.2, 8.3.4 and 8.3.5, but not 8.3.3. The function G given by

$$G(\mathbf{q}^0, \mathbf{p}^0, \mathbf{q}, \mathbf{p}) = \frac{\mathbf{q}^0\mathbf{p}^0}{\mathbf{q}^0\mathbf{p}^0 + 1}\,\frac{1}{n}\sum_{\nu=1}^{n}\frac{p_\nu}{p_\nu^0} + \frac{1}{\mathbf{q}^0\mathbf{p}^0 + 1}\max\left\{\frac{p_1}{p_1^0}, \ldots, \frac{p_n}{p_n^0}\right\}$$

satisfies Axioms 8.3.1–8.3.3 and 8.3.5, but not 8.3.4. The function G given by

$$G(\mathbf{q}^0, \mathbf{p}^0, \mathbf{q}, \mathbf{p}) = \mathbf{a}\mathbf{p}/\mathbf{a}\mathbf{p}^0, \qquad \mathbf{a} = (a_1, \ldots, a_n),$$
$$a_1 > 0, \ldots, a_n > 0 \text{ real const},$$

satisfies Axioms 8.3.1–8.3.4, but not 8.3.5. ■

---

[7] The formula presented by Swamy [1965, p. 620] considers only the special case where $\lambda_1 = \cdots = \lambda_n$.

Examples of price indices $\mathcal{P}$ satisfying Axioms 8.3.1–8.3.5 are given by

$$\mathcal{P}(\mathbf{q}^0, \mathbf{p}^0, \mathbf{q}, \mathbf{p}) = \mathbf{q}^0\mathbf{p}/\mathbf{q}^0\mathbf{p}^0 \qquad (\textit{Laspeyres' index } [1871]), \tag{8.3.7}$$

$$\mathcal{P}(\mathbf{q}^0, \mathbf{p}^0, \mathbf{q}, \mathbf{p}) = \mathbf{q}\mathbf{p}/\mathbf{q}\mathbf{p}^0 \qquad (\textit{Paasche's index } [1874]), \tag{8.3.8}$$

$$\mathcal{P}(\mathbf{q}^0, \mathbf{p}^0, \mathbf{q}, \mathbf{p}) = [(\mathbf{q}^0\mathbf{p})/\mathbf{q}^0\mathbf{p}^0)\,(\mathbf{q}\mathbf{p}/\mathbf{q}\mathbf{p}^0)]^{1/2} \qquad (\textit{Fisher's ideal index } [1922]) \tag{8.3.9}$$

$$\mathcal{P}(\mathbf{q}^0, \mathbf{p}^0, \mathbf{q}, \mathbf{p}) = \left(\frac{p_1}{p_1^0}\right)^{\alpha_1}\left(\frac{p_2}{p_2^0}\right)^{\alpha_2}\cdots\left(\frac{p_n}{p_n^0}\right)^{\alpha_n}, \quad \alpha_1 > 0, \alpha_2 > 0, \ldots, \alpha_n > 0 \text{ real const}, \textstyle\sum \alpha_\nu = 1, \tag{8.3.10}$$

$$\mathcal{P}(\mathbf{q}^0, \mathbf{p}^0, \mathbf{q}, \mathbf{p}) = \frac{[(q_1^0 p_1)^{-\varrho} + \cdots + (q_n^0 p_n)^{-\varrho}]^{-1/\varrho}}{[(q_1^0 p_1^0)^{-\varrho} + \cdots + (q_n^0 p_n^0)^{-\varrho}]^{-1/\varrho}}, \qquad \varrho \neq 0 \text{ a real const}, \tag{8.3.11}$$

$$\mathcal{P}(\mathbf{q}^0, \mathbf{p}^0, \mathbf{q}, \mathbf{p}) = [\beta_1(p_1/p_1^0)^{-\varrho} + \cdots + \beta_n(p_n/p_n^0)^{-\varrho}]^{-1/\varrho}, \quad \varrho \neq 0, \beta_1 > 0, \ldots, \beta_n > 0 \text{ real const}, \textstyle\sum \beta_\nu = 1. \tag{8.3.12}$$

At this point it is instructive to compare (8.3.7), (8.3.8) with (8.1.6); (8.3.9) with (8.1.10); (8.3.10) with (8.1.9); (8.3.11) with (8.1.7); (8.3.12) with (8.1.8)

8.3.13 **Remark.** Given an arbitrary number k of price indices $\mathcal{P}_1, \ldots, \mathcal{P}_k$, we obtain new price indices in the same way as described in Remark 8.1.13.

8.3.14 **Remark.** Every price index $\mathcal{P}$ satisfies

$$\mathcal{P}(\mathbf{q}^0, \mathbf{p}^0, \mathbf{q}, \lambda\mathbf{p}^0) = \lambda \qquad (\textit{Proportionality Test}; \text{ compare with 8.1.17}),$$

$$\mathcal{P}(\mathbf{q}^0, \lambda\mathbf{p}^0, \mathbf{q}, \mathbf{p}) = (1/\lambda)\,\mathcal{P}(\mathbf{q}^0, \mathbf{p}^0, \mathbf{q}, \mathbf{p}) \qquad (\text{see Test 8.1.18}),$$

$$\min\left\{\frac{p_1}{p_1^0}, \ldots, \frac{p_n}{p_n^0}\right\} \leqq \mathcal{P}(\mathbf{q}^0, \mathbf{p}^0, \mathbf{q}, \mathbf{p}) \leqq \max\left\{\frac{p_1}{p_1^0}, \ldots, \frac{p_n}{p_n^0}\right\} \qquad (\textit{Mean Value Test}; \text{ compare with 8.1.19}).$$

8.4 Fisher's System of Tests for Price Indices $\mathcal{P}$

From the historical point of view, the axiomatic theory of the price indices started not with Axioms 8.3.1–8.3.5 but with the following system of tests, which are due to Fisher [1922] and are therefore referred to as *Fisher's tests*. We shall formulate these tests as functional equations that are valid for all $(\mathbf{q}_0, \mathbf{p}_0, \mathbf{q}, \mathbf{p}) \in \mathbb{R}_{++}^{4n}$.

T.1 *Proportionality Test.* If all prices change λ-fold ($\lambda \in \mathbb{R}_{++}$), then the index value is λ:

$$\mathcal{P}(\mathbf{q}^0, \mathbf{p}^0, \mathbf{q}, \lambda\mathbf{p}^0) = \lambda \qquad \text{for all} \quad \lambda \in \mathbb{R}_{++}; \tag{8.4.1}$$

see also Test 8.1.17.

T.2 *Circular Test.* If the (vectors of) quantities and prices change from $\mathbf{q}^0, \mathbf{p}^0$ to $\mathbf{q}^1, \mathbf{p}^1$ and then further to $\mathbf{q}, \mathbf{p}$, then the price index for the whole change is the product of the price indices for the two changes from which it is composed:

$$\mathcal{P}(\mathbf{q}^0, \mathbf{p}^0, \mathbf{q}^1, \mathbf{p}^1)\,\mathcal{P}(\mathbf{q}^1, \mathbf{p}^1, \mathbf{q}, \mathbf{p}) = \mathcal{P}(\mathbf{q}^0, \mathbf{p}^0, \mathbf{q}, \mathbf{p}); \tag{8.4.2}$$

see also Test 8.2.2.

8.4.3 **Remark.** Every price index $\mathcal{P}$ satisfies the Proportionality Test, but there exist price indices $\mathcal{P}$ that do not satisfy the Circular Test; see, for instance, examples (8.3.9) and (8.3.12). The following tests (8.4.4), (8.4.6), (8.4.7) are straightforward consequences of the Circular Test:

$$\mathcal{P}(q^0, \mathbf{p}^0, \mathbf{q}^0, \mathbf{p}^0) = 1. \tag{8.4.4}$$

The Proportionality Test implies even more:

$$\mathcal{P}(\mathbf{q}^0, \mathbf{p}^0, \mathbf{q}^0, \mathbf{p}^0) = 1 \qquad \text{(Identity Axiom).} \tag{8.4.5}$$

$$\mathcal{P}(\mathbf{q}^0, \mathbf{p}^0, \mathbf{q}, \mathbf{p})\,\mathcal{P}(\mathbf{q}, \mathbf{p}, \mathbf{q}^0, \mathbf{p}) = 1 \qquad \text{(Time Reversal Test).} \tag{8.4.6}$$

$$\mathcal{P}(\mathbf{q}^0, \mathbf{p}^0, \mathbf{q}^1, \mathbf{p}^1)\,\mathcal{P}(\mathbf{q}^1, \mathbf{p}^1, \mathbf{q}, \mathbf{p},)\,\mathcal{P}(\mathbf{q}, \mathbf{p}, \mathbf{q}^0, \mathbf{p}^0) = 1. \tag{8.4.7}$$

T.3 *Determinateness Test.* If any scalar argument in $\mathcal{P}$ tends to zero, then $\mathcal{P}(\mathbf{q}^0, \mathbf{p}^0, \mathbf{q}, \mathbf{p})$ tends to a unique positive real number (which depends on the other arguments).

8.4.8 **Remark.** Obviously, the Determinateness Test contains a (rather weak) continuity assumption. The formulation of this test as presented by Swamy [1965, p. 620] differs from the formulation above, which is Fisher's [1922] original one and which has also been considered by Frisch [1930]. Neither Laspeyres' (see (8.3.7)) nor Paasche's (see (8.3.8)) price index satisfies Swamy's Determinateness Test. Neither Swamy [1965] nor Samuelson and Swamy [1974, p. 572] consider Determinateness Test T.3 very relevant: "This condition, it seems to us, is an odd one and not at all a desirable one." At this point we note that example (8.3.10) satisfies all above-mentioned axioms and tests with the exception of T.3. The following Theorems 8.5.1, 8.5.14, 8.5.20, Corollaries 8.5.16, 8.5.17 and Remarks 8.5.9, 8.5.10, 8.5.19, 8.5.26 do not use T.3.

T.4 *Commensurability Test.* See Commensurability Axiom 8.3.5.

T.5 *Factor Reversal Test.* By interchanging $\mathbf{q}^0$ and $\mathbf{p}^0$ as well as $\mathbf{q}$ and $\mathbf{p}$ in the price index $\mathcal{P}$, the resulting $\mathcal{P}(\mathbf{p}^0, \mathbf{q}^0, \mathbf{p}, \mathbf{q})$ may be considered the value of a quantity index if $\mathcal{P}$ is a price index. The product of the values of the two indices shall be a ratio of values; that is,

$$\mathcal{P}(\mathbf{q}^0, \mathbf{p}^0, \mathbf{q}, \mathbf{p})\,\mathcal{P}(\mathbf{p}^0, \mathbf{q}^0, \mathbf{p}, \mathbf{q}) = \mathbf{qp}/\mathbf{q}^0\mathbf{p}^0. \tag{8.4.9}$$

We add the following tests, which are weakened versions of Tests T.2 and T.5, respectively.

T.2′ *Base Test* (Frisch [1930, p. 398]). If the (vectors of) quantities and prices change from $\mathbf{q}^0$, $\mathbf{p}^0$ to $\mathbf{q}^1$, $\mathbf{p}^1$ and then further to $\mathbf{q}$, $\mathbf{p}$, then there exists an index S such that[8]

$$\mathcal{P}(\mathbf{q}^0, \mathbf{p}^0, \mathbf{q}^1, \mathbf{p}^1)\, S(\mathbf{q}^1, \mathbf{p}^1, \mathbf{q}, \mathbf{p}) = \mathcal{P}(\mathbf{q}^0, \mathbf{p}^0, \mathbf{q}, \mathbf{p}) \qquad \text{(see (8.4.2))} \qquad (8.4.10)$$

or

$$S(\mathbf{q}^0, \mathbf{p}^0, \mathbf{q}^1, \mathbf{p}^1)\, \mathcal{P}(\mathbf{q}^1, \mathbf{p}^1, \mathbf{q}, \mathbf{p}) = \mathcal{P}(\mathbf{q}^0, \mathbf{p}^0, \mathbf{q}, \mathbf{p}) \qquad \text{(see (8.4.2)).} \qquad (8.4.11)$$

T.5′ *Product Test* (Frisch [1930, p. 399]). Instead of T.5 we require only

$$\mathcal{P}(\mathbf{q}^0, \mathbf{p}^0, \mathbf{q}, \mathbf{p})\, Q(\mathbf{q}^0, \mathbf{p}^0, \mathbf{q}, \mathbf{p}) = \mathbf{qp}/\mathbf{q}^0\mathbf{p}^0 \qquad \text{(see (8.2.22), (8.4.9))} \qquad (8.4.12)$$

to hold, where $Q\colon \mathbb{R}^{4n}_{++} \to \mathbb{R}_{++}$ is a quantity index satisfying axioms analogous to those satisfied by the price index $\mathcal{P}$.

8.5 Implications of Fisher's Tests[9]

8.5.1 **Theorem.** *Let F be a function (8.3.0) that satisfies Base Test T.2′ and Commensurability Test (or Axiom) T.4. Then there exist functions G, H, Φ from $\mathbb{R}^n_{++}$ into $\mathbb{R}_{++}$ such that*

$$F(\mathbf{q}^0, \mathbf{p}^0, \mathbf{q}, \mathbf{p}) = \frac{G(q_1p_1, \ldots, q_np_n)}{H(q_1^0p_1^0, \ldots, q_n^0p_n^0)}\, \Phi\left(\frac{p_1}{p_1^0}, \ldots, \frac{p_n}{p_n^0}\right). \qquad (8.5.2)$$

The function Φ is multiplicative:

$$\Phi(\lambda_1\mu_1, \ldots, \lambda_n\mu_n) = \Phi(\lambda_1, \ldots, \lambda_n)\, \Phi(\mu_1, \ldots, \mu_n) \qquad (8.5.3)$$

Every function given by (8.5.2) with (8.5.3) satisfies both T.2′ and T.4.

Proof. The last statement can be verified by inserting (8.5.2) in conjunction with (8.5.3) into T.2′ and T.4. To prove the first assertion, we start with T.2′ or, equivalently, with

$$F(\mathbf{q}^0, \mathbf{p}^0, \mathbf{q}, \mathbf{p}) = \frac{F(\mathbf{q}^1, \mathbf{p}^1, \mathbf{q}, \mathbf{p})}{S(\mathbf{q}^1, \mathbf{p}^1, \mathbf{q}^0, \mathbf{p}^0)}\,.$$

[8] Note that S depends on only four of the six vectors occurring in functional equations (8.4.10), (8.4.11).

[9] This and the following section contain results presented in Eichhorn [1973b, 1976].

By defining

$$F(1, \ldots, 1, 1, \ldots, 1, \mathbf{q}, \mathbf{p}) = : g(\mathbf{q}, \mathbf{p}),$$
$$S(1, \ldots, 1, 1, \ldots, 1, \mathbf{q}^0, \mathbf{p}^0) = : h(\mathbf{q}^0, \mathbf{p}^0)$$

this becomes

$$F(\mathbf{q}^0, \mathbf{p}^0, \mathbf{q}, \mathbf{p}) = g(\mathbf{q}, \mathbf{p})/h(\mathbf{q}^0, \mathbf{p}^0). \tag{8.5.4}$$

Now we apply Commensurability Test T.4 to (8.5.4) in order to obtain

$$\frac{g(q_1/\lambda_1, \ldots, q_n/\lambda_n, \lambda_1 p_1, \ldots, \lambda_n p_n)}{g(\mathbf{q}, \mathbf{p})} = \frac{h(q_1^0/\lambda_1, \ldots, q_n^0/\lambda_n, \lambda_1 p_1^0, \ldots, \lambda_n p_n^0)}{h(\mathbf{q}^0, \mathbf{p}^0)}.$$

With $\mathbf{q}^0 = (1, \ldots, 1)$, $\mathbf{p}^0 = (1, \ldots, 1)$, this becomes

$$g(q_1/\lambda_1, \ldots, q_n/\lambda_n, \lambda_1 p_1, \ldots, \lambda_n p_n) = \Phi(\lambda_1, \ldots, \lambda_n)\, g(\mathbf{q}, \mathbf{p}) \tag{8.5.5}$$

where

$$\Phi(\lambda_1, \ldots, \lambda_n) = \frac{h(1/\lambda_1, \ldots, 1/\lambda_n, \lambda_1, \ldots, \lambda_n)}{h(1, \ldots, 1, 1, \ldots, 1)}.$$

In the same way we obtain

$$h(q_1^0/\lambda_1, \ldots, q_n^0/\lambda_n, \lambda_1 p_1^0, \ldots, \lambda_n p_n^0) = \Phi(\lambda_1, \ldots, \lambda_n)\, h(\mathbf{q}^0, \mathbf{p}^0) \tag{8.5.6}$$

with the same Φ as in (8.5.5). Equation (8.5.5) (as well as Eq. (8.5.6)) implies (8.5.3).

Because of T.4 and (8.5.5),

$$\begin{aligned} g(\mathbf{q}, \mathbf{p}) &= g(q_1 p_1/p_1, \ldots, q_n p_n/p_n, p_1 \cdot 1, \ldots, p_n \cdot 1) \\ &= \Phi(p_1, \ldots, p_n)\, G(q_1 p_1, \ldots, q_n p_n) \end{aligned} \tag{8.5.7}$$

where

$$G(q_1 p_1, \ldots, q_n p_n) : = g(q_1 p_1, \ldots, q_n p_n, 1, \ldots, 1).$$

Analogously,

$$h(\mathbf{q}^0, \mathbf{p}^0) = \Phi(p_1^0, \ldots, p_n^0) H(q_1^0 p_1^0, \ldots, q_n^0 p_n^0). \tag{8.5.8}$$

The theorem is now proved by inserting (8.5.7), (8.5.8) into (8.5.4) and by making use of (8.5.3). ■

8.5.9 **Remark.** If in Theorem 8.5.1 we replace "Base Test T.2′" by "Circular Test T.2", then H in formula (8.5.2) must be changed to G, since T.2 is equivalent to

$$F(\mathbf{q}^0, \mathbf{p}^0, \mathbf{q}, \mathbf{p}) = \frac{F(\mathbf{q}^1, \mathbf{p}^1, \mathbf{q}, \mathbf{p})}{F(\mathbf{q}^1, \mathbf{p}^1, \mathbf{q}^0, \mathbf{p}^0)} = \frac{g(\mathbf{q}, \mathbf{p})}{g(\mathbf{q}^0, \mathbf{p}^0)}.$$

8.5.10 **Remark.** If there exists a point $(\bar{\mathbf{q}}_0, \bar{\mathbf{p}}_0)$ such that $(\mathbf{q}, \mathbf{p}) \to F(\bar{\mathbf{q}}^0, \bar{\mathbf{p}}^0, \mathbf{q}, \mathbf{p})$ is continuous at (at least) one point $(\bar{\mathbf{q}}, \bar{\mathbf{p}})$, then formula (8.5.2) can be written as

$$F(\mathbf{q}^0, \mathbf{p}^0, \mathbf{q}, \mathbf{p}) = \frac{G(q_1 p_1, \ldots, q_n p_n)}{H(q_1^0 p_1^0, \ldots, q_n^0 p_n^0)} \left(\frac{p_1}{p_1^0}\right)^{c_1} \left(\frac{p_2}{p_2^0}\right)^{c_2} \cdots \left(\frac{p_n}{p_n^0}\right)^{c_n} \tag{8.5.11}$$

where $c_1, c_2, \ldots, c_n$ are real constants. This follows from the fact that a multiplicative function Φ: $\mathbb{R}^n_{++} \to \mathbb{R}_{++}$ that is continuous at (at least) one point can be written as

$$\Phi(\lambda_1, \lambda_2, \ldots, \lambda_n) = \lambda_1^{c_1}\lambda_2^{c_2} \cdots \lambda_n^{c_n} \qquad (c_1, c_2, \ldots, c_n \text{ real const});$$

see Remark 1.9.23 and Theorem 3.6.7. Formula (8.5.11) is due to Frisch [1930, p. 404]; his derivation is made under rather strong regularity assumptions on F with the aid of results from the theory of partial differential equations.

8.5.12 **Remark.** Frisch [1930, p. 405] concludes from (8.5.11) that Base Test T.2′, Commensurability Test T.4, and Determinateness Test T.3 "cannot be fulfilled at the same time (if the index number possesses partial derivatives)." However, this is not correct: Taking

$$G(q_1p_1, \ldots, q_np_n) = (\mathbf{qp})^{1/2}, \qquad H(q_1^0p_1^0, \ldots, q_n^0p_n^0) = (\mathbf{q}^0\mathbf{p}^0)^{1/2},$$
$$c_1 = c_2 = \cdots = c_n = 0,$$

in (8.5.11) we obtain

$$F(\mathbf{q}^0, \mathbf{p}^0, \mathbf{q}, \mathbf{p}) = (\mathbf{qp}/\mathbf{q}^0\mathbf{p}^0)^{1/2}, \tag{8.5.13}$$

which satisfies Tests T.2, T.3, T.4, and T.5. Note that (8.5.13) does not satisfy Linear Homogeneity Axiom 8.1.2, so that F given by (8.5.13) is not a price index $\mathcal{P}$.

8.5.14 **Theorem.** *Let F: $\mathbb{R}^{4n}_{++} \to \mathbb{R}_{++}$ satisfy Base Test T.2′, Commensurability Test T.4, and Factor Reversal Test T.5. Then there exists a multiplicative function Φ : $\mathbb{R}^n_{++} \to \mathbb{R}_{++}$ such that*

$$F(\mathbf{q}^0, \mathbf{p}^0, \mathbf{q}, \mathbf{p}) = \left[\Phi\left(\frac{q_1^0p_1}{q_1p_1^0}, \ldots, \frac{q_n^0p_n}{q_np_n^0}\right)\frac{\mathbf{qp}}{\mathbf{q}^0\mathbf{p}^0}\right]^{1/2}. \tag{8.5.15}$$

The function F given by (8.5.15) satisfies T.2, T.4, and T.5.

Proof. In order that (8.5.2) fulfill T.5, the product of (8.5.2) and of

$$F(\mathbf{p}^0, \mathbf{q}^0, \mathbf{p}, \mathbf{q}) = \frac{G(q_1p_1, \ldots, q_np_n)}{H(q_1^0p_1^0, \ldots, q_n^0p_n^0)}\Phi\left(\frac{q_1}{q_1^0}, \ldots, \frac{q_n}{q_n^0}\right)$$

must be equal to $\mathbf{p}/\mathbf{q}^0\mathbf{p}^0$. Hence

$$\frac{\Phi(q_1/q_1^0, \ldots, q_n/q_n^0)}{\Phi(p_1/p_1^0, \ldots, p_n/p_n^0)} F(\mathbf{q}^0, \mathbf{p}^0, \mathbf{q}, \mathbf{p})^2 = \frac{\mathbf{qp}}{\mathbf{q}^0\mathbf{p}^0}.$$

This is equivalent to (8.5.15), since Φ is multiplicative. The last assertion of Theorem 8.5.14 is obvious. ■

8.5.16 **Corollary.** *If a continuity assumption as made in Remark 8.5.10 is added to the assumptions of Theorem 8.5.14, then this implies the differentiability of F.*

Proof. As mentioned in Remark 8.5.10, the continuity assumption implies

$$\Phi(\lambda_1, \lambda_2, \ldots, \lambda_n) = \lambda_1^{c_1}\lambda_2^{c_2} \cdots \lambda_n^{c_n} \qquad (c_1, c_2, \ldots, c_n \text{ real const}).$$

But then F given by (8.5.15) is differentiable. ■

Since (8.5.15) does not satisfy Proportionality Test T.1, we have the following corollary:

8.5.17 **Corollary.** *Tests T.1, T.2′, T.4, and T.5 are inconsistent in the sense that there cannot exist any function* $F : \mathbb{R}^{4n}_{++} \to \mathbb{R}_{++}$ *that satisfies them all.*

A proof of this was given by Swamy [1965, pp. 621–622] under the additional assumption that F possesses partial derivatives. Note that since T.3 is not required, our proof runs without any continuity (or differentiability) assumption.

8.5.18 **Corollary.** *The function F given by (8.5.13) is uniquely determined by Tests T.2–T.5.*

Proof. Determinateness Test T.3 implies the boundedness of Φ in (8.5.15) whenever a scalar argument of Φ is varying in a sufficiently small interval with left boundary 0. But then the multiplicativity of Φ implies

$$\Phi\left(\frac{q_1^0 p_1}{q_1 p_1^0}, \ldots, \frac{q_n^0 p_n}{q_n p_n^0}\right) = \left(\frac{q_1^0 p_1}{q_1 p_1^0}\right)^{c_1} \cdots \left(\frac{q_n^0 p_n}{q_n p_n^0}\right)^{c_n}, \qquad c_1, \ldots, c_n \quad \text{real const};$$

see the proof of Theorem 3.6.7 and apply Remark 1.9.23 with property (1.2.13). Then (8.5.15) satisfies Determinateness Test T.3 if and only if $c_1 = \cdots = c_n = = 0$; that is, if and only if $\Phi(\lambda_1, \ldots, \lambda_n) \equiv 1$. ■

8.5.19 **Remark.** Further consequences of Theorem 8.5.14 are the following. If a function $F: \mathbb{R}^{4n}_{++} \to \mathbb{R}_{++}$ satisfies Tests T.2′, T.4, and T.5, then the following homogeneity relations are valid for all $\lambda \in \mathbb{R}_{++}$:

$$F(\mathbf{q}^0, \lambda\mathbf{p}^0, \mathbf{q}, \lambda\mathbf{p}) = F(\mathbf{q}^0, \mathbf{p}^0, \mathbf{q}, \mathbf{p}) \qquad \text{(Dimensionality Axiom 8.3.4)}, \quad (8.5.20)$$

$$F(\lambda\mathbf{q}^0, \mathbf{p}^0, \lambda\mathbf{q}, \mathbf{p}) = F(\mathbf{q}^0, \mathbf{p}^0, \mathbf{q}, \mathbf{p}), \qquad (8.5.21)$$

$$F(\lambda\mathbf{q}^0, \lambda\mathbf{p}^0, \lambda\mathbf{q}, \lambda\mathbf{p}) = F(\mathbf{q}^0, \mathbf{p}^0, \mathbf{q}, \mathbf{p}). \qquad (8.5.22)$$

It should be remarked that Corollary 8.5.17 remains valid without Commensurability Test T.4.

8.5.20 **Theorem.** (Wald [1937, pp. 181–182]). *There does not exist any function* $F : \mathbb{R}^{4n}_{++} \to \mathbb{R}_{++}$ *that satisfies tests T.1, T.2, and T.5′ simultaneously.*

Proof (Wald [1937, pp. 181–182]). Consider three time periods. In the first period, the quantities and prices change from $\mathbf{q}^0$, $\mathbf{p}^0$ to $\mathbf{q}^1$, $\mathbf{p}^1$; in the second, from $\mathbf{q}^1$, $\mathbf{p}^1$ to $\mathbf{q}^2$, $\mathbf{p}^2$; and in the third, from $\mathbf{q}^2$, $\mathbf{p}^2$ to $\mathbf{q}^3$, $\mathbf{p}^3$. We assume

$$\mathbf{p}^0 = \mathbf{p}^2, \qquad \mathbf{p}^1 = \mathbf{p}^3, \qquad \mathbf{q}^0 = \mathbf{q}^1, \qquad \mathbf{q}^2 = \mathbf{q}^3.$$

If Proportionality Test T.1 is satisfied, we have

$$F(\mathbf{q}^0, \mathbf{p}^0, \mathbf{q}^2, \mathbf{p}^2) = F(\mathbf{q}^1, \mathbf{p}^1, \mathbf{q}^3, \mathbf{p}^3) = 1 \tag{8.5.21}$$

and, in view of the quantity index,

$$G(\mathbf{q}^0, \mathbf{p}^0, \mathbf{q}^1, \mathbf{p}^1) = G(\mathbf{q}^0, \mathbf{p}^0, \mathbf{q}^3, \mathbf{p}^3) = 1. \tag{8.5.22}$$

If, in addition, Product Test T.5′ is also satisfied, then, from (8.5.22)

$$F(\mathbf{q}^0, \mathbf{p}^0, \mathbf{q}^1, \mathbf{p}^1)\, G(\mathbf{q}^0, \mathbf{p}^0, \mathbf{q}^1, \mathbf{p}^1) = F(\mathbf{q}^0, \mathbf{p}^0, \mathbf{q}^1, \mathbf{p}^1) = \frac{\mathbf{q}^1\mathbf{p}^1}{\mathbf{q}^0\mathbf{p}^0} = \frac{\mathbf{q}^0\mathbf{p}^3}{\mathbf{q}^0\mathbf{p}^0} \tag{8.5.23}$$

and

$$F(\mathbf{q}^2, \mathbf{p}^2, \mathbf{q}^3, \mathbf{p}^3)\, G(\mathbf{q}^2, \mathbf{p}^2, \mathbf{q}^3, \mathbf{p}^3) = F(\mathbf{q}^2, \mathbf{p}^2, \mathbf{q}^3, \mathbf{p}^3) = \frac{\mathbf{q}^3\mathbf{p}^3}{\mathbf{q}^2\mathbf{p}^2} = \frac{\mathbf{q}^3\mathbf{p}^3}{\mathbf{q}^3\mathbf{p}^0}. \tag{8.5.24}$$

By considering (8.5.21)–(8.5.24) and Circular Test T.2, namely,

$$F(\mathbf{q}^0, \mathbf{p}^0, \mathbf{q}^1, \mathbf{p}^1)\, F(\mathbf{q}^1, \mathbf{p}^1, \mathbf{q}^3, \mathbf{p}^3) = F(\mathbf{q}^0, \mathbf{p}^0, \mathbf{q}^2, \mathbf{p}^2)\, F(\mathbf{q}^2, \mathbf{p}^2, \mathbf{q}^3, \mathbf{p}^3),$$

we conclude that

$$(\mathbf{q}^0\mathbf{p}^3)/(\mathbf{q}^0\mathbf{p}^0) = (\mathbf{q}^3\mathbf{p}^3)/(\mathbf{q}^3\mathbf{p}^0). \tag{8.5.25}$$

Since the vectors $\mathbf{q}^0$, $\mathbf{p}^0$, $\mathbf{q}^3$, $\mathbf{p}^3$ can be chosen in such a way that identity (8.5.25) is *not* fulfilled, we have obtained a contradiction. This proves the theorem. ■

8.5.26 **Remark.** Since every function F satisfying Tests T.1 and T.2′ also satisfies Circular Test T.2, Theorem 8.5.20 remains valid if we replace T.2 by T.2′.

8.5.27 **Theorem.** *Tests T.1–T.4 are inconsistent in the sense that there cannot exist any function* $F\colon \mathbb{R}^{4n}_{++} \to \mathbb{R}_{++}$ *that satisfies them all.*

Proof. According to Theorem 8.5.1 and Remark 8.5.9, every function F that satisfies both Circular Test T.2 and Commensurability Test T.4 can be written as

$$F(\mathbf{q}^0, \mathbf{p}^0, \mathbf{q}, \mathbf{p}) = \frac{G(q_1p_1, \ldots, q_np_n)}{G(q_1^0p_1^0, \ldots, q_n^0p_n^0)}\, \Phi\left(\frac{p_1}{p_1^0}, \ldots, \frac{p_n}{p_n^0}\right) \tag{8.5.28}$$

where $G : \mathbb{R}^n_{++} \to \mathbb{R}_{++}$ is arbitrary and $\Phi : \mathbb{R}^n_{++} \to \mathbb{R}_{++}$ is multiplicative. From (8.5.28) it follows that

$$\frac{F(\mathbf{q}^0, \mathbf{p}^0, \mathbf{q}, \lambda\mathbf{p}^0)}{F(\mathbf{q}^0, \mathbf{p}^0, \lambda\mathbf{q}, \mathbf{p}^0)} = \frac{\Phi(\lambda, \ldots, \lambda)}{\Phi(1, \ldots, 1)} \quad \text{for all} \quad \lambda \in \mathbb{R}_{++}, \quad \mathbf{q}^0, \mathbf{p}^0, \mathbf{q}, \mathbf{p}. \tag{8.5.29}$$

Because of Proportionality Test T.1, the left-hand side of this equation is equal to λ. The multiplicativity and positivity of Φ yields $\Phi(1, \ldots, 1) = 1$ on the right-hand side. So we have

$$\Phi(\lambda, \ldots, \lambda) = \lambda \qquad \text{for all} \quad \lambda \in \mathbb{R}_{++}. \tag{8.5.30}$$

Since Φ is multiplicative, this can be written as

$$\Phi(\lambda, 1, \ldots, 1)\Phi(1, \lambda, 1, \ldots, 1) \ldots \Phi(1, \ldots, 1, \lambda) = \lambda$$

or, by multiplying both sides by

$$\frac{G(\lambda, 1, \ldots, 1)}{G(1, 1, \ldots, 1)} \frac{G(1, \lambda, 1, \ldots, 1)}{G(1, 1, 1, \ldots, 1)} \cdots \frac{G(1, \ldots, 1, \lambda)}{G(1, \ldots, 1, 1)},$$

$$\frac{G(\lambda, 1, \ldots, 1)}{G(1, 1, \ldots, 1)} \Phi(\lambda, 1, \ldots, 1) \cdots \frac{G(1, \ldots, 1, \lambda)}{G(1, \ldots, 1, 1)} \Phi(1, \ldots, 1, \lambda)$$
$$= \lambda \frac{G(\lambda, 1, \ldots, 1)}{G(1, 1, \ldots, 1)} \cdots \frac{G(1, \ldots, 1, \lambda)}{G(1, \ldots, 1, 1)},$$

that is, by using (8.5.28) and (8.5.30),

$$\begin{aligned} &F(1, \ldots, 1, 1, \ldots, 1, 1, \ldots, 1, \lambda, \ldots, 1) \\ &\cdots F(1, \ldots, 1, 1, \ldots, 1, 1, \ldots, 1, 1, \ldots, \lambda) \\ &= \lambda F(1, \ldots, 1, 1, \ldots, 1, \lambda, \ldots, 1, 1, \ldots, 1) \\ &\cdots F(1, \ldots, 1, 1, \ldots, 1, 1, \ldots, \lambda, 1, \ldots, 1). \end{aligned}$$

This equation and the existence of the limits in Determinateness Test T.3 imply that at least one of the factors on the left-hand side tends to zero for $\lambda \to 0$. But this contradicts T.3. ■

We note that this proof did not require any regularity condition on F (except for the conditions imposed by T.1–T.4).

8.5.31 **Remark.** Any *three* of the tests T.1–T.4 *are* consistent. For instance, the function F given by (8.5.13) satisfies T.2–T.4; Fisher's ideal index given by (8.3.9) satisfies T.1, T.3, T.4; the index $\mathcal{D}$ given by (8.3.10) satisfies T.1, T.2, T.4; and the function F given by

$$F(\mathbf{q}^0, \mathbf{p}^0, \mathbf{q}, \mathbf{p}) = \mathbf{ap}/\mathbf{ap}^0, \qquad \mathbf{a} = (a_1, \ldots, a_n), \quad a_1 > 0, \ldots, a_n > 0 \text{ real const},$$

satisfies T.1–T.3.

The rather disappointing results illustrated by Theorem 8.5.20, Remark 8.5.26, and Theorem 8.5.27 suggest an attempt at weakening Fisher's tests T.1–T.5 in order to obtain consistent sets of tests.

8.6 Weakened Systems of Tests

In the following discussion let us replace Circular Test T.2 by the (weaker) Base Test T.2′, Factor Reversal Test T.5 by the (weaker) Product Test T.5′, and Proportionality Test T.1 by the following test:

T.1′ *Weak Proportionality Test.* If the quantities do not change, then a λ-fold ($\lambda \in \mathbb{R}_{++}$) change of prices yields an index value of λ:

$$\mathcal{P}(\mathbf{q}^0, \mathbf{p}^0, \mathbf{q}^0, \lambda\mathbf{p}^0) = \lambda \qquad \text{for all} \quad \lambda \in \mathbb{R}_{++}, \mathbf{q}^0, \mathbf{p}^0. \tag{8.6.1}$$

We note that, for instance, the function F given by

$$F(\mathbf{q}^0, \mathbf{p}^0, \mathbf{q}, \mathbf{p}) = \mathbf{qp}/\mathbf{q}^0\mathbf{p}^0 \tag{8.6.2}$$

satisfies T.1′, but not T.1.

8.6.3 **Theorem.** *Tests T.1′, T.2′, T.3, T.4, T.5′ are independent in the following sense: Any four of them can be satisfied by a function $F: \mathbb{R}^{4n}_{++} \to \mathbb{R}_{++}$ that does not fulfill the remaining test.*

Proof. The function F given by (8.6.2) satisfies T.1′, T.2′ (even T.2), T.3, T.4, but not T.5′. The function F given by

$$F(\mathbf{q}^0, \mathbf{p}^0, \mathbf{q}, \mathbf{p}) = \left[\frac{\mathbf{qp}}{\mathbf{q}^0\mathbf{p}^0}\,\frac{\mathbf{ap}}{\mathbf{ap}^0}\,\frac{\mathbf{bq}^0}{\mathbf{bq}}\right]^{1/2}, \qquad \mathbf{a}, \mathbf{b} \text{ vectors with } n \text{ positive components,}$$

satisfies T.1′, T.2′ (even T.2), T.3, T.5′,[10] but not T.4. The function F given by (8.5.15) with

$$\Phi(\lambda_1, \lambda_2, \ldots, \lambda_n) = \lambda_1^{c_1}\lambda_2^{c_2}\cdots\lambda_n^{c_n}, \qquad c_1 > 0,\ c_2 > 0,\ \ldots,\ c_n > 0 \text{ real const,} \quad \sum c_\nu = 1,$$

satisfies T.1′, T.2′ (even T.2), T.4, T.5′ (even T.5), but not T.3. Fisher's ideal index (8.3.9) satisfies T.1′ (even T.1), T.3, T.4, T.5′ (even T.5), but not T.2′. Finally, the function F given by (8.5.13) satisfies T.2′ (even T.2), T.3, T.4, T.5′ (even T.5), but not T.1′. ■

8.6.4 **Theorem.** *There does not exist any function $F: \mathbb{R}^{4n}_{++} \to \mathbb{R}_{++}$ that satisfies Tests T.1′, T.2′, T.3, T.4, and T.5′ at the same time.*

---

[10] Let then $Q(\mathbf{q}^0, \mathbf{p}^0, \mathbf{q}, \mathbf{p}) = \left[\frac{\mathbf{qp}}{\mathbf{q}^0\mathbf{p}^0}\,\frac{\mathbf{ap}^0}{\mathbf{ap}}\,\frac{\mathbf{bq}}{\mathbf{bq}^0}\right]^{1/2}.$

Proof. As we saw in the proof of Theorem 8.5.1, a function F satisfying Base Test T.2′ can be written as

$$F(\mathbf{q}^0, \mathbf{p}^0, \mathbf{q}, \mathbf{p}) = g(\mathbf{q}, \mathbf{p})/h(\mathbf{q}^0, \mathbf{p}^0). \tag{8.6.5}$$

If F satisfies simultaneously T.2′ and Weak Proportionality Test T.1′, then the identity $g(\mathbf{q}, \mathbf{p}) \equiv h(\mathbf{q}^0, \mathbf{p}^0)$ follows from (8.6.5) with $\mathbf{q} = \mathbf{q}^0$ and $\mathbf{p} = \mathbf{p}^0$; that is, F satisfies Circular Test T.2.

According to Theorem 8.5.1 and Remark 8.5.9, every function F satisfying both Circular Test T.2 and Commensurability Test T.4 can be written in the form (8.5.28). The same is true for a function $F^*\colon \mathbb{R}^{4n}_{++} \to \mathbb{R}_{++}$ satisfying the analoga of Tests T.1′, T.2′, T.4 for a quantity index:

$$F^*(\mathbf{q}^0, \mathbf{p}^0, \mathbf{q}, \mathbf{p}) = \frac{G^*(q_1p_1, \ldots, q_np_n)}{G^*(q_1^0p_1^0, \ldots, q_n^0p_n^0)} \Phi^* \left(\frac{q_1}{q_1^0}, \ldots, \frac{q_n}{q_n^0}\right). \tag{8.6.6}$$

By setting $\mathbf{q}^0 = \mathbf{p}^0 = \mathbf{q} = (1, \ldots, 1), \mathbf{p} = (\lambda, \ldots, \lambda)$ in (8.5.28) we obtain, from T.1′,

$$\frac{G(\lambda, \ldots, \lambda)}{G(1, \ldots, 1)} \Phi(\lambda, \ldots, \lambda) = \lambda. \tag{8.6.7}$$

Similarly, (8.6.6) implies

$$\frac{G^*(\lambda, \ldots, \lambda)}{G^*(1, \ldots, 1)} \Phi^*(\lambda, \ldots, \lambda) = \lambda. \tag{8.6.8}$$

In order that (8.5.28) and (8.6.6) satisfy Product Test T.5′ for the arguments $\mathbf{q}^0 = \mathbf{p}^0 = \mathbf{p} = (1, \ldots, 1), \mathbf{q} = (\lambda, \ldots, \lambda)$, the following must be true:

$$\frac{G(\lambda, \ldots, \lambda)}{G(1, \ldots, 1)} \Phi(1, \ldots, 1) \frac{G^*(\lambda, \ldots, \lambda)}{G^*(1, \ldots, 1)} \Phi^*(\lambda, \ldots, \lambda) = \lambda. \tag{8.6.9}$$

Since Φ is multiplicative and positive valued, it follows that $\Phi(1, \ldots, 1) = 1$. Hence from (8.6.8) and (8.6.9),

$$G(\lambda, \ldots, \lambda) \equiv G(1, \ldots, 1),$$

and therefore, from (8.6.7),

$$\Phi(\lambda, \ldots, \lambda) = \lambda. \tag{8.6.10}$$

The final part of the proof runs along the same line of reasoning as does the proof of Theorem 8.5.27 from formula (8.5.30) on. ■

How far must Tests T.1′, T.2′, T.3, T.4, T.5′ be weakened in order to obtain a consistent set? Answers to this question are given by Theorem 8.6.3: Take the examples in the proof of Theorem 8.6.3. Each of them satisfies exactly four of the five Tests T.1′, T.2′, T.3, T.4, T.5′. Weaken the remaining test in such a way that the weakened test is satisfied by the example. For instance, Fisher's ideal index (8.3.9) satisfies T.1, T.3, T.4, T.5, but neither Circular Test T.2 nor Base Test T.2′. But it satisfies Time Reversal Test (8.4.6). Being a consequence of T.2, the Time Reversal Test, call it T.2″, is a weakened form of the Circular Test. So Tests T.1, T.2″, T.3, T.4, T.5 form a consistent set of five tests.

Another consistent set of five tests is T.2, T.3, T.4, T.5, and the following:

$$\mathcal{P}(\mathbf{q}^0, \mathbf{p}^0, \lambda\mathbf{q}^0, \lambda\mathbf{p}^0) = \lambda \qquad \text{for all} \quad \lambda \in \mathbb{R}_{++}, \mathbf{q}^0, \mathbf{p}^0. \qquad (\text{T}.1'')$$

Note that T.1″ is another weakened form of Proportionality Test T.1.

8.6.11 **Remark.** In his Karlsruhe dissertation, Voeller [1974] analyzed and solved the problem of consistency and independence with respect to *every* subset of the set of tests T.1, T.1′, T.2, T.2′, T.3, T.4, T.5, T.5′. These results can be found in the lecture notes [1976] by Eichhorn and Voeller.

9

Systems of Functional Equations Determining the Effectiveness of a Production Process

A *production process* can be considered as a quadruple

$$(K, t, \mathbf{x}, \mathbf{u}) \in \mathbb{R}_+^{2+n+m} \tag{9.0.1}$$

where $K \in \mathbb{R}_+$ is the capital necessary for establishing and running the production, and $t \in \mathbb{R}_+$ is the time period required to produce the output vector $\mathbf{u} \in \mathbb{R}_+^m$ with the aid of the input vector $\mathbf{x} \in \mathbb{R}_+^n$.

In this chapter (which contains parts of the author's papers [1972b, in German; 1974a]) we consider two different notions of the *effectiveness*[1] of a production process: *technical effectiveness* and *economic effectiveness*. Both terms will be defined as real-valued functions that satisfy certain functional equations.

Let $\mathbf{q} \in \mathbb{R}_+^n$ be the (given, constant) prices of the inputs $\mathbf{x} \in \mathbb{R}_+^n$. Then the variable cost $k \in \mathbb{R}_+$ of process (9.0.1) is $k = \mathbf{xq}$. If we are interested only in the variable cost and the time period required to produce the output vector $\mathbf{u}$, then we will consider, instead of the quadruple (9.0.1), only the triple

$$(t, k, \mathbf{u}) \in \mathbb{R}_+^{2+m}, \tag{9.0.2}$$

which can also be called a production process.

By the *technical effectiveness of production process (9.0.2)* we understand a function

$$T : \mathbb{R}_+^{2+m} \to \mathbb{R}_+, \qquad (t, k, \mathbf{u}) \to T(t, k, \mathbf{u}) \tag{9.0.3}$$

[1] We speak of effectiveness, rather than efficiency, since the phrase "efficient production process" has another meaning in the literature on production theory; see, e.g., Shephard [1970, p. 180] or Remark 9.8.8.

Wolfgang Eichhorn, Functional Equations in Economics.

ISBN 0–201–01948–5/01949–3 PBK

that is strictly decreasing with respect to t and k, strictly increasing with respect to $\mathbf{u}$, and, moreover, satisfies seven assumptions, all of them in form of functional equations. This system S of equations will be formulated in Section 9.1. In Sections 9.2–9.5 we consider axiomatic questions like consistency, independence, dependence, and sufficiency in connection with S. Section 9.6 gives the general solution of S, namely, all functions T that satisfy the equations of S simultaneously.

In Section 9.7 we introduce the notion of the *economic effectiveness of production process (9.0.1)*. As distinguished from a technologist, an economist is more interested in the price vector $\mathbf{p} \in \mathbb{R}_+^m$ that can be realized for the output vector $\mathbf{u}$, that is, in the profitability of process (9.0.1). Since measures of profitability are of the form $\mathbf{up}/\mathbf{xq}$ and $\mathbf{up} - \mathbf{xq}$, we define the *economic effectiveness E of production process (9.0.1)* to be a function that depends on K, t, $\mathbf{up}/\mathbf{xq}$, and $\mathbf{up} - \mathbf{xq}$, and that, moreover, satisfies five assumptions, four of them in the form of functional equations. In the concluding section (9.8) we determine all functions E that satisfy the system of assumptions.

9.1 A System of Functional Equations Determining the Technical Effectiveness of a Production Process

By the *technical effectiveness T of production process (9.0.2)* we mean a function (9.0.3) that is strictly decreasing with respect to t and k, strictly increasing with respect to $\mathbf{u}$, and, in addition, satisfies the following seven functional equations for all $\lambda > 0$, $t > 0$, $k > 0$, $\mathbf{u} \geqq \mathbf{0}$:

$$T(\lambda t, \lambda k, \lambda \mathbf{u}) = T(t, k, \mathbf{u}), \tag{9.1.1}$$

$$T(t, \lambda k, \lambda \mathbf{u}) = \phi(\lambda)\, T(t, k, \mathbf{u}), \quad \phi: \mathbb{R}_{++} \to \mathbb{R}_{++}, \text{ strictly incresasing}, \quad \phi(1) = 1, \tag{9.1.2}$$

$$T(\lambda t, k, \lambda \mathbf{u}) = \psi(\lambda)\, T(t, k, \mathbf{u}), \quad \psi: \mathbb{R}_{++} \to \mathbb{R}_{++}, \text{ strictly increasing}, \quad \psi(1) = 1, \tag{9.1.3}$$

$$T(\lambda t, \lambda k, \mathbf{u}) = \chi(\lambda)\, T(t, k, \mathbf{u}), \quad \chi: \mathbb{R}_{++} \to \mathbb{R}_{++}, \text{ strictly decreasing}, \quad \chi(1) = 1, \tag{9.1.4}$$

$$T(t, k, \lambda \mathbf{u}) = \varrho(\lambda)\, T(t, k, \mathbf{u}), \quad \varrho: \mathbb{R}_{++} \to \mathbb{R}_{++}, \text{ strictly increasing}, \quad \varrho(1) = 1, \tag{9.1.5}$$

$$T(t, \lambda k, \mathbf{u}) = \sigma(\lambda)\, T(t, k, \mathbf{u}), \quad \sigma: \mathbb{R}_{++} \to \mathbb{R}_{++}, \text{ strictly decreasing}, \quad \sigma(1) = 1, \tag{9.1.6}$$

$$T(\lambda t, k, \mathbf{u}) = \tau(\lambda)\, T(t, k, \mathbf{u}), \quad \tau: \mathbb{R}_{++} \to \mathbb{R}_{++}, \text{ strictly decreasing}, \quad \tau(1) = 1. \tag{9.1.7}$$

A special case of system (9.1.1)–(9.1.3), namely (9.1.1), (9.1.2), and

$$T(\lambda t, k, \lambda u) = \lambda T(t, k, u) \qquad (u \in \mathbb{R}_+), \tag{9.1.3'}$$

was considered by Vincze [1960]. For various generalizations we refer to Hosszú and Vincze [1961], and to Eichhorn [1972b].

Let us call assumptions (9.1.1)–(9.1.7) axioms. They are easily motivated. For instance, Axiom 9.1.1 says that the effectiveness of a process $(t, k, \mathbf{u})$ is not changed if the process is multiplied by $\lambda > 0$. Multiplication by λ may (but need not) mean that the same machinery is operating in period λt as in t.

9.2 Consistency

9.2.1 **Theorem.** *Axioms 9.1.1–9.1.7 are consistent in the following sense: There exist functions T, ϕ, ψ, χ, ϱ, σ, τ such that 9.1.1–9.1.7 is fulfilled.*

Proof. Let $|\mathbf{u}|$ be the Euclidean norm $(u_1^2 + \cdots + u_m^2)^{1/2}$ of $\mathbf{u}$, and let α and β be arbitrary positive constants. The function T given by

$$T(t, k, \mathbf{u}) = |\mathbf{u}|^{\alpha+\beta}/t^\alpha k^\beta \tag{9.2.2}$$

satisfies 9.1.1–9.1.7 with specific functions ϕ, ψ, χ, ϱ, σ, τ. ■

Here and in the following, we assume that variables are *positive* whenever a formula does not make sense in the case of nonnegative variables.

9.3 Independence

9.3.1 **Theorem.** *Any two of the Axioms 9.1.1–9.1.7 are independent in the following sense: A function satisfying one of them need not necessarily satisfy the other one.*

Proof. In the following table we find in row i and column j a function of t, k, and $|\mathbf{u}|$ that satisfies Axiom 9.1.i but not Axiom 9.1.j, $i \neq j$:

	1	2	3	4	5	6	7
1		$tk^{-2}\lvert\mathbf{u}\rvert$	$t^{-2}k\lvert\mathbf{u}\rvert$	$tk\lvert\mathbf{u}\rvert^{-2}$	$tk\lvert\mathbf{u}\rvert^{-2}$	$t^{-2}k\lvert\mathbf{u}\rvert$	$tk^{-2}\lvert\mathbf{u}\rvert$
2	$tk\lvert\mathbf{u}\rvert$		$t^{-2}k\lvert\mathbf{u}\rvert$	$t^{-1}k\lvert\mathbf{u}\rvert$	$tk^2\lvert\mathbf{u}\rvert^{-1}$	$tk^2\lvert\mathbf{u}\rvert^{-1}$	$t^{-1}k^2\lvert\mathbf{u}\rvert^{-1}$
3	$tk\lvert\mathbf{u}\rvert$	$tk^{-2}\lvert\mathbf{u}\rvert$		$tk\lvert\mathbf{u}\rvert$	$t^2k\lvert\mathbf{u}\rvert^{-1}$	$tk\lvert\mathbf{u}\rvert$	$tk\lvert\mathbf{u}\rvert$
4	$t^{-1}k^{-1}\lvert\mathbf{u}\rvert$	$t^{-1}k^{-1}\lvert\mathbf{u}\rvert^{-1}$	$t^{-1}k^{-1}\lvert\mathbf{u}\rvert^{-1}$		$t^{-1}k^{-1}\lvert\mathbf{u}\rvert^{-1}$	$t^{-2}k\lvert\mathbf{u}\rvert$	$tk^{-2}\lvert\mathbf{u}\rvert$
5	$tk\lvert\mathbf{u}\rvert$	$tk^{-2}\lvert\mathbf{u}\rvert$	$t^{-2}k\lvert\mathbf{u}\rvert$	$tk\lvert\mathbf{u}\rvert$		$tk\lvert\mathbf{u}\rvert$	$tk\lvert\mathbf{u}\rvert$
6	$tk^{-1}\lvert\mathbf{u}\rvert$	$tk^{-1}\lvert\mathbf{u}\rvert^{-1}$	$t^{-1}k^{-1}\lvert\mathbf{u}\rvert^{-1}$	$t^2k^{-1}\lvert\mathbf{u}\rvert$	$tk^{-1}\lvert\mathbf{u}\rvert^{-1}$		$tk^{-1}\lvert\mathbf{u}\rvert$
7	$t^{-1}k\lvert\mathbf{u}\rvert$	$t^{-1}k^{-1}\lvert\mathbf{u}\rvert^{-1}$	$t^{-1}k\lvert\mathbf{u}\rvert^{-1}$	$t^{-1}k^2\lvert\mathbf{u}\rvert$	$t^{-1}k\lvert\mathbf{u}\rvert^{-1}$	$t^{-1}k\lvert\mathbf{u}\rvert$	

There exist subsets of four *independent* equations from 9.1.1–9.1.7, but any five of them are dependent (see Theorem 9.4.1). *Examples of independent quadruples are* {9.1.2, 9.1.3, 9.1.4, 9.1.6}, {9.1.2, 9.1.3, 9.1.4, 9.1.7}, {9.1.2, 9.1.3, 9.1.6, 9.1.7}. For instance, the first quadruple is satisfied by $T(t, k, \mathbf{u}) = t^{-1}k^{-3}|\mathbf{u}|^2$ except for 9.1.2, by $T(t, k, \mathbf{u}) = t^{-3}k^{-1}|\mathbf{u}|^2$ except for 9.1.3, by $T(t, k, \mathbf{u}) = t^2k^{-1}|\mathbf{u}|^2$ except for 9.1.4, and by $T(t, k, \mathbf{u}) = t^{-2}k|\mathbf{u}|^3$ except for 9.1.6. The independence of the two other quadruples can be shown in an analogous manner. ■

9.4 Dependence

9.4.1 **Theorem.** *Any five of the Axioms 9.1.1–9.1.7 are dependent in the following sense: There exists at least one quadruple among any five equations such that a function satisfying the quadruple necessarily satisfies the remaining axiom.*

The proof is a consequence of the following nine propositions.

9.4.2 *Propositions*

(i) *Every function T satisfying Eqs. 9.1.1 and 9.1.2 also satisfies 9.1.7. Briefly:* 9.1.1, 9.1.2 ⇒ 9.1.7.

(ii) 9.1.1, 9.1.3 ⇒ 9.1.6.

(iii) 9.1.1, 9.1.4 ⇒ 9.1.5.

(iv) 9.1.1, 9.1.7 ⇒ 9.1.2.

(v) 9.1.1, 9.1.6 ⇒ 9.1.3.

(vi) 9.1.1, 9.1.5 ⇒ 9.1.4.

(vii) 9.1.6, 9.1.7 ⇒ 9.1.4.

(viii) 9.1.2, 9.1.3, 9.1.4 ⇒ 9.1.5.

(ix) 9.1.2, 9.1.3, 9.1.6 ⇒ 9.1.5.

Proofs[2]

(i) $$T(\lambda t, k, \mathbf{u}) = T(t, k/\lambda, \mathbf{u}/\lambda) \qquad \text{(by 9.1.1)}$$
$$= \phi(1/\lambda)\, T(t, k, \mathbf{u}) \qquad \text{(by 9.1.2).}$$

This is 9.1.7, since $\phi(1/\lambda) =: \tau(\lambda)$ is strictly decreasing, as follows from 9.1.2, where ϕ is assumed to be strictly increasing.

[2] I am indebted to J. Aczél for proposals simplifying earlier versions of the following proofs.

Propositions (ii)–(vi) can be proved in an analogous manner.

$$\begin{aligned}
\text{(vii)}\ T(\lambda t, \lambda k, \mathbf{u}) &= \sigma(\lambda)\, T(\lambda t, k, \mathbf{u}) && \text{(by 9.1.6)}\\
&= \sigma(\lambda)\, \tau(\lambda)\, T(t, k, \mathbf{u}) && \text{(by 9.1.7)}\\
&=: \chi(\lambda)\, T(t, k, \mathbf{u}) && (\chi(\lambda) := \sigma(\lambda)\, \tau(\lambda)).
\end{aligned}$$

This proves proposition (vii), since the assumptions that both functions σ and τ are strictly decreasing imply the same for the function χ.

$$\begin{aligned}
\text{(viii)}\quad T(t, k, \mu^2\mathbf{u}) &= \phi(\mu)\, T(t, k/\mu, \mu\mathbf{u}) && \text{(by 9.1.2)}\\
&= \phi(\mu)\, \chi(1/\mu)\, T(\mu t, k, \mu\mathbf{u}) && \text{(by 9.1.4)}\\
&= \phi(\mu)\, \chi(1/\mu)\, \psi(\mu)\, T(t, k, \mathbf{u}) && \text{(by 9.1.3).}
\end{aligned}$$

Let us now write

$$\mu^2 =: \lambda, \qquad \phi(\sqrt{\lambda})\, \chi(1/\sqrt{\lambda})\, \psi(\sqrt{\lambda}) =: \varrho(\lambda).$$

According to the assumptions made on the functions ϕ, ψ, and χ in 9.1.2–9.1.4, the function ϱ is strictly increasing, which proves Proposition (viii).

The proof of Proposition (ix) follows the same line of reasoning. ■

9.4.3 **Remark.** It should be noted that each of the functions ϕ, ψ, χ, ϱ, σ, τ in 9.1.2–9.1.7 is necessarily a positive or a negative power.

Proof. From 9.1.2 it follows that ϕ is *multiplicative*, that is,

$$\phi(\lambda\mu) = \phi(\lambda)\, \phi(\mu) \qquad (\lambda > 0,\ \mu > 0). \tag{9.4.4}$$

The same is true for ψ, χ, ϱ, σ, τ in 9.1.3–9.1.7. According to Remark 1.9.23, every solution of (9.4.4), which is strictly monotonic in an arbitrarily small interval, is given by $\phi(\lambda) = \lambda^c$, where $c \neq 0$ is a real constant. ■

9.5 Sufficiency

We call a subset of Axioms 9.1.1.–9.1.7 *sufficient* if any function that satisfies this subset also satisfies the entire set of axioms.

9.5.1 **Theorem.** *There does not exist any sufficient pair among Axioms 9.1.1–9.1.7.*

Proof. The functions listed at place (i, j) with $i < j$ of the following matrix satisfy the functional equations 9.1.i and 9.1.j, but do not have the properties 9.1.h ($h \in \{1, 2, \ldots, 7\}$), where h is listed at place (j, i).

	1	2	3	4	5	6	7
1		$t^{-1}k^2\|\mathbf{u}\|^{-1}$	$t^2k^{-1}\|\mathbf{u}\|^{-1}$	$t^{-2}k\|u\|$	$tk^{-2}\|u\|$	$t^2k^{-1}\|u\|^{-1}$	$t^{-1}k^2\|u\|^{-1}$
2	3, 4, 5, 6		$t^2k^2\|u\|^{-1}$	$t^{-3}k^2\|u\|^{-1}$	$tk\|u\|$	$t^2k^{-1}\|u\|^2$	$t^{-1}k^3\|u\|^{-1}$
3	2, 4, 5, 7	1, 4, 5, 6, 7		$t^2k^{-3}\|u\|^{-1}$	$tk\|u\|$	$t^3k^{-1}\|u\|^{-1}$	$t^{-1}k^2\|u\|^2$
4	3, 6	1, 3, 5, 6	1, 2, 5, 7		$t^{-3}k\|u\|$	$tk^{-2}\|u\|^{-2}$	$t^{-2}k\|u\|^{-2}$
5	2, 7	1, 4, 6, 7	1, 4, 6, 7	1, 3, 6		$t^3k^{-2}\|u\|$	$t^{-2}k^3\|u\|$
6	2, 4, 5, 7	1, 4, 7	1, 2, 4, 5, 7	1, 2, 3, 5, 7	1, 2, 4, 7		$t^{-1}k^{-1}\|u\|^{-1}$
7	3, 4, 5, 6	1, 3, 4, 5, 6	1, 4, 6	1, 2, 3, 5, 6	1, 3, 4, 6	1, 2, 3, 5	

9.5.2 **Theorem.** *There exist triples among Axioms 9.1.1–9.1.7 that are sufficient, for example {9.1.1, 9.1.2, 9.1.3}, {9.1.1, 9.1.2, 9.1.6}, {9.1.1, 9.1.3, 9.1.7}, {9.1.1, 9.1.6, 9.1.7}. Each of these triples is independent. A sufficient triple always contains axiom 9.1.1.*

Proof. (i) The last assertion follows from the fact that the function given by

$$T(t, k, \mathbf{u}) = |\mathbf{u}|^3/tk$$

satisfies the axioms, except for 9.1.1.

(ii) If one of the triples were dependent, then at least one pair of the three axioms would yield the remaining axiom. Then this pair would be sufficient, which contradicts Theorem 9.5.1.

(iii) We show here that the triple {9.1.1, 9.1.2, 9.1.6} is sufficient:

$$\begin{aligned} T(t, k, \mathbf{u}) = T\left(t \cdot 1, t\frac{k}{t}, t\frac{\mathbf{u}}{t}\right) &= T(1, k/t, \mathbf{u}/t) && \text{(by 9.1.1)} \\ &= (1/t^\alpha)\, T(1, k, \mathbf{u}) && \text{(by 9.1.2)} \\ &= (1/t^\alpha k^\beta)\, T(1, 1, \mathbf{u}) && \text{(by 9.1.6)} \\ &= f(\mathbf{u})/t^\alpha k^\beta, \end{aligned}$$

where $\alpha > 0$, $\beta > 0$, and $f(\mathbf{u}) := T(1, 1\ \mathbf{u})$ is homogeneous of degree $\alpha + \beta$ because of 9.1.1. Obviously,

$$T(t, k, \mathbf{u}) = \frac{f(\mathbf{u})}{t^\alpha k^\beta} \begin{cases} \alpha > 0, \quad \beta > 0 & \text{real const,} \\ f\colon \mathbb{R}_+^m \to \mathbb{R}_+ & \text{homogeneous of degree } \alpha + \beta, \end{cases} \tag{9.5.3}$$

satisfies Axioms 9.1.1–9.1.7; that is, the triple {9.1.1, 9.1.2, 9.1.6} is sufficient. The sufficiency of the triples {9.1.1, 9.1.2, 9.1.3}, {9.1.1, 9.1.3, 9.1.7}, {9.1.1, 9.1.6, 9.1.7} can be proved analogously. ∎

9.6 General Solution of the System in Section 9.1

9.6.1 **Theorem.** *Let T be any function (9.0.3) satisfying Axioms 9.1.1–9.1.7. Then there exist constants $\alpha > 0$, $\beta > 0$, and a function $f: \mathbb{R}_+^m \to \mathbb{R}_+$ that is homogeneous of degree $\alpha + \beta$, such that T is given by (9.5.3). Every function of this kind satisfies Axioms 9.1.1–9.1.7.*

Proof. See part (iii) of the proof of Theorem 9.5.2. ■

9.6.2 **Remark.** If T in Theorem 9.6.1 is supposed to be the technical effectiveness of the production process (9.0.2), that is, if T, in addition to satisfying 9.1.1–9.1.7, is supposed to be both strictly increasing with respect to $\mathbf{u}$ and strictly decreasing with respect to t and k, then f of (9.5.3) must be strictly increasing. If only one commodity is produced, that is, if $\mathbf{u} = u \in \mathbb{R}_+$, then, clearly, (9.5.3) becomes

$$T(t, k, u) = (Cu^{\alpha+\beta})/(t^\alpha k^\beta)$$

where C is a positive real constant. The determination of α and β or of the ratio α/β is an empirical matter (see Vincze [1960, p. 38]). Systems of axioms that determine f in (9.5.3) in a more specific form have been given by this author [1972b].

9.7 A System of Functional Equations Determining the Economic Effectiveness of a Production Process

Let the production process

$$(K, t, \mathbf{x}, \mathbf{u}) \in \mathbb{R}_+^{2+n+m} \qquad \text{(see (9.0.1))} \qquad (9.7.0)$$

be given, where $K \in \mathbb{R}_+$ is the capital necessary for establishing and running the production, and $t \in \mathbb{R}_+$ is the time period required to produce the output vector $\mathbf{u} \in \mathbb{R}_+^m$ with the aid of the input vector $\mathbf{x} \in \mathbb{R}_+^n$. Let $\mathbf{q} \in \mathbb{R}_{++}^n$ be the vector of the prices of the inputs and $\mathbf{p} \in \mathbb{R}_+^m$ be the vector of the prices of the outputs. In what follows we assume $\mathbf{x} \neq \mathbf{0}$.

We define the *economic effectiveness of production process (9.7.0)* to be a function E that depends on K, t and the "measures of profitability," namely,

$$\mathbf{up}/\mathbf{xq} = : \xi \qquad \text{and} \qquad \mathbf{up} - \mathbf{xq} = : \eta,$$

and which satifies the following assumptions for all possible values of the variables:

$$E(K, t, \xi, \eta) = \begin{cases} E_+(K, t, \xi, \eta) > 0 & \text{if} \quad \eta > 0, \\ 0 & \text{if} \quad \eta = 0, \\ E_-(K, t, \xi, \eta) < 0 & \text{if} \quad \eta < 0, \end{cases} \tag{9.7.1}$$

where

$E_+ : \mathbb{R}^2_+ \times]1, \infty[\times \mathbb{R}_{++} \to \mathbb{R}_{++}$ and $E_- : \mathbb{R}^2_+ \times [0, 1[\times \mathbb{R}_{--} \to \mathbb{R}_{--}$;

$$E(K, \lambda t, \xi, \lambda\eta) = E(K, t, \xi, \eta) \quad \text{for all} \quad \lambda > 0; \tag{9.7.2}$$

$$E(\lambda K, t, \xi, \lambda\eta) = E(K, t, \xi, \eta) \quad \text{for all} \quad \lambda > 0; \tag{9.7.3}$$

$$E_+(K, t, \xi, \lambda\eta) = \mu(\lambda)\, E_+(K, t, \xi, \eta)$$
for all $\lambda > 0$ with strictly increasing $\mu : \mathbb{R}_{++} \to \mathbb{R}_{++}$, $\mu(1) = 1$; (9.7.4a)

$$E_-(K, t, \xi, \lambda\eta) = \mu^*(\lambda)\, E_-(K, t, \xi, \eta)$$
for all $\lambda > 0$ with strictly increasing $\mu^* : \mathbb{R}_{++} \to \mathbb{R}_{++}$, $\mu^*(1) = 1$; (9.7.4b)

$$E_+(K, t, \lambda\xi, \eta) = \nu(\lambda)\, E_+(K, t, \xi, \eta)$$
for all $\lambda \in]1, \infty[$ with strictly increasing $\nu :]1, \infty[\to \mathbb{R}_{++}$; (9.7.5a)

$$E_-(K, t, \lambda\xi, \eta) = \nu^*(\lambda)\, E_-(K, t, \xi, \eta)$$
for all $\lambda \in [0, 1]$ with strictly decreasing $\nu^* : [0, 1[\to \mathbb{R}_{++}$. (9.7.5b)

Let us consider assumptions (9.7.1)–(9.7.5) a bit further. Assumption (9.7.1) is a normalizing condition, and seems to be quite natural. Assumption (9.7.2) says in particular that the production processes

$$(K, t, \mathbf{x}, \mathbf{u}) \quad \text{and} \quad (K, \lambda t, \lambda \mathbf{x}, \lambda \mathbf{u}) \quad (\lambda > 0)$$

are equally effective. This means, for instance, that the economic effectiveness of a machinery is not changed if it works for λt time units instead of t time units. As to assumption (9.7.3), the economic effectiveness of the production processes

$$(K, t, \mathbf{x}, \mathbf{u}) \quad \text{and} \quad (\lambda K, t, \lambda \mathbf{x}, \lambda \mathbf{u}) \quad (\lambda > 0)$$

is identical. For instance, two identical production processes operating together have the same economic effectiveness as each of them. This requirement is reasonable from the point of view of return on investment. Assumption (9.7.4) says the following: If

$$K^* = K, \quad t^* = t, \quad \mathbf{u}^*\mathbf{p}/\mathbf{x}^*\mathbf{q} = \mathbf{up}/\mathbf{xq}, \quad \mathbf{u}^*\mathbf{p} - \mathbf{x}^*\mathbf{q} = \lambda(\mathbf{up} - \mathbf{xq}) \quad (\lambda > 0)$$

is valid for the two production processes

$$(K, t, \mathbf{x}, \mathbf{u}) \quad \text{and} \quad (K^*, t^*, \mathbf{x}^*, \mathbf{u}^*),$$

then the economic effectiveness of $(K^*, t^*, \mathbf{x}^*, \mathbf{u}^*)$ is a multiple of the economic effectiveness of $(K, t, \mathbf{x}, \mathbf{u})$, where this multiple depends on (and increases strictly with) λ. Assumption (9.7.5) can be interpreted in a similar manner.

9.8 General Solution of the System in Section 9.7

9.8.1 **Theorem.** *Every function E that satisfies assumptions (9.7.1)–(9.7.5) can be represented by*[3]

$$E(K, t, \xi, \eta)$$
$$= \begin{cases} c\xi^{\alpha}(\eta/Kt)^{\beta} & \text{for } (K, t, \xi, \eta) \in \mathbb{R}^2_+ \times]1, \infty[\times \mathbb{R}_{++}, \\ 0 & \text{for } (K, t, \xi, \eta) \in \mathbb{R}^2_+ \times \{1\} \times \{0\}, \\ -c^*\xi^{-\alpha^*}|\eta/Kt|^{\beta^*} & \text{for } (K, t, \xi, \eta) \in \mathbb{R}^2_+ \times [0, 1[\times \mathbb{R}_{--}, \end{cases} \qquad (9.8.2)$$

where the constants $c, c^*, \alpha, \alpha^*, \beta, \beta^*$ are positive real numbers. Every function E given by (9.8.2) with positive constants $c, c^*, \alpha, \alpha^*, \beta, \beta^*$ satisfies assumptions (9.7.1)–(9.7.5).

Proof. The second assertion is obvious. In order to prove the first one we show at first

$$\begin{aligned} E(K, t, \xi, \eta) &= E(K, t\cdot 1, \xi, t(\eta/t)) \\ &= E(K, 1, \xi, (\eta/t)) \qquad \text{(by (9.7.2))} \\ &= E(1, 1, \xi, (\eta/Kt)) \qquad \text{(by (9.7.3))}. \end{aligned}$$

Assumptions (9.7.4) and (9.7.5) imply the multiplicativity of μ, μ^*, ν, ν^*; that is, for μ (and accordingly for μ^*, ν, ν^*)

$$\mu(\lambda_1\lambda_2) = \mu(\lambda_1)\,\mu(\lambda_2) \qquad \text{for all} \quad \lambda_1 > 0, \quad \lambda_2 > 0.$$

Since μ, μ^*, ν, ν^* are supposed to be strictly monotonic, we can apply Remark 1.9.23, in order to obtain

$$\mu(\lambda) = \lambda^{\beta}, \qquad \mu^*(\lambda) = \lambda^{\beta^*}, \qquad \nu(\lambda) = \lambda^{\alpha}, \qquad \nu^*(\lambda) = \lambda^{-\alpha^*},$$
$$\alpha, \alpha^*, \beta, \beta^* \qquad \text{positive real const.}$$

Hence

$$\begin{aligned} E_+\left(1, 1, \xi, \frac{\eta}{Kt}\right) &= E_+\left(1, 1, \xi, c_1, \frac{\eta}{Kt}\frac{1}{c_1}\right) \\ &= \left(c_1\frac{\eta}{Kt}\right)^{\beta} E_+\left(1, 1, \xi, \frac{1}{c_1}\right) \qquad \text{(by (9.7.4))} \end{aligned}$$

[3] In the following formula, $x^{-\gamma} := \infty$ if $x = 0$, $\gamma > 0$.

where $c_1 > 0$. We obtain similarly

$$E_-(1, 1, \xi, \eta/Kt) = |c_2(\eta/Kt)|^{\beta^*} E_-(1, 1, \xi, 1/c_2) \qquad (c_2 < 0).$$

Let $c_3 := 1 - \varepsilon/2$, where $\varepsilon \in]0, \frac{1}{2}[$. Then $c_3\xi > 1$ for all $\xi \in [1 + \varepsilon, \infty[$. Now,

$$E_+\left(1, 1, \xi, \frac{1}{c_1}\right) = E_+\left(1, 1, c_3\xi\frac{1}{c_3}, \frac{1}{c_1}\right)$$

$$= (c_3\xi)^\alpha E_+\left(1, 1, \frac{1}{c_3}, \frac{1}{c_1}\right) \qquad \text{(by (9.7.5))}$$

and, similarly, for all $\xi \in [0, 1 - \varepsilon]$, $\varepsilon \in]0, 1]$,

$$E_-\left(1, 1, \xi, \frac{1}{c_2}\right) = (c_4\xi)^{-\alpha^*} E_-\left(1, 1, \frac{1}{c_4}, \frac{1}{c_2}\right) \qquad (c_4 := 1+\varepsilon).$$

This completes the proof. Obviously,

$$c = c_1^\beta c_3^\alpha E_+\left(1, 1, \frac{1}{c_3}, \frac{1}{c_1}\right), \qquad -c^* = |c_2|^{\beta^*} c_4^{-\alpha^*} E_-\left(1, 1, \frac{1}{c_4}, \frac{1}{c_2}\right). \quad ■$$

9.8.3 **Corollary.** *Let the economic effectiveness E of the production process* $(K, t, \mathbf{x}, \mathbf{u}) \in \mathbb{R}_+^{2+n+m}$ *be given, where* $\mathbf{x} \neq \mathbf{0}$. *Let* $\mathbf{q} \in \mathbb{R}_{++}^n$ *and* $\mathbf{p} \in \mathbb{R}_+^m$ *be the vectors of the prices of the inputs and the outputs, respectively. If* $\mathbf{up} - \mathbf{xq} \geqq 0$, *then there exist constants* $c > 0, \alpha > 0, \beta > 0$ *such that*

$$E(K, t, \mathbf{up}/\mathbf{xq}, \mathbf{up} - \mathbf{xq}) = c(\mathbf{up}/\mathbf{xq})^\alpha ((\mathbf{up} - \mathbf{xq})/Kt)^\beta. \tag{9.8.4}$$

If $\mathbf{up} - \mathbf{xq} < 0$, *then there exist constants* $c^* > 0$, $\alpha^* > 0$, $\beta^* > 0$ *such that*

$$E(K, t, \mathbf{up}/\mathbf{xq}, \mathbf{up} - \mathbf{xq}) = -c^* (\mathbf{up}/\mathbf{xq})^{-\alpha^*} |(\mathbf{up} - \mathbf{xq})/Kt|^{\beta^*}. \tag{9.8.5}$$

9.8.6 **Remark.** According to (9.8.4), the economic effectiveness of a (profitable) production process is a power $\alpha > 0$ of the "profitability" $\mathbf{up}/\mathbf{xq}$ of the process times a power $\beta > 0$ of the gross profit $\mathbf{up} - \mathbf{xq}$ per capital and time unit times a positive constant c. For comparing the economic effectiveness of two different processes the magnitude of the quotient α/β is essential. It has to be chosen depending on what is more important in the particular situation, the value of $\mathbf{up}/\mathbf{xq}$ or the value of $(\mathbf{up} - \mathbf{xq})/Kt$. If $c = 1$, $\alpha = 1$, $\beta \to 0$, or $c = 1$, $\beta = 1$, $\alpha \to 0$, the economic effectiveness tends to well-known economic indices.

9.8.7 **Remark.** As can be easily seen from (9.8.4), the economic effectiveness E of a profitable production process $(K, t, \mathbf{x}, \mathbf{u})$ is strictly increasing with respect to $\mathbf{u}$ and strictly decreasing with respect to K, t, and $\mathbf{x}$. It is interesting to note that these monotonicity properties of E follow from assumptions (9.7.1)–(9.7.5), which do not state them explicitly.

9.8.8 **Remark.** Let S be a set of production processes. A process $(K^*, t^*, \mathbf{x}^*, \mathbf{u}^*) \in S$ is called *efficient* if there is no process $(K, t, \mathbf{x}, \mathbf{u}) \in S$ with

$$(-K, -t, -\mathbf{x}, \mathbf{u}) \geq (-K^*, -t^*, -\mathbf{x}^*, \mathbf{u}^*).$$

From the strict monotonicity properties of E (see Remark 9.8.7) it follows that *every production process with maximum economic effectiveness is efficient.*

10

Systems of Functional Equations and the Law of Diminishing Returns

In two famous papers Menger [1936] analyzed "the laws of return as well as their relations to one another and to other propositions." One of the aims of these papers was to show that a production function statisfying the properties thus far considered by economists does not necessarily fulfill the

10.0.1 "law" of everywhere diminishing marginal returns with respect to variation of a single factor[1]

or the

10.0.2 "law" of eventually diminishing marginal returns with respect to variation of a single factor.[1]

Note that 10.0.2 follows from 10.0.1, but 10.0.2 does not imply 10.0.1. Menger further showed that the

10.0.3 "law" of eventually diminishing average returns[2] with respect to variation of a single factor

does not follow either from most production-theoretic assumptions thus far considered. For instance, he introduced a production function that satisfies 10.0.2, but not 10.0.3. Furthermore, he gave an example of a production function that satisfies 10.0.3, but not 10.0.2.

These results, which exposed the incorrectness of several "proofs" of the laws of diminishing returns in economic literature, suggest the question:

[1] For the definition of the law of diminishing marginal returns see 4.3.3, 4.3.4.

[2] For the definition of the law of diminishing average returns see 4.3.15.

Wolfgang Eichhorn, Functional Equations in Economics.

ISBN 0-201-01948-5/01949-3 PBK

Do there exist any systems of assumptions that are, on the one hand, significant from the economic point of view, and that allow, on the other hand, for deducing at least one, but preferably all three, of the above-mentioned "laws"?

In this chapter (a revised version of the author's paper [1968c, in German]), we will show that such a system of assumptions does exist. The main part of this system will be formulated as a system of functional equations, which will be introduced in Section 10.1. Thereafter, we prove the consistency (10.2) and the independence (10.3) of the assumptions. We prove further (10.4) that Laws 10.0.1 and 10.0.2 cannot be derived from any true subset of the system of assumptions, but (10.5) that Laws 10.0.1–10.0.3 can be derived from the whole system. As a by-product of our analysis, we obtain another characterization of the Cobb–Douglas production function with n factors (10.6). After a remark about the incompatibility of the "law of initially increasing marginal returns and eventually diminishing marginal returns" with the linear homogeneity assumption (10.7), the chapter conludes with a remark that emphasizes different properties of the laws of diminishing marginal returns and diminishing average returns in connection with a linearly homogeneous production function.

Neither differentiability nor continuity assumptions are made in the theorems of this chapter.

10.1 Three Assumptions Providing a System of Functional Equations for Production Functions

Let

$$\Phi : \mathbb{R}^n_+ \to \mathbb{R}_+, \qquad \mathbf{x} \to \Phi(\mathbf{x}) \tag{10.1.0}$$

be a production function,[3] where $\mathbf{x} = (x_1, \ldots, x_n) \in \mathbb{R}^n_+$, $n \geqq 2$, denotes the vector of n input quantities and $\Phi(\mathbf{x})$ is the maximum output obtainable from $\mathbf{x}$. In this chapter we are interested in the class of all production functions (10.1.0) that satisfy the following three assumptions.

A.1 *Significance of the jth Input* ($j \in \{1, \ldots, n\}$). Given an arbitrary vector $\mathbf{x} \in \mathbb{R}^n_{++}$, there exists at least one pair $x_j' \in \mathbb{R}_+$, $x_j'' \in \mathbb{R}_+$ with $x_j' < x_j''$ such that

$$\Phi(x_1, \ldots, x_{j-1}, x_j', x_{j+1}, \ldots, x_n) < \Phi(x, \ldots, x_{j-1}, x_j'', x_{j+1}, \ldots, x_n). \tag{10..1.1}$$

Our second assumption is the linear homogeneity assumption, which is well known from many papers on the theory of production, cost, distribution,

[3] See Section 13.3 for Shephard's axioms of a production function.

equilibrium, and growth. For a justification of this assumption see Section 4.3.

A.2. *Linear Homogeneity*

$$\Phi(\lambda \mathbf{x}) = \lambda \Phi(\mathbf{x}) \qquad \text{for all} \quad \mathbf{x} \in \mathbb{R}_+^n,\ \lambda \in \mathbb{R}_+. \tag{10.1.2}$$

If not every essential input is represented by a component of **x**, then the assumption of *linear* homogeneity generally has to be omitted. This reflection motivates our third assumption, which nevertheless keeps the homogeneity:

A.3. *Homogeneity with Respect to the Inputs* $1, \ldots, j-1, j+1, \ldots, n$.[4] There exists $j \in \{1, \ldots, n\}$ such that for any two vectors

$$\mathbf{x} \in \mathbb{R}_+^n \quad \text{and} \quad (\lambda x_1, \ldots, \lambda x_{j-1}, x_j, \lambda x_{j+1}, \ldots, \lambda x_n) \quad \text{with} \quad \lambda \in \mathbb{R}_+$$

we have

$$\Phi(\lambda x_1, \ldots, \lambda x_{j-1}, x_j, \lambda x_{j+1}, \ldots, \lambda x_n) = \lambda^{r_j} \Phi(\mathbf{x}) \tag{10.1.3}$$

where $r_j \in \mathbb{R}_{++}$ is a constant.

In other words, we assume that our (linearly homogeneous) production function Φ has at least one input, say j, for which the following property holds: If this input is held constant, the resulting function of the remaining $n-1$ inputs is homogeneous of degree r_j, where r_j may be any positive scalar.

Note that Eqs. (10.1.2) and (10.1.3) can be considered a system of $n+1$ functional equations if assumption A.3 is valid for all $j = 1, \ldots, n$ and j runs from 1 to n.

10.2 Existence of Production Functions Satisfying the Assumptions

A classic example of a production function that satisfies Assumptions A.1–A.3 is the CD (Cobb and Douglas [1928]) production function represented by

$$\Phi(\mathbf{x}) = C x_1^{\alpha_1} x_2^{\alpha_2} \cdots x_n^{\alpha_n} \qquad \begin{array}{l}(C > 0, \alpha_1 > 0, \ldots, \alpha_n > 0 \\ \text{real const}, \sum \alpha_\nu = 1).\end{array} \tag{10.2.1}$$

Here, r_j of Eq. (10.1.3) is equal to $1 - \alpha_j$.

A more general example is given by

$$\Phi(\mathbf{x}) = x_j^{\alpha_j} \Psi(x_1, \ldots, x_{j-1}, x_{j+1}, \ldots, x_n) \qquad (0 < \alpha_j < 1) \tag{10.2.2}$$

where the production function

$$\Psi \colon \mathbb{R}_+^{n-1} \to \mathbb{R}_+$$

is homogeneous of degree $r_j = 1 - \alpha_j$, otherwise arbitrary.

---

[4] Compare this assumption with Test 7.1.4.

10.3 Independence of the Assumptions

Examples (10.3.1)–(10.3.3) show that Assumptions A.1–A.3 formulated in Section 10.1 are *independent* in the following sense: A function that satisfies any two of them does not necessarily satisfy the remaining one. In other words, any two of the assumptions do not imply the third.

The function $\phi\colon \mathbb{R}^n_+ \to \mathbb{R}_+$ given by

$$\phi(\mathbf{x}) = x_1^2 x_2^2 \cdots x_n^2 \tag{10.3.1}$$

satisfies Assumptions A.1 and A.3, but not A.2. The function $\psi\colon \mathbb{R}^n_+ \to \mathbb{R}_+$ given by

$$\psi(\mathbf{x}) = x_1 + x_2 + \cdots + x_n \tag{10.3.2}$$

satisfies A.1 and A.2, but not A.3. Note that both functions ϕ and ψ satisfy Shephard's [1970, p. 22] properties 13.3.1–13.3.6 of a production function. The function $\chi\colon \mathbb{R}^n_+ \to \mathbb{R}_+$ given by

$$\chi(\mathbf{x}) = x_1^{1/(n-2)} x_2^{1/(n-2)} \cdots x_{j-1}^{1/(n-2)} x_j^{-1/(n-2)} x_{j+1}^{1/(n-2)} \cdots x_n^{1/(n-2)} \quad (n \geqq 4) \tag{10.3.3}$$

satisfies assumptions (10.1.2) and (10.1.3), but not (10.1.1) (since the exponent of x_j is negative).

With the aid of examples (10.3.1)–(10.3.3) we establish not only the independence of Assumptions A.1–A.3 but also the conclusions of the next section.

10.4 The Law of Eventually Diminishing Marginal Returns Does not Follow from Any Pair of the Assumptions

In order to prove this, we differentiate the functions ϕ, ψ, χ (see (10.3.1)–(10.3.3)) with respect to x_j. The respective derivatives are, considered as functions of x_j, *not* strictly decreasing for sufficiently large x_j, as is required by the law of eventually diminishing marginal returns.

By use of (10.3.1), Assumptions A.1 and A.3 do not imply the law of eventually diminishing average returns either. But we mention that this law follows from the linear homogeneity Assumption A.2 in conjunction with the assumption of *strict* monotonicity of the underlying production function (see Section 10.8).

10.5 Derivation of the Law of Diminishing Returns from the Assumptions

Let

$$\Phi : \mathbb{R}^n_+ \to \mathbb{R}_+ \qquad (n \geqq 2) \tag{10.5.1}$$

be an arbitrary function that satisfies Assumptions A.1–A.3 of Section 10.1. Then, for all $x_j > 0$,

$$\begin{aligned} \Phi(\mathbf{x}) &= \Phi(x_j(\mathbf{x}/x_j)) \\ &= x_j \Phi(x_1/x, \ldots, x_{j-1}/x_j, 1, x_{j+1}/x_j, \ldots, x_n/x_j) \qquad \text{(by A.2)} \\ &= x_j^{1-r_j} \Phi(x_1, \ldots, x_{j-1}, 1, x_{j+1}, \ldots, x_n) \qquad \text{(by A.3)} \end{aligned}$$

with $0 < (1 - r_j) < 1$ because of A.1 and A.3. Hence, considering Φ as a production function, Laws 10.0.1–10.0.3 are satisfied with respect to the jth input. We have proved

10.5.2 **Theorem.** *Assumptions A.1–A.3 (i.e., significance of the jth input, linear homogeneity, and homogeneity with respect to the inputs* $1, \ldots, j-1, j+1, \ldots, n$*) imply the laws (10.0.1–10.0.3) of diminishing returns with respect to the jth input.*

10.6 Characterization of the Cobb–Douglas Production Function with *n* Inputs

In the following we assume that Assumptions A.1 and A.3 of Section 10.1 are satisfied for all $j = 1, \ldots, n$. Then an arbitrary function 10.5.1 satisfying A.1–A.3 can be written, for all $\mathbf{x} \in \mathbb{R}^n_{++}$, as

$$\begin{aligned} \Phi(\mathbf{x}) &= \Phi\left(x_1 x_2 \cdots x_n \frac{\mathbf{x}}{x_1 x_2 \cdots x_n}\right) \\ &= x_1 x_2 \cdots x_n \Phi\left(\frac{1}{x_2 x_3 \cdots, x_n}, \frac{1}{x_1 x_3 \cdots x_n}, \ldots, \frac{1}{x_1 x_2 \cdots x_{n-1}}\right) \qquad \text{(by A.2)} \\ &= x_1^{1-r_1} x_2^{1-r_2} \cdots x_n^{1-r_n} \Phi(1, 1, \ldots, 1) \qquad \text{(by repeated application of A.3).} \end{aligned}$$

Let us abbreviate $1 - r_\nu$ by α_ν for $\nu = 1, 2, \ldots, n$. From A.2 it follows that $\sum \alpha_\nu = 1$, and from A.1 and A.3 that $0 < \alpha_\nu < 1$. Thus, we have derived the CD function (see (10.2.1); $C = \Phi(1, 1, \ldots, 1)$). Conversely, every CD function satisfies A.1–A.3. We summarize:

10.6.1 **Theorem.** *A function* $\Phi\colon \mathbb{R}^n_+ \to \mathbb{R}_+$ *is, for all* $\mathbf{x} \in \mathbb{R}^n_{++}$, *the Cobb–Douglas production function given by*

$$\Phi(\mathbf{x}) = Cx_1^{\alpha_1}x_2^{\alpha_2}\cdots x_n^{\alpha_n}, \qquad (C > 0, \alpha_1 > 0, \alpha_2 > 0, \ldots, \alpha_n > 0 \text{ real const}, \textstyle\sum \alpha_\nu = 1), \tag{10.6.2}$$

if and only if it satisfies Assumptions A.1–A.3 of Section 10.1 for all $j = 1, \ldots, n$.

As can be easily seen from (10.6.2), the following corollary is valid:

10.6.3 **Corollary.** *Let the set* $\{j_1, j_2, \ldots, j_k\}, 2 \leqq k \leqq n-1$, *be an arbitrary complex of the factors of the production function* $\Phi\colon \mathbb{R}^n_+ \to \mathbb{R}_+$. *If Assumptions A.1–A.3 of Section 10.1 on* Φ *are valid for all* $j = 1, \ldots, n$, *then* Φ *satisfies the laws of diminishing marginal as well as average returns with respect to proportional variation of the factor complex* $\{j_1, j_2, \ldots, j_k\}$.[5]

10.7 Incompatibility of the Law of Initially Increasing and Eventually Diminishing Marginal Returns with the Linear Homogeneity Assumption

Theorems 10.5.1, 10.6.1, and Corollary 10.6.3 contain the laws of diminishing returns in the strict sense, that is, Assumptions A.1–A.3 imply that the marginal as well as the average returns diminish *everywhere.* We point out here that this is natural for every system of assumptions on production functions that contains (or implies) both the linear homogeneity of the underlying production function and the law of diminishing marginal returns with respect to proportional variation of *each* subset of the factors. We have already proved this; see Corollary 4.3.10.

At this point we note that there *do* exist linearly homogeneous production functions that satisfy the law of initially increasing and eventually diminishing *average* returns. An example of such a function is given by

$$\Phi(x_1, x_2) = x_2 + \frac{x_1^2 x_2^{1/2}}{x_1^{3/2} + x_2^{3/2}}. \tag{10.7.1}$$

This function is linearly homogeneous and satisfies the law of initially increasing and eventually diminishing marginal returns (with respect to x_1) as well as the law of eventually diminishing average returns (with respect to x_1 and x_2).

[5] For the definition of these laws see 4.3.3, 4.3.4, and 4.3.15.

10.8 Derivation of the Law of Eventually Diminishing Average Returns from the Assumptions of Linear Homogeneity and Strict Monotonicity for Sufficiently Small Input Quantities

As a consequence of Theorem 4.3.16 (concerning the law of diminishing average returns) and the result of Section 10.7, we note

10.8.1 **Remark.** If we speak, in connection with a linearly homogeneous production function, of the law of diminishing returns and if we understand this law as being valid in the case of variation of each single factor as well as each factor complex, then either the law of everywhere diminishing marginal returns or the law of everywhere or eventually diminishing average returns can be meant, but *not* the law of initially increasing and eventually diminishing marginal returns

Part IV

Functional Equations for Vector-Valued and Set-Valued Functions of Several Variables

11

Functional Equations for Vector-Valued Functions

In this chapter we consider functional equations that express the (i) additivity, (ii) linear homogeneity, (iii) linearity, (iv) homogeneity, and (v) ray-homotheticity of vector-valued functions. As an application of definitions (i)–(iii) introduced in Section 11.1 we derive in Section 11.2 the rules of matrix algebra or, as it is generally called, of linear mappings. Excellent examples of the usefulness of linear mappings in economics are, among others, the original models of

(a) input output analysis (Leontief [1941]),
(b) activity analysis (Koopmans [1951, 1953]),
(c) expanding economies (von Neumann [1937]),
(d) multisectoral economic growth (see, e.g., Nikaido [1968, chapter II]).

Since these models are well known, we will here consider another application of linear mappings, namely, to the multiple-product oligopoly. Some of the results obtained thereby are at first sight paradoxical (see Section 11.3) but for that very reason noteworthy.

In Section 11.4 we shall derive results on vector-valued functions satisfying functional equations that occur in generalizing the linear or linearly homogeneous models of multisectoral economic growth (see, e.g., Nikaido [1968, chapter II] or Solow and Samuelson [1953], respectively). In this context the notion of a ray-homothetic vector-valued function will be introduced.

The concluding section (11.5) treats the so-called budget equation. This equation can be considered a functional equation for the (vector-valued) demand function of a household.

ISBN 0-201-01948-3/01949-3 PBK

Wolfgang Eichhorn, Functional Equtions in Economics.

11.1 Additivity, Linear Homogeneity, and Linearity of Vector-Valued Functions

A function

$$\mathbf{F} : \mathbb{R}^n \to \mathbb{R}^m \tag{11.1.1}$$

is called *additive* if it satisfies the functional equation

$$\mathbf{F}(\mathbf{x} + \mathbf{y}) = \mathbf{F}(\mathbf{x}) + \mathbf{F}(\mathbf{y}) \qquad \text{for all} \quad (\mathbf{x}, \mathbf{y}) \in \mathbb{R}^{2n}. \tag{11.1.2}$$

Since Eq. (11.1.2) can be considered an m-tuple

$$F_\mu(\mathbf{x} + \mathbf{y}) = F_\mu(\mathbf{x}) + F_\mu(\mathbf{y}) \qquad (\mu = 1, \ldots, m) \tag{11.1.3}$$

of (scalar-valued) functional equations that have been solved in Section 3.1, we know the following.

If an additive function (11.1.1) satisfies a regularity condition such as

(i) continuity at a single point, or
(ii) boundedness in an arbitrarily small ε-neighborhood of a point,

then by Corollary 1.2.10, $\mathbf{F}$ is both continuous everywhere and *homogeneous of the first degree:*

$$\mathbf{F}(\lambda \mathbf{x}) = \lambda \mathbf{F}(\mathbf{x}) \qquad \text{for all} \quad (\lambda, \mathbf{x}) \in \mathbb{R}^{n+1}. \tag{11.1.4}$$

A function (11.1.1) that satisfies both Eqs. (11.1.2) and (11.1.4) is called a *linear function* or a *linear mapping*. A linear function $\mathbf{F}$: $\mathbb{R}^n \to \mathbb{R}^n$ is called a *linear transformation of* $\mathbb{R}^n$. The problem of representation of linear vector-valued functions leads to the notion of a matrix and to the rules of matrix algebra.

11.2 Application: Rules of Matrix Algebra

In this section, the well-known rules of matrix algebra will be derived from functional equations (11.1.2) and (11.1.4), which characterize the linear functions.

Let

$$\begin{aligned} \mathbf{e}_1 &= (1, 0, 0, \ldots, 0, 0) \\ \mathbf{e}_2 &= (0, 1, 0, \ldots, 0, 0) \\ &\ \vdots \\ \mathbf{e}_n &= (0, 0, 0, \ldots, 0, 1) \end{aligned}$$

be the unit vectors of $\mathbb{R}^n$. With these we can write $\mathbf{x} = (x_1, x_2, \ldots, x_n) \in \mathbb{R}^n$ as

$$\mathbf{x} = x_1\mathbf{e}_1 + x_2\mathbf{e}_2 + \cdots + x_n\mathbf{e}_n. \tag{11.2.1}$$

The following vectors are column vectors, as expressed by the prime.

Let the function $\mathbf{F}\colon \mathbb{R}^n \to \mathbb{R}^m$ be linear. Then

$$\left.\begin{aligned} \mathbf{F}(\mathbf{x})' &= \mathbf{F}(x_1\mathbf{e}_1 + x_2\,\mathbf{e}_2 + \cdots + x_n\mathbf{e}_n)' && \text{(by (11.2.1))} \\ &= \mathbf{F}(x_1\mathbf{e}_1)' + \mathbf{F}(x_2\mathbf{e}_2)' + \cdots + \mathbf{F}(x_n\mathbf{e}_n)' && \text{(by (11.1.2))} \\ &= x_1\mathbf{F}(\mathbf{e}_1)' + x_2\mathbf{F}(\mathbf{e}_2)' + \cdots + x_n\mathbf{F}(\mathbf{e}_n)' && \text{(by (11.1.4)).} \end{aligned}\right\} \tag{11.2.2}$$

The function $\mathbf{F}$ maps every vector of $\mathbb{R}^n$ into $\mathbb{R}^m$, in particular the unit vectors $\mathbf{e}_1, \mathbf{e}_2, \ldots, \mathbf{e}_n$. The images of these vectors are elements of $\mathbb{R}^m$ that can be written uniquely as linear combinations of the unit vectors $\mathbf{v}_1, \mathbf{v}_2, \ldots, \mathbf{v}_m$ of $\mathbb{R}^m$ (the $a_{\mu\nu}$ being real numbers):

$$\begin{aligned} \mathbf{F}(\mathbf{e}_1)' &= a_{11}\mathbf{v}_1' + a_{21}\mathbf{v}_2' + \cdots + a_{m1}\mathbf{v}_m' \\ \mathbf{F}(\mathbf{e}_2)' &= a_{12}\mathbf{v}_1' + a_{22}\mathbf{v}_2' + \cdots + a_{m2}\mathbf{v}_m' \\ &\vdots \\ \mathbf{F}(\mathbf{e}_n)' &= a_{1n}\mathbf{v}_1' + a_{2n}\mathbf{v}_2' + \cdots + a_{mn}\mathbf{v}_m'. \end{aligned}$$

Inserting this in (11.2.2) we obtain

$$\begin{aligned} \mathbf{F}(\mathbf{x})' &= (a_{11}x_1 + a_{12}x_2 + \cdots + a_{1n}x_n)\,\mathbf{v}_1' \\ &\quad + (a_{21}x_1 + a_{22}x_2 + \cdots + a_{2n}x_n)\,\mathbf{v}_2' \\ &\quad \vdots \\ &\quad + (a_{m1}x_1 + a_{m2}x_2 + \cdots + a_{mn}x_n)\,\mathbf{v}_m' \\ &= \begin{pmatrix} a_{11}x_1 + a_{12}x_2 + \cdots + a_{1n}x_n \\ a_{21}x_1 + a_{22}x_2 + \cdots + a_{2n}x_n \\ \vdots \\ a_{m1}x_1 + a_{m2}x_2 + \cdots + a_{mn}x_n \end{pmatrix}. \end{aligned} \tag{11.2.3}$$

From here it follows that every linear function $\mathbf{F}\colon \mathbb{R}^n \to \mathbb{R}^m$ is uniquely determined by a rectangular matrix

$$\begin{pmatrix} a_{11} & a_{12} & \cdots & a_{1n} \\ a_{21} & a_{22} & \cdots & a_{2n} \\ \vdots & \vdots & & \vdots \\ a_{m1} & a_{m2} & \cdots & a_{mn} \end{pmatrix} =: \mathbf{A} \tag{11.2.4}$$

of $m \cdot n$ real numbers $a_{\mu\nu}$ that are called the *elements of* $\mathbf{A}$.

Because of identity (11.2.3) we define the *product* $\mathbf{Ax}'$ *of matrix (11.2.4) and the column vector*

$\mathbf{x}' = (x_1, x_2, \ldots, x_n)'$ to be the column vector

$$\begin{pmatrix} a_{11} & a_{12} & \cdots & a_{1n} \\ a_{21} & a_{22} & \cdots & a_{2n} \\ \vdots & \vdots & & \vdots \\ a_{m1} & a_{m2} & \cdots & a_{mn} \end{pmatrix} \begin{pmatrix} x_1 \\ x_2 \\ \vdots \\ x_n \end{pmatrix} := \begin{pmatrix} a_{11}x_1 + a_{12}x_2 + \cdots + a_{1n}x_n \\ a_{21}x_1 + a_{22}x_2 + \cdots + a_{2n}x_n \\ \vdots \\ a_{m1}x_1 + a_{m2}x_2 + \cdots + a_{mn}x_n \end{pmatrix}.$$

We point out here that *there is a one-to-one correspondence between the linear functions* $\mathbf{F}: \mathbb{R}^n \to \mathbb{R}^m$ *and the real matrices of the form (11.2.4)* whenever bases are fixed in both $\mathbb{R}^n$ and $\mathbb{R}^m$. If, for instance, the bases $\mathbf{e}_1, \mathbf{e}_2, \ldots, \mathbf{e}_n$ of $\mathbb{R}^n$ and $\mathbf{v}_1, \mathbf{v}_2, \ldots, \mathbf{v}_m$ of $\mathbb{R}^m$ are introduced, then given a linear function $\mathbf{F}: \mathbb{R}^n \to \mathbb{R}^m$, there exists one and only one real matrix (11.2.4) such that

$$\mathbf{F}(\mathbf{x})' = \mathbf{A}\mathbf{x}' \qquad \text{for all} \quad \mathbf{x} \in \mathbb{R}^n. \tag{11.2.5}$$

Conversely, given a real matrix (11.2.4), by (11.2.5) one and only one linear function $\mathbf{F}: \mathbb{R}^n \to \mathbb{R}^m$ is defined.

Addition of matrices. Given the linear functions

$$\mathbf{F}: \mathbb{R}^n \to \mathbb{R}^m, \qquad \mathbf{G}: \mathbb{R}^n \to \mathbb{R}^m$$

the *sum* $(\mathbf{F} + \mathbf{G})$ is defined by

$$(\mathbf{F} + \mathbf{G})(\mathbf{x}) := \mathbf{F}(\mathbf{x}) + \mathbf{G}(\mathbf{x}).$$

The linearity of both functions $\mathbf{F}$ and $\mathbf{G}$ yields the linearity of the function $(\mathbf{F} + \mathbf{G})$. Now let $\mathbf{F}$ and $\mathbf{G}$ be defined by matrices $\mathbf{A}$ and $\mathbf{B}$, respectively:

$$\mathbf{F}(\mathbf{x})' = \mathbf{A}\mathbf{x}', \qquad \mathbf{G}(\mathbf{x})' = \mathbf{B}\mathbf{x}'.$$

Let the matrix $\mathbf{C}$ correspond to $(\mathbf{F} + \mathbf{G})$ as the matrices

$$\mathbf{A} = \begin{pmatrix} a_{11} & a_{12} & \cdots & a_{1n} \\ a_{21} & a_{22} & \cdots & a_{2n} \\ \vdots & \vdots & & \vdots \\ a_{m1} & a_{m2} & \cdots & a_{mn} \end{pmatrix} \quad \text{and} \quad \mathbf{B} = \begin{pmatrix} b_{11} & b_{12} & \ldots & b_{1n} \\ b_{21} & b_{22} & \cdots & b_{2n} \\ \vdots & \vdots & & \vdots \\ b_{m1} & b_{m2} & \cdots & b_{mn} \end{pmatrix} \tag{11.2.6}$$

correspond to $\mathbf{F}$ and $\mathbf{G}$, respectively. Then, obviously,

$$\mathbf{C} = \begin{pmatrix} a_{11} + b_{11}, & a_{12} + b_{12}, & \ldots, & a_{1n} + b_{1n} \\ a_{21} + b_{21}, & a_{22} + b_{22}, & \ldots, & a_{2n} + b_{2n} \\ \vdots & \vdots & & \vdots \\ a_{m1} + b_{m1}, & a_{m2} + b_{m2}, & \ldots, & a_{mn} + b_{mn} \end{pmatrix}.$$

Hence, if we write

$$(\mathbf{A} + \mathbf{B})\,\mathbf{x}' \quad \text{for} \quad \mathbf{A}\mathbf{x}' + \mathbf{B}\mathbf{x}',$$

we have defined the *sum of the matrices* **A** *and* **B**:

$$\mathbf{A}+\mathbf{B}:=\begin{pmatrix} a_{11} & \cdots & a_{1n} \\ \vdots & & \vdots \\ a_{m1} & \cdots & a_{mn}\end{pmatrix}+\begin{pmatrix} b_{11} & \cdots & b_{1n} \\ \vdots & & \vdots \\ b_{m1} & \cdots & b_{mn}\end{pmatrix}:=\begin{pmatrix} a_{11}+b_{11}, & \ldots, & a_{1n}+b_{1n} \\ \vdots & & \vdots \\ a_{m1}+b_{m1}, & \ldots, & a_{mn}+b_{mn}\end{pmatrix}.$$

Subtraction of matrices. The *difference* $(\mathbf{F}-\mathbf{G})$ of two linear functions **F** and **G** is defined analogously to the sum $(\mathbf{F}+\mathbf{G})$. Hence, for the corresponding matrices (11.2.6) and $(\mathbf{A}-\mathbf{B})$ we obtain

$$\mathbf{A}-\mathbf{B}:=\begin{pmatrix} a_{11} & \cdots & a_{1n} \\ \vdots & & \vdots \\ a_{m1} & \cdots & a_{mn}\end{pmatrix}-\begin{pmatrix} b_{11} & \cdots & b_{1n} \\ \vdots & & \vdots \\ b_{m1} & \cdots & q_{mn}\end{pmatrix}:=\begin{pmatrix} a_{11}-b_{11}, & \ldots, & a_{1n}-b_{1n} \\ \vdots & & \vdots \\ a_{m1}-b_{m1}, & \ldots, & a_{mn}-b_{mn}\end{pmatrix}.$$

Product of a matrix and a real number. We want

$$\mathbf{F}(\lambda\mathbf{x}')=\mathbf{A}(\lambda\mathbf{x})' \qquad (\lambda \text{ a real number})$$

to be *associative* in the sense that

$$\mathbf{A}(\lambda\mathbf{x})'=(\mathbf{A}\lambda)\,\mathbf{x}'.$$

Thus we define

$$\mathbf{A}\lambda:=\begin{pmatrix} a_{11} & \cdots & a_{1n} \\ \vdots & & \vdots \\ a_{m1} & \cdots & a_{mn}\end{pmatrix}\lambda:=\begin{pmatrix} a_{11}\lambda, & \ldots, & a_{1n}\lambda \\ \vdots & & \vdots \\ a_{m1}\lambda, & \ldots, & a_{mn}\lambda\end{pmatrix}$$

to be the *product of the matrix* **A** *and the real number* λ.

Product of two matrices. Let the functions

$$\mathbf{F}:\mathbb{R}^n\to\mathbb{R}^m, \qquad \mathbf{G}:\mathbb{R}^m\to\mathbb{R}^k$$

be given. We denote by $(\mathbf{G}\circ\mathbf{F})$ the *composition* or *product of* **F** *and* **G**. This is a function from $\mathbb{R}^n$ into $\mathbb{R}^k$ defined by

$$(\mathbf{G}\circ\mathbf{F})(\mathbf{x}):=\mathbf{G}(\mathbf{F}(\mathbf{x})).$$

If **F** and **G** are linear, then $(\mathbf{G}\circ\mathbf{F})$ is also linear, as can be seen from

$$(\mathbf{G}\circ\mathbf{F})(\lambda\mathbf{x})=\mathbf{G}(\mathbf{F}(\lambda\mathbf{x}))=\mathbf{G}(\lambda\mathbf{F}(\mathbf{x}))=\lambda\mathbf{G}(\mathbf{F}(\mathbf{x}))=\lambda(\mathbf{G}\circ\mathbf{F})(\mathbf{x})$$

and

$$\begin{aligned}(\mathbf{G}\circ\mathbf{F})(\mathbf{x}+\mathbf{y})&=\mathbf{G}(\mathbf{F}(\mathbf{x}+\mathbf{y}))=\mathbf{G}(\mathbf{F}(\mathbf{x})+\mathbf{F}(\mathbf{y}))\\&=\mathbf{G}(\mathbf{F}(\mathbf{x}))+\mathbf{G}(\mathbf{F}(\mathbf{y}))=(\mathbf{G}\circ\mathbf{F})(\mathbf{x})+(\mathbf{G}\circ\mathbf{F})(\mathbf{y}).\end{aligned}$$

Let the matrices that correspond to the linear functions **F** and **G** be

$$\mathbf{A}=\begin{pmatrix} a_{11} & a_{12} & \cdots & a_{1n} \\ \vdots & \vdots & & \vdots \\ a_{m1} & a_{m2} & \cdots & a_{mn}\end{pmatrix} \quad \text{and} \quad \mathbf{B}=\begin{pmatrix} b_{11} & b_{12} & \cdots & b_{1m} \\ \vdots & \vdots & & \vdots \\ b_{k1} & b_{k2} & \cdots & b_{km}\end{pmatrix}, \qquad (11.2.7)$$

respectively; that is, let

$$\mathbf{F}(\mathbf{x})' = \mathbf{A}\mathbf{x}' \qquad \text{and} \qquad \mathbf{G}(\mathbf{y})' = \mathbf{B}\mathbf{y}'.$$

Using

$$\mathbf{y} = \mathbf{F}(\mathbf{x}) = (\mathbf{A}\mathbf{x}')' = \mathbf{x}\mathbf{A}'$$

where $\mathbf{A}'$ is the *transpose of* $\mathbf{A}$, that is,

$$\mathbf{A}' = \begin{pmatrix} a_{11} & \cdots & a_{m1} \\ a_{12} & \cdots & a_{m2} \\ \vdots & & \vdots \\ a_{1n} & \cdots & a_{mn} \end{pmatrix},$$

we obtain

$$(\mathbf{G} \circ \mathbf{F})(\mathbf{x})' = \mathbf{G}(\mathbf{F}(\mathbf{x}))' = \mathbf{G}(\mathbf{y})' = \mathbf{B}\mathbf{y}' = \mathbf{B}(\mathbf{x}\mathbf{A}')' = \mathbf{B}(\mathbf{A}\mathbf{x}').$$

If we denote the k row vectors of $\mathbf{B}$ by $\mathbf{b}_1, \mathbf{b}_2, \ldots, \mathbf{b}_n$ and the n column vectors of $\mathbf{A}$ by $\mathbf{a}_1', \mathbf{a}_2', \ldots, \mathbf{a}_n'$, then the matrix $\mathbf{C}$ that corresponds to $(\mathbf{G} \circ \mathbf{F})$ is

$$\mathbf{C} := \begin{pmatrix} \mathbf{b}_1\mathbf{a}_1', & \mathbf{b}_1\mathbf{a}_2', & \ldots, & \mathbf{b}_1\mathbf{a}_n' \\ \mathbf{b}_2\mathbf{a}_1', & \mathbf{b}_2\mathbf{a}_2', & \ldots, & \mathbf{b}_2\mathbf{a}_n' \\ \vdots & \vdots & & \vdots \\ \mathbf{b}_k\mathbf{a}_1', & \mathbf{b}_k\mathbf{a}_2', & \cdots, & \mathbf{b}_k\mathbf{a}_n' \end{pmatrix} \tag{11.2.8}$$

where

$$\mathbf{b}_i\mathbf{a}_j' := b_{i1}a_{1j} + b_{i2}a_{2j} + \cdots + b_{im}a_{mj}.$$

This follows from the identity

$$\mathbf{B}(\mathbf{A}\mathbf{x}') = \mathbf{C}\mathbf{x}' \qquad \text{for all} \quad \mathbf{x} \in \mathbb{R}^n,$$

which gives rise to the definition that matrix (11.2.8) is the *product* **BA** *of matrices (11.2.7)*.

11.2.9 **Remark.** The product **BA** of two matrices **B** and **A** is well defined if and only if the number of columns of **B** is equal to the number of rows of **A**. This corresponds to the fact that the composition (product) $(\mathbf{G} \circ \mathbf{F})$ of two linear functions

$$\mathbf{F} : \mathbb{R}^n \to \mathbb{R}^m, \qquad \mathbf{G} : \mathbb{R}^p \to \mathbb{R}^k$$

is possible if and only if $m = p$.

11.2.10 **Remark.** From the preceding definition of the product of two matrices it follows that matrix multiplication is *associative*:

$$\mathbf{A}(\mathbf{B}\mathbf{C}) = (\mathbf{A}\mathbf{B})\mathbf{C},$$

but *not* necessarily *commutative*: There exist matrices **A**, **B** such that both products **AB** and **BA** are well defined, but **AB** $\neq$ **BA**. For instance,

$$\begin{pmatrix}1 & 2\\3 & 0\end{pmatrix}\begin{pmatrix}2 & 1\\0 & 3\end{pmatrix} = \begin{pmatrix}2 & 7\\6 & 3\end{pmatrix} \neq \begin{pmatrix}5 & 4\\9 & 0\end{pmatrix} = \begin{pmatrix}2 & 1\\0 & 3\end{pmatrix}\begin{pmatrix}1 & 2\\3 & 0\end{pmatrix}.$$

This corresponds to the fact that there exist linear functions **F** and **G** such that both compositions $(\mathbf{G} \circ \mathbf{F})$ and $(\mathbf{F} \circ \mathbf{G})$ exist, but $(\mathbf{G} \circ \mathbf{F}) \neq (\mathbf{F} \circ \mathbf{G})$.

11.3 Application of Linear Mappings: Multiple-Product Oligopoly with Linear Cost and Sales Functions

There exists a great variety of linear economic models that could serve as excellent examples for applications of linear mappings. The following examples, the results of which are quite surprising at first sight, are taken from the author's papers [1971, 1972d, 1973a]; see also Eichhorn, Funke, and Stehling [1977]. All of these papers, which were published in German, consider the *multiple-product oligopoly*. This kind of oligopoly has been treated before only by Selten [1970], but in an essentially different form.

We consider an oligopoly model given by the following assumptions.

M.1 There are n producers, $P_1, \ldots, P_n$, producing a set of k noncomplementary commodities. For simplicity, we denote the k commodities by the natural numbers $1, \ldots, k$.

Let I_ν denote the set of those natural numbers (in natural order) that correspond to the commodities produced by the νth ($\nu = 1, \ldots, n$) producer. We denote the number of elements of the set I_ν by $|I_\nu|$. Obviously, $|I_\nu| \leqq k$.

M.2 The producers sell their products directly to many price-taking consumers. We assume that marketing is carried out only by a price policy; that is, the set Σ_ν of the strategies of the producer P_ν is

$$\Sigma_\nu : = \{(p_\varrho^\nu) \mid \varrho \in I_\nu, p_\varrho^\nu \in \mathbb{R}_{++}\} \qquad (\nu = 1, \ldots, n)$$

where

$$(p_\varrho^\nu) = : \mathbf{p}^\nu \qquad (\varrho \in I_\nu)$$

denotes the (column) vector of prices set by producer P_ν.

Note that within $\mathbf{p}^\nu$ the price of the τth commodity has a uniquely determined place which we call the τ^*th component of $\mathbf{p}^\nu$ in what follows.

Let the column vector

$$\mathbf{x}^\nu = (x_\varrho^\nu) \qquad (\varrho \in I_\nu)$$

denote the sales vector of the producer P_ν and let the column vector

$$\mathbf{b}^\nu = (b_\varrho^\nu) \qquad (\varrho \in I_\nu)$$

be the vector of the "saturation quantities with respect to the supply of producer P_ν."

M.3 The difference $\mathbf{x}^\nu - \mathbf{b}^\nu$ is a *linear* function $\mathbf{F}^\nu$ of the price vector $\mathbf{p}^\nu$ of the producer P_ν as well as of the price vectors $\mathbf{p}^\lambda$ of his competitors P_λ ($\lambda = 1, \ldots, \nu - 1, \nu + 1, \ldots, n$):

$$\mathbf{x}^\nu - \mathbf{b}^\nu = \mathbf{F}^\nu(\mathbf{p}^1, \ldots, \mathbf{p}^n).$$

With the aid of matrices

$$\mathbf{A}^{\nu\mu} = (a_{\varrho\sigma}^{\nu\mu}) \qquad \begin{cases} \varrho \in I_\nu;\ \nu = 1, \ldots, n, \\ \sigma \in I_\mu;\ \mu = 1, \ldots, n, \end{cases}$$

this can be written as

$$\mathbf{x}^\nu = \sum_{\mu=1}^{n} \mathbf{A}^{\nu\mu}\mathbf{p}^\mu + \mathbf{b}^\nu \qquad (\nu = 1, \ldots, n).$$

M.4 The vector $\mathbf{b}^\nu$ of the saturation quantities is positive, and the matrices $\mathbf{A}^{\nu\mu}$ satisfy the inequalities

$$\mathbf{A}^{\nu\mu} \geqq \mathbf{0}, \quad \text{that is,} \quad a_{\varrho\sigma}^{\nu\mu} \geqq \mathbf{0} \quad \text{if} \quad \nu \neq \mu;$$

$$a_{\varrho\varrho}^{\nu\nu} < 0; \quad a_{\varrho\sigma}^{\nu\nu} \geqq 0 \quad \text{if} \quad \varrho \neq \sigma;$$

where $\nu = 1, \ldots, n$; $\mu = 1, \ldots, n$; $\varrho \in I_\nu$; $\sigma \in I_\mu$ or I_ν, respectively.

The inequality $a_{\varrho\varrho}^{\nu\nu} < 0$ says that sales by producer P_ν of the ϱth commodity will decrease whenever he raises his price p_ϱ^ν for the ϱth commodity. The remaining inequalities of Assumption M.4 indicate that the commodities of our oligopoly market are noncomplementary goods.

M.5 The following "hypermatrix"

$$\underline{\mathbf{A}} := \begin{pmatrix} \mathbf{A}^{11} & \mathbf{A}^{12} & \cdots & \mathbf{A}^{1n} \\ \mathbf{A}^{21} & \mathbf{A}^{22} & \cdots & \mathbf{A}^{2n} \\ \vdots & \vdots & \ddots & \vdots \\ \mathbf{A}^{n1} & \mathbf{A}^{n2} & \cdots & \mathbf{A}^{nn} \end{pmatrix}$$

is a matrix with a *symmetrically dominant* (negative; see M.4) *diagonal* in the sense of Selten [1970, p. 26]: If the units of the quantities of the commodities are suitably chosen,[6] then in every row of the matrix $(\underline{\mathbf{A}} + \underline{\mathbf{A}}')$, where $\underline{\mathbf{A}}'$ is

[6] We assume in our model that this has already been done.

the transpose of $\underline{A}$, the sum of the absolute values of the off-diagonal elements is smaller than the absolute value of the diagonal element. (The off-diagonal elements are nonnegative; see M.4.)

In other words, we assume that the direct price impacts are dominant. Assumptions of this kind are usual in price theory (see, e.g., Selten [1970, p. 26]).

11.3.1 **Remark.** A matrix with a symmetrically dominant negative diagonal in the sense of Selten is always a matrix with a dominant negative diagonal in the ordinary sense (see, e.g., McKenzie [1960]): If the units of the commodities are suitably chosen, then in every row of such a matrix the sum of the absolute values of the off-diagonal elements is smaller than the absolute value of the diagonal element.

M.6 The variable cost of producing the quantity vector $\mathbf{x}^\nu$ is a linear function of $\mathbf{x}^\nu$. In other words, the cost function K_{P_ν} of the producer P_ν is given by[7]

$$K_{P_\nu}(\mathbf{x}^\nu) = \alpha^\nu + \boldsymbol{\beta}^{\nu\prime}\mathbf{x}^\nu$$

where $\alpha^\nu > 0$ is the fixed cost of P_ν and $\boldsymbol{\beta}^\nu = (\beta_\varrho^\nu) > \mathbf{0}$, $\varrho \in I_\nu$, is the vector of the partial marginal cost of P_ν.

From Assumptions M.3 and M.6 it follows that the profit function Π_{P_ν} of the producer P_ν is given by

$$\begin{aligned} \Pi_{P_\nu}(\mathbf{p}^1, \ldots, \mathbf{p}^n) &= \mathbf{p}^{\nu\prime}\mathbf{x}^\nu - K_{P_\nu}(\mathbf{x}^\nu) \\ &= (\mathbf{p}^\nu - \boldsymbol{\beta}^\nu)'\left(\sum_{\mu=1}^{n} \mathbf{A}^{\nu\mu}\mathbf{p}^\mu + \mathbf{b}^\nu\right) - \alpha^\nu. \end{aligned} \tag{11.3.2}$$

In order to calculate the profit-maximizing price vector $\mathbf{p}^\nu$ of producer P_ν, we set the partial derivatives of the profit function Π_{P_ν} with respect to the components p_ϱ^ν, $\varrho \in I_\nu$, of $\mathbf{p}^\nu$ equal to zero. Since these derivatives are linear functions of $\mathbf{p}^1, \ldots, \mathbf{p}^n$, the problem of determining the optimal prices $\mathbf{p}^\nu$ can be solved with the aid of matrix calculus.

First we have

$$\begin{aligned} &\frac{\partial \Pi_{P_\nu}(\mathbf{p}^1, \ldots, \mathbf{p}^n)}{\partial p_\varrho^\nu} \\ &= (0, \ldots, 1, \ldots, 0)\left(\sum_{\mu=1}^{n} \mathbf{A}^{\nu\mu}\mathbf{p}^\mu + \mathbf{b}^\nu\right) + (\mathbf{p}^\nu - \boldsymbol{\beta}^\nu)'\,\mathbf{A}^{\nu\nu}\begin{pmatrix} 0 \\ \vdots \\ 1 \\ \vdots \\ 0 \end{pmatrix} = 0.^{8} \end{aligned} \tag{11.3.3}$$

---

[7] The prime turns the column vector $\boldsymbol{\beta}^\nu$ into a row vector.

[8] The 1's in the vectors $(0, \ldots, 1, \ldots, 0)$ and $(0, \ldots, 1, \ldots, 0)'$ represent the τ^*th component; see the definition of τ^* following Assumption M.2.

Next, let ϱ run through I_ν. Then (11.3.3) can be written as the following system of linear equations.

$$(\mathbf{A}^{\nu\nu} + \mathbf{A}^{\nu\nu\prime})\,\mathbf{p}^\nu = -\mathbf{A}^{\nu 1}\mathbf{p}^1 - \cdots - \mathbf{A}^{\nu,\nu-1}\mathbf{p}^{\nu-1} - \mathbf{A}^{\nu,\nu+1}\mathbf{p}^{\nu+1} - \cdots - \mathbf{A}^{\nu n}\mathbf{p}^n + \mathbf{A}^{\nu\nu\prime}\boldsymbol{\beta}^\nu - \mathbf{b}^\nu. \quad (11.3.4)$$

This system has one and only one solution $\mathbf{p}^\nu$ that maximizes the profit (11.3.2) of the producer P_ν, this solution depending on the prices $\mathbf{p}^1, \ldots, \mathbf{p}^{\nu-1}, \mathbf{p}^{\nu+1}, \ldots, \mathbf{p}^n$ of the competitors. This follows from Assumption M.5, which ensures that the inverse of the matrix $\mathbf{A}^{\nu\nu} + \mathbf{A}^{\nu\nu\prime}$ exists and that the symmetric matrix

$$\left(\frac{\partial^2 \Pi_{P_\nu}(\mathbf{p}^1, \ldots, \mathbf{p}^n)}{\partial p^\nu_\varkappa\, \partial p^\nu_\lambda}\right) = \mathbf{A}^{\nu\nu} + \mathbf{A}^{\nu\nu\prime}$$

is globally negative definit[9]. As follows from Assumption M.4, the right-hand side of system (11.3.4) is negative whenever the vector $\mathbf{b}^\nu$ of the saturation quantities is sufficiently large; that is, greater than $\mathbf{A}^{\nu\nu\prime}\boldsymbol{\beta}^\nu$. Under this assumption every solution vector $\mathbf{p}^\nu$ of (11.3.4) is positive, since the matrix $(\mathbf{A}^{\nu\nu} + \mathbf{A}^{\nu\nu\prime})$ has both a dominant negative diagonal and nonnegative off-diagonal elements (see Assumptions M.4 and M.5); for the proof of this see McKenzie [1960, Theorem 4].

Let us write system (11.3.4) for all $\nu = 1, \ldots, n$. Then we obtain the following system of systems of linear equations:

$$\begin{array}{ccccccccc}
(\mathbf{A}^{11} + \mathbf{A}^{11\prime})\,\mathbf{p}^1 & + & \mathbf{A}^{12}\mathbf{p}^2 & + \cdots + & \mathbf{A}^{1n}\mathbf{p}^n & = & \mathbf{A}^{11\prime}\boldsymbol{\beta}^1 - \mathbf{b}^1 \\
\mathbf{A}^{21}\mathbf{p}^1 & + & (\mathbf{A}^{22} + \mathbf{A}^{22\prime})\,\mathbf{p}^2 & + \ldots + & \mathbf{A}^{2n}\mathbf{p}^n & = & \mathbf{A}^{22\prime}\boldsymbol{\beta}^2 - \mathbf{b}^2 \\
\vdots & & \vdots & & \vdots & & \vdots \\
\mathbf{A}^{n1}\mathbf{p}^1 & + & \mathbf{A}^{n2}\mathbf{p}^2 & + \cdots + & (\mathbf{A}^{nn} + \mathbf{A}^{nn\prime})\,\mathbf{p}^n & = & \mathbf{A}^{nn\prime}\boldsymbol{\beta}^n - \mathbf{b}^n.
\end{array}$$

With the abbreviations

$$\underline{\mathbf{T}} := -\begin{pmatrix} \mathbf{A}^{11} + \mathbf{A}^{11\prime} & \mathbf{A}^{12} & \cdots & \mathbf{A}^{1n} \\ \mathbf{A}^{21} & \mathbf{A}^{22} + \mathbf{A}^{22\prime} & \cdots & \mathbf{A}^{2n} \\ \vdots & \vdots & \ddots & \vdots \\ \mathbf{A}^{n1} & \mathbf{A}^{n2} & \cdots & \mathbf{A}^{nn} + \mathbf{A}^{nn\prime} \end{pmatrix},$$

$$\underline{\mathbf{S}} := -\begin{pmatrix} \mathbf{A}^{12\prime} & \mathbf{0} & \cdots & \mathbf{0} \\ \mathbf{0} & \mathbf{A}^{22\prime} & \cdots & \mathbf{0} \\ \vdots & \vdots & \ddots & \vdots \\ \mathbf{0} & \mathbf{0} & \cdots & \mathbf{A}^{nn\prime} \end{pmatrix},$$

$$\underline{\mathbf{p}} := \begin{pmatrix} \mathbf{p}^1 \\ \vdots \\ \mathbf{p}^n \end{pmatrix}, \qquad \underline{\boldsymbol{\beta}} := \begin{pmatrix} \boldsymbol{\beta}^1 \\ \vdots \\ \boldsymbol{\beta}^n \end{pmatrix}, \qquad \underline{\mathbf{b}} := \begin{pmatrix} \mathbf{b}^1 \\ \vdots \\ \mathbf{b}^n \end{pmatrix}$$

[9] See McKenzie [1960. p. 49] in conjunction with Remark 11.3.1.

this system can be written as

$$\underline{\mathbf{T}}\mathbf{p} = \underline{\mathbf{S}}\boldsymbol{\beta} + \mathbf{b}. \tag{11.3.5}$$

We solve this equation for $\mathbf{p}$ and obtain

$$\bar{\mathbf{p}} := \underline{\mathbf{T}}^{-1}\underline{\mathbf{S}}\boldsymbol{\beta} + \underline{\mathbf{T}}^{-1}\mathbf{b}, \tag{11.3.6}$$

which is the (uniquely determined) *equilibrium price vector* (in the sense of Nash [1951]; see (13.3.25)) of model M.1–M.6. The inverse $\underline{\mathbf{T}}^{-1}$ of the matrix $\underline{\mathbf{T}}$ exists, since $\underline{\mathbf{T}}$ has, as a consequence of Assumption M.5, a dominant diagonal. According to Assumption M.4, the matrix $\underline{\mathbf{T}}$ has positive diagonal elements, whereas the other elements of $\underline{\mathbf{T}}$ are nonpositive. This situation permits the application of a result of McKenzie [1960, Theorem 4]: If the right-hand side of Eq. (11.3.5) is positive,[10] then the equilibrium price vector $\bar{\mathbf{p}}$ is positive. We summarize:

11.3.7 **Theorem.** *The model M.1–M.6 of a multiple-product oligopoly has a unique Nash equilibrium. The equilibrium price vector of the model is positive whenever the vector of the saturation quantities is sufficiently large.*

In what follows, we are interested in comparing the equilibrium price vector (11.3.6) with the (we hope, unique) price vector $\hat{\mathbf{p}}$ that maximizes the joint profit

$$\Pi := \Pi_{P_1} + \Pi_{P_2} + \cdots + \Pi_{P_n}$$

of the n oligopolists $P_1, P_2, \ldots, P_n$ (if they form a cartel, e.g.).

In order to determine $\hat{\mathbf{p}}$, let us consider the system

$$\frac{\partial \Pi(\mathbf{p}^1, \cdots, \mathbf{p}^n)}{\partial p_\varrho^\lambda} = 0 \qquad (\varrho \in I_\lambda;\ \lambda = 1, \ldots, n)$$

which can be written as

$$\begin{array}{l}
(\mathbf{A}^{11} + \mathbf{A}^{11\prime})\,\mathbf{p}^1 + (\mathbf{A}^{12} + \mathbf{A}^{21\prime})\,\mathbf{p}^2 + \cdots + (\mathbf{A}^{1n} + \mathbf{A}^{n1\prime})\,\mathbf{p}^n = \sum_{\tau=1}^{n} \mathbf{A}^{\tau 1\prime}\boldsymbol{\beta}^\tau - \mathbf{b}^1 \\
\qquad\vdots \qquad\qquad\qquad \vdots \qquad\qquad\qquad \vdots \qquad\qquad \vdots \qquad\qquad\quad \vdots \qquad\qquad\quad \vdots \\
(\mathbf{A}^{n1} + \mathbf{A}^{1n\prime})\,\mathbf{p}^1 + (\mathbf{A}^{n2} + \mathbf{A}^{2n\prime})\,\mathbf{p}^2 + \cdots + (\mathbf{A}^{nn} + \mathbf{A}^{nn\prime})\,\mathbf{p}^n = \sum_{\tau=1}^{n} \mathbf{A}^{\tau n\prime}\boldsymbol{\beta}^\tau - \mathbf{b}^n.
\end{array}$$

Using these abbreviations together with

$$\underline{\mathbf{R}} := -\begin{pmatrix} \mathbf{0} & \mathbf{A}^{21\prime} & \cdots & \mathbf{A}^{n1\prime} \\ \mathbf{A}^{12\prime} & \mathbf{0} & \cdots & \mathbf{A}^{n2\prime} \\ \vdots & \vdots & \ddots & \vdots \\ \mathbf{A}^{1n\prime} & \mathbf{A}^{2n\prime} & \cdots & \mathbf{0} \end{pmatrix},$$

[10] That is the case if the (positive; see M.4) vector $\mathbf{b}$ of the saturation quantities is sufficiently large, i.e., $\mathbf{b} > -\underline{\mathbf{S}}\boldsymbol{\beta}$.

we can write this system as

$$\underline{\mathbf{T}}\underline{\mathbf{p}} + \underline{\mathbf{R}}\underline{\mathbf{p}} = \underline{\mathbf{S}}\underline{\boldsymbol{\beta}} + \underline{\mathbf{R}}\underline{\boldsymbol{\beta}} + \underline{\mathbf{b}}. \tag{11.3.8}$$

According to Assumption M.5, the symmetric matrix $(\underline{\mathbf{T}} + \underline{\mathbf{R}}) = -(\underline{\mathbf{A}} + \underline{\mathbf{A}}')$ has a dominant diagonal; that is, the inverse exists. Then the (unique) solution of system (11.3.8) is the desired price vector $\hat{\underline{\mathbf{p}}}$. The solution $\hat{\underline{\mathbf{p}}}$ of (11.3.8) maximizes the profit Π, since the matrix of the second derivatives of Π, namely $(\underline{\mathbf{A}} + \underline{\mathbf{A}}')$, is negative definite because of Assumption M.5. In order to compare $\hat{\underline{\mathbf{p}}}$ with the equilibrium price vector $\bar{\underline{\mathbf{p}}}$, we write

$$\hat{\underline{\mathbf{p}}} = \bar{\underline{\mathbf{p}}} + \underline{\mathbf{w}} \tag{11.3.9}$$

where the vector $\underline{\mathbf{w}}$ represents the yet unknown difference between $\hat{\underline{\mathbf{p}}}$ and $\bar{\underline{\mathbf{p}}}$. Since $\bar{\underline{\mathbf{p}}}$ is the solution of system (11.3.5), insertion of (11.3.9) into (11.3.8) yields the system

$$(\underline{\mathbf{T}} + \underline{\mathbf{R}})\,\underline{\mathbf{w}} = -\,\underline{\mathbf{R}}(\bar{\underline{\mathbf{p}}} - \underline{\boldsymbol{\beta}}). \tag{11.3.10}$$

According to Assumption M.4, the matrix $-\underline{\mathbf{R}}$ has only nonnegative elements, whereas the matrix $(\underline{\mathbf{T}} + \underline{\mathbf{R}}) = -(\underline{\mathbf{A}} + \underline{\mathbf{A}}')$ has nonpositive off-diagonal elements and, due to Assumption M.5, a dominant positive diagonal. If the equilibrium prices are greater than or equal to the marginal cost,

$$\bar{\underline{\mathbf{p}}} \geqq \underline{\boldsymbol{\beta}},$$

that is,

$$\underline{\mathbf{T}}^{-1}\underline{\mathbf{b}} \geqq \underline{\boldsymbol{\beta}} - \underline{\mathbf{T}}^{-1}\underline{\mathbf{S}}\underline{\boldsymbol{\beta}} \tag{11.3.11}$$

(see (11.3.6); $\underline{\mathbf{b}}$ is the vector of the saturation quantities), then Eq. (11.3.10) implies $\underline{\mathbf{w}} \geqq \underline{\mathbf{0}}$, that is, $\hat{\underline{\mathbf{p}}} \geqq \bar{\underline{\mathbf{p}}}$; see McKenzie [1960, Theorem 4].

We summarize this as Theorem 11.3.12, where we state *property (11.3.11) as: the saturation quantities are sufficiently large.*

11.3.12 **Theorem.** *Let $\bar{\underline{\mathbf{p}}}$ be the equilibrium price vector of oligopoly model M.1–M.6. If the saturation quantities are sufficiently large, then the price vector $\hat{\underline{\mathbf{p}}}$ that maximizes the joint profit of the oligopolists is greater than or equal to $\bar{\underline{\mathbf{p}}}$.*

In other words: *As compared with a profit-maximizing cartel of the oligopolists, the consumers in our model face lower prices if there is price competition among the oligopolists which leads to the equilibrium price vector.*

11.3.13 **Remark.** It should be noted here that this result rests heavily on the assumption (M.4) of noncomplementary commodities. If we drop this assumption, then, *paradoxically*, $\hat{\underline{\mathbf{p}}} < \bar{\underline{\mathbf{p}}}$ is possible, as can be seen from the following simple example: Let the sales functions of two duopolists who supply only one commodity each be given by

$$x = -\,5p - q + 100, \qquad y = -\,p - 5q + 100,$$

where x, y are the quantities and p, q the prices of the commodities, respectively. Obviously, the sales of the first (second) duopolist decline if the second (first) duopolist raises his price. In other words, the commodities are complementary goods. Let the cost functions of the duopolists be identical:

$$K_1(x) = 120 + 2x, \qquad K_2(y) = 120 + 2y.$$

The equilibrium price vector

$$(\bar{p}, \bar{q}) = (10, 10)$$

is greater than the price vector

$$(\hat{p}, \hat{q}) = (28/3, 28/3)$$

that maximizes the joint profit of the duopolists. The corresponding profits are

$$\Pi_1(\bar{p}, \bar{q}) = 200 = \Pi_2(\bar{p}, \bar{q}), \qquad \Pi_1(\hat{p}, \hat{q}) = 608/3 = 202.67 = \Pi_2(\hat{p}, \hat{q}).$$

Further noteworthy examples of this kind can be found very easily if we replace Assumption M.4 of our model by the assumption that there exists at least one pair of complementary commodities.

In a somewhat different model, Selten [1970, p. 188] showed that paradoxical situations as described by the example of Remark 11.3.13 *always* occur in the case of complementary commodities.

Let us now modify oligopoly model M.1–M.6 slightly by both adding an assumption M.7 and replacing Assumptions M.2 and M.3 by Assumptions M.2′ and M.3′:

M.2′ Each of the n producers $P_1, \ldots, P_n$ sells the $|I_1|, \ldots, |I_n|$ commodities produced by him to exactly one of n dealers $D_1, \ldots, D_n$. Each of the n dealers buys his articles from only one producer. Without loss of generality, let D_1 buy from $P_1, \ldots, D_n$ from P_n. The (vector of) prices that the dealer D_ν has to pay to the producer P_ν will be denoted by the (column) vector

$$\mathbf{q}^\nu = (q_\varrho^\nu) \qquad (\varrho \in I_\nu,\ q_\varrho^\nu \in \mathbb{R}_+).$$

The dealers who sell their goods to many price-taking consumers buy only as much as they can sell (Fig. 11.3.14).

Hence, the sales vector of both the producer P_ν and the dealer D_ν can be denoted by

$$\mathbf{x}^\nu = (x_\varrho^\nu) \qquad (\varrho \in I_\nu),$$

as before. The same is true with the vector $\mathbf{b}^\nu$ of the saturation quantities. From now on the (column) vector

$$\mathbf{p}^\nu = (p_\varrho^\nu) \qquad (\varrho \in I_\nu,\ p_\varrho^\nu \in \mathbb{R}_+)$$

will denote the price vector of the *dealer* $D_\nu (\nu = 1, \ldots, n)$.

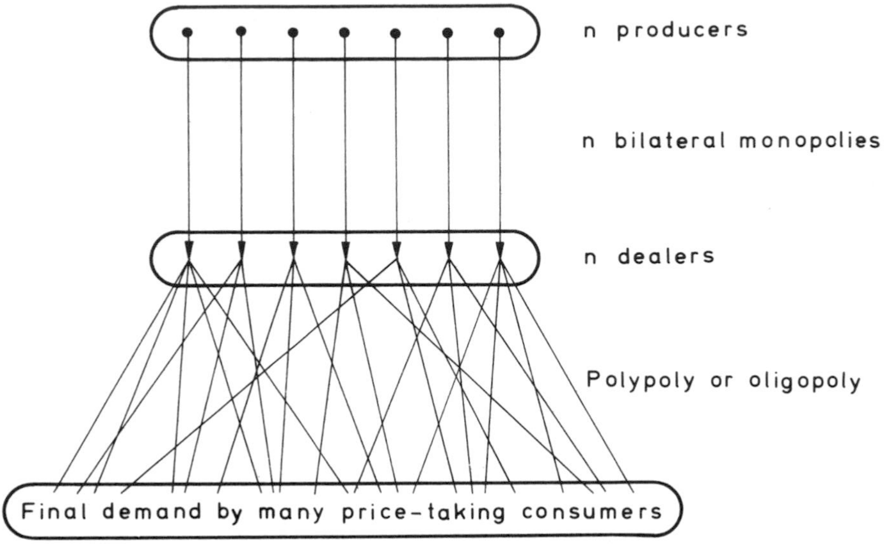

11.3.14 Figure. Market situation as described in Assumption M.2′.

M.3′ This is Assumption M.3 with the exception that "producer P_ν" and "competitors P_λ" have to be replaced by "dealer D_ν" and "competitors D_λ," respectively.

M.7 The part of the variable cost of the dealer D_ν that is different from $\mathbf{q}^{\nu\prime}\mathbf{x}^\nu$ is a *linear* function of the sales vector $\mathbf{x}^\nu$:

$$K_{D_\nu}(\mathbf{x}^\nu) = \gamma^\nu + \boldsymbol{\delta}^{\nu\prime}\mathbf{x}^\nu$$

where $\gamma^\nu > 0$ is the fixed cost of D_ν and $\boldsymbol{\delta}^\nu = (\delta^\nu_\varrho) > \mathbf{0}$, $\varrho \in I_\nu$, is the vector of the partial marginal cost of D_ν.

The model given by Assumptions M.1, M.2′, M.3′, M.4–M.7 is somewhat more general than that given by M.1–M.6, since it allows for considering some sort of *vertical* pricing in addition to the horizontal pricing studied before. In the following, we are interested in the impact of vertical cartels of the n pairs $\{P_1, D_1\}, \ldots, \{P_n, D_n\}$ on the equilibrium prices of our model.

As an example of a market that satisfies Assumptions M.1 and M.2′ consider a gasoline sales market, where each of n producers of k fuel qualities sells to "his" ring of gas stations, provided that this ring can be considered a single firm.

With the foregoing notation, the profit functions Π_{P_ν} and Π_{D_ν} of the νth producer and dealer, respectively, and the profit function $\Pi_\nu = \Pi_{P_\nu} + \Pi_{D_\nu}$ of the pair $\{P_\nu, D_\nu\}$ are given by

$$\Pi_{P_\nu}(\mathbf{q}^\nu, \mathbf{p}^1, \ldots, \mathbf{p}^n) = (\mathbf{q}^\nu - \boldsymbol{\beta}^\nu)'\left(\sum_{\mu=1}^{n} \mathbf{A}^{\nu\mu}\mathbf{p}^\mu + \mathbf{b}^\nu\right) - \alpha^\nu, \tag{11.3.15}$$

$$\Pi_{D_\nu}(\mathbf{q}^\nu, \mathbf{p}^1, \ldots, \mathbf{p}^n) = (\mathbf{p}^\nu - \mathbf{q}^\nu - \boldsymbol{\delta}^\nu)'\left(\sum_{\mu=1}^{n} \mathbf{A}^{\nu\mu}\mathbf{p}^\mu + \mathbf{b}^\nu\right) - \gamma^\nu, \tag{11.3.16}$$

$$\Pi_\nu(\mathbf{p}^1, \ldots, \mathbf{p}^n) = (\mathbf{p}^\nu - \boldsymbol{\beta}^\nu - \boldsymbol{\delta}^\nu)'\left(\sum_{\mu=1}^{n} \mathbf{A}^{\nu\mu}\mathbf{p}^\mu + \mathbf{b}^\nu\right) - \alpha^\nu - \gamma^\nu, \tag{11.3.17}$$

respectively.

The same arguments that yielded system (11.3.5) in our treatment of model M.1–M.6 now lead to the system

$$\underline{\mathbf{T}}\underline{\mathbf{p}} = \underline{\mathbf{S}}(\underline{\mathbf{q}} + \underline{\boldsymbol{\delta}}) + \underline{\mathbf{b}} \qquad \text{where} \quad \underline{\mathbf{q}} = \begin{pmatrix} \mathbf{q}^1 \\ \vdots \\ \mathbf{q}^n \end{pmatrix}, \quad \underline{\boldsymbol{\delta}} = \begin{pmatrix} \boldsymbol{\delta}^1 \\ \vdots \\ \boldsymbol{\delta}^n \end{pmatrix}, \tag{11.3.18}$$

from which the (Nash) equilibrium price vector, say $\tilde{\underline{\mathbf{p}}}$, of the dealer–consumer market can be calculated as depending on the price vector $\underline{\mathbf{q}}$ set by the producers.

If the producer $P_\nu(\nu = 1, \ldots, n)$ and "his" dealer D_ν form a cartel in order to maximize the total profit (11.3.17), then we obtain the equilibrium price vector, say $\check{\underline{\mathbf{p}}}$, from

$$\underline{\mathbf{T}}\underline{\mathbf{p}} = \underline{\mathbf{S}}(\underline{\boldsymbol{\beta}} + \underline{\boldsymbol{\delta}}) + \underline{\mathbf{b}}. \tag{11.3.19}$$

We note that this system is formally similar to system (11.3.18), since the profit functions given by (11.3.16) and (11.3.17) are formally similar.

Let us now compare the equilibrium price vectors $\tilde{\underline{\mathbf{p}}}$ and $\check{\underline{\mathbf{p}}}$. Under realistic assumptions we obtain the following result, which is somewhat astonishing, at least at first sight:

11.3.20 **Theorem.** *In the model M.1, M.2′, M.3′, M.4–M.7, let the vector of the partial marginal cost* $\underline{\boldsymbol{\beta}}$ *of the producers satisfy* $\underline{\mathbf{S}}\underline{\boldsymbol{\beta}} > \underline{\mathbf{0}}$.[11] *Let the price demand of the producer* P_ν *to his dealer* D_ν *be*

$$\mathbf{q}^\nu = \lambda^\nu \boldsymbol{\beta}^\nu \qquad \textit{with} \quad \lambda^\nu > 1 \qquad (\nu = 1, \ldots, n);$$

---

[11] For given $\underline{\boldsymbol{\beta}}$ this is the case whenever the positive diagonal elements of $\underline{\mathbf{S}}$ are sufficiently dominant, i.e., whenever the direct price impacts are sufficiently dominant.

that is, let the price vector of the v-th producer be a certain positive percentage higher than the vector of his partial marginal cost. If, now, the producer P_ν and the dealer D_ν ($\nu = 1, \ldots, n$) form a cartel in order to maximize their joint profit, the equilibrium price vector is smaller than the equilibrium price vector when there is no joint vertical profit maximization.

Proof. We have to compare $\check{\underline{\mathbf{p}}}$ in

$$\underline{\mathbf{T}}\check{\underline{\mathbf{p}}} = \underline{\mathbf{S}} \begin{pmatrix} \boldsymbol{\beta}^1 + \boldsymbol{\delta}^1 \\ \vdots \\ \boldsymbol{\beta}^n + \boldsymbol{\delta}^n \end{pmatrix} + \underline{\mathbf{b}} \qquad (11.3.19')$$

with $\tilde{\underline{\mathbf{p}}}$ in

$$\underline{\mathbf{T}}\tilde{\underline{\mathbf{p}}} = \underline{\mathbf{S}} \begin{pmatrix} \lambda^1\boldsymbol{\beta}^1 + \boldsymbol{\delta}^1 \\ \vdots \\ \lambda^n\boldsymbol{\beta}^n + \boldsymbol{\delta}^n \end{pmatrix} + \underline{\mathbf{b}} \quad (\lambda^1 > 1, \ldots, \lambda^n > 1). \qquad (11.3.18')$$

If we subtract (11.3.19′) from (11.3.18′), we obtain

$$\underline{\mathbf{T}}(\tilde{\underline{\mathbf{p}}} - \check{\underline{\mathbf{p}}}) = \underline{\mathbf{S}} \begin{pmatrix} (\lambda^1 - 1)\,\boldsymbol{\beta}^1 \\ \vdots \\ (\lambda^n - 1)\,\boldsymbol{\beta}^n \end{pmatrix} \qquad (\lambda^1 > 1, \ldots, \lambda^n > 1),$$

and this is $> \underline{\mathbf{0}}$ because of the assumption $\underline{\mathbf{S}}\underline{\boldsymbol{\beta}} > \underline{\mathbf{0}}$. But then the properties of $\underline{\mathbf{T}}$, which follow from Assumption M.5, imply $\tilde{\underline{\mathbf{p}}} - \check{\underline{\mathbf{p}}} > \underline{\mathbf{0}}$ (see McKenzie [1960, Theorem 4). ■

11.3.21 **Remark.** The inequality $\underline{\mathbf{S}}\underline{\boldsymbol{\beta}} < \underline{\mathbf{0}}$ has no solution $\underline{\boldsymbol{\beta}} > \underline{\mathbf{0}}$, since the positive diagonal of $\underline{\mathbf{S}}$ is dominant as a consequence of assumption M.5. This implies that in our model the case $\tilde{\underline{\mathbf{p}}} < \check{\underline{\mathbf{p}}}$ cannot occur, even if the assumption $\underline{\mathbf{S}}\underline{\boldsymbol{\beta}} > \underline{\mathbf{0}}$ is *not* made.

11.4 Homogeneous and Ray-Homothetic Vector-Valued Functions in the Theory of Multisectoral Growth

In the theory of multisectoral growth, systems of first-order difference equations of the following form play an important role:

$$\mathbf{x}(t + 1) = \mathbf{H}(\mathbf{x}(t)) \qquad (t = 0, 1, 2, \ldots). \qquad (11.4.1)$$

Given an initial commodity vector $\mathbf{x}(0)$, such a system permits the calculation of the sequence of the commodity vectors produced in a closed economy in the course of time. Here, $\mathbf{x}(t + 1) \in \mathbb{R}^n_+$ is the commodity vector that, on the one hand, has been obtained by the production process from the commodity vector

$\mathbf{x}(t) \in \mathbb{R}^n_+$ during the tth production period and that, on the other hand, serves as the input vector within the $(t + 1)$th production period. The vector-valued function

$$\mathbf{H}: \mathbb{R}^n_+ \to \mathbb{R}^n_+ \tag{11.4.2}$$

describes the production structure of the economy under consideration by transforming the nonnegative vector $\mathbf{x}(t)$ to the nonnegative vector $\mathbf{x}(t + 1)$.

The theory of nonnegative matrices as developed, for instance, by Nikaido [1968, Chapter II] has entailed a complete exploration of the model of multisectoral economic growth given by (11.4.1), (11.4.2) with *linear* $\mathbf{H}$.

Many of the qualitative properties of the (autonomous dynamic) system (11.4.1) with *linear* $\mathbf{H}$ can be carried over to systems (11.4.1), where $\mathbf{H}$ belongs to certain classes of *nonlinear* functions (11.4.2). For instance, Solow and Samuelson [1953] analyzed (11.4.1) in the case where $\mathbf{H}$ is *homogeneous of the first degree.* Their results concerning the existence and behavior of so-called *balanced growth solutions*[12] have been generalized by Muth [1954], Suits [1954], Morishima [1964], Nikaido [1964, 1968], Stehling [1973, 1974b], and Vahrenkamp [1974, 1977].

The basic assumptions of Nikaido are

$$\mathbf{H} : \mathbb{R}^n_+ \to \mathbb{R}^n_+; \qquad n \geqq 2; \quad \mathbf{H}(\mathbf{x}) \not\equiv \mathbf{0}; \tag{11.4.3}$$

$$\mathbf{H} \text{ is continuous on } \mathbb{R}^n_+; \tag{11.4.4}$$

$$\mathbf{H}(\lambda\mathbf{x}) = \lambda^r\mathbf{H}(\mathbf{x}) \qquad \text{for all} \quad \lambda \in \mathbb{R}_{++}, \mathbf{x} \geq \mathbf{0} \quad \text{with some } r \in [0, 1]. \tag{11.4.5}$$

He showed (see [1964; 1968, pp. 162ff.]) that even for nonautonomous systems, such as

$$\left.\begin{array}{l} \mathbf{x}(t + 1) = \mathbf{H}(\mathbf{x}(t)) + K(t)\,\mathbf{a} \qquad (t = 0, 1, 2, \ldots) \\ \text{where } \mathbf{a} \geq \mathbf{0} \text{ is a constant vector of } \mathbb{R}^n_+ \text{ and } K \text{ is} \\ \text{a real-valued function satisfying } K(t) > 0,\ K(0) = 1, \end{array}\right\} \tag{11.4.6}$$

the class of the balanced growth solutions[12] plays an important role in proving the following assertion. For $r \in\,]0, 1[$, every solution of (11.4.6) converges to a balanced growth solution which is uniquely determined under some additional assumptions, namely, the monotonicity and indecomposability of $\mathbf{H}$ and the positivity of the vector $\mathbf{a}$.

Suits and Vahrenkamp, who considered only autonomous systems like (11.4.1), and Stehling [1974b] weakened the homogeneity assumption (11.4.5). Nevertheless they obtained, under some additional assumptions, some of

---

[12] Balanced growth solutions are of the form $\mathbf{x}(t) = \varrho(t)\mathbf{c}$ where $\mathbf{c} \in \mathbb{R}^n_+$ is a constant vector and ϱ is a real-valued function.

Nikaido's results for ordinary homogeneous functions **H**. Vahrenkamp [1974, 1977] introduced the rather interesting notion of *cone homogeneity;* that is, the function **H** maps, for every fixed $\mathbf{x} \in \mathbb{R}^n_+$, the ray

$$\{\lambda\mathbf{x} \mid \lambda \in \mathbb{R}_+\} \tag{11.4.7}$$

into an ε-cone around the ray

$$\{\mu\mathbf{H}(\mathbf{x}) \mid \mu \in \mathbb{R}_+\} \tag{11.4.8}$$

rather than onto (or into) the ray (11.4.8).

Here we are interested only in the solutions of the functional equations obtained by Suits, Stehling, and Vahrenkamp in their attempts at weakening Eq. (11.4.5).

As Stehling [1973] pointed out in a slightly different context, for the purposes of multisectoral growth theory the functional equation

$$\left.\begin{array}{l} \mathbf{H}(\lambda_1 x_1, \ldots, \lambda_n x_n) = \phi(\lambda_1, \ldots, \lambda_n)\, \mathbf{H}(x_1, \ldots, x_n) \\ \text{with } (\boldsymbol{\lambda}, \mathbf{x}) \in \mathbb{R}^{2n}_+,\ \mathbf{H}\colon \mathbb{R}^n_+ \to \mathbb{R}^n_+, \\ \phi\colon \mathbb{R}^n_+ \to \mathbb{R},\ \phi(1, \ldots, 1) = 1 \end{array}\right\} \tag{11.4.9}$$

does not provide any generalization of Eq. (11.4.5) with $r \in [0, \infty[$. We show here:

11.4.10 **Theorem.** *Let* **H**, ϕ *be arbitrary functions satisfying Eq. (11.4.9) where* $\mathbf{H}(\mathbf{x}) > \mathbf{0}$ *for at least one* $\mathbf{x} \geq \mathbf{0}$, *and* ϕ *is nondecreasing in an arbitrarily small n-dimensional interval. Then there exist nonnegative real constants*

$$r_1, \ldots, r_n, \qquad c_1, \ldots, c_n \qquad \textit{with} \quad (c_1, \ldots, c_n) \neq \mathbf{0} \tag{11.4.11}$$

such that for all $\boldsymbol{\lambda} > \mathbf{0}$, $\mathbf{x} > \mathbf{0}$

$$\phi(\lambda_1, \ldots, \lambda_n) = \lambda_1^{r_1}\lambda_2^{r_2} \cdots \lambda_n^{r_n} \tag{11.4.12}$$

and

$$\mathbf{H}(x_1, \ldots, x_n) = (c_1, \ldots, c_n)\, x_1^{r_1}x_2^{r_2} \cdots x_n^{r_n}. \tag{11.4.13}$$

Conversely, every pair of functions $\phi\colon \mathbb{R}^n_+ \to \mathbb{R}$, $\mathbf{H}\colon \mathbb{R}^n_+ \to \mathbb{R}^n_+$ *given by (11.4.12) and (11.4.13) satisfies Eq. (11.4.9).*

Proof. The second assertion is obvious. The proof of the first assertion can be formulated in the same way as the proof of Theorem 3.6.7 (take a suitable component of Eq. (11.4.9)). Theorem 3.6.7 was proven under the assumption of *strict* monotonicity of one of the functions occurring in the functional equation, whereas in Theorem 11.4.10 only the monotonicity of ϕ is presupposed. This does not matter, since Theorem 1.9.13, which is needed for both proofs, is formulated for the case of ordinary monotonicity. ■

Suits, Stehling [1974b], and Vahrenkamp have weakened homogeneity assumption (11.4.5) into

$$\left.\begin{array}{lll} \mathbf{H}(\lambda\mathbf{x}) = \psi(\lambda, \mathbf{x})\,\mathbf{H}(\mathbf{x}) & \text{for all} & (\lambda, \mathbf{x}) \in \mathbb{R}_{++} \times \mathbb{R}^n_+, \\ \mathbf{H}: \mathbb{R}^n_+ \to \mathbb{R}^n_+, & & \psi: \mathbb{R}_{++} \times \mathbb{R}^n_+ \to \mathbb{R}_{++}, \\ \psi(1, \mathbf{x}) = \psi(\lambda, \mathbf{0}) = 1 & \text{for all} & \lambda \in \mathbb{R}_{++}, \mathbf{x} \in \mathbb{R}^n_+. \end{array}\right\} \quad (11.4.14)$$

We note that (11.4.14) is equivalent to

$$\left.\begin{array}{lll} \mathbf{H}(\lambda\mathbf{x}) = \lambda^{r(\lambda, \mathbf{x})}\,\mathbf{H}(\mathbf{x}) & \text{for all} & (\lambda, \mathbf{x}) \in \mathbb{R}_{++} \times \mathbb{R}^n_+, \\ \mathbf{H}: \mathbb{R}^n_+ \to \mathbb{R}^n_+, & & r: \mathbb{R}_{++} \times \mathbb{R}^n_+ \to \mathbb{R}, \\ r(\lambda, \mathbf{0}) = 0 & \text{for all} & \lambda \in \mathbb{R}_{++}. \end{array}\right\} \quad (11.4.15)$$

Since a function $\mathbf{H}$ satisfying Eq. (11.4.14) or the equivalent Eq. (11.4.15) is not necessarily homogeneous of a fixed degree along a given ray (11.4.7), we will *not* call it ray homogeneous, as Vahrenkamp does. We call a function $\mathbf{H}$ satisfying (11.4.14) *ray homothetic* in accordance with a paper by Färe and Shephard [1975] on generalizations of the homogeneity concept for production correspondences (see Section 12.4).

11.4.16 **Remark.** If $\mathbf{H} = H$, where $H: \mathbb{R}^n_+ \to \mathbb{R}_+$, the generalization (11.4.14) of (11.4.5) would admit *every* function $H: \mathbb{R}^n_+ \to \mathbb{R}_+$ satisfying $H(\mathbf{x}) \neq 0$ for all $\mathbf{x} \neq \mathbf{0}$. Every such function satisfies a functional equation of the form

$$H(\lambda\mathbf{x}) = \psi(\lambda, \mathbf{x})\,H(\mathbf{x}),$$

which can be seen by setting

$$\psi(\lambda, \mathbf{x}) := H(\lambda\mathbf{x})/H(\mathbf{x}). \quad (11.4.17)$$

However, the class of the ray-homothetic functions $\mathbf{H}: \mathbb{R}^n_+ \to \mathbb{R}^n_+$, where $n \geqq 2$, is considerably smaller than the class of the functions $\mathbf{H}: \mathbb{R}^n_+ \to \mathbb{R}^n_+$.

In this context, it is interesting to note the following results by Stehling [1974b].

11.4.18 **Theorem.** *Let the functions* $\mathbf{H}$ *and* ψ *satisfy functional equation (11.4.14); that is, let* $\mathbf{H}$ *be ray homothetic. Denote the set of all* $\mathbf{x} \in R^n_+$ *with* $\mathbf{H}(\mathbf{x}) \neq \mathbf{0}$ *by* L *and the set of all* $\mathbf{x} \in \mathbb{R}^n_+$ *with* $\mathbf{H}(\mathbf{x}) = \mathbf{0}$ *by* M $(= \mathbb{R}^n_+ \setminus L)$. *Then the following statements are true:*

(i) *If* $\mathbf{x} \in L$, *then* $\lambda\mathbf{x} \in L$ *for all* $\lambda \in \mathbb{R}_{++}$.

(ii) *If* $\mathbf{x} \in M$, *then* $\lambda\mathbf{x} \in M$ *for all* $\lambda \in \mathbb{R}_{++}$.

(iii) *There exists a function* $g: L \to \mathbb{R}_{++}$ *such that*

$$\psi(\lambda, \mathbf{x}) = g(\lambda\mathbf{x})/g(\mathbf{x}) \quad \textit{for all} \quad (\lambda, \mathbf{x}) \in \mathbb{R}_{++} \times L. \quad (11.4.19)$$

Proof. Assertions (i) and (ii) are obvious. For the proof of assertion (iii) we follow Cross [1968] (see also Aczél [1969, pp. 57–58]). We calculate $\mathbf{H}(\lambda\mu\mathbf{x})$, where both μ and λ belong to $\mathbb{R}_{++}$, in two different ways:

$$\mathbf{H}(\lambda\mu\cdot\mathbf{x}) = \psi(\lambda\mu, \mathbf{x})\,\mathbf{H}(\mathbf{x});$$

$$\mathbf{H}(\lambda\cdot\mu\mathbf{x}) = \psi(\lambda, \mu\mathbf{x})\,\mathbf{H}(\mu\mathbf{x}) = \psi(\lambda, \mu\mathbf{x})\,\psi(\mu, \mathbf{x})\,\mathbf{H}(\mathbf{x}).$$

Hence, whenever $\mathbf{x} \in L$, the function ψ satisfies the functional equation

$$\psi(\lambda\mu, \mathbf{x}) = \psi(\lambda, \mu\mathbf{x})\,\psi(\mu, \mathbf{x}). \tag{11.4.20}$$

If $\mathbf{x} \geqq \mathbf{0}$, put $\lambda = (\mu\,|\mathbf{x}|)^{-1}$ into (11.4.20) in order to get

$$\psi(1/|\mathbf{x}|, \mathbf{x}) = \psi(1/\mu|\mathbf{x}|, \mu\mathbf{x})\,\psi(\mu, \mathbf{x}).$$

Hence,

$$\psi(\mu, \mathbf{x}) = \frac{\psi(1/|\mathbf{x}|, \mathbf{x})}{\psi(1/\mu|\mathbf{x}|, \mu\mathbf{x})}.$$

With

$$\psi(1/|\mathbf{x}|, \mathbf{x}) =: 1/g(\mathbf{x})$$

this becomes (11.4.19). If $\mathbf{x} = \mathbf{0}$, we obtain $\psi(\lambda, \mathbf{0}) \equiv 1$ from (11.4.19), as required by (11.4.14). ■

Stehling [1974b] also has proved the converse of (iii):

11.4.21 **Theorem.** *Let $L \subseteqq \mathbb{R}^n_+$ be an arbitrary set and let $g\colon L \to \mathbb{R}_{++}$ be an arbitrary function. For every function $\psi\colon \mathbb{R}_{++} \times \mathbb{R}^n_+ \to \mathbb{R}_{++}$ given by*

$$\psi(\lambda, \mathbf{x}) = \begin{cases} g(\lambda\mathbf{x})/g(\mathbf{x}) & \text{for } \mathbf{x} \in L \subseteqq \mathbb{R}^n_+, \\ 1 & \text{for } \mathbf{x} \in \mathbb{R}^n_+ \setminus L \end{cases} \tag{11.4.22}$$

there exists a vector-valued function $\mathbf{H}\colon \mathbb{R}^n_+ \to \mathbb{R}^n_+$ such that $\mathbf{H}$ and ψ together satisfy (11.4.14); that is, $\mathbf{H}$ is ray homothetic.

Proof. Define $\mathbf{H}$ by

$$H_\nu(\mathbf{x}) := \begin{cases} g(\mathbf{x}) & \text{for all } \mathbf{x} \in L, \\ 0 & \text{for all } \mathbf{x} \in \mathbb{R}^n_+ \setminus L, \end{cases}$$
$$(\nu = 1, 2, \ldots, n).$$

Then, clearly, for $\nu = 1, 2, \ldots, n$

$$H_\nu(\lambda\mathbf{x}) = \begin{cases} \dfrac{H_\nu(\lambda\mathbf{x})}{H_\nu(\mathbf{x})} H_\nu(\mathbf{x}) = \dfrac{g(\lambda\mathbf{x})}{g(\mathbf{x})} H_\nu(\mathbf{x}) & \text{for } \mathbf{x} \in L, \\ 1 \cdot H_\nu(\mathbf{x}) & \text{for } \mathbf{x} \in \mathbb{R}^n_+ \setminus L, \end{cases}$$
$$= \psi(\lambda, \mathbf{x})\,H_\nu(\mathbf{x}). \quad ■$$

11.4.23 **Remark.** As Vahrenkamp [1977] pointed out, *the ray-homothetic functions* $\mathbf{H}: \mathbb{R}_+^n \to \mathbb{R}_+^n$ *form a semigroup with respect to composition.*

Proof. We have to show that the composition of any two functions

$$\mathbf{F}: \mathbb{R}_+^n \to \mathbb{R}_+^n \quad \text{and} \quad \mathbf{G}: \mathbb{R}_+^n \to \mathbb{R}_+^n$$

given by

$$\mathbf{F}(\lambda\mathbf{x}) = \varrho(\lambda, \mathbf{x})\, \mathbf{F}(\mathbf{x}), \qquad \varrho: \mathbb{R}_{++} \times \mathbb{R}_+^n \to \mathbb{R}_{++}, \tag{11.4.24}$$

$$\mathbf{G}(\lambda\mathbf{x}) = \sigma(\lambda, \mathbf{x})\, \mathbf{G}(\mathbf{x}), \qquad \sigma: \mathbb{R}_{++} \times \mathbb{R}_+^n \to \mathbb{R}_{++}, \tag{11.4.25}$$

can be written as

$$(\mathbf{G} \circ \mathbf{F})(\lambda\mathbf{x}) = \tau(\lambda, \mathbf{x})(\mathbf{G} \circ \mathbf{F})(\mathbf{x}) \qquad \text{with some} \quad \tau: \mathbb{R}_{++} \times \mathbb{R}_+^n \to \mathbb{R}_{++}.$$

This is the case:

$$\begin{aligned}(\mathbf{G} \circ \mathbf{F})(\lambda\mathbf{x}) := \mathbf{G}(\mathbf{F}(\lambda\mathbf{x})) &= \mathbf{G}(\varrho(\lambda, \mathbf{x})\, \mathbf{F}(\mathbf{x})) && \text{(by (11.4.24))}\\ &= \sigma(\varrho(\lambda, \mathbf{x}), \mathbf{F}(\mathbf{x}))\, \mathbf{G}(\mathbf{F}(\mathbf{x})) && \text{(by (11.4.25))}\\ &= \tau(\lambda, \mathbf{x})(\mathbf{G} \circ \mathbf{F})(\mathbf{x})\end{aligned}$$

where $\tau(\lambda, \mathbf{x}) := \sigma(\varrho(\lambda, \mathbf{x}), \mathbf{F}(\mathbf{x}))$. ■

11.5 A Functional Equation for Vector-Valued Demand Functions: The Budget Equation

Let

$$\mathbf{p} = (p_1, \ldots, p_n) \in \mathbb{R}_+^n$$

denote the prices of n commodities in which a household is interested. Also let

$$z \in \mathbb{R}_+$$

be its corresponding budget, and let

$$\mathbf{h}: \mathbb{R}_+^n \times \mathbb{R}_+ \to \mathbb{R}_+^n, \qquad (\mathbf{p}, z) \to \mathbf{h}(\mathbf{p}, z), \tag{11.5.1}$$

be its demand function assigning to each vector $(\mathbf{p}, z)$ the vector of quantities bought by the household in the price–budget situation $(\mathbf{p}, z)$.

The *budget equation* is

$$\mathbf{h}(\mathbf{p}, z)\, \mathbf{p}' = z. \tag{11.5.2}$$

When $\mathbf{h}$ is not known, (11.5.2) can be considered a functional equation for determining vector-valued functions $\mathbf{h}$. Since the budget equation (11.5.2) represents one of the properties (or axioms) satisfied by a demand function (11.5.1), the set of possible demand functions is a subset of the set of solutions of (11.5.2). Axioms for demand functions can be found in the literature on the theory of revealed preference; see, for instance, Samuelson [1938], Houthakker [1950], Uzawa [1960, 1971], Afriat [1962], Katzner [1970], Hurwicz and Richter [1971], Sonnenschein [1971], Stigum [1973], and Fuchs-Seliger [1977].

11.5.3 **Theorem.** *Let* $(h_1, \ldots, h_n)$ *be any solution of the budget equation (11.5.2). Then there exist functions*

$$g_\nu : \mathbb{R}^{n+1}_{++} \to \mathbb{R}_+ \qquad (\nu = 1, \ldots, n) \tag{11.5.4}$$

satisfying

$$g_1(\mathbf{p}, z) + \cdots + g_n(\mathbf{p}, z) = 1 \qquad \text{for all} \quad (\mathbf{p}, z) \in \mathbb{R}^{n+1}_{++} \tag{11.5.5}$$

such that for all $(\mathbf{p}, z) \in \mathbb{R}^{n+1}_{++}$,

$$h_\nu(\mathbf{p}, z) = g_\nu(\mathbf{p}, z)(z/p_\nu) \qquad (\nu = 1, \ldots, n). \tag{11.5.6}$$

Conversely, every $\mathbf{h}$ *given on* $\mathbb{R}^{n+1}_{++}$ *by (11.5.6) in conjunction with (11.5.5), (11.5.4) is a solution of the "budget equation with restricted domain," that is, a solution of (11.5.2) with* $(\mathbf{p}, z) \in \mathbb{R}^{n+1}_{++}$.

Proof. The second assertion can be proved immediately by inserting (11.5.6) into (11.5.2). Since for $(\mathbf{p}, z) \in \mathbb{R}^{n+1}_{++}$ every function value $h_\nu(\mathbf{p}, z)$ can be written in the form

$$g_\nu(\mathbf{p}, z)(z/p_\nu),$$

the first statement is also valid. ■

It is an obvious consequence of the budget equation (11.5.2) that the demand curves with respect to the νth commodity are bounded from above by hyperbolas that are strictly decreasing functions of the price of the νth commodity. In other words, a demand curve need not necessarily decrease everywhere (it may even increase in certain intervals), but since the budget is bounded, there is always a *tendency* toward decrease of demand when the corresponding price increases.

11.5.7 **Corollary.** *Every component* h_ν *of any given solution* $\mathbf{h}$ *of the budget equation (11.5.2) satisfies the inequality*

$$h_\nu(\mathbf{p}, z) \leqq (z/p_\nu) \qquad \text{for all} \quad p_\nu \in \mathbb{R}_{++}, \qquad (p_1, \ldots, p_{\nu-1}, p_{\nu+1}, \ldots, p_n, z) \in \mathbb{R}^n_+.$$

11.5.8 **Remark.** When there is *no money illusion*, that is, when the demand function $\mathbf{h}$ is homogeneous of degree 0, formulas (11.5.6), (11.5.5) can be written in the form

$$h_\nu(\mathbf{p}, z) = f_\nu(\mathbf{p}/z)(z/p_\nu) \qquad (\nu = 1, \ldots, n)$$

and

$$f_1(\mathbf{p}/z) + \cdots + f_n(\mathbf{p}/z) = 1 \qquad \text{for all} \quad (\mathbf{p}, z) \in \mathbb{R}^{n+1}_{++},$$

respectively, where

$$f_\nu(\mathbf{p}/z) := g_\nu(\mathbf{p}/z, 1) = g_\nu(z(\mathbf{p}/z), z \cdot 1) = g_\nu(\mathbf{p}, z).$$

12

Functional Equations for Set-Valued Functions (Correspondences)

In this chapter we will consider functions that map $\mathbb{R}^n_+$ into the *power set of* $\mathbb{R}^m_+$, that is, the set of all subsets of $\mathbb{R}^m_+$. In contrast to vector-valued functions

$$\mathbf{F} : \mathbb{R}^n_+ \to \mathbb{R}^m_+,$$

we denote set-valued functions by

$$\underline{\mathbf{F}} : \mathbb{R}^n_+ \to \text{power set of } \mathbb{R}^m_+. \tag{12.0.1}$$

For each $\mathbf{x} \in \mathbb{R}^n_+$ the image $\underline{\mathbf{F}}(\mathbf{x})$ is a subset of vectors of $\mathbb{R}^m_+$ which generally consists of more than one element.

In many cases, set-valued functions or *correspondences* of the form (12.0.1) are better tools for analyzing economic situations than scalar-valued or vector-valued functions. Consider, for instance, a household that determines the sets of commodity vectors $\mathbf{u} \in \mathbb{R}^m_+$ it can buy with amounts $z \in \mathbb{R}_+$ of money. We can express this as follows. The household determines its *budget correspondence*

$$\begin{aligned} &\underline{\mathbf{B}} : \mathbb{R}^{m+1}_+ \to \text{power set of } \mathbb{R}^m_+ \\ &(\mathbf{p}, z) \to \underline{\mathbf{B}}(\mathbf{p}, z) = \{\mathbf{u} \mid \mathbf{u}\mathbf{p}' \leqq z,\ \mathbf{p} \in \mathbb{R}^m_+ \text{ the prices of the goods}\}. \end{aligned} \tag{12.0.2}$$

By definition (12.0.2), a budget correspondence satisfies the following functional equations for all $\lambda \in \mathbb{R}_{++}$, $\mathbf{p} \in \mathbb{R}^m_+$, $z \in \mathbb{R}_+$, $z_1 \in \mathbb{R}_+$, $z_2 \in \mathbb{R}_+$:

$$\underline{\mathbf{B}}(\lambda\mathbf{p}, \lambda z) = \underline{\mathbf{B}}(\mathbf{p}, z) \quad \text{(homogeneity of degree zero);} \tag{12.0.3}$$

$$\begin{aligned} \underline{\mathbf{B}}(\mathbf{p}, z_1 + z_2) &= \underline{\mathbf{B}}(\mathbf{p}, z_1) + \underline{\mathbf{B}}(\mathbf{p}, z_2) \quad \text{(additivity with respect to } z) \\ &=: \{\mathbf{u} \mid \mathbf{u} = \mathbf{v} + \mathbf{w},\quad \mathbf{v} \in \underline{\mathbf{B}}(\mathbf{p}, z_1),\quad \mathbf{w} \in \underline{\mathbf{B}}(\mathbf{p}, z_2)\}; \end{aligned} \tag{12.0.4}$$

$$\underline{\mathbf{B}}(\mathbf{p}, \lambda z) = \lambda\underline{\mathbf{B}}(\mathbf{p}, z) =: \{\lambda\mathbf{u} \mid \mathbf{u}\mathbf{p}' \leqq z\} \quad \text{(linear homogeneity with respect to } z) \tag{12.0.5}$$

$$\underline{\mathbf{B}}(\lambda\mathbf{p}, z) = 1/\lambda\ \underline{\mathbf{B}}(\mathbf{p}, z) \quad \text{(homogeneity of degree } -1 \text{ with respect to } \mathbf{p}). \tag{12.0.6}$$

ISBN 0-201-01948-5/01949-3 PBK

Let the household have a preference ordering $\succsim$ on $\mathbb{R}_+^m$ so that for any pair $\mathbf{u}$, $\mathbf{v}$ of commodity vectors at least one of the relations $\mathbf{u} \succsim \mathbf{v}$ ("$\mathbf{u}$ is at least as preferred as $\mathbf{v}$") or $\mathbf{v} \succsim \mathbf{u}$ holds. Then the household's *demand correspondence*

$$\underline{\mathbf{D}}: \mathbb{R}_+^{m+1} \to \text{power set of } \mathbb{R}_+^m$$

is given by

$$\underline{\mathbf{D}}(\mathbf{p}, z) = \{\mathbf{u} \in \underline{\mathbf{B}}(\mathbf{p}, z) \mid \mathbf{u} \succsim \mathbf{v} \text{ for all } \mathbf{v} \in \underline{\mathbf{B}}(\mathbf{p}, z)\}.$$

Obviously, it also satisfies functional equations (12.0.3)–(12.0.6).

This chapter is devoted to functional equations for *production correspondences*. The main reason for this is that, due to the work of Shephard [1970, 1974b], the theory of production correspondences is highly developed.

Intuitively, an *output production correspondence* $\underline{\mathbf{P}}$ assigns to each input vector $\mathbf{x} \in \mathbb{R}_+^n$ the set $\underline{\mathbf{P}}(\mathbf{x})$ of output vectors $\mathbf{u} \in \mathbb{R}_+^m$ that are obtainable with $\mathbf{x}$ per unit time. Furthermore, an *input production correspondence* $\underline{\mathbf{L}}$ is given by

$$\underline{\mathbf{L}}(\mathbf{u}) = \{\mathbf{x} \mid \mathbf{x} \in \mathbb{R}_+^n \text{ yields at least the output vector } \mathbf{u} \in \mathbb{R}_+^m\}.$$

Systems of axioms for production correspondences have been given by Shephard [1970, 1974b]; see 13.3.10–13.3.15. In this chapter, an input production correspondence $\underline{\mathbf{L}}$ is always supposed to satisfy at least the following axiom.

12.0.7 **Axiom.** $\underline{\mathbf{L}}(\mathbf{0}) = \mathbb{R}_+^n$, $\mathbf{0} \notin \underline{\mathbf{L}}(\mathbf{u})$ for $\mathbf{u} \geq \mathbf{0}$.

In Section 12.1, we shall consider *linear* production correspondences, that is, production correspondences that are both additive and linearly homogeneous. A representation theorem will be proved. Sections 12.2–12.5 will deal with homogeneous, quasihomogeneous, semihomogeneous, and ray-homothetic production correspondences. It will be shown that these classes of correspondences yield linear expansion paths and that the graph of the cost function belonging to a homogeneous production correspondence does *not* have the "classic" shape of a cost curve. If both an output production correspondence and the corresponding input production correspondence are ray homothetic, then under rather natural additional assumptions they are semihomogeneous.

12.1 Linear Production Correspondences

An output production correspondence

$$\begin{aligned} &\underline{\mathbf{P}}: \mathbb{R}_+^n \to \text{power set of } \mathbb{R}_+^m, \\ &\mathbf{x} \to \underline{\mathbf{P}}(\mathbf{x}) = \{\mathbf{u} \mid \mathbf{u} \text{ is obtainable with } \mathbf{x}\} \end{aligned} \tag{12.1.1}$$

is called *linearly homogeneous* or *homogeneous of degree* 1 if

$$\underline{\mathbf{P}}(\lambda\mathbf{x}) = \lambda\underline{\mathbf{P}}(\mathbf{x}) \tag{12.1.2}$$

holds for all $(\mathbf{x}, \lambda) \in \mathbb{R}_+^{n+1}$. The right-hand side of functional equation (12.1.2) is defined to be the set

$$\{\lambda\mathbf{u} \mid \mathbf{u} \in \underline{\mathbf{P}}(\mathbf{x})\}.$$

We can express (12.1.2) as follows: The set of output vectors obtainable with the input vector $\lambda\mathbf{x}$ is equal to the set of the vectors $\lambda\mathbf{u}$, where $\mathbf{u}$ is an output vector obtainable with $\mathbf{x}$.

Note that this definition and the following assertions and definitions analogously apply to input production correspondences. Compare the definitions in this section with those in Section 11.1.

An output production correspondence (12.1.1) is called *additive* if it satisfies the functional equation

$$\underline{\mathbf{P}}(\mathbf{x} + \mathbf{y}) = \underline{\mathbf{P}}(\mathbf{x}) + \underline{\mathbf{P}}(\mathbf{y}) \tag{12.1.3}$$

for all $(\mathbf{x}, \mathbf{y}) \in \mathbb{R}_+^{2n}$. Here, the right-hand side is defined to be the set

$$\{\mathbf{u} + \mathbf{v} \mid \mathbf{u} \in \underline{\mathbf{P}}(\mathbf{x}), \quad \mathbf{v} \in \underline{\mathbf{P}}(\mathbf{y})\}.$$

Equation (12.1.3) means that the set of output vectors that can be produced by the input vector $\mathbf{x} + \mathbf{y}$ is equal to the set of output vectors obtainable by applying the input vectors $\mathbf{x}$ and $\mathbf{y}$ separately and adding up.

We call a production correspondence *linear* if it is both additive and linearly homogeneous.

12.1.4 **Theorem.** *Let the linear output production correspondence* $\underline{\mathbf{P}}$ *and the input vectors* $\mathbf{x}_1, \ldots, \mathbf{x}_k$ *be given. If the sets* $\underline{\mathbf{P}}(\mathbf{x}_1), \ldots, \underline{\mathbf{P}}(\mathbf{x}_k)$ *of the output vectors obtainable with* $\mathbf{x}_1, \ldots, \mathbf{x}_k$*, respectively, are known, then for every input vector* $\mathbf{x}^*$ *of the cone*

$$\{\mathbf{x} \mid \mathbf{x} = \lambda_1\mathbf{x}_1 + \cdots + \lambda_k\mathbf{x}_k;\quad \lambda_1 \in \mathbb{R}_+, \ldots, \lambda_k \in \mathbb{R}_+\}, \tag{12.1.5}$$

the set $\underline{\mathbf{P}}(\mathbf{x}^*)$ *can be represented by a suitably chosen linear combination*

$$\mu_1\underline{\mathbf{P}}(\mathbf{x}_1) + \cdots + \mu_k\underline{\mathbf{P}}(\mathbf{x}_k) \qquad (\mu_1 \in \mathbb{R}_+, \ldots, \mu_k \in \mathbb{R}_+)$$

of the sets $\underline{\mathbf{P}}(\mathbf{x}_1), \ldots, \underline{\mathbf{P}}(\mathbf{x}_k)$.

Proof. Let $\mathbf{x}^*$ be a point of the cone (12.1.5). Then there exist nonnegative real numbers $\lambda_1^*, \ldots, \lambda_k^*$ such that

$$\mathbf{x}^* = \lambda_1^*\mathbf{x}_1 + \cdots + \lambda_k^*\mathbf{x}_k.$$

Since $\underline{\mathbf{P}}$ is linear,

$$\begin{aligned}\underline{\mathbf{P}}(\mathbf{x}^*) &= \underline{\mathbf{P}}(\lambda_1^*\mathbf{x}_1 + \cdots + \lambda_k^*\mathbf{x}_k)\\ &= \underline{\mathbf{P}}(\lambda_1^*\mathbf{x}_1) + \cdots + \underline{\mathbf{P}}(\lambda_k^*\mathbf{x}_k) \qquad \text{(by (12.1.3))}\\ &= \lambda_1^*\underline{\mathbf{P}}(\mathbf{x}_1) + \cdots + \lambda_n^*\underline{\mathbf{P}}(\mathbf{x}_k) \qquad \text{(by (12.1.2))},\end{aligned}$$

which proves the theorem. ■

An immediate consequence of Theorem 12.1.4 is

12.1.6 **Corollary.** *In Theorem* 12.1.4, *let* $k = n$ *and*

$$\mathbf{x}_1 = \tau_1\mathbf{e}_1, \ldots, \mathbf{x}_n = \tau_n\mathbf{e}_n \qquad (\tau_1 \in \mathbb{R}_{++}, \ldots, \tau_n \in \mathbb{R}_{++}),$$

where the $\mathbf{e}_\nu$*'s are the unit vectors of* $\mathbb{R}^n$. *Then the set* (12.1.5) *can be replaced by* $\mathbb{R}^n_+$, *that is,* $\underline{\mathbf{P}}$ *can be represented on the whole of* $\mathbb{R}^n_+$ *by suitably choosing linear combinations of* $\underline{\mathbf{P}}(\mathbf{e}_1), \ldots, \underline{\mathbf{P}}(\mathbf{e}_n)$.

12.2 Homogeneous Production Correspondences and Linear Expansion Paths

An output production correspondence

$$\begin{aligned}&\underline{\mathbf{P}} : \mathbb{R}^n_+ \to \text{power set of } \mathbb{R}^m_+,\\ &\mathbf{x} \to \underline{\mathbf{P}}(\mathbf{x}) = \{\mathbf{u} \mid \mathbf{u} \text{ is obtainable with } \mathbf{x}\}\end{aligned} \tag{12.2.1}$$

is called *homogeneous of degree r* ($r \in \mathbb{R}_{++}$) if

$$\underline{\mathbf{P}}(\lambda\mathbf{x}) = \lambda^r\underline{\mathbf{P}}(\mathbf{x}) \qquad (\lambda^r := e^{r \log \lambda} \quad \text{for} \quad \lambda > 0;\ 0^r := 0) \tag{12.2.2}$$

holds for all $(\lambda, \mathbf{x}) \in \mathbb{R}^{n+1}_+$. The right-hand side is defined to be the set

$$\{\lambda^r\mathbf{u} \mid \mathbf{u} \in \underline{\mathbf{P}}(\mathbf{x})\}.$$

We point out here that from (12.2.2) it easily follows that

$$\underline{\mathbf{L}}(\lambda\mathbf{u}) = \lambda^{1/r}\underline{\mathbf{L}}(\mathbf{u}) \tag{12.2.3}$$

whenever the input production correspondence

$$\begin{aligned}&\underline{\mathbf{L}} : \mathbb{R}^m_+ \to \text{power set of } \mathbb{R}^n_+,\\ &\mathbf{u} \to \underline{\mathbf{L}}(\mathbf{u}) = \{\mathbf{x} \mid \mathbf{x} \text{ yields at least } \mathbf{u}\}\end{aligned} \tag{12.2.4}$$

is the *inverse* $\underline{\mathbf{P}}^{-1}$ *of* $\underline{\mathbf{P}}$, defined by $\underline{\mathbf{P}}^{-1}(\mathbf{u}) := \{\mathbf{x} \mid \underline{\mathbf{P}}(\mathbf{x}) \ni \mathbf{u}\}$.

In what follows, let $\varkappa(\mathbf{x})$ be the (variable) *cost of the input* vector $\mathbf{x} \in \mathbb{R}^n_+$ and $\varrho(\mathbf{u})$ the *revenue earned by selling the output vector* $\mathbf{u} \in \mathbb{R}^m_+$. If $\mathbf{q}$ and $\mathbf{p}$ denote the vectors of the prices of the inputs and outputs, respectively, then $\varkappa$ and ϱ can be written as

$$\varkappa(\mathbf{x}) = \mathbf{qx} \quad \text{and} \quad \varrho(\mathbf{u}) = \mathbf{pu}. \tag{12.2.5}$$

If the prices are constant, it easily follows from (12.2.5) that

$$\varkappa(\mu\mathbf{x}_1) \geqq \varkappa(\mu\mathbf{x}_2) \quad \text{for all} \quad \mu \in \mathbb{R}_+, \mathbf{x}_1, \mathbf{x}_2 \text{ with } \varkappa(\mathbf{x}_1) \geqq \varkappa(\mathbf{x}_2) \tag{12.2.6}$$

and

$$\varrho(\nu\mathbf{u}_1) \geqq \varrho(\nu\mathbf{u}_2) \quad \text{for all} \quad \nu \in \mathbb{R}_+, \mathbf{u}_1, \mathbf{u}_2 \text{ with } \varrho(\mathbf{u}_1) \geqq \varrho(\mathbf{u}_2). \tag{12.2.7}$$

In the next theorem, we need only properties (12.2.6) and (12.2.7) of $\varkappa$ and ϱ; that is, the prices may depend on time and quantities, at least to a certain extent.

If the output production correspondence $\underline{\mathbf{P}}$ and, hence, the input production correspondence $\underline{\mathbf{P}}^{-1}$ of a production system (e.g., a firm or a sector of an economy) are given, then the (minimum) cost of producing the output vector $\mathbf{u} \in \mathbb{R}^m_+$ can be calculated:

$$K(\mathbf{u}) = \min\{\varkappa(\mathbf{x}) \mid \mathbf{x} \in \underline{\mathbf{P}}^{-1}(\mathbf{u})\} + \text{fixed cost}. \tag{12.2.8}$$

This can be expressed as follows. Apart from the fixed cost, the (minimum) cost of the output vector $\mathbf{u}$ is the (variable) cost $\varkappa(\mathbf{x})$ of a cheapest input vector $\mathbf{x}$ that yields $\mathbf{u}$.

Such an input vector $\mathbf{x}$ is called a *minimal cost combination for* $\mathbf{u}$ *with respect to* $\underline{\mathbf{P}}$ *and* $\varkappa$. The existence of minimal cost combinations is assured, for example, whenever the function $\varkappa$ is continuous and the set $\underline{\mathbf{P}}^{-1}(\mathbf{u})$ is both closed and bounded from below.[1]

The next theorem (see Eichhorn and Oettli [1968]; Eichhorn [1970, pp. 85ff.]) answers the question how the minimal cost combinations will vary if the output is changed from $\mathbf{u}^*$ to $\lambda\mathbf{u}^*$ with $\lambda \in \mathbb{R}_{++}$.

12.2.9 **Theorem.** *Let* $\underline{\mathbf{P}}$ *be an output production correspondence that is homogeneous of degree* $r(r \in \mathbb{R}_{++})$. *Let the cost* $\varkappa(\mathbf{x})$ *of the input vector* $\mathbf{x}$ *satisfy condition* (12.2.6). *If* $\mathbf{x}^*$ *is a minimal cost combination for* $\mathbf{u}^*$ *with respect to* $\underline{\mathbf{P}}$ *and* $\varkappa$, *then for all* $\lambda \in \mathbb{R}_{++}$, $\lambda^{1/r}\mathbf{x}^*$ *is a minimal cost combination for* $\lambda\mathbf{u}^*$ *with respect to* $\underline{\mathbf{P}}$ *and* $\varkappa$.

Proof. We show first that

$$\lambda\mathbf{u}^* \in \underline{\mathbf{P}}(\lambda^{1/r}\mathbf{x}^*), \tag{12.2.10}$$

that is, $\lambda\mathbf{u}^*$ is obtainable with $\lambda^{1/r}\mathbf{x}^*$.

---

[1] Let $\underline{\mathbf{P}}^{-1}$ satisfy Shephard's [1970, pp. 189–190] system of axioms (see 13.3.18ff.). Then the set $\mathbf{P}^{-1}(\mathbf{u})$ is both closed and bounded from below. Let the vector $\mathbf{q}$ of prices in (12.2.5) be constant. Then the function $\varkappa$ given by (12.2.5) is continuous.

By assumption, $\mathbf{u}^* \in \underline{\mathbf{P}}(\mathbf{x}^*)$. Hence,

$$\lambda\mathbf{u}^* \in \lambda\underline{\mathbf{P}}(\mathbf{x}^*) = (\lambda^{1/r})^r\, \underline{\mathbf{P}}(\mathbf{x}^*) = \underline{\mathbf{P}}(\lambda^{1/r}\mathbf{x}^*) \qquad \text{(by (12.2.2))},$$

and this is (12.2.10).

In order to complete the proof, we have to show that

$$\varkappa(\mathbf{x}) \geqq \varkappa(\lambda^{1/r}\mathbf{x}^*) \qquad \text{for all} \quad \mathbf{x} \in \underline{\mathbf{P}}^{-1}(\lambda\mathbf{u}^*), \tag{12.2.11}$$

that is, every input vector $\mathbf{x}$ that yields at least $\lambda\mathbf{u}^*$ is not cheaper than $\lambda^{1/r}\mathbf{x}^*$. Indeed, multiply $\lambda\mathbf{u}^* \in \underline{\mathbf{P}}(\mathbf{x})$ by λ^{-1} in order to obtain

$$\mathbf{u}^* \in \lambda^{-1}\underline{\mathbf{P}}(\mathbf{x}) = (\lambda^{-1/r})^r\underline{\mathbf{P}}(\mathbf{x}) = \underline{\mathbf{P}}(\lambda^{-1/r}\mathbf{x}) \qquad \text{(by (12.2.2))},$$

that is, $\mathbf{u}^*$ is obtainable with $\lambda^{-1/r}\mathbf{x}$. Since $\mathbf{x}^*$ is assumed to be a minimal cost combination for $\mathbf{u}^*$ with respect to $\underline{\mathbf{P}}$ and $\varkappa$,

$$\varkappa(\lambda^{-1/r}\mathbf{x}) \geqq \varkappa(\mathbf{x}^*).$$

By (12.2.6), this inequality implies (12.2.11). ■

12.2.12 **Remark.** Theorem 12.2.9 shows that for homogeneous $\underline{\mathbf{P}}$ and $\varkappa$ satisfying (12.2.6), the following is true: Given any scalar multiple $\lambda\mathbf{u}^*$ of $u^*(\lambda \in \mathbb{R}_{++})$ there exists a scalar multiple of $\mathbf{x}^*$ such that this multiple of $\mathbf{x}^*$ is a minimal cost combination for $\lambda\mathbf{u}^*$. We will refer to this by saying that a homogeneous output production correspondence $\underline{\mathbf{P}}$ yields *linear input expansion paths.*

According to the next theorem (see Eichhorn and Oettli [1969]; Eichhorn [1970, pp. 85ff.]), such a $\underline{\mathbf{P}}$ also yields linear output expansion paths.

We call an output vector $\mathbf{u}^*$ a *maximal revenue combination for the input vector* $\mathbf{x}^*$ *with respect to* $\underline{\mathbf{P}}$ *and* ϱ if

$$\varrho(\mathbf{u}^*) \geqq \varrho(\mathbf{u}) \qquad \text{for all} \quad \mathbf{u} \in \underline{\mathbf{P}}(\mathbf{x}^*),$$

that is, the revenue made possible by $\mathbf{u}^*$ is greater than or equal to the revenue yielded by any other output vector $\mathbf{u}$ that can be obtained with the given input vector $\mathbf{x}^*$.

12.2.13 **Theorem.** *Let* $\underline{\mathbf{P}}$ *be an output production correspondence that is homogeneous of degree* $r(r \in \mathbb{R}_{++})$. *Let the revenue* $\varrho(\mathbf{u})$ *obtainable with the output vector* $\mathbf{u}$ *satisfy condition* (12.2.7). *If* $\mathbf{u}^*$ *is a maximal revenue combination for the input vector* $\mathbf{x}^*$ *with respect to* $\underline{\mathbf{P}}$ *and* ϱ, *then for all* $\lambda \in \mathbb{R}_{++}$, $\lambda^r\mathbf{u}^*$ *is a maximal revenue combination for* $\lambda\mathbf{x}^*$ *with respect to* $\underline{\mathbf{P}}$ *and* ϱ.

We can prove this theorem analogously to Theorem 12.2.9. We omit the proof since Theorem 12.2.13 is a special case of Theorem 12.5.1.

12.3 Cost Functions in the Case of Homogeneous Production Correspondences

It is interesting to know how the (minimum) cost of producing the output vector $\lambda\mathbf{u}^* \neq 0$, namely

$$K(\lambda\mathbf{u}^*) = \min\{\varkappa(\mathbf{x}) \mid \mathbf{x} \in \underline{\mathbf{P}}^{-1}(\lambda\mathbf{u}^*)\} + \text{fixed cost},$$

will vary with $\lambda \in \mathbb{R}_{++}$. Under the assumptions of Theorem 12.2.9, we have

$$K(\lambda\mathbf{u}^*) = \varkappa(\lambda^{1/r}\mathbf{x}^*) + \text{fixed cost} \qquad (\lambda \in \mathbb{R}_{++})$$

or, if $\varkappa$ is given by (12.2.5) with a constant and positive price vector $\mathbf{q}$,

$$K(\lambda\mathbf{u}^*) = c\lambda^{1/r} + \text{fixed cost} \qquad (c := \mathbf{q}\mathbf{x}^* > 0,^2 \text{ const}). \qquad (12.3.1)$$

Hence, for production systems with homogeneous $\underline{\mathbf{P}}$ and constant prices of the inputs there exist no "classic cost functions," that is, strictly increasing functions which are strictly concave on an interval $[0, a]$ and strictly convex to the right of $a \in \mathbb{R}_{++}$ (see Fig. 12.3.2).

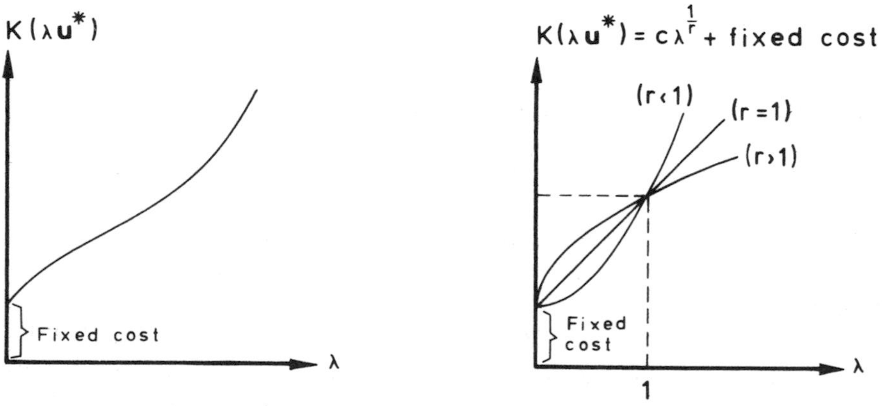

12.3.2 Figure. Graphs of a „classic cost function" and of the cost functions given by (12.3.1) for three different r's.

A more detailed analysis of this topic can be found in Eichhorn [1972a].

---

[2] By assumption, $\mathbf{q} > \mathbf{0}$, and $\mathbf{u}^* \geq \mathbf{0}$, whence, by Shephard's axiom 13.3.10, $\mathbf{x}^* \geq \mathbf{0}$ and $\mathbf{q}\mathbf{x}^* > 0$.

12.4 Generalized Homogeneous Production Correspondences

The following generalization of the notion of a homogeneous production correspondence is due to Färe and Shephard [1975].

An output production correspondence (12.1.1) is called *ray homothetic* if it satisfies a functional equation of the form

$$\underline{\mathbf{P}}(\lambda \mathbf{x}) = \psi(\lambda, \mathbf{x})\, \underline{\mathbf{P}}(\mathbf{x}) \qquad \text{for all} \quad (\lambda, \mathbf{x}) \in \mathbb{R}_{++} \times \mathbb{R}_{+}^{n}, \tag{12.4.1}$$
$$\psi : \mathbb{R}_{++} \times \mathbb{R}_{+}^{n} \to \mathbb{R}_{++}, \quad \psi(1, \mathbf{x}) = \psi(\lambda, \mathbf{0}) = 1 \quad \text{for all} \quad \lambda \in \mathbb{R}_{++}, \mathbf{x} \in \mathbb{R}_{+}^{n}.$$

Compare this with the definition of the ray-homothetic vector-valued functions **H** introduced in Section 11.4. The definition of the ray-homothetic input production correspondences is analogous.

Obviously, every homogeneous output (or input) production correspondence is ray homothetic.

From (12.4.1) it follows that

$$\underline{\mathbf{P}}(\mathbf{x}) = \underline{\mathbf{P}}\left(|\mathbf{x}| \frac{\mathbf{x}}{|\mathbf{x}|}\right) = \psi\left(|\mathbf{x}|, \frac{\mathbf{x}}{|\mathbf{x}|}\right) \underline{\mathbf{P}}\left(\frac{\mathbf{x}}{|\mathbf{x}|}\right) \qquad \text{for all} \quad \mathbf{x} \geq \mathbf{0}. \tag{12.4.2}$$

Let $\lambda \to \psi(\lambda, \mathbf{x})$ be monotonically increasing and let ψ as defined in (12.4.1) not depend on $\mathbf{x}$ when $|\mathbf{x}| = 1$. Then (12.4.2) can be written as

$$\underline{\mathbf{P}}(\mathbf{x}) = f(|\mathbf{x}|)\, \underline{\mathbf{P}}(\mathbf{x}/|\mathbf{x}|), \tag{12.4.3}$$

where $f\colon \mathbb{R}_{++} \to \mathbb{R}_{++}$ is monotonically increasing, $f(1) = 1$, $\mathbf{x} \geq \mathbf{0}$, $f(|\mathbf{x}|) = \psi(|\mathbf{x}|, \mathbf{x}/|\mathbf{x}|)$.

An output (or input) production correspondence that satisfies a functional equation of the form (12.4.3) is called *quasihomogeneous* (see Section 4.7; Eichhorn and Oettli [1968]; Eichhorn [1970, pp. 100–102]). Hence, every quasihomogeneous output (or input) production correspondence is ray homothetic.

Eichhorn [1969, 1970, pp. 104–111; Section 4.7] and Shephard [1974a] have studied semihomogeneous production functions and production correspondences, respectively. An output production correspondence (12.1.1) is called *semihomogeneous* if it satisfies a functional equation of the form

$$\begin{aligned} &\underline{\mathbf{P}}(\lambda \mathbf{x}) = \lambda^{h(\mathbf{x}/|\mathbf{x}|)}\, \underline{\mathbf{P}}(\mathbf{x}), \qquad \text{where} \quad (\lambda, \mathbf{x}) \in \mathbb{R}_{++} \times \mathbb{R}_{+}^{n}, \mathbf{x} \geqq \mathbf{0}, \\ &h : \{\mathbf{y} \mid \mathbf{y} \in \mathbb{R}_{+}^{n}, |\mathbf{y}| = 1\} \to \mathbb{R}_{++}. \end{aligned} \tag{12.4.4}$$

The definition of the semihomogeneous input production correspondences (12.2.4) is analogous.

Since $\lambda^{h(\mathbf{x}/|\mathbf{x}|)}$ in (12.4.4) is a special form of $\psi(\lambda, \mathbf{x})$ in (12.4.1), every semihomogeneous production correspondence is ray homothetic.

12.4.5 **Remark.** As in the proof of Theorem 11.4.18 it can be shown that the following proposition is true: Whenever $\mathbf{x} \in L := \{\mathbf{x} \mid \mathbf{x} \in \mathbb{R}^n_+, \underline{\mathbf{P}}(\mathbf{x}) \neq \{\mathbf{0}\}, \underline{\mathbf{P}}(\mathbf{x}) \neq \emptyset\}$, the function ψ in (12.4.1) can be given in the form

$$\psi(\lambda, \mathbf{x}) = g(\lambda\mathbf{x})/g(\mathbf{x}) \qquad \text{where} \quad g : L \to \mathbb{R}_{++}.$$

12.4.6 **Remark.** The following example shows that there exist ray-homothetic output production correspondences $\underline{\mathbf{P}}$ that are neither homogeneous nor quasihomogeneous nor semihomogeneous: Let $\underline{\mathbf{P}}$ be given by

$$\underline{\mathbf{P}}(\mathbf{x}) = \{\mathbf{u} \mid u_1 = \Phi(\mathbf{x}), \ldots, u_m = \Phi(\mathbf{x})\}$$

where $\Phi \colon \mathbb{R}^n_+ \to \mathbb{R}_+$ is a scalar-valued production function given by

$$\Phi(\mathbf{x}) = x_1^{1/2} + x_2^{1/3} + \cdots + x_n^{1/(n+1)} \; (n \geqq 2).$$

It is obvious that such a $\underline{\mathbf{P}}$ satisfies neither (12.2.2), (12.4.3), nor (12.4.4). But it is ray homothetic:

$$\underline{\mathbf{P}}(\lambda\mathbf{x}) = (\Phi(\lambda\mathbf{x})/\Phi(\mathbf{x}))\, \underline{\mathbf{P}}(\mathbf{x}) \qquad (\Phi(\mathbf{0})/\Phi(\mathbf{0}) := 1).$$

In the next section we shall show that ray-homothetic output (input) production correspondences always yield linear output (input) expansion paths.[3] Since the homogeneous, quasihomogeneous, and semihomogeneous production correspondences are ray homothetic, these classes of production correspondences have this expansion path property, too.

12.5 Ray-Homothetic Production Correspondences and Linear Expansion Paths

The following theorem is due to Färe and Shephard [1977].

12.5.1. *Theorem. Let* $\underline{\mathbf{P}}$ *be a ray-homothetic output production correspondence; that is, let* $\underline{\mathbf{P}}$ *satisfy functional equation (12.4.1). Let the revenue* $\varrho(\mathbf{u})$ *obtainable with the output vector* $\mathbf{u}$ *satisfy condition* (12.2.7). *If* $\mathbf{u}^*$ *is a maximal revenue combination for the input vector* $\mathbf{x}^*$ *with respect to* $\underline{\mathbf{P}}$ *and* ϱ, *then for all* $\lambda \in \mathbb{R}_{++}$, $\psi(\lambda, \mathbf{x}^*)\,\mathbf{u}^*$ *is a maximal revenue combination for* $\lambda\mathbf{x}^*$ *with respect to* $\underline{\mathbf{P}}$ *and* ϱ. *In other words, a ray-homothetic output production correspondence yields linear output expansion paths.*

---

[3] See, in this connection, Remark 12.2.12. Note that a *homogeneous* output production correspondence always yields both linear output *and* input expansion paths; see Theorems 12.2.9 and 12.2.13.

Proof. The relation $\mathbf{u}^* \in \underline{\mathbf{P}}(\mathbf{x}^*)$ is equivalent to the relation

$$\psi(\lambda, \mathbf{x}^*)\, \mathbf{u}^* \in \underline{\mathbf{P}}(\lambda \mathbf{x}^*)$$

because of

$$\underline{\mathbf{P}}(\lambda \mathbf{x}^*) = \psi(\lambda, \mathbf{x}^*)\, \underline{\mathbf{P}}(\mathbf{x}^*).$$

Since $\mathbf{u}^*$ is assumed to be a maximum revenue combination for $\mathbf{x}^*$, we have

$$\varrho(\mathbf{u}) \leqq \varrho(\mathbf{u}^*) \qquad \text{for all} \quad \mathbf{u} \in \underline{\mathbf{P}}(\mathbf{x}^*).$$

Now, let $\mathbf{v}$ be an arbitrary output vector obtainable with $\lambda \mathbf{x}^*$, that is,

$$\mathbf{v} \in \underline{\mathbf{P}}(\lambda \mathbf{x}^*) = \psi(\lambda, \mathbf{x}^*)\, \underline{\mathbf{P}}(\mathbf{x}^*).$$

This is equivalent to

$$\mathbf{v}/\psi(\lambda, \mathbf{x}^*) \in \underline{\mathbf{P}}(\mathbf{x}^*).$$

Hence, by the optimality of $\mathbf{u}^*$,

$$\varrho(\mathbf{v}/\psi(\lambda, \mathbf{x}^*)) \leqq \varrho(\mathbf{u}^*),$$

or, by (12.2.7),

$$\varrho(\mathbf{v}) \leqq \varrho(\psi(\lambda, \mathbf{x}^*)\, \mathbf{u}^*)),$$

which was to be proved. ■

12.5.2 **Remark.** An analogous theorem can be formulated for the ray-homothetic *input* production correspondences $\underline{\mathbf{L}}$. They yield linear *input* expansion paths.

From this remark and Theorem 12.5.1 it follows that for a production system to yield linear output as well as linear input expansion paths it is sufficient that both its output correspondence $\underline{\mathbf{P}}$ and its input correspondence $\underline{\mathbf{L}} = \underline{\mathbf{P}}^{-1}$ be ray homothetic.

12.5.3 **Theorem.** *Let both the output production correspondence* $\underline{\mathbf{P}}$ *and the corresponding input correspondence* $\underline{\mathbf{L}} = \underline{\mathbf{P}}^{-1}$ *be ray homothetic; that is,*

$$\begin{aligned} &\underline{\mathbf{P}}(\lambda \mathbf{x}) = \psi(\lambda, \mathbf{x})\, \underline{\mathbf{P}}(\mathbf{x}) \qquad \textit{for all} \quad (\lambda, \mathbf{x}) \in \mathbb{R}_{++} \times \mathbb{R}^n_+, \\ &\psi: \mathbb{R}_{++} \times \mathbb{R}^n_+ \to \mathbb{R}_{++}, \qquad \psi(1, \mathbf{x}) = 1 \qquad \textit{for all} \quad \mathbf{x} \in \mathbb{R}^n_+, \end{aligned} \tag{12.5.4}$$

and

$$\begin{aligned} &\underline{\mathbf{L}}(\mu \mathbf{u}) = \chi(\mu, \mathbf{u})\, \underline{\mathbf{L}}(\mathbf{u}) \qquad \textit{for all} \quad (\mu, \mathbf{u}) \in \mathbb{R}_{++} \times \mathbb{R}^m_+, \\ &\chi: \mathbb{R}_{++} \times \mathbb{R}^m_+ \to \mathbb{R}_{++}, \qquad \chi(1, \mathbf{u}) = 1 \qquad \textit{for all} \quad \mathbf{u} \in \mathbb{R}^m_+. \end{aligned} \tag{12.5.5}$$

Moreover, let $\lambda \to \psi(\lambda, \mathbf{x})$ *and* $\mu \to \chi(\mu, \mathbf{u})$ *be strictly increasing from* 0 *to* $+\infty$. *Then the assumption of weak disposability*[4] *of both the inputs and the outputs*

[4] $\underline{\mathbf{P}}(\mathbf{x}) \subseteqq \underline{\mathbf{P}}(\lambda \mathbf{x})$ for all $\lambda \in [1, \infty[$, $\mathbf{x} \in \underline{\mathbf{L}}(\nu \mathbf{u})$ implies $\mathbf{x} \in \underline{\mathbf{L}}(\mathbf{u})$ for all $\nu \in [1, \infty[$.

implies the semihomogeneity (12.4.4) of $\underline{\mathbf{P}}$ *and* $\underline{\mathbf{L}}$, *whereas the assumption of free disposability of inputs*[5] *implies the homogeneity (12.2.2) of* $\underline{\mathbf{P}}$ *on* $\mathbb{R}^n_{++}$.

Proof.[6] It is obvious that the following relations are equivalent:

$$\mathbf{x} \in \underline{\mathbf{L}}(\mu\mathbf{u}) = \chi(\mu, \mathbf{u})\, \underline{\mathbf{L}}(\mathbf{u}) \qquad \text{by (12.5.5)}, \tag{12.5.6}$$

$$\mathbf{x}/\chi(\mu, \mathbf{u}) \in \underline{\mathbf{L}}(\mathbf{u}), \tag{12.5.7}$$

$$\mathbf{u} \in \underline{\mathbf{P}}(\mathbf{x}/\chi(\mu, \mathbf{u})) = \psi(1/\chi(\mu, \mathbf{u}), \mathbf{x})\, \underline{\mathbf{P}}(\mathbf{x}) \qquad \text{(by (12.5.4)}, \tag{12.5.8}$$

$$\frac{\mathbf{u}}{\psi(1/\chi(\mu, \mathbf{u}), \mathbf{x})} \in \underline{\mathbf{P}}(\mathbf{x}), \tag{12.5.9}$$

$$\mathbf{x} \in \underline{\mathbf{L}}\left(\frac{\mathbf{u}}{\psi(1/\chi(\mu, \mathbf{u}), x)}\right) = \chi\left(\frac{1}{\psi(1/\chi(\mu, \mathbf{u}), x)}, \mathbf{u}\right) \underline{\mathbf{L}}(\mathbf{u}) \qquad \text{(by (12.5.5))}. \tag{12.5.10}$$

Thus, by (12.5.6) and (12.5.10), for all $\mathbf{u} \in S$, where $S := \{\mathbf{u} \mid \underline{\mathbf{L}}(\mathbf{u}) \neq \emptyset, \underline{\mathbf{L}}(\mathbf{u}) \neq \mathbb{R}^n_+\}$,[7]

$$\chi(\mu, \mathbf{u}) = \chi\left(\frac{1}{\psi(1/\chi(\mu, \mathbf{u}), \mathbf{x})}, \mathbf{u}\right). \tag{12.5.11}$$

Since $\mu \to \chi(\mu, \mathbf{u})$ is assumed to be strictly increasing, identity (12.5.11) implies

$$1/\mu = \psi(1/\chi(\mu, \mathbf{u}), \mathbf{x}). \tag{12.5.12}$$

Since $\lambda \to \psi(\lambda, \mathbf{x})$ has the inverse ψ^{-1}, (12.5.12) can be written in the form

$$\psi^{-1}(1/\mu, \mathbf{x})\, \chi(\mu, \mathbf{u}) = 1. \tag{12.5.13}$$

From the assumption of weak disposability of outputs, that is,

$$\underline{\mathbf{L}}(\nu\mathbf{u}) \subseteq \underline{\mathbf{L}}(\mathbf{u}) \qquad \text{for} \quad \nu \in [1, +\infty[,$$

or equivalently, from

$$\underline{\mathbf{L}}(\mathbf{u}) \subseteq \underline{\mathbf{L}}(\sigma\mathbf{u}) \qquad \text{for} \quad \sigma \in\,]0, 1],$$

it follows that

$$\mathbf{x} \in \underline{\mathbf{L}}(\mu\mathbf{u}) \subseteq \underline{\mathbf{L}}(\mu\sigma\mathbf{u}) \qquad \text{for} \quad \sigma \in\,]0, 1].$$

We now repeat the arguments from (12.5.6) on and start with $\mathbf{x} \in \underline{\mathbf{L}}(\mu \cdot \sigma\mathbf{u})$ instead of $\mathbf{x} \in \underline{\mathbf{L}}(\mu\mathbf{u})$. Thus we obtain, analogously to (12.5.13),

$$\psi^{-1}(1/\mu, \mathbf{x})\, \chi(\mu, \sigma\mathbf{u}) = 1 \qquad (\sigma \in\,]0, 1]). \tag{12.5.14}$$

---

[5] $\mathbf{x} \leqq \mathbf{x}^*$ implies $\underline{\mathbf{P}}(\mathbf{x}) \subseteq \underline{\mathbf{P}}(\mathbf{x}^*)$.

[6] I am indebted to Rolf Färe and Ronald W. Shephard for the idea of this proof.

[7] Note that there exists no output vector $\mathbf{u}$ such that $\underline{\mathbf{L}}(\mathbf{u}) = \{\mathbf{0}\}$; see Shephard's axiom 13.3.18. Furthermore, we have $\mathbf{0} \notin S$ by Shephard's axiom 13.3.18.

Equations (12.5.13) and (12.5.14) imply

$$\chi(\mu, \sigma\mathbf{u}) = \chi(\mu, \mathbf{u}). \tag{12.5.15}$$

Also from (12.5.5) by taking $\underline{\mathbf{L}}(\mu\sigma\cdot\mathbf{u})$, we get the following functional equation for all $\mathbf{u} \in S$:

$$\chi(\mu\sigma, \mathbf{u}) = \chi(\mu, \sigma\mathbf{u})\, \chi(\sigma, \mathbf{u}). \tag{12.5.16}$$

From (12.5.15) and (12.5.16) we obtain

$$\chi(\mu\sigma, \mathbf{u}) = \chi(\mu, \mathbf{u})\, \chi(\sigma, \mathbf{u}). \tag{12.5.17}$$

For any given $\mathbf{u}$ this functional equation is defined only for (μ, σ) on the restricted domain $\mathbb{R}_{++} \times\,]0, 1]$. Application of Theorem 2.6.3 yields

$$\chi(\mu, \mathbf{u}) = \mu^{g(\mathbf{u}/|\mathbf{u}|)} \qquad (g: \{\mathbf{v} \mid \mathbf{v} \in \mathbb{R}^m_+, |\mathbf{v}| = 1\} \to \mathbb{R}_{++}) \tag{12.5.18}$$

as the general strictly increasing solution of (12.5.17), (12.5.15). Note that $\mathbf{u} \in S$, whence $\mathbf{u} \neq \mathbf{0}$ by Shephard's axiom 12.0.7.

By applying similar arguments to $\underline{\mathbf{P}}$ we obtain

$$\psi(\lambda, \mathbf{x}) = \lambda^{h(\mathbf{x}/|\mathbf{x}|)} \qquad (h: \{\mathbf{y} \mid \mathbf{y} \in \mathbb{R}^n_+, |\mathbf{y}| = 1\} \to \mathbb{R}_{++}) \tag{12.5.19}$$

for all $\mathbf{x} \in T$ where $T := \{\mathbf{x} \mid \underline{\mathbf{P}}(\mathbf{x}) \neq \{\mathbf{0}\}\}$.

Checking back, we find that χ and ψ given by (12.5.18) and (12.5.19) satisfy Eq. (12.5.14) with the reciprocal relationship

$$h(\mathbf{x}/|\mathbf{x}|)\, g(\mathbf{u}/|\mathbf{u}|) = 1 \tag{12.5.20}$$

for all pairs $(\mathbf{x}, \mathbf{u})$ where $\mathbf{x} \in T$ and $\mathbf{u} \in S$, $\mathbf{u} \in \underline{\mathbf{P}}(\mathbf{x})$.

Thus we have proved the first assertion of Theorem 12.5.3 for all $\mathbf{u} \in S$, $\mathbf{x} \in T$. Whenever $\mathbf{u} \notin S$ or $\mathbf{x} \notin T$, that is, $\mathbf{u}$ satisfies $\underline{\mathbf{L}}(\mathbf{u}) = \emptyset$ or $\underline{\mathbf{L}}(\mathbf{u}) = \mathbb{R}^n_+$, or $\mathbf{x}$ satisfies $\underline{\mathbf{P}}(\mathbf{x}) = \{\mathbf{0}\}$, then Eqs. (12.5.4) and (12.5.5) imply $\underline{\mathbf{P}}(\lambda\mathbf{x}) = \{\mathbf{0}\}$ for all $\lambda \in \mathbb{R}_{++}$ and $\underline{\mathbf{L}}(\mu\mathbf{u}) = \emptyset$ or $\underline{\mathbf{L}}(\mu\mathbf{u}) = \mathbb{R}^n_+$ for all $\mu \in \mathbb{R}_{++}$, respectively. These are properties of semihomogeneous correspondences.

Since $\mathbf{x}$ and $\mathbf{u}$ depend on each other, Eq. (12.5.20) does *not* imply

$$\mathbf{h}(\mathbf{x}/|\mathbf{x}|) = r, \qquad g(\mathbf{u}/|\mathbf{u}|) = 1/r \quad (r \in \mathbb{R}_{++}, \text{const}),$$

that is, the homogeneity of $\underline{\mathbf{P}}$ and $\underline{\mathbf{L}}$.

But with the aid of the assumption of free disposability of inputs, that is,

$$\underline{\mathbf{P}}(\mathbf{x}) \subseteq \underline{\mathbf{P}}(\mathbf{x}^*) \qquad \text{whenever} \quad \mathbf{x}^* \geqq \mathbf{x},$$

the homogeneity of $\underline{\mathbf{P}}$ on $\mathbb{R}^n_+$ can be derived from the assumptions of Theorem 12.5.3.

It follows from (12.5.12) that ψ does not depend on $\mathbf{x} \in \underline{\mathbf{L}}(\mathbf{u})$, where $\mathbf{u} \in S$. Thus by Theorem 2.6.3, for all $\mathbf{x} \in \underline{\mathbf{L}}(\mathbf{u})$ where $\mathbf{u} \in S$,

$$\psi(\lambda, \mathbf{x}) = \lambda^r \qquad (r \in \mathbb{R}_{++}). \tag{12.5.21}$$

Moreover, from:

(a) $\mathbf{u} \in S$ implies $\mu\mathbf{u} \in S$ for all $\mu \in \mathbb{R}_{++}$ (by (12.5.5));

(b) $\mu \to 0$ implies $\chi(\mu, \mathbf{u}) \to 0$ for all $\mathbf{u} \in \mathbb{R}_+^m$ (by the second assumption of Theorem (12.5.3);

(c) $\mathbf{x} \in \underline{\mathbf{L}}(\mathbf{u})$ implies $\chi(\mu, \mathbf{u})\,\mathbf{x} \in \underline{\mathbf{L}}\,(\mu\,\mathbf{u})$ for all $\mu \in \mathbb{R}_{++}$ (by (12.5.5));

(d) $\mathbf{x} \in \underline{\mathbf{L}}(\mathbf{u})$ implies $\mathbf{x}^* \in \underline{\mathbf{L}}(\mathbf{u})$ for all $\mathbf{x}^* \geqq \mathbf{x}$ (by free disposability of inputs);

it follows that (12.5.21) holds for *every* $\mathbf{x} \in \mathbb{R}^n_{++}$; that is, $\underline{\mathbf{P}}$ is homogeneous of degree $r (r \in \mathbb{R}_{++})$ on $\mathbb{R}^n_{++}$. ■

12.5.22 **Corollary.** *The second assertion of Theorem 12.5.3 remains true whenever "ray homothetic" is replaced by "quasihomogeneous" or "semi-homogeneous."*

Proof. As was shown in Section 12.4, quasihomogeneous as well as semi-homogeneous production correspondences are ray homothetic. ■

12.5.23 **Remark.** There exist various other conditions under which semi-homogeneity also implies homogeneity; see Shephard [1974a] for production correspondences and Goldman and Shephard [1972] or Section 4.7 for production functions.

12.5.24 **Remark.** Färe and Shephard [1977] have shown that for a wide class of production correspondences ray homotheticity is not only sufficient for the existence of linear expansion paths (see Theorem 12.5.1) but also necessary.

13

Notation and Definitions

13.1 Symbols

13.1.1 **Sets.** We denote sets by capital italic letters. Let A and B be two sets. We mean by

$A \subseteqq B$	or	$B \supseteqq A$	that A is a subset of B;
$A \subset B$	or	$B \supset A$	that A is a true subset of B;
$A = B$	or	$B = A$	that $A \subseteqq B$ and $B \subseteqq A$;
$A := B$	or	$B =: A$	that A is defined by B;
$a \in A$	or	$A \ni a$	that a is an element of A.

We denote by

$A \backslash B$ the set of all elements of A that do not belong to B;

$A \cap B$ the intersection of A and B;

$\bigcap_{\nu=1}^{\infty} A_\nu$ the intersection of the sets $A_1, A_2, A_3, \ldots$;

$A \cup B$ the union of A and B;

$\bigcup_{\nu=1}^{\infty} A_\nu$ the union of the sets $A_1, A_2, A_3, \ldots$.

By

$$\{a \mid a \text{ satisfies conditions } C_1, C_2, \ldots, C_k\}$$

we mean the set of all a that satisfy the conditions $C_1, C_2, \ldots, C_k$ simultaneously. The following sets occur very often in this book:

ISBN 0–201–01948–5/01949–3 PBK

$\mathbb{R}$	set of real numbers;
$\mathbb{R}_+$	set of nonnegative real numbers;
$\mathbb{R}_{++}$	set of positive real numbers;
$\mathbb{R}_-$	set of nonpositive real numbers;
$\mathbb{R}_{--}$	set of negative real numbers;
$\emptyset$	empty set.

Let $S_1, S_2, \ldots, S_n$ be arbitrary nonempty sets. Then

$$S_1 \times S_2 \times \cdots \times S_n$$

is the Cartesian product of $S_1, S_2, \ldots, S_n$. When $S_1 = S_2 = \cdots = S_n =: S$ we write

$$S^n: = S \times S \times \cdots \times S.$$

Let a and b be two real numbers. We write

$$\begin{array}{llll} a = b & \text{or} & b = a & \text{if } a \text{ is equal to } b; \\ a < b & \text{or} & b > a & \text{if } a \text{ is smaller than } b; \\ a \leqq b & \text{or} & b \geqq a & \text{if } a \text{ is smaller than or equal to } b. \end{array}$$

Let $\sim$ be any of the symbols $=, <, >, \leqq, \geqq, \subseteqq, \supseteqq, \subset, \supset, \in, \ni$. Then $\not\sim$ means that $\sim$ does not hold.

Now, assume $a < b$. The following symbols denote intervals:

$$[a, b] : = \{x \mid x \in \mathbb{R}, a \leqq x \leqq b\}; \qquad [a, b[: = \{x \mid x \in \mathbb{R}, a \leqq c < b\};$$

$$]a, b] : = \{x \mid x \in \mathbb{R}, a < x \leqq b\}; \qquad]a, b[: = \{x \mid x \in \mathbb{R}, a < x < b\};$$

$$[a, \infty[: = \{x \mid x \in \mathbb{R}, x \geqq a\}; \qquad]a, \infty[: = \{x \mid x \in \mathbb{R}, x > a\}.$$

If $a_1, a_2, \ldots, a_n$ are real numbers,

$$\sum_{\nu=1}^{n} a_\nu \quad \text{means} \quad a_1 + a_2 + \cdots + a_n.$$

13.1.2 **Vectors, Matrices.** Vectors are denoted by lowercase boldface letters, matrices by capital boldface letters. If $\mathbf{a}$ is a row (column) vector, then $\mathbf{a}'$ is a column (row) vector. Let $\mathbf{A}$ be a matrix. Then $\mathbf{A}'$ is the transpose of $\mathbf{A}$. If the inverse of $\mathbf{A}$, exists (briefly; $\exists$) it is denoted by $\mathbf{A}^{-1}$. Let

$$\mathbf{a} = (a_1, a_2, \ldots, a_n), \qquad \mathbf{b} = (b_1, b_2, \ldots, b_n)$$

be vectors of $\mathbb{R}^n$. Then

$$\begin{array}{lllll} \mathbf{a} = \mathbf{b} & \text{or} & \mathbf{b} = \mathbf{a} & \text{means} & a_1 = b_1, \ldots, a_n = b_n; \\ \mathbf{a} \leqq \mathbf{b} & \text{or} & \mathbf{b} \geqq \mathbf{a} & \text{means} & a_1 \leqq b_1, \ldots, a_n \leqq b_n; \\ \mathbf{a} \leq \mathbf{b} & \text{or} & \mathbf{b} \geq \mathbf{a} & \text{means} & a_1 \leqq b_1, \ldots, a_n \leqq b_n, \mathbf{a} \neq \mathbf{b}; \\ \mathbf{a} < \mathbf{b} & \text{or} & \mathbf{b} > \mathbf{a} & \text{means} & a_1 < b_1, \ldots, a_n < b_n. \end{array}$$

The *Euclidean length* of $\mathbf{a}$ is

$$|\mathbf{a}| := (a_1^2 + a_2^2 + \cdots + a_n^2)^{1/2}.$$

In Chapter 11, we denote by $\underline{\mathbf{b}}$, $\underline{\boldsymbol{\beta}}$, $\underline{\mathbf{p}}$, $\underline{\mathbf{w}}$ vectors whose components are vectors and by $\underline{\mathbf{R}}$, $\underline{\mathbf{S}}$, $\underline{\mathbf{T}}$, $\underline{\mathbf{T}}^{-1}$ *hypermatrices* (i.e., matrices whose elements are matrices).

13.1.3 **Functions.** Let A and B be sets and F a (unique) mapping from A into B or onto B, that is, a function with domain A and range B. Then we write

$$F: A \to B.$$

If $a \in A$ is mapped onto $b \in B$, then we denote b by $F(a)$ and write

$$a \to F(a).$$

If B is $\mathbb{R}^n$ or the *power set of* $\mathbb{R}^n$ (i.e., the set of all subsets of $\mathbb{R}^n$), then we write $\mathbf{F}$ or $\underline{\mathbf{F}}$, respectively. Let $A = \mathbb{R}^m$. By

$$a_\mu \to F(\mathbf{a}) \qquad (\mu \in \{1, \ldots, m\},\ \mathbf{a} = (a_1, \ldots, a_m))$$

we mean the mapping that assigns to each $a_\mu \in \mathbb{R}$

$$F(a_1, \ldots, a_{\mu-1}, a_\mu, a_{\mu+1}, \ldots, a_m) \in B,$$

where $(a_1, \ldots, a_{\mu-1}, a_{\mu+1}, \ldots, a_m)$ is fixed.

Let F: $\mathbb{R} \to \mathbb{R}$ be given. Then $F(x) \to r$ for $x \to s$ means that $F(x)$ tends to r when x tends to s. If ∞ appears in place of r or s, then read "tends to infinity" (which means that there does not exist any real number as an upper bound).

Assume that the inverse F^{-1} of F exists. If F maps $a \in A$ on $b \in B$, then we denote a, which is the image of b under F^{-1}, by $F^{-1}(b)$. Let the function $G: C \to \mathbb{R}$ map $c \in C$ on $d = G(c) \in \mathbb{R}$, where $G(c) \neq 0$. Sometimes we denote $1/G(c)$ by $G(c)^{-1}$, which has to be distinguished from $G^{-1}(c)$.

Let the functions

$$F: A \to B, \qquad G: C \to D$$

be given. By $F = G$ or $G = F$ we mean that F and G are ***equal***, that is,

$$A = C,\ B = D,\quad F(a) = G(a) \qquad \text{for all} \quad a \in A.$$

Instead of "$F(a) = c$ for all $a \in A$" we write briefly $F(a) \equiv c$. Thus, $F(a) \not\equiv c$ means that "$F(a) = c$ for all $a \in A$" does not hold.

Let the functions

$$F: A \to B, \qquad G: C \to D$$

satisfy $B \subseteq C$. Then a mapping $H: A \to D$ is defined by

$$a \to H(a) := G(F(a)) \qquad \text{for all} \quad a \in A,$$

and we write $H = G \circ F$.

13.2 Mathematics

Sets. The sets

$$\{1, 2, 3, \ldots\}, \tag{13.2.1}$$

$$\{0, 1, -1, 2, -2, 3, -3, \ldots\}, \tag{13.2.2}$$

and

$$\{x \mid x \text{ is } 0 \text{ or a fraction of two integers} \neq 0\} \tag{13.2.3}$$

are the sets of all *positive integers (natural numbers)*, *integers*, and *rational numbers*, respectively.

Each rational number can be written as a repeating or terminating decimal. Each repeating or terminating decimal is a rational number. The nonrepeating, nonterminating decimals, such as

$$\sqrt{2} = 1{,}4142\ldots, \qquad \pi = 3{,}1415\ldots,$$

form the set of *irrational numbers*.

The set

$$\begin{aligned} \mathbb{R} := &\{x \mid x \text{ is a decimal}\} \\ = &\{x \mid x \text{ is a rational or an irrational number}\} \end{aligned} \tag{13.2.4}$$

is called the *set of real numbers*.

13.2.5 Let S be a set of real numbers. It is called

(1) *bounded from below* if there exists $a \in \mathbb{R}$ such that $x \geqq a$ for all $x \in S$,
(2) *bounded from above* if there exists $b \in \mathbb{R}$ such that $x \leqq b$ for all $x \in S$,
(3) *bounded* if there exists $a \in \mathbb{R}$, $b \in \mathbb{R}$ with $a < b$ such that $x \in [a, b]$ for all $x \in S$.

The real numbers a and b are called *lower* und *upper bounds*, respectively.

13.2.6 Let $S_1, S_2, \ldots, S_n$ be arbitrary nonempty sets. The *Cartesian product*

$$S_1 \times S_2 \times \cdots \times S_n$$

of $S_1, S_2, \ldots, S_n$ is the set of all ordered n-tuples or vectors

$$(s_1, s_2, \ldots, s_n) \qquad \text{where} \quad s_1 \in S_1, s_2 \in S_2, \ldots, s_n \in S_n.$$

We write

$$S^n := S \times S \times \cdots \times S$$

when there are n identical factors on the right-hand side.

13.2.7 A set S is said to be *ordered* if there is a relation $\precsim$ for its elements $s, t, u, \ldots$ satisfying some of the following axioms.

$$s \precsim t \text{ and } t \precsim s \text{ imply } s = t \text{ (antisymmetry)} \tag{13.2.8}$$

$$s \precsim t \text{ and } t \precsim u \text{ imply } s \precsim u \text{ (transitivity)} \tag{13.2.9}$$

$$\text{For any } s \in S,\ t \in S \text{ either } s \precsim t \text{ or } t \precsim s. \tag{13.2.10}$$

13.2.11 In particular, axioms (13.2.8) and (13.2.9) are said to define a *partial order*, whereas axioms (13.2.8)–(13.2.10) are said to determine a *total* or *full order*. Note that the relation $\leqq$ determines a total order for real numbers, but that it determines only a partial order for real vectors (cf. Section 13.1.2).

13.2.12 The sets R of the rational numbers and $\mathbb{R}$ of the real numbers have *Archimedean order* with respect to $\leqq$; that is, for every r of R or $\mathbb{R}$ there exists a natural number n such that $n > r$.

A set is called a *space* if there is defined a distance between any two of its elements.

Spaces. In this book we are interested in sets of ordered n-tuples of real numbers, that is, in the set $\mathbb{R}^n$ and in subsets of $\mathbb{R}^n$. These sets become *spaces* by defining a distance between any two elements (points)

$$\mathbf{x} = (x_1, x_2, \ldots, x_n) \quad \text{and} \quad \mathbf{y} = (y_1, y_2, \ldots, y_n)$$

of $\mathbb{R}^n$. We use here the *Euclidean distance* defined by

$$|\mathbf{y} - \mathbf{x}| := [(y_1 - x_1)^2 + (y_2 - x_2)^2 + \cdots + (y_n - x_n)^2]^{1/2} \tag{13.2.13}$$

that is, the length of $(\mathbf{y} - \mathbf{x}) \in \mathbb{R}^n$.

The set

$$N_\varepsilon(\mathbf{x}) := \{\mathbf{y} \mid \mathbf{y} \in \mathbb{R}^n, |\mathbf{y} - \mathbf{x}| < \varepsilon, \varepsilon \in \mathbb{R}_{++}\} \tag{13.2.14}$$

is called an *ε-neighborhood of* $\mathbf{x}$. It is an example of an open set.

13.2.15 A set $S \subseteqq \mathbb{R}^n$ is *open* if for any $\mathbf{x} \in S$ there exists $\varepsilon \in \mathbb{R}_{++}$ such that $N_\varepsilon(\mathbf{x}) \subseteqq S$.

13.2.16 Let R be the set of all rational numbers. We can show that the set R^n is *dense* in $\mathbb{R}^n$; that is, *every* ε-neighborhood of any $\mathbf{x} \in \mathbb{R}^n$ contains points $\mathbf{y} \in R^n, \mathbf{y} \neq \mathbf{x}$.

13.2.17 A set $S \subset \mathbb{R}^n$ is *bounded* if there exists $\varepsilon \in \mathbb{R}_{++}$ such that $S \subset N_\varepsilon(\mathbf{0})$.

13.2.18 A point $\mathbf{x} \in \mathbb{R}^n$ is said to be an *accumulation* or *limit point* of a set $S \subseteqq \mathbb{R}^n$ if every ε-neighborhood of $\mathbf{x}$ contains some point of S other than $\mathbf{x}$.

13.2.19 A set $S \subseteqq \mathbb{R}^n$ is called *closed* if it contains its accumulation points.

13.2.20 A set $S \subseteq \mathbb{R}^n$ is said to be *connected* if any points $\mathbf{x} \in S$, $\mathbf{y} \in S$ can be joined by a polygonal line lying entirely in S. A polygonal line is obtained by joining a finite number of straight line segments end to end. An open and connected set $S \subseteq \mathbb{R}^n$ is called a *domain*.

Groups. For any two vectors

$$\mathbf{x} = (x_1, x_2, \ldots, x_n) \in \mathbb{R}^n, \qquad \mathbf{y} = (y_1, y_2, \ldots, y_n) \in \mathbb{R}^n$$

their *sum* is defined to be

$$\mathbf{x} + \mathbf{y} := (x_1 + y_1, x_2 + y_2, \ldots, x_n + y_n) \tag{13.2.21}$$

where $x_\nu + y_\nu$ is the ordinary sum of the real numbers x_ν and y_ν ($\nu = 1, 2, \ldots, n$). Note that $(\mathbf{x} + \mathbf{y}) \in \mathbb{R}^n$. From definition (13.2.21) it follows that vector addition is *commutative*, that is,

$$\mathbf{x} + \mathbf{y} = \mathbf{y} + \mathbf{x}; \tag{13.2.22}$$

and *associative*, that is,

$$\mathbf{x} + (\mathbf{y} + \mathbf{z}) = (\mathbf{x} + \mathbf{y}) + \mathbf{z} \qquad (\mathbf{z} \in \mathbb{R}^n); \tag{13.2.23}$$

and that there exists a *neutral element* $\mathbf{0} \in \mathbb{R}^n$ such that

$$\mathbf{x} + \mathbf{0} = \mathbf{0} + \mathbf{x} = \mathbf{x} \qquad \text{for all} \quad \mathbf{x} \in \mathbb{R}^n, \tag{13.2.24}$$

namely $\mathbf{0} := (0, 0, \ldots, 0)$. Further, for every $\mathbf{x} \in \mathbb{R}^n$ there exists a unique *inverse element* with respect to vector addition, $\mathbf{x}^{-1}$ say, such that

$$\mathbf{x} + \mathbf{x}^{-1} = \mathbf{x}^{-1} + \mathbf{x} = \mathbf{0}, \tag{13.2.25}$$

namely

$$\mathbf{x}^{-1} := (-x_1, -x_2, \ldots, -x_n) =: -\mathbf{x}.$$

Properties (13.2.22)–(13.2.25) say that the set $\mathbb{R}^n$ is an Abelian or commutative group with respect to vector addition (13.2.21).

13.2.26 An arbitrary set S with elements $\mathbf{x}, \mathbf{y}, \mathbf{z}, \ldots$ and a composition $+$ which assigns to each pair $\mathbf{x}, \mathbf{y}$, of S exactly one element of S, namely $\mathbf{x} + \mathbf{y}$, is called a *group* if axioms (13.2.23)–(13.2.25) are satisfied. It is said to be an *Abelian* or *commutative group* if, in addition, (13.2.22) is valid for every pair $\mathbf{x}, \mathbf{y}$ of S.

13.2.27 An arbitrary set S with elements $\mathbf{x}, \mathbf{y}, \mathbf{z}, \ldots$ and a composition $+$ satisfying (13.2.23) is said to be a *semigroup*.

Vector spaces. In this book we are interested in the real *vector space* or real *linear space* that is formed by $\mathbb{R}^n$ in conjunction with distance (13.2.13) and with both

(1) vector addition (13.2.21) (implying that we have a commutative group with respect to vector addition), and
(2) scalar multiplication.

Scalar multiplication is an operation that assigns to each pair of a real number r and a vector $\mathbf{x} = (x_1, x_2, \ldots, x_n) \in \mathbb{R}^n$ the vector

$$r\mathbf{x} := (rx_1, rx_2, \ldots, rx_n) \qquad (13.2.28)$$

of $\mathbb{R}^n$, where rx_ν is the ordinary product of the real numbers r and x_ν ($\nu = 1, 2, \ldots, n$). Note that scalar multiplication is *distributive:*

$$r(\mathbf{x} + \mathbf{y}) = r\mathbf{x} + r\mathbf{y}, \qquad (r + s)\mathbf{x} = r\mathbf{x} + s\mathbf{y} \qquad (13.2.29)$$
$$(r \in \mathbb{R}, \mathbf{x} \in \mathbb{R}^n, \mathbf{y} \in \mathbb{R}^n, s \in \mathbb{R});$$

and *associative:*

$$(rs)\mathbf{x} = r(s\mathbf{x}) \qquad (r \in \mathbb{R}, s \in \mathbb{R}, \mathbf{x} \in \mathbb{R}^n). \qquad (13.2.30)$$

13.2.31 Let $\mathbf{a}_1, \mathbf{a}_2, \ldots, \mathbf{a}_m$ be m vectors of $\mathbb{R}^n$. They are called *linearly independent* if the so-called *linear combination*

$$\lambda_1\mathbf{a}_1 + \lambda_2\mathbf{a}_2 + \cdots + \lambda_m\mathbf{a}_m \qquad (\lambda_1, \lambda_2, \ldots, \lambda_m \text{ real numbers}) \quad (13.2.32)$$

is always different from $\mathbf{0} = (0, 0, \ldots, 0)$ except for $\lambda_1 = \lambda_2 = \cdots = \lambda_m = 0$. Otherwise they are said to be *linearly dependent.*

13.2.33 A subset S of $\mathbb{R}^n$ is said to be *convex* if

$$(1 - \lambda)\mathbf{x} + \lambda\mathbf{y} \in S \qquad \text{whenever} \quad \mathbf{x} \in S, \mathbf{y} \in S, \text{ and } \lambda \in]0, 1[.$$

Functions. Let A and B be sets. A mapping F of A into B that maps each $a \in A$ onto one and only one $b \in B$ is calleda *function from A into B* (or a *function with domain A and range B*). This is usually written $F: A \to B$. $F(a) \in B$, that is, the *value of F at* $a \in A$, is called the *image* (or *image point*) *of the element (point)* $a \in A$ *under F*. If *every* point $b \in B$ is an image under F, then F is said to be a function from A *onto* B.

13.2.34 If the function F represents a *one-to-one mapping* (i.e., if the function is such that any two different values of A will always yield two different values of B), then the function F will have an *inverse function*

$$F^{-1}: B^* \to A \qquad \text{where} \quad B^* \subseteq B.$$

If the one-to-one mapping is *onto*, then $B^* = B$.

13.2.35 Two groups G and $\dot{G}$, with compositions $+$ and $\dot{+}$, respectively, are called *isomorphic* if there exists a one-to-one mapping F from G onto $\dot{G}$

such that for any two elements a and b of G

$$F(a + b) = F(a) \dot{+} F(b)$$

is always satisfied.

In the following we consider real-valued functions F of n real variables, that is,

$$F\colon D \to \mathbb{R}, \qquad \text{where} \quad D \subseteqq \mathbb{R}^n. \tag{13.2.36}$$

13.2.37 Functions $F\colon D \to \mathbb{R}_{++}$ or $F\colon D \to \mathbb{R}_{+}$ are called *positive-valued* or *nonnegative-valued*, respectively. They are bounded from below.

13.2.38 A function (13.2.36) is *bounded from below* if there exists a real number r satisfying

$$r \leqq F(\mathbf{x}) \qquad \text{for all} \quad \mathbf{x} \in D.$$

The number r is then called a *lower bound* of the function (values of) F. If an *upper bound* of F exists, that is a real number s satisfying

$$s \geqq F(\mathbf{x}) \qquad \text{for all} \quad \mathbf{x} \in D,$$

then F is said to be *bounded from above*. A function (13.2.36) having both an upper and a lower bound is called *bounded*.

13.2.39 A function (13.2.36) is said to be *strictly increasing* if

$$F(\mathbf{x}) < F(\mathbf{y}) \qquad \text{whenever} \quad \mathbf{x} \lneqq \mathbf{y}\ (\mathbf{x} \in D,\ \mathbf{y} \in D).$$

It is called *increasing* (or *nondecreasing*) if we have $\leqq$ instead of $<$. The definitions of "*strictly decreasing*" and "*decreasing*" (or "*nonincreasing*") are analogous. A *monotonic* function is a function which is either nondecreasing or nonincreasing.

13.2.40 A function (13.2.36) with convex domain $D \subseteqq \mathbb{R}^n$ is said to be *convex* if

$$F((1 - \lambda)\mathbf{x} + \lambda\mathbf{y}) \leqq (1-\lambda)\, F(\mathbf{x}) + \lambda\, F(\mathbf{y}) \quad \text{whenever} \quad \mathbf{x} \in D,\ \mathbf{y} \in D,\ \lambda \in\,]0, 1[.$$

It is called *strictly convex (concave, strictly concave)* if we have $<$ ($\geqq$, $>$) instead of $\leqq$ whenever $\mathbf{x} \neq \mathbf{y}$.

13.2.41 In what follows, let the domain D of the function (13.2.36) be an open and connected set of $\mathbb{R}^n$. The function 13.2.36 is said to have a *relative maximum at the point* $\mathbf{x}_0 \in D$ if there exists an ε-neighborhood

$$N_\varepsilon(\mathbf{x}_0) := \{\mathbf{x} \mid |\mathbf{x} - \mathbf{x}_0| < \varepsilon,\ \mathbf{x} \in D,\ \varepsilon \in \mathbb{R}_{++}\} \subset D$$

such that

$$F(\mathbf{x}) \leqq F(\mathbf{x}_0) \qquad \text{for all} \quad \mathbf{x} \in N_\varepsilon(\mathbf{x}_0).$$

A *relative minimum* is defined similarly.

13.2.42 Let the function (13.2.36) have *partial derivatives at the point* $\mathbf{x}_0$, i.e., let the limits

$$\lim_{\lambda \to 0} \frac{(F(\mathbf{x}_0 + \lambda \mathbf{e}_\nu) - F(\mathbf{x}_0)}{\lambda}$$

exist for $\nu = 1, \ldots, n$ where $\mathbf{e}_\nu$ denotes the ν-th unit vector. We denote them by

$$\frac{\partial F}{\partial x_\nu}(\mathbf{x}_0) \qquad (\nu = 1, \ldots, n).$$

If F has a relative maximum or minimum at $\mathbf{x}_0$, then

$$\frac{\partial F}{\partial x_1}(\mathbf{x}_0) = 0, \ldots, \frac{\partial F}{\partial x_n}(\mathbf{x}_0) = 0. \qquad (13.2.43)$$

Note that (13.2.43) is *not* sufficient for the existence of a relative maximum or minimum at $\mathbf{x}_0$. For instance, the function F given by $F(\mathbf{x}) = x_1 x_2 \ldots x_n$ satisfies (13.2.43) at $\mathbf{x}_0 = \mathbf{0}$ but has neither a maximum nor a minimum at this point (if $D = \mathbb{R}^n$, for example).

13.2.44 A symmetric matrix $\mathbf{A}$, i.e., a matrix

$$\mathbf{A} = \begin{pmatrix} a_{11} & \ldots & a_{1n} \\ \vdots & & \vdots \\ a_{n1} & \ldots & a_{nn} \end{pmatrix} \qquad \text{with} \quad a_{\nu\mu} = a_{\mu\nu} \begin{cases} \nu = 1, \ldots, n \\ \mu = 1, \ldots, n \end{cases}$$

is said to be *positive definite* or *negative definite* if the quadratic function

$$Q\colon \mathbb{R}^n \to \mathbb{R} \qquad \text{given by} \quad Q(\mathbf{x}) = \mathbf{x}\mathbf{A}\mathbf{x}'$$

is, for all $\mathbf{x} \neq \mathbf{0}$, greater than zero or smaller than zero, respectively. Note that the prime turns the row vector $\mathbf{x}$ into a column vector.

13.2.45 The function (13.2.36) is said to have *continuous* partial derivatives of second order on an ε-neighborhood $N_\varepsilon(\mathbf{x}_0) \subset D$ if the partial derivatives

$$\frac{\partial}{\partial x_\mu}\left(\frac{\partial F}{\partial x_\nu}\right) =: \frac{\partial^2 F}{\partial x_\nu \, \partial x_\mu} \qquad (\nu = 1, \ldots, n;\ \mu = 1, \ldots, n) \qquad (13.2.46)$$

are continuous functions (cf. 13.2.50 below) of $\mathbf{x} \in N_\varepsilon(\mathbf{x}_0)$. The partial derivatives (13.2.46) are defined by

$$\lim_{\lambda \to 0} \frac{\dfrac{\partial F}{\partial x_\nu}(\mathbf{x} + \lambda \mathbf{e}_\mu) - \dfrac{\partial F}{\partial x_\nu}(\mathbf{x})}{\lambda} \qquad (\mathbf{x} \in N_\varepsilon(\mathbf{x}_0),\ \lambda \text{ sufficiently small}).$$

13.2.47 **Theorem.** *Let the function (13.2.36) have continuous partial derivatives of second order in* $N_\varepsilon(\mathbf{x}_0) \subset D$. *Let (13.2.43) be satisfied. If, then, the symmetric*[1] *matrix*

$$\begin{pmatrix} \frac{\partial^2 F}{\partial x_1^2}(\mathbf{x}_0) & \frac{\partial^2 F}{\partial x_1 \partial x_2}(\mathbf{x}_0) & \cdots & \frac{\partial^2 F}{\partial x_1 \partial x_n}(\mathbf{x}_0) \\ \vdots & \vdots & & \vdots \\ \frac{\partial^2 F}{\partial x_n \partial x_1}(\mathbf{x}_0) & \frac{\partial^2 F}{\partial x_n \partial x_2}(\mathbf{x}_0) & \cdots & \frac{\partial^2 F}{\partial x_n^2}(\mathbf{x}_0) \end{pmatrix} \qquad (13.2.48)$$

is positive definite or negative definite then F has a relative minimum or a relative maximum at $\mathbf{x}_0$, *respectively.*

Note that the converse of this theorem is not true. For instance, the function F given by

$$F(\mathbf{x}) = x_1^4 + x_2^4 + \ldots + x_n^4$$

has an absolute minimum at $\mathbf{x}_0 = \mathbf{0}$, but the matrix (13.2.48) at $\mathbf{x}_0 = \mathbf{0}$ is the zero matrix which is *not* positive definite.

From now on, we consider vector-valued functions $\mathbf{F}$ of n real variables, i.e.,

$$\mathbf{F}: D \to \mathbb{R}^m, \qquad \text{where} \quad D \subseteq \mathbb{R}^n. \qquad (13.2.49)$$

13.2.50 A function (13.2.4) is said to be *continuous at the point* $\mathbf{x}_0 \in D$ if, given any $\varepsilon \in \mathbb{R}_{++}$, there exists a $\delta \in \mathbb{R}_{++}$ such that

$$|\mathbf{F}(\mathbf{x}) - \mathbf{F}(\mathbf{x}_0)| < \varepsilon$$

whenever

$$|\mathbf{x} - \mathbf{x}_0| < \delta.$$

It is said to be *continuous on D* if it is continuous at every point $\mathbf{x} \in D$.

13.2.51 The linear functions $\mathbf{F}: \mathbb{R}^n \to \mathbb{R}^m$ are examples of functions which are continuous on $\mathbb{R}^n$. The *linear functions* have been defined and the *rules of matrix algebra* have been deduced in Chapter 11.

13.2.52 In Section 11.2 we pointed out that, given a linear function $\mathbf{F}: \mathbb{R}^n \to \mathbb{R}^m$, there exists a real matrix (11.2.4) such that[2]

$$\mathbf{F}(\mathbf{x})' = \mathbf{A}\mathbf{x}' \qquad \text{for all} \quad \mathbf{x} \in \mathbb{R}^n.$$

---

[1] Under the first assumption of the theorem the formula $\dfrac{\partial^2 F}{\partial x_\mu \partial x_\nu}(\mathbf{x}_0) = \dfrac{\partial^2 F}{\partial x_\nu \partial x_\mu}(\mathbf{x}_0)$ is valid.

[2] In what follows, the vectors $\mathbf{F}$, $\mathbf{G}$, $\mathbf{L}$, $\mathbf{x}$, $\mathbf{x}_0$, $\mathbf{y}$, $\mathbf{y}_0$, $\mathbf{e}_\nu$, $\mathbf{0}$ are assumed to be row vectors. A dash turns them into column vectors.

Let $n = m$. If, then, the row (or column) vectors of $\mathbf{A}$ are linearly independent, the inverse $\mathbf{F}^{-1}\colon \mathbb{R}^m \to \mathbb{R}^m$ of $\mathbf{F}$ exists and is given by

$$\mathbf{F}^{-1}(\mathbf{y})' = \mathbf{A}^{-1}\mathbf{y}' \qquad \text{for all} \quad \mathbf{y} \in \mathbb{R}^m.$$

Here $\mathbf{A}^{-1}$ is the *inverse* of the matrix $\mathbf{A}$. It is defined by the identity

$$\mathbf{A}^{-1}\mathbf{A} = \mathbf{I} = \mathbf{A}\mathbf{A}^{-1},$$

where

$$\mathbf{I} := \begin{pmatrix} 1 & 0 & \dots & 0 \\ 0 & 1 & \dots & 0 \\ \vdots & \vdots & \ddots & \vdots \\ 0 & 0 & \dots & 1 \end{pmatrix}$$

is the *identity matrix* of m rows and columns. Note that $\mathbf{A}^{-1}$ exists if and only if the row (or column) vectors of $\mathbf{A}$ are linearly independent.

13.2.53 The function $\mathbf{F}\colon D \to \mathbb{R}^m$, D an open and connected set of $\mathbb{R}^n$, is said to be *differentiable at the point* $\mathbf{x}_0 \in D$ if there exists a linear function

$$\mathbf{L}\colon \mathbb{R}^n \to \mathbb{R}^m,$$

the so-called *complete* or *exact differential of* $\mathbf{F}$ *at* $\mathbf{x}_0$, such that

$$\frac{(\mathbf{F}(\mathbf{x}) - \mathbf{F}(\mathbf{x}_0)) - \mathbf{L}(\mathbf{x} - \mathbf{x}_0)}{|\mathbf{x} - \mathbf{x}_0|} \to \mathbf{0} \in \mathbb{R}^m \quad \text{as} \quad \mathbf{x} \to \mathbf{x}_0. \tag{13.2.54}$$

The function $\mathbf{F}$ is said to be *differentiable on* D if it is differentiable at every point $\mathbf{x} \in D$.

Obviously, differentiability of $\mathbf{F}$ at $\mathbf{x}_0$ means that $\mathbf{F}$ can be approximated, around $\mathbf{x}_0$, by a linear function, the approximation being the better the smaller the distance from $\mathbf{x}_0$ is chosen.

13.2.55 Given a fixed *basis* of $\mathbb{R}^n$ (i.e., n linearly independent vectors of $\mathbb{R}^n$) and a fixed basis of $\mathbb{R}^m$ there exists one and only matrix $\mathbf{A}$ (cf. (11.2.4)) such that $\mathbf{L}(x)$ of (13.2.54) can be written as

$$\mathbf{L}(\mathbf{x})' = \mathbf{A}\mathbf{x}'. \tag{13.2.56}$$

This matrix $\mathbf{A}$ is called the *Jacobian matrix belonging to* $\mathbf{F}$ *at* $\mathbf{x}_0$ or the *derivative of* $\mathbf{F}$ *at* $\mathbf{x}_0$.

Let the function $\mathbf{F}\colon D \to \mathbb{R}^m$, where D is an open and connected set of $\mathbb{R}^n$, be differentiable at $\mathbf{x}_0 \in D$. Then (13.2.54) holds for every $\mathbf{x} \in D$ tending to $\mathbf{x}_0$, especially for

$$\mathbf{x} = \mathbf{x}_0 + \lambda\mathbf{e}_\nu \to \mathbf{x}_0 \begin{cases} \mathbf{e}_\nu \text{ the } \nu\text{-th unit vector,} \\ \lambda \in \mathbb{R},\ (\mathbf{x}_0 + \lambda\mathbf{e}_\nu) \in D,\ \nu \in \{1, \dots, n\}. \end{cases} \tag{13.2.57}$$

Inserting (13.2.57) into (13.2.54) we obtain, in view of (13.2.56),

$$\frac{\mathbf{F}(\mathbf{x}_0) + \lambda \mathbf{e}_\nu)' - \mathbf{F}(\mathbf{x}_0)' - \mathbf{A}(\lambda \mathbf{e}_\nu)'}{|\lambda \mathbf{e}_\nu|} \to \mathbf{0}' \text{ as } \lambda \to 0. \tag{13.2.58}$$

Now, since $|\lambda \mathbf{e}_\nu| = |\lambda|$ and $\mathbf{A}\,(\lambda \mathbf{e}_\nu)' = \lambda \mathbf{A}\mathbf{e}_\nu'$, formula (13.2.58) can be written as

$$\frac{\mathbf{F}(\mathbf{x}_0 + \lambda \mathbf{e}_\nu)' - \mathbf{F}(\mathbf{x}_0)' - \lambda \mathbf{A}\mathbf{e}_\nu'}{\lambda} \frac{\lambda}{|\lambda|} \to \mathbf{0}' \text{ as } \lambda \to 0,$$

that is,

$$\lim_{\lambda \to 0} \frac{\mathbf{F}(\mathbf{x}_0 + \lambda \mathbf{e}_\nu)' - \mathbf{F}(\mathbf{x}_0)'}{\lambda} = \mathbf{A}\mathbf{e}_\nu' = \begin{pmatrix} a_{1\nu} \\ a_{2\nu} \\ \vdots \\ a_{m\nu} \end{pmatrix}.$$

The elements ("components") of the left-hand side of this equation are the partial derivatives[3] of the real-valued functions $F_1, \ldots, F_m$ (i.e., the components of $\mathbf{F}$) with respect to x_ν at $\mathbf{x}_0$. So we have

13.2.59 **Theorem.** *The Jacobian matrix or derivative of a function* $\mathbf{F}$ *at* $\mathbf{x}_0$ *is the matrix of the partial derivatives of the components of* $\mathbf{F}$ *at* $\mathbf{x}_0$*:*

$$\begin{pmatrix} \frac{\partial F_1}{\partial x_1}(\mathbf{x}_0) & \cdots & \frac{\partial F_1}{\partial x_n}(\mathbf{x}_0) \\ \vdots & & \vdots \\ \frac{\partial F_m}{\partial x_1}(\mathbf{x}_0) & \cdots & \frac{\partial F_m}{\partial x_n}(\mathbf{x}_0) \end{pmatrix} =: \frac{d\mathbf{F}}{d\mathbf{x}}(\mathbf{x}_0).$$

13.2.60 **Chain rule.** *Let the following functions be given:*

$\mathbf{F} : D \to T,\ \mathbf{x} \to \mathbf{F}(\mathbf{x}),\ D \subseteqq \mathbb{R}^n,$ *D open and connected,* $T \subseteqq \mathbb{R}^m$

$\mathbf{G} : S \to \mathbb{R}^p,\ \mathbf{y} \to \mathbf{G}(\mathbf{y}),\ S \supseteqq T,$ *S open and connected,*

$\mathbf{G} \circ \mathbf{F} : D \to \mathbb{R}^p,\ \mathbf{x} \to (\mathbf{G} \circ \mathbf{F})(\mathbf{x}) = \mathbf{G}(\mathbf{F}(\mathbf{x})).$

If $\mathbf{F}$ *is differentiable at* $\mathbf{x}_0 \in D$ *and* $\mathbf{G}$ *is differentiable at* $\mathbf{y} = \mathbf{F}(\mathbf{x}_0)$, *then* $\mathbf{G} \circ \mathbf{F}$ *is differentiable at* $\mathbf{x}_0$, *and the respective Jacobian matrices satisfy the so-called chain rule:*

$$\frac{d(\mathbf{G} \circ \mathbf{F})}{d\mathbf{x}}(\mathbf{x}_0) = \frac{d\mathbf{G}}{d\mathbf{x}}(\mathbf{y}_0)\, \frac{d\mathbf{F}}{d\mathbf{x}}(\mathbf{x}_0)'. \tag{13.2.61}$$

Note that the second matrix on the right-hand side of (13.2.61) is the transpose of the Jacobian matrix of $\mathbf{F}$ at $\mathbf{x}_0$.

---

[3] See 13.2.42.

Proof of (13.2.61). Let **B** be the Jacobian matrix belonging to **G** at $\mathbf{y}_0$. Then

$$\mathbf{G}(\mathbf{y})' - \mathbf{G}(\mathbf{y}_0)' = \mathbf{B}(\mathbf{y} - \mathbf{y}_0)' + |\mathbf{y} - \mathbf{y}_0|\, \mathbf{G}^*(\mathbf{y})', \qquad (13.2.62)$$

where

$$\mathbf{G}^*(\mathbf{y})' := \begin{cases} \dfrac{\mathbf{G}(\mathbf{y})' - \mathbf{G}(\mathbf{y}_0)' - \mathbf{B}(\mathbf{y} - \mathbf{y}_0)'}{|\mathbf{y} - \mathbf{y}_0|} & \text{for } \mathbf{y} \neq \mathbf{y}_0 \\ \mathbf{0} & \text{for } \mathbf{y} = \mathbf{y}_0. \end{cases}$$

Now we write $\mathbf{F}(\mathbf{x})$ instead of $\mathbf{y}$ in (13.2.62):

$$(\mathbf{G}\circ\mathbf{F})(\mathbf{x})' - (\mathbf{G}\circ\mathbf{F})(\mathbf{x}_0)' = \mathbf{B}(\mathbf{F}(\mathbf{x}) - \mathbf{F}(\mathbf{x}_0))' + |\mathbf{F}(\mathbf{x}) - \mathbf{F}(\mathbf{x}_0)|\mathbf{G}^*(\mathbf{F}(\mathbf{x}))'.$$

We divide this by $\lambda \neq 0$ and insert $\mathbf{x} = \mathbf{x}_0 + \lambda\mathbf{e}_\nu$:

$$\frac{(\mathbf{G}\circ\mathbf{F})(\mathbf{x}_0 + \lambda\mathbf{e}_\nu)' - (\mathbf{G}\circ\mathbf{F})(\mathbf{x}_0)'}{\lambda} \qquad (13.2.64)$$

$$= \mathbf{B}\,\frac{\mathbf{F}(\mathbf{x}_0 + \lambda\mathbf{e}_\nu)' - \mathbf{F}(\mathbf{x}_0)'}{\lambda} + \frac{|\mathbf{F}(\mathbf{x}_0 + \lambda\mathbf{e}_\nu) - \mathbf{F}(\mathbf{x}_0)|}{\lambda}\,\mathbf{G}^*(\mathbf{F}(\mathbf{x}_0 + \lambda\mathbf{e}_\nu))'.$$

Since

$$\lim_{\lambda\to 0} \mathbf{G}^*(\mathbf{F}(\mathbf{x}_0 + \lambda\mathbf{e}_\nu)) = \lim_{\mathbf{y}\to\mathbf{y}_0} \mathbf{G}^*(\mathbf{y}) = \mathbf{0}$$

and

$$\lim_{\lambda\to 0} \frac{|\mathbf{F}(\mathbf{x}_0 + \lambda\mathbf{e}_\nu) - \mathbf{F}(\mathbf{x}_0)|}{\lambda} = \text{const.},$$

(13.2.64) becomes (13.2.61) as $\lambda \to 0$. ■

13.2.65 **Special case of (13.2.61).** Let $p = n = 1$. Then

$$G(\mathbf{y}) = G(y_1, \ldots, y_m) = G(F_1(x), \ldots, F_m(x)),$$

and (13.2.61) becomes the well-known formula

$$\frac{\mathrm{d}(G\circ F)}{\mathrm{d}x}(\mathbf{x}_0) = \left(\frac{\partial G}{\partial y_1}(\mathbf{y}_0), \ldots, \frac{\partial G}{\partial y_m}(\mathbf{y}_0)\right)\left(\frac{\mathrm{d}F_1}{\mathrm{d}x}(x_0), \ldots, \frac{\mathrm{d}F_m}{\mathrm{d}x}(x_0)\right)'$$

$$= \frac{\partial G}{\partial y_1}(\mathbf{y}_0)\frac{\mathrm{d}F_1}{\mathrm{d}x}(x_0) + \ldots + \frac{\partial G}{\partial y_m}(\mathbf{y}_0)\frac{\mathrm{d}F_m}{\mathrm{d}x}(x_0)$$

which is often briefly written as

$$\frac{\mathrm{d}G}{\mathrm{d}x} = \frac{\partial G}{\partial y_1}\frac{\mathrm{d}y_1}{\mathrm{d}x} + \ldots + \frac{\partial G}{\partial y_m}\frac{\mathrm{d}y_m}{\mathrm{d}x}.$$

13.3 Economics

Properties of a scalar-valued production function. A scalar-valued production function

$$F : \mathbb{R}^n_+ \to \mathbb{R}_+ \tag{13.3.0}$$

assigns to each input vector $\mathbf{x} \in \mathbb{R}^n_+$ the maximum output obtainable with $\mathbf{x} = (x_1, \ldots, x_n)$ per unit time, namely $F(\mathbf{x})$. Note that this intuitive definition does not exclude production systems where indivisible inputs are involved: If, for instance, inputs are indivisible,

$$F(643.75, \ldots, 98.21) := F(643, \ldots, 98).$$

Shephard [1967, p. 212; 1970, p. 22] assumes the following six properties for a production function F:

(13.3.1) $F(\mathbf{0}) = 0$ ("nothing comes from nothing").

(13.3.2) $\{u \mid u = F(\mathbf{x}), \mathbf{x} \in D \subset \mathbb{R}^n_+, D \text{ bounded}\}$ is bounded.

(13.3.3) If $\mathbf{x}^* \geqq \mathbf{x}$, then $F(\mathbf{x}^*) \geqq F(\mathbf{x})$ ("free disposability of inputs").

(13.3.4) For any $\mathbf{x} \geq \mathbf{0}$ such that $F(\lambda\mathbf{x}) > 0$ for some $\lambda \in \mathbb{R}_{++}$, $F(\lambda\mathbf{x}) \to \infty$ as $\lambda \to \infty$ ("attainability of output").

(13.3.5) F is *quasiconcave on* $\mathbb{R}^n_+$, that is, for any two input vectors $\mathbf{x}$ and $\mathbf{y}$

$$F((1-\theta)\mathbf{x} + \theta\mathbf{y}) \geqq \mathrm{Min}\{F(\mathbf{x}), F(\mathbf{y})\} \qquad \text{for all} \quad \theta \in [0, 1].$$

(13.3.6) F is upper semicontinuous on $\mathbb{R}^n_+$, that is, for any $\mathbf{x} \in \mathbb{R}^n_+$ and arbitrary $\alpha \in \mathbb{R}_{++}$ there exists an ε-neighborhood $N_\varepsilon(\mathbf{x}) := \{\mathbf{y} \mid \mathbf{y} \in \mathbb{R}^n, |\mathbf{y} - \mathbf{x}| < \varepsilon, \ \varepsilon \in \mathbb{R}_{++}\}$ such that $F(\mathbf{x}^*) < F(\mathbf{x}) + \alpha$ for any $\mathbf{x}^* \in N_\varepsilon(\mathbf{x}) \cap \mathbb{R}^n_+$.

13.3.7 **Remark.** Properties (13.3.0), (13.3.1), and (13.3.2) are obviously characteristic of any production structure producing a single commodity. Therefore, when we speak of a *production function* in the context of this book, we always mean a *function satisfying these three properties*. Since free disposability of inputs involves a social decision, we do not require (13.3.3) from *every* production function. In Section 4.5 we determined production functions that are neither quasiconcave (cf. (13.3.5)) nor satisfy (13.3.3). If n of (13.3.0) is not the maximum number of inputs involved in the production of the output commodity, then (13.3.4) is not necessarily true.

13.3.8 **Remark.** We point out here that properties (13.3.1)–(13.3.6) may also be considered properties of a utility function $F: \mathbb{R}^n_+ \to \mathbb{R}_+$.

Properties of a set-valued production function (output or input correspondence). An output correspondence

$$\underline{\mathbf{P}}: \mathbb{R}^n_+ \to \text{power set of } \mathbb{R}^m_+ \tag{13.3.9}$$

assigns to each input vector $\mathbf{x} \in \mathbb{R}^n_+$ the set of all output vectors $\mathbf{u} \in \mathbb{R}^m_+$ obtainable with $\mathbf{x}$ per unit time, namely $\underline{\mathbf{P}}(\mathbf{x})$.

Shephard [1974b, p. 1] takes as "globally applicable" the following six properties for an output correspondence $\underline{\mathbf{P}}$:

(13.3.10) $\underline{\mathbf{P}}(\mathbf{0}) = \{\mathbf{0}\}$, and for some $\mathbf{u} > \mathbf{0}$ there exists $\mathbf{x} \geq \mathbf{0}$ such that $\mathbf{u} \in \underline{\mathbf{P}}(\mathbf{x})$.

(13.3.11) $\underline{\mathbf{P}}(\mathbf{x})$ is bounded for every fixed $\mathbf{x} \in \mathbb{R}^n_+$.

(13.3.12) $\underline{\mathbf{P}}(\lambda\mathbf{x}) \supseteqq \underline{\mathbf{P}}(\mathbf{x})$ for all $\lambda \in [1, \infty[$ and all $\mathbf{x} \in \mathbb{R}^n_+$ ("weak disposability of inputs").

(13.3.13) $\mathbf{u} \in \underline{\mathbf{P}}(\mathbf{x})$ implies $\mu\mathbf{u} \in \underline{\mathbf{P}}(\mathbf{x})$ for all $\mu \in [0, 1]$ ("weak disposability of outputs").

(13.3.14) If $\mathbf{x} \geq \mathbf{0}$ and there exists $\mathbf{u} \geq \mathbf{0}$ such that $\mathbf{u} \in \underline{\mathbf{P}}(\mathbf{x})$, then for all $\mu \in \mathbb{R}_{++}$ there exists $\lambda \in \mathbb{R}_{++}$ such that $\mu\mathbf{u} \in \underline{\mathbf{P}}(\lambda\mathbf{x})$ (i.e., in conjunction with the second part of (13.3.10), "attainability of outputs").

(13.3.15) $\underline{\mathbf{P}}$ is upper semicontinuous on $\mathbb{R}^n_+$. [$\underline{\mathbf{P}}$ is *upper semicontinuous at* $\mathbf{x}^0$ *if* $\mathbf{x}^\nu \to \mathbf{x}^0$ for $\nu \to \infty$, $\mathbf{u}^\nu \in \underline{\mathbf{P}}(\mathbf{x}^\nu)$ ($\nu \in \{1, 2, 3, \ldots\}$) and $\mathbf{u}^\nu \to \mathbf{u}^0$ imply $\mathbf{u}^0 \in \underline{\mathbf{P}}(\mathbf{x}^0)$].

If we add

$$\underline{\mathbf{P}}(\mathbf{x}) \neq \emptyset \qquad \text{for all} \quad \mathbf{x} \in \mathbb{R}^n_+$$

to (13.3.10) and

$$\exists \mathbf{u} > \mathbf{0} \qquad \text{such that} \quad \underline{\mathbf{L}}(\mathbf{u}) \neq \emptyset \tag{13.3.16}$$

to (13.3.18), then properties (13.3.10)–(13.3.15) for $\underline{\mathbf{P}}$ are equivalent to the following properties (cf. Shephard [1974b, p. 3]) for the input correspondence

$$\underline{\mathbf{L}}: \mathbb{R}^m_+ \to \text{power set of } \mathbb{R}^n_+ \tag{13.3.17}$$

defined by

$$\underline{\mathbf{L}}(\mathbf{u}) := \{\mathbf{x} \mid \mathbf{x} \text{ yields at least } \mathbf{u} \text{ per unit time}\}.$$

(13.3.18) $\underline{\mathbf{L}}(\mathbf{0}) = \mathbb{R}^n_+$ and $\mathbf{0} \notin \underline{\mathbf{L}}(\mathbf{u})$ for $\mathbf{u} > \mathbf{0}$.

(13.3.19) $|\mathbf{u}^\nu| \to \infty$ for $\nu \to \infty$ ($\nu \in \{1, 2, 3, \ldots\}$) implies $\bigcap_{\nu=1}^{\infty} \underline{\mathbf{L}}(\mathbf{u}^\nu) = \emptyset$.

(13.3.20) If $\mathbf{x} \in \underline{\mathbf{L}}(\mathbf{u})$, then $\lambda\mathbf{x} \in \underline{\mathbf{L}}(\mathbf{u})$ for all $\lambda \in [1, \infty[$ (weak disposability of inputs).

(13.3.21) $\underline{\mathbf{L}}(\lambda\mathbf{u}) \subseteqq \underline{\mathbf{L}}(\mathbf{u})$ for all $\lambda \in [1, \infty[$ and all $\mathbf{u} \in \mathbb{R}^m_+$ (weak disposability of outputs).

(13.3.22) If $\mathbf{x} \geq \mathbf{0}$ and $\mathbf{x} \in \underline{\mathbf{L}}(\mathbf{u})$ for some $\mathbf{u} \geq \mathbf{0}$, then for all $\mu \in \mathbb{R}_{++}$ there exists $\lambda \in \mathbb{R}_{++}$ such that $\lambda\mathbf{x} \in \underline{\mathbf{L}}(\mu\mathbf{u})$ (i.e., in conjunction with (13.3.16), attainability of outputs).

(13.3.23) $\underline{\mathbf{L}}$ is upper semicontinuous on $\mathbb{R}^m_+$.

The economic or technical meaning of properties (13.3.10)–(13.3.14) or, equivalently, (13.3.18)–(13.3.22), is obvious. Property (13.3.15) ((13.3.23)) is merely a mathematical convenience. It is synonymous with closure of the graph

$$\{(\mathbf{x}, \mathbf{u}) \mid (\mathbf{x}, \mathbf{u}) \in \mathbb{R}^n_+ \times \mathbb{R}^m_+, \mathbf{u} \in \underline{\mathbf{P}}(\mathbf{x})\}$$

permitting valuable definitions and results for the theory based on properties (13.3.10)–(13.3.15) (or, equivalently, (13.3.18)–(13.3.23)).

13.3.24 **Remark.** When we speak of an *output correspondence* (or *input correspondence*) in the context of this book, we always mean a correspondence (13.3.9) (or (13.3.17)) that satisfies only (13.3.10), (13.3.11) (or (13.3.18), (13.3.19)).

Nash equilibrium vectors in the theory of oligopoly. A game-theoretic approach to oligopoly theory considers the n oligopolists as players, each having a set of strategies (consisting of alternative price vectors, e.g.). Let $\Sigma_1, \Sigma_2, \ldots, \Sigma_n$ denote these sets. It is assumed that the profit (payoff) of each oligopolist (player) depends only on the vector $(\sigma_1, \sigma_2, \ldots, \sigma_n)$ of strategies chosen. Note that

$$\sigma_1 \in \Sigma_1, \sigma_2 \in \Sigma_2, \ldots, \sigma_n \in \Sigma_n,$$

that is,

$$(\sigma_1, \sigma_2, \ldots, \sigma_n) \in \Sigma_1 \times \Sigma_2 \times \cdots \times \Sigma_n.$$

In other words, the profit functions (payoff functions) $\Pi_1, \Pi_2, \ldots, \Pi_n$ of the oligopolists (players) are mappings

$$\Pi_\nu : \Sigma_1 \times \Sigma_2 \times \cdots \times \Sigma_n \to \mathbb{R}.$$

A vector $(\sigma_1^*, \sigma_2^*, \ldots, \sigma_n^*)$ is called a Nash *equilibrium vector* or Nash *equilibrium point* if, for all $\nu \in \{1, 2, \ldots, n\}$,

$$\Pi_\nu(\sigma_1^*, \sigma_2^*, \ldots, \sigma_n^*) \geqq \Pi_\nu(\sigma_1^*, \ldots, \sigma_{\nu-1}^*, \sigma_\nu, \sigma_{\nu+1}^*, \ldots \sigma_n^*) \qquad \text{for all} \quad \sigma_\nu \in \Sigma_\nu \tag{13.3.25}$$

(cf. Nash [1951]).

References

Aczél, J. (1966). *Lectures on Functional Equations and Their Applications* (Mathematics in Science and Engineering, Vol. *19*). Academic Press, New York.

Aczél, J. (1969). *On Applications and Theory of Functional Equations* (Elemente der Mathematik vom Höheren Standpunkt aus, Vol. *5*). Basel and Stuttgart.

Aczél, J. (1975). "On a system of functional equations determining price and productivity indices", *Utilitas Mathematica 7*, 345–362.

Aczél, J., and Daróczy, Z. (1975). On Measures of Information and Their Characterizations (Mathematics in Science and Engineering, Vol. *115*). New York, San Francisco, London,

Aczél, J., and Eichhorn, W. (1974a). "Systems of functional equations determining price and productivity indices", *Utilitas Mathematica 5*, 213–226.

Aczél, J., and Eichhorn, W. (1974b). "A note on additive indices", *Journal of Economic Theory 8*, 525–529.

Aczél, J., Baker, J. A., Djoković, D. Ž., Kannappan, P. L., and Radó, F. (1971). "Extensions of certain homomorphisms of subsemigroups to homomorphisms of groups," *Aequationes Mathematicae* 6, 263–271.

Afriat, S. N. (1962). "Preference scales and expenditure systems," *Econometrica 30*, 305–323.

Afriat, S. N. (1967). "The cost-of-living index," in *Essays in Mathematical Economics*, pp. 335–365. Princeton Univ. Press, Princeton, N.J.

Afriat, S. N. (1972). "The theory of international comparisons of real income and prices," in *International Comparisons of Prices and Output*, pp. 13–69. New York, London.

Allen, R. G. D. (1967). *Macro-Economic Theory*. Macmillan, London, Melbourne, Toronto, St. Martin's Press, New York.

Allen, R. G. D. (1975). *Index Numbers in Theory and Practice*. Macmillan, London.

Arrow, K. J., Chenery, H. B., Minhas, B. S., and Solow, R. M. (1961) . "Capital-labour substitution and economic efficiency," *Rev. Economics and Statistics* 43, 225–250.

Banerjee, K. S. (1975). *Cost of Living Index Numbers*. Marcel Decker, New York.

Beckmann, M. J. (1974). "Invariant relationships for homothetic production functions," in *Production Theory* (Proc. Intern. Seminar, Univ.of Karlsruhe, May–July 1973), pp. 3–18 (Lecture Notes in Economics and Mathematical Systems, Vol. 99). Springer–Verlag, Berlin, Heidelberg, New York.

Bellman, R. (1971). "Functional equations in the theory of dynamic programming, 18: A problem connected with the value of information," *Math. Biosc.* 11, 1–3.

Bellman, R., and Kalaba, R. (1957). "On the role of dynamic programming in statistical communication theory," *IRE Trans. Prof. Group on Information Theory* IT–3, 197–203.

Blackorby, C., and Russell, R. R. (1978). "Indices and subindices of the cost of living and the standard of living," *Intern. Economic Rev.*

Cauchy, A. L. (1821). *Cours d'analyse de l'École Polytechnique*, Vol. 1, *Analyse algébrique*, V. Paris. (*Oeuvres*, Ser. 2, Vol. 3, pp. 98–113, 220. Gauthier-Villars et Fils, Imprimeurs-Libraires, Paris.)

Chattopadhyay, P. (1966). "Diminishing returns and linear homogeneity: Further comment," *Amer. Economic Rev.* 56, 181–182.

Cobb, C. W., and Douglas, P. H. (1928). "A theory of production," *Amer. Economic Rev.* 18, *Suppl.*, pp. 139–165.

Cross, G. (1968). "Note on a generalized homogeneous function," *Aequationes Math.* 1, 298–300.

Daróczy, Z., and Losonczi, L. (1967). "Über die Erweiterung der auf einer Punktmenge additiven Funktionen," *Publ. Math. Debrecen* 14, 239–245.

Debreu, G. (1960). "Topological methods in cardinal utility theory," in *Mathematical Methods in the Social Sciences*, pp. 16–26. Stanford University Press, Stanford.

Diewert, W. E. (1976). "Exact and superlative index numbers," *J. Econometrics* 4, 115–145.

Douglas, P. H. (1934). *Theory of Wages*. Macmillan, New York.

Eichhorn, W. (1968a). "Behandlung zweier auf die Untersuchung von Funktionalgleichungen führender produktionstheoretischer Probleme," *Jahrb. Nationalökonomie und Statistik* 181, 334–342.

Eichhorn, W. (1968b). "Diminishing returns and linear homogeneity: Final comment," *Amer. Economic Rev.* 58, 150–162.

Eichhorn, W. (1968c). "Deduktion der Ertragsgesetze aus Prämissen," *Z. Nationalökonomie* 28, 191–205. This article has since been published in *Mathematische Wirtschaftstheorie* (Neue Wissenschaftliche Bibliothek, Vol. 75, *Wirtschaftswissenschaften)*, pp. 28–42. Kiepenheuer & Witsch, Köln.

Eichhorn, W. (1969). "Eine Verallgemeinerung des Begriffs der homogenen Produktionsfunktion," *Unternehmensforschung* 13, 99–109.

Eichhorn, W. (1970). *Theorie der homogenen Produktionsfunktion.* (Lecture Notes in Operations Research and Mathematical Systems, Vol. 22). Springer-Verlag, Berlin, Heidelberg, New York.

Eichhorn, W. (1971). "Zur statischen Theorie des Mehrproduktenoligopols," *Operations Research-Verfahren* 10, 16–33.

Eichhorn, W. (1972a). "Zur Kostentheorie der Mehrproduktenunternehmung," in *Festschrift für Walter Georg Waffenschmidt zur Vollendung seines 85. Geburtstags*, pp. 25–31. Verlag Anton Hain, Meisenheim.

Eichhorn, W. (1972b). "Effektivität von Produktionsverfahren," *Operations Research-Verfahren* 12, 98–115.

Eichhorn, W. (1972c). "Optimaler Werbeaufwand je Produkt und für das Sortiment in einem Monopol- und einem Oligopolmodell," *Operations Research-Verfahren* 14, 75–84.

Eichhorn, W. (1972d). "Zur dynamischen Theorie des Mehrproduktenoligopols," *Jahrb. Nationalökonomie und Statistik* 186, 498–515.

Eichhorn, W. (1973a). *Modelle der vertikalen Preisbildung* (Mathematical Systems in Economics, Vol. 6). Verlag Anton Hain, Meisenheim.

Eichhorn, W. (1973b). "Zur axiomatischen Theorie des Preisindex," *Demonstratio Math.* 6, 561–573.

Eichhorn, W. (1974a). "Systems of functional equations determining the effectiveness of a production process," in *Mathematical Models in Economics*, pp. 433–439. Polish Scientific Publishers, Warszawa; North-Holland, Amsterdam, London, New York.

Eichhorn, W. (1974b). "Characterization of the CES production functions by quasilinearity," in *Production Theory* (Proc. Intern. Seminar, Univ. of Karlsruhe, May–July 1973), pp. 21–33 (Lecture Notes in Economics and Mathematical Systems, Vol. 99). Springer-Verlag, Berlin, Heidelberg, New York.

Eichhorn, W. (1976). "Fisher's tests revisited," *Econometrica* 44, 247–256.

Eichhorn, W., and Kolm, S.-C. (1974). "Technical progress, neutral inventions, and Cobb-Douglas," in *Production Theory* (Proc. Intern. Seminar, Univ. of Karlsruhe, May–July 1973), pp. 35–45 (Lecture Notes in Economics and Mathematical Systems, Vol. 99). Springer-Verlag, Berlin, Heidelberg, New York.

Eichhorn, W., and Müller, U. (1967). "Substitutionsgebiete, Minimalkostenlinien und Isoquanten homogener Produktionsfunktionen," *Z. ges. Staatswiss.* 123, 698–710.

Eichhorn, W., and Müller, U. (1968). "Über homogene, speziell linear-homogene Produktionsfunktionen und das Ertragsgesetz," *Weltwirtschaftliches Arch.* 100, 290–305.

Eichhorn, W., and Oettli, W. (1968). "Mehrproduktunternehmungen mit linearen Expansionswegen," *Operations Research-Verfahren* 6, 101–117.

Eichhorn, W., and Voeller, J. (1976). *Theory of the Price Index: Fisher's Test Approach and Generalizations* (Lecture Notes in Operations Research and Mathematical Systems, Vol. 140). Springer-Verlag, Berlin, Heidelberg, New York.

Eichhorn, W., Funke, H., and Stehling, F. (1977). "Spieltheoretische Behandlung der Preisbildung vor und nach Unternehmenszusammenschlüssen," in *Mathematical Economics. and Game Theory*. Essays in Honor of Oscar Morgenstern. pp. 376–387 (Lecture Notes in Economics and Mathematical Systems, Vol. 141). Springer- Verlag, Berlin, Heidelberg, New York.

Färe, R., and Shephard, R. W. (1977). "Ray-homothetic production functions," Econometrica 45, 133–146.

Fischer, P. (1974). "On Bellman's functional equation," *J. Math. Anal. Appl.* 46, 212–227.

Fischer, P. (1975). "On Bellman's functional equation, II," *J. Math. Anal. Appl.* 49, 786–793.

Fisher, F. M., and Shell, K. (1972). *The Economic Theory of Price Indices—Two Essays on the Effect of Taste, Quality, and Technological Change*. Academic Press, New York, London.

Fisher, I. (1911). *The Purchasing Power of Money*. Macmillan, New York.

Fisher, I. (1922). *The Making of Index Numbers*. Houghton Mifflin Co., The Riverside Press, Cambridge, Mass. (3d ed., rev., 1927); reprinted by Augustus M. Kelley, New York, 1967.

Fontenay, P. B. de (1964). "Diminishing returns and linear homogeneity: Comment," *Amer. Economic Rev.* 54, 750.

Friedman, J. W. (1973). "Concavity of production functions and nonincreasing returns to scale," *Econometrica* 41, 981–984.

Frisch, R. (1930). "Necessary and sufficient conditions regarding the form of an index number which shall meet certain of Fisher's tests," *J. Amer. Statist. Assoc.* 25, 397–406.

Frisch, R. (1936). "Annual survey of general economic theory: The problem of index numbers," *Econometrica* 4, 1–38.

Frisch, R. (1954). "Some basic principles of price of living measurements: A survey article," *Econometrica* 22, 407–421.

Frisch, R. (1965). *Theory of Production.* D. Reidel Publishing Company, Dordrecht, The Netherlands.

Fuchs, L. (1963). *Partially Ordered Algebraic Structures.* Pergamon Press, Oxford, London, New York, Paris.

Fuchs-Seliger, S. (1977). "Bemerkungen zur Widerspruchsfreiheit der Axiome in der Theorie der Revealed Preference," in *Mathematical Economics and Game Theory.* Essays in Honor of Oskar Morgenstern, pp. 217–225. (Lecture Notes in Economics and Mathematical Systems, Vol. 141). Springer-Verlag, Berlin, Heidelberg, New York.

Gehrig, W. (1976). *Neutraler technisher Fortschritt und Produktionsfunktionen mit beliebig vielen Produktionsfaktoren* (Mathematical Systems in Economics, Vol. 20). Verlag Anton Hain, Meisenheim.

Goldman, S. M., and Shephard, R. W. (1972). "On Eichhorn's generalization of homogeneous production functions," *Unternehmensforschung* 16, 215–219.

Gorman, W. M. (1968)., "The structure of utility functions," *Rev. Economic Studies* 35, 367–390.

Green, H. A. J. (1964). *Aggregation in Economic Analysis.* Princeton Univ. Press, Princeton, N. J.

Hardy, G. H., Littlewood, J. E., and Pólya, G. (1934). *Inequalities.* Cambridge Univ. Press, Cambridge (reprinted 1967).

Hasenkamp, G. (1978). "Economic and atomistic index numbers: Contrasts and similarities," to appear in *Theory and Applications of Economic Indices* (Proc. Intern. Symposium on Economic Index Numbers, Univ. of Karlsruhe, April and July, 1976). Physica-Verlag, Würzburg, Wien.

Hosszú, M., and Vincze, E. (1961). "Über die Verallgemeinerungen eines Funktionalgleichungssystems der Wirtschaftlichkeit," *Publ. Math. Inst. Hungar. Acad. Sci.* 6, 313–321.

Houthakker, H. S. (1950). "Revealed preference and the utility function," *Economica* 17 159–174.

Hurwicz, L., and Richter, M. K. (1971). "Revealed preference without demand continuity assumptions," in *Preferences, Utility, and Demand*, pp. 59–77. Harcourt Brace Jovanovich, New York.

Kalmbach, P. (1972). *Wachstum und Verteilung in neoklassischer und postkeynesianischer Sicht.* Duncker & Humblot, Berlin.

Kats, A. (1970). "Comments on the definition of homogeneous and homothetic functions," *J. Economic Theory* 2, 310–313.

Katzner, D. W. (1970). *Static Demand Theory.* Macmillan, New York and London.

Kelly, J. (1956). "A new interpretation of information rate," *Bell System Tech. J.* 35, 917–926.

Klein, L. R. (1946a). "Macroeconomics and the theory of rational behavior," *Econometrica* 14, 93–108.

Klein, L. R. (1946b). "Remarks on the theory of aggregation," *Econometrica* 14, 303–312.

Klein, L. R., and Rubin, H. (1948). "Constant utility index of the cost-of-living," *Rev. Economic Studies* 15, 84–87.

Koopmans, T. C. (1951). "Analysis of production as an efficient combination of activities," in *Activity Analysis of Production and Allocation*, pp. 33–97. Wiley, New York.

Koopmans, T. C. (1953). "Activity analysis and its applications," *Amer. Economic Rev.* 43, 406–414.

Krein, M., and Milman, D. (1940). "On extreme points of regular convex sets," *Studia Math.* 9, 133–138.

Krelle, W. (1961). *Preistheorie.* J. C. B. Mohr (Paul Siebeck), Tübingen and Zürich.

Krelle, W. (with W. Scheper) (1969). *Produktionstheorie.* J. C. B. Mohr (Paul Siebeck), Tübingen.

Lancaster, K. (1968). *Mathematical Economics.* Macmillan, New York.

Laspeyres, E. (1871). "Die Berechnung einer mittleren Waarenpreissteigerung," *Jahr. Nationalökonomie und Statistik* 16, 296–314.

Leontief, W. (1941). *The Structure of American Economy, 1919–1939.* Oxford Univ. Press, London and New York.

Leontief, W. (1947). "Introduction to a theory of the international structure of functional relationships," *Econometrica* 15, 361–373.

Levenson, A. M., and Solon, B. (1966). "Returns to scale and the spacing of isoquants," *Amer. Economic Rev.* 56, 501–505.

Liebhafsky, H. H. (1964). "Diminishing returns and linear homogeneity: Comment," *Amer. Economic Rev.* 54, 739–744.

Lipsey, R. G. (1975). *An Introduction to Positive Economics* (4th ed.). Weidenfeld and Nicolson, London.

McElroy, F. W. (1969). "Returns to scale, Euler's theorem, and the form of production functions," *Econometrica* 37, 275–279.

McKenzie, L. (1960). "Matrices with dominant diagonals and economic theory," in *Mathematical Methods in the Social Sciences*, pp. 47–62. Stanford Univ. Press, Stançord, Calif.

Menger, K. (1936). "Bemerkungen zu den Ertragsgesetzen," *Z. Nationalökonomie* 7, 25–56; 388–397. These two articles have been translated into English and published, under the title "The logic of the laws of return: A study in meta-economics," in *Economic Activity Analysis*, pp. 419–482. Wiley, New York and London.

Moeseke, P. van (1945). "Diminishing returns and linear homogeneity: Comment," *Amer. Economic Rev.* 55, 536–539.

Morishima, M. (1964). *Equilibrium, Stability and Growth. A Multi-Sectoral Analysis.* Oxford University Press, London and New York.

Muellbauer, J. (1975). "The cost of living and taste and quality change," *J. Economic Theory* 10, 269–283.

Muth, J. F. (1954). "A note on balanced growth," *Econometrica* 22, 493–495.

Nash, J. F. (1951). "Noncooperative games," *Ann. of Math.* 54, 286–295.

Nataf, A. (1948). "Sur la possibilité de construction de certain macromodéles," *Econometrica* 16, 232–244.

Neumann, J. von (1937). "Über ein ökonomisches Gleichungssystem und eine Verallgemeinerung des Brouwerschen Fixpunktsatzes," *Ergebn. Math. Kolloq.* 8 (1935–1936), 73–83. [English translation: "A model of general economic equilibrium," *Rev. Economic Studies* 13 (1945–1946), 1–9.]

Nikaido, H. (1964). "Balanced growth in multi-sectoral income propagation under autonomous expenditure schemes," *Rev. Economic Studies* 31, 25–42.

Nikaido, H. (1968). *Convex Structures and Economic Theory* (Mathematics in Science and Engineering, Vol. 51). Academic Press, New York.

Nutter, G. W. (1963). "Diminishing returns and linear homogeneity, " *Amer. Economic Rev.* 53, 1084–1085.

Nutter, G. W. (1964). "Diminishing returns and linear homogeneity: Reply," *Amer. Economic Rev.* 54, 751–753.

Nutter, G. W. (1965). "Diminishing returns and linear homogeneity: Reply," *Amer. Economic Rev.* 55, 539.

Paasche, H. (1874). "Über die Preisentwicklung der letzten Jahre, nach den Hamburger Börsennotierungen," *Jahr. Nationalökoncmie und Statistik* 23, 168–178.

Paroush, J. (1964). "A note on CES production function," *Econometrica* 32, 213–214.

Pexider, J. V. (1903). "Notiz über Funktionaltheoreme," *Monatsh. Math. und Physik* 14, 293–301.

Phlips, L. (1974). *Applied Consumption Analysis*. North-Holland, Amsterdam and Oxford; American Elsevier, New York.

Phlips, L., and Sanz-Ferrer, R. (1975). "A taste-dependent true index of the cost of living," *Rev. Economics and Statistics* 57, 495–501.

Piron, R. (1966). "Diminishing returns and linear homogeneity: Further comment," *Amer. Econcmic Rev.* 56, 183–186.

Pckrcpp, F. (1972a). "A note on the problem of aggregation," *Rev. Economic Studies* 39, 221–230.

Pokropp, F. (1972b). *Aggregation von Produktionsfunktionen* (Lecture Notes in Economics and Mathematical Systems, Vol. 74). Springer-Verlag, Berlin, Heidelberg, New York.

Pollak, R. A. (1971). "The theory of the cost of living index," Research Discussion Paper 11 (Research Division, Office of Prices and Living Conditions, U.S. Bureau of Labor Statistics, Washington, D.C. 20212).

Pollak, R. A. (1975). "Subindices of the cost of living index," *Intern. Economic Rev.* 16, 135–150.

Rader, T. (1972). *Theory of Microeconomics*. Academic Press, New York.

Rao, A. G. (1970). *Quantitative Theories in Advertising*. Wiley, New York.

Reed, H. L. (1942). *Money, Currency and Banking*. McGraw-Hill, New York and London.

Rowe, J. W., Jr. (1964). "Diminishing returns and linear homogeneity: Comment," *Amer. Economic Rev.* 54, 532–535.

Rowe, J. W., Jr. (1965). "Diminishing returns and linear homogeneity: Comment," *Amer. Economic Rev.* 55, 532–535.

Samuelson, P. A. (1938). "A note on the pure theory of consumer's behavior," *Economica* 5, 61–71.

Samuelson, P. A. (1948). *Foundations of Economic Analysis*. Harvard University Press, Cambridge.

Samuelson, P. A., and Swamy, S. (1974). "Invariant economic index numbers and canonical duality: Survey and synthesis," *Amer. Economic Rev.* 64, 566–593.

Sato, R. (1964). "Diminishing returns and linear homogeneity: Comment," *Amer. Economic Rev.* 54, 745–746.

Sato, K. (1975). *Production Functions and Aggregation* (Contributions to Economic Analysis, Vol. 90). North-Holland, Amsterdam, Oxford; American Elsevier, New York.

Sato, R., and Beckmann, M. J. (1968). "Neutral inventions and production functions," *Rev. Economic Studies* 35, 57–66.

Schips, B. (1970). "Substitutionselastizität und Produktionsfunktionen," *Operations Research-Verfahren* 9, 105–115.

Schneider, D. (1964). "Diminishing returns and linear homogeneity: Comment," *Amer. Economic Rev.* 54, 747–749.

Selten, R. (1970). *Preispolitik der Mehrproduktenunternehmung in der statischen Theorie*

(Ökonometrie und Unternehmensforschung, Vol. 16). Springer-Verlag, Berlin, Heidelberg, New York.

Shephard, R. W. (1953). *Cost and Production Functions.* Princeton Univ. Press, Princeton, N.J.

Shephard, R. W. (1967). "The notion of a production function," *Unternehmensforschung* 11, 209–232.

Shephard, R. W. (1970). *Theory of Cost and Production Functions* (Princeton Studies in Mathematical Economics, Vol. 4). Princeton Univ. Press. Princeton, N.J.

Shephard, R. W. (1974a). "Semi-homogeneous production functions and scaling of production," in *Production Theory* (Proc. Intern. Seminar, Univ. of Karlsruhe, May–July 1973), pp. 253–285. (Lecture Notes in Economics and Mathematical Systems, Vol. 99). Springer-Verlag, Berlin, Heidelberg, New York.

Shephard, R. W. (1974b). *Indirect Production Functions* (Mathematical Systems in Economics, Vol. 10). Verlag Anton Hain, Meisenheim.

Solow, R. M., and Samuelson, P. A. (1953). "Balanced growth under constant returns to scale," *Econometrica* 21, 412–424.

Sonnenschein, H. (1971). "On the continuity of demand functions which satisfy the strong axiom of revealed preference," in *Preference, Utility, and Demand*, pp. 271–276. Harcourt Brace Jovanovich, New York.

Stehling, F. (1973). "Über gleichgewichtige Lösungen nichtlinearer Differenzengleichungssysteme endlicher Ordnung, " *Operations Research-Verfahren* 17, 341–351.

Stehling, F. (1974a). "Neutral inventions and CES production functions," in *Production Theory* (Proc. Intern. Seminar, Univ. of Karlsruhe, May–July 1973), pp. 65–94 (Lecture Notes in Economics and Mathematical Systems, Vol. 99). Springer-Verlag, Berlin, Heidelberg, New York.

Stehling, F. (1974b). "Balanced growth of open economies under variable degree of homogeneity," in *Production Theory* (Proc. Intern. Seminar, Univ. of Karlsruhe, May–July 1973), pp. 147–176 (Lecture Notes in Economics and Mathematical Systems, Vol. 99). Springer-Verlag, Berlin, Heidelberg, New York.

Stehling, F. (1974c). *Zur Charakterisierung einiger wichtiger Klassen von Produktionsfunktionen.* Habilitationsschrift. Univ. of Karlsruhe.

Stehling, F. (1975). "Eine neue Charakterisierung der CD- und ACMS-Produktionsfunktionen," *Operations Research-Verfahren* 21, 222–238.

Stehling, F. (1977). "Wilhelm Krelles Produktionskoeffiziente n und neutraler technischer Fortschritt," in *Quantitative Wirtschaftsforschung.* Festschrift zum 60. Geburtstag von Wilhelm Krelle. J. C. B. Mohr (Paul Siebeck), Tübingen.

Stigum, B. P. (1973). "Revealed preference—a proof of Houthakker's theorem," *Econometrica* 41, 411–423.

Suits, D. B. (1954). "Dynamic growth under diminishing returns to scale," *Econometrica* 22, 496–501.

Swamy, S. (1965). "Consistency of Fisher's tests," *Econometrica* 33, 619–623.

Tintner, G. (1948). "Homogeneous systems in mathematical economics," *Econometrica* 16, 273–294.

Ulmer, M. J. (1949). *The Economic Theory of Cost-of-Living Index Numbers.* Columbia Univ. Press, New York.

Uzawa, H. (1960). "Preference and rational choice in the theory of consumption," in *Mathematical Methods in the Social Sciences*, pp. 129–148. Stanford Univ. Press, Stanford, Calif.

Uzawa, H. (1961). "Neutral inventions and the stability of growth equilibrium," *Rev. Economic Studies* 28, 117–123.

Uzawa, H. (1962). "Production functions with constant elasticities of substitution," *Rev. Economic Studies* 29, 291–299.

Uzawa, H. (1971). "Preferences and rational choice in the theory of consumption," in *Preferences, Utility, and Demand*, pp. 7–28. Harcourt Brace Jovanovich, New York.

Vahrenkamp, R. (1974). "On weak homogeneity," in *Production Theory* (Proc. Intern. Seminar, Univ. of Karlsruhe, May–July 1973), pp. 177–203. (Lecture Notes in Economics and Mathematical Systems, Vol. 99). Springer-Verlag, Berlin, Heidelberg, New York.

Vahrenkamp, R. (1977). *Kegelbalanciertes Wachstum*. (Mathematical Systems in Economics). Verlag Anton Hain, Meisenheim.

Vincze, E. (1960). "Über das Problem der Berechnung der Wirtschaftlichkeit," *Acta Tech. Acad. Sci. Hungar.* 28, 33–41.

Voeller, J. (1974). *Theorie des Preis- und Lebenshaltungskostenindex*, Ph.D. Dissertation, Univ. of Karlsruhe.

Wald, A. (1937). "Zur Theorie der Preisindexziffern," *Z. Nationalökonomie* 8, 179–219.

Wald, A. (1939). "A new formula for the cost-of-living," *Econometrica* 7, 319–331.

Warburton, C. (1953). "Elementary algebra and the equation of exchange," *Amer. Economic Rev.* 43, 358–361.

Whitaker, J. K., and McCallum, B. T. (1971). "On homotheticity of production functions," *Western Economic J.* 9, 57–63.

Author Index

Author Index

Numbers set in *italics* designate the page numbers on which the complete citation is given.

Subject Index

Subject Index

Numbers set in *italics* designate the page numbers on which the entry is defined.